Software Engineering
with UML

Software Engineering with UML

Bhuvan Unhelkar

CRC Press
Taylor & Francis Group
Boca Raton London New York

CRC Press is an imprint of the
Taylor & Francis Group, an **informa** business
AN AUERBACH BOOK

CRC Press
Taylor & Francis Group
6000 Broken Sound Parkway NW, Suite 300
Boca Raton, FL 33487-2742

© 2018 by Taylor & Francis Group, LLC
CRC Press is an imprint of Taylor & Francis Group, an Informa business

No claim to original U.S. Government works

Printed on acid-free paper

International Standard Book Number-13: 978-1-138-29743-2 (Hardback)

Visit the Taylor & Francis Web site at
http://www.taylorandfrancis.com

and the CRC Press Web site at
http://www.crcpress.com

Janalee and Allen Heinemann

Who succinctly abstracts humanity in all its joys and grace:

Worth Modeling!

Contents

Note: Appendix A, including additional case studies, Appendix B: Mid-Term, and Appendix C: Final Exam are available online at https://www.crcpress.com/9781138297432.

Foreword

A few months ago, I was talking with one of my colleagues, and our conversation meandered into modeling skills, or rather the lack thereof, in the new generation of software engineers. More specifically, my colleague lamented the lack of knowledge about the Unified Modeling Language (UML) and object-oriented (OO) design skills among developers these days. Time and again we had both run into very smart developers whose effectiveness was nowhere near what it should be mainly owing to their lack of modeling skills and experience. Worse yet, many of them were proud of it! Yikes!

To be fair, though, one of the problems seems to be the lack of emphasis on good modeling and design in software engineering curricula. Adding to this problem is the fact that so few good books have been written on UML in the past five years. The need for books and other teaching materials that explain software engineering with UML and show its application in practice cannot be over-emphasized. This modeling material also needs to keep up with the changes in software engineering such as the development of services, analytics, and mobile apps. Yet, even online forums, sites, and blogs that discuss software modeling do so sparingly. Budding programmers rarely get to see good examples of models and are not able to develop their skills and techniques in applying these models in enhancing the quality and productivity of their work.

And there is a dire need for both quality and productivity to improve in practice. From controllers in street lights to aviation systems and battlefield targeting, software systems permeate every aspect of our society. These software systems need proper definitions, architectures, designs, testing, and sensible deployment. A commonly-understood, standardized modeling language is imperative. The UML defines the standard modeling artifacts when it comes to OO technology.* The use of UML has significantly enhanced the quality and acceptability of software applications by enabling formal requirements modeling, undertaking quality designs, and providing sound basis for iterative development of solutions.

In this book, Dr. Unhelkar applies UML to these critical societal functions. While the primary focus of this book is to teach UML standards, techniques, diagrams, and models, they are all couched within the fundamentals of OO software engineering. These OO fundamentals—classification, abstraction, inheritance, association, encapsulation, and polymorphism—set the tone for the use of UML in subsequent chapters. The contents within each chapter reflect the experiences of Dr. Unhelkar in teaching and practicing software engineering with the UML. The book is replete with short, simple examples that explain the fundamentals of OO software engineering; then there the book explains the use of each of the UML diagrams and their relevance in practice. It also has one of the key things that I always look for in a book—a running example of practical case study that helps make the material relevant to both students and practitioners of software

---

* The Object Primer 3rd Edition: Agile Modeling Driven Development with UML 2.—See more at http://www.agilemodeling.com/essays/umlDiagrams.htm

engineering. The presentation of common errors in modeling, discussion questions, team-based project work, and quizzes makes this book invaluable to readers. I think this book goes a long way toward helping rectify the situation around the lack of modeling in teaching and practice.

Now, you may wonder why am I writing the foreword for this book. I've been associated with UML since its inception in the mid-1990s; I wrote the first publicly published article about UML for *Object Magazine* in 1996, and my second book, *Building Object Applications That Work*, published in 1997, was the first book to cover UML. In 2002, my book *Agile Modeling* featured UML extensively, showing how to take a lightweight approach to modeling and documentation. In 2005, the *Object Primer 3rd Edition* went into even more detail about how UML and modeling in general are key aspects of enterprise-class Agile software development. So I have a fairly deep background in UML and OO software design and have written about it extensively. During my visits to Australia, I was also invited by Dr. Unhelkar to present at the Special Interest Group of the Australian Computer Society. In the mid-2000s, my focus shifted from UML and objects to software process in general, culminating in my continuous work with Mark Lines on the Disciplined Agile (DA) framework. Despite this change in focus, I remain extremely interested in developing good software models using UML standards.

I recommend this book to anyone who is serious about software engineering. The fundamental skills and knowledge about software engineering and UML outlined here will be of immense value to both students and practitioners. I take this opportunity to compliment Dr. Unhelkar on authoring this much needed yet simple and practical book on a vital topic within software engineering.

Scott Ambler
Toronto, Canada

Scott Ambler is a Senior Consulting Partner with Scott Ambler + Associates, working with organizations around the world to help them improve their software processes. Ambler is globally known for training, coaching, and mentoring in disciplined Agile and lean strategies at both the project and organizational level. Ambler is (co-)author of several books and white papers on object-oriented software development, software process, disciplined Agile delivery (DAD), Agile model-driven development (AMDD), Agile database techniques, and the Enterprise Unified Process (EUP)™. He is also a regular invitee for keynote addresses in conferences worldwide. He is a Fellow of the International Association of Software Architects and the Disciplined Agile Consortium. He was a Senior Contributing Editor with *Dr. Dobb's Journal* and occasionally writes for Cutter Consortium and IBM Developerworks. Please visit ScottAmbler.com for further details.

Preface

Modeling saves time and energy.[*]

Welcome to *Software Engineering with UML*. This book acknowledges and uses the Object Management Group's Unified Modeling Language (UML 2.5) standard to engineer high-quality software solutions. In an age of ever-increasing demand on software developers, clarity of communication and conveyance of understanding are prerequisites for success. Rapidly changing technologies for development, crunching time to produce working solutions, unpredictable business and legal environments, exploding data, cross-platform testing, globally dispersed development teams, and incessant requirements dictated by highly knowledgeable users place a premium on the technical and professional skills of a software engineer.

The premises of this book are that communication is the key to good software engineering and that modeling forms the basis of such communication. UML-based models facilitate and enhance communication between business analysts, users, designers, architects, and testers of the system under development. UML version 2.5 covers 14 different modeling constructs (package, use case, activity, interaction overview, class, sequence, communication, object, state machine, component, deployment, composite structure, timing, and profile diagrams). UML diagrams are based on a robust meta-model, which also enables extensibility mechanisms (stereotypes, tags, and notes).

An object-oriented approach to developing software introduces fundamentals for high-quality software development. Therefore, the topic of object orientation is interwoven throughout this book—in discussing the fundamentals of software engineering and applying those fundamentals in modeling, and developing software solutions.

UML grew out of a need to standardize a varying sets of notations and design approaches. Today it has evolved and stabilized for use across multiple software engineering functions such as capturing and modeling requirements of the problem to be solved, designing and prototyping the software solution, and understanding the constraints and impact of the solution on the existing enterprise-level architecture. UML is presented in this book as three interrelated models: model of the problem space (MOPS), model of the solution space (MOSS), and model of the architectural space (MOAS). These models are not watertight compartments but, rather, a way of delineating the tools (diagrams) provided by the UML based on a role and its purpose within a software project. As an ISO standard, UML certainly forms an integral part of a software engineer's toolkit.

Methods (processes) for developing software solutions form an important and integral part of software engineering. This material touches key areas of software development methods. Helpful

---

[*] From a Tony Robbins seminar.

hints are provided on how a software engineer can work in an Agile development environment and also understand the wider project management aspect of producing software solutions.

In the era of mobile apps, Cloud-based services, the Internet of Things (IoT), and Big Data analytics, a skeptic might be prone to discount the value of modeling (and in particular UML). Successful software development shows that disciplined modeling remains integral to communications across multiple stakeholders involved in developing solutions. The aim in this book is to make software engineers appreciate the importance and the relevance of software modeling in creating high-quality software programs.

Budding software engineers need to learn from the outset that developing good solutions involves a lot more than "coding." While programming is a necessity in the field of software, it is *not* sufficient. For example, user interface design, nonfunctional requirements (NFRs), quality assurance, and testing are crucial topics in software engineering that are more or less beyond the UML. This book covers these additional topics to ensure the appropriate breadth and sufficient depth that are necessary for teaching and learning software engineering.

This book is based on the author's teaching, researching, and experiencing the nitty-gritty and nuances in the field of software engineering. Students and practitioners alike will find themselves building on the knowledge gained here and applying it to the intricacies of software engineering. The book is designed to be of value to both undergraduate and postgraduate courses in software modeling through appropriate selection of chapters and corresponding emphasis on exercises and case studies. The value for practitioners is embedded in the example-based explanations and practical hints and tips through the discussions.

Audience

The primary audiences of this book are:

- *Students (undergrad)*: These are the basic- to intermediate-level readers learning software engineering at an undergraduate level. These readers are keen to understand the basics of software engineering followed by a standard way to model requirements and create design solutions using UML.
- *Students (postgrad)*: These are readers looking for greater details on building an overall holistic software solution. These readers go deeper into the architectural and design aspects of solutions, and they are also keen to understand the process and management aspects of software projects. The impact of advanced concepts (e.g., reuse, granularity, patterns) on software solutions is also of interest to these readers.
- *Business analysts/requirements modelers*: These readers are learning to capture and model requirements using UML standards (notably use cases, activity diagrams, and business-level basic class diagrams). These people work primarily to develop the model of the problem space (MOPS).
- *Quality professionals*: These are the quality analysts and testers aiming to improve their work in enhancing the quality of a solution by inspecting the models, undertaking walk-throughs, and verifying and validating the models. These readers also need the UML to understand and communicate with the users, designers, and architects of the software solutions.
- *Teachers*: These include professors who are keen to pitch the right material at the right level. Teachers will find this book an excellent text for a typical one-semester subject (unit) totally supported by presentation material and case studies (available on the publisher's website).

- *Trainers*: Trainers conducting a 2- to 3-day industrial course in software modeling or business analysis will find that this book supports their training efforts. The book's value to trainers lies in the succinct organization of chapters with the opportunity to choose the chapters depending on the audience and time provided to conduct trainings. The team project case study enables experiential learning in industrial training courses.
- *Consultants/practitioners*: These are readers who will find the practical content and a running case study through the chapters to be of immense value.

Assumed Knowledge

This book assumes a general (introductory) understanding of software development (for example, what is a software system and what is meant by analysis and design?). Students can develop this understanding through any programming- or database-related course or by reading and absorbing the basics of analysis and designs. Practitioners easily gain this understanding through their experience. Such an introductory understanding of software development makes it easier and quicker to grasp the concepts of software engineering, object orientation, and UML-based modeling discussed in this book.

Contents

This book is divided into 21 chapters, each reflecting a topic of discussion relevant to a 90-minute industrial training session or a 2-hour lecture. Assuming an introduction, a concluding lecture, and a midterm test, this book covers a teaching period of approximately 14 weeks for an undergrad course in software modeling (or program design). An alternative selection of chapters and greater emphasis on the team project case study result in material for a graduate course in software engineering.

At the end of each chapter, readers will find discussion questions (which can be treated like exercises). It is highly recommended that these discussion questions are completed immediately after the lecture or reading of the chapter. The discussion questions are designed to help students consolidate the concepts discussed in the chapter. Each chapter also has the steps outlined for a case study. The case study must be performed on a team to enable students to appreciate the challenges and advantages in using UML in real-life software projects. Three to four students are expected to participate in this team project. The team project work is performed during the tutorials in labs outside the lecture times. The team project requires the use of a UML-based CASE tool (for example, StarUML or Visio™).

Pedagogy

This book is written for the purpose of teaching and learning UML within the context of object orientation. This book is relevant for both undergraduate and graduate students. The examples in the book are derived from the author's practical industrial experience, yet the teaching experience ensures the book will fall short with respect to academic rigor and authenticity. The book is a combination of the author's experience in various practical consulting roles—including business analysis, project management, system design, quality assurance, and testing—combined with years of teaching and coordinating UML courses at both undergraduate and graduate levels across universities in Australia, the USA, China, and India.

Web Support

Suggested structure and formats for presentations of this material, typical assessments with timings and marks, as well as administrative requirements for this subject are available on the CRC Press/Taylor & Francis Group website (https://www.crcpress.com/9781138297432). Web support for this book includes:

- All presentation materials including all figures and slides for each chapter
- Suggestions on tutorial sessions and roughly worked examples for the team project
- Administrative and lab requirements for the project work including suggested CASE tools
- Suggestions on assessments and marks and time distribution
- Appendix A: Case Study Problem Statements for Team Projects with additional case studies not included in this book.
- Appendix B: Mid-Term
- Appendix C: Final Exam

Critiques

Readers are invited to submit criticism of this work. It would be an honor to receive genuine criticism and comments on this material that, I am sure, will not only enrich my own knowledge and understanding of the topics discussed in this book but also add to the general wealth of modeling knowledge available to the ICT community. Therefore, I extend a *thank you* in advance to all potential critics of this work.

Bhuvan Unhelkar

www.unhelkar.com

Glossary of Acronyms

BA	Business Analyst (not to be confused with business architect)
BDFAB	Big Data Framework for Agile Business
BDM	Business Domain Model—represented by class diagram at a high level (i.e., not containing technical details)
BO	Business Objective (basis for software projects)
BPM	Business Process Model—representing workflow or business processes
BPMN	Business Process Model and Notation
CAMS	Composite Agile Method and Strategy
CBT	Computer-Based Training (for users before deploying a system; automated in many cases)
CC	Cloud Computing (anything on the Cloud—includes computing, storage, analytics, platform, and infrastructure)
CMM	Capability Maturity Model—provides basis for measuring and comparing process maturities of various organizations and projects; initiative of Software Engineering Institute at Carnegie Mellon University
CMMi	Capability Maturity Model integration
CMS	Content Management System—dealing primarily with the contents of a website and its management
CRM	Customer Relationship Management—a comprehensive system including interfaces, processes, and databases to handle all aspects of customer-related processes (from identifying, marketing, and selling through to support and retirement)
CWM	Common Warehouse Metamodel
DAD	Disciplined Agile Development
DE	Domain Expert—in a particular domain or industry like banking, airlines, or hospitals
DM	Data Modelers—focusing on creating models to represent databases in backend
EA	Enterprise Architecture—brings together various (primarily technical) aspects of an enterprise/organization
ERP	Enterprise Resource Planning—typically representing large and complex software systems that include all functions of an organization (e.g., SAP, PeopleSoft, Oracle)
GUI	Graphic User Interface—also known as screens or forms
HMS	Hospital Management System—a case study used in this text to demonstrate practical application of software engineering with UML
ICT	Information and Communication Technology
ID	Interface Designer—specialist in designing various types of interfaces including, but not limited to, graphics.

IIoT	Industrial Internet of Things
IIP	Iterative, Incremental, Parallel—software development life cycle ideally suited for OO development
IOD	Interaction Overview Diagram—part of UML providing high-level overview of interaction diagrams
IoE	Internet of Everything—a more generic term to include IoT
IoT	Internet of Things—represents daily use devices that are connected to the base and with each other through the Internet
ISAM	Indexed Sequential Access Method—a method to access data through indexes
IT	Information Technology—increasingly being referred to as ICT
MDA	Model-Driven Architecture (OMG initiative)
Metamodel	Model of a Model that dictates the rules for the creation of modeling mechanisms like the UML
MOAS	Model Of Architecture Space—created primarily by the system architect in the background space using UML notations and diagrams
MOF	Meta-Object Facility—owned by OMG and forms basis for the creation of new methods
MOPS	Model Of Problem Space—created primarily by business analyst in problem space using UML notations and diagrams
MoSCoW	Must–Should–Could–Won't (four categories/priorities in terms of requirements of a software system)
MOSS	Model Of Solution Space—created primarily by system designer in solution space using UML notations and diagrams
NFR	NonFunctional Requirement—also known as operational requirement
NFRS	NonFunctional Requirement Specifications—also nonfunctional requirements
OMG	Object Management Group—responsible for unification of modeling notations resulting in UML
OO	Object Oriented—earlier considered only as a programming technique, OO now permeates all aspects of software engineering
PIoT	Personal Internet of Things
PM	Project Manager
QA	Quality Assurance
QC	Quality Control
QM	Quality Management
RM	Requirements Modeler
SA	System Architect
SD	System Designer
SDLC	Software Development Life Cycle
SEP	Software Engineering Process (also software process)
SMD	State machine Diagram—also known as state chart or state diagram
SOAP	Simple Object Access Protocol
UDDI	Universal Description, Discovery, and Integration
UML	Unified Modeling Language
V&V	Verification and Validation
WS	Web Services
XML	eXtensible Markup Language

Acknowledgements

Abbass Ghanbary
Abhay Saxena
Alexandrina Kostova
Amit Tiwary
Anand Kuppuswami
Andy Lyman
Anurag Agarwal
Asim Chauhan
Bhargav Bhatt
Cihan Cobanoglu
Colleen Berish
Daniel A. Thuraiappah
Ekata Mehul
Girish Nair
Haydar Jawad
James Curran
Javed Matin
Karan Karandikar
Keith Sherringham
Lila Rajabion
M.N. Sharif

Milind Barve
Mohammed Maharmeh
Motilal Bhatia
Nosh Mistry
Prashant Risbud
Prince Soundararajan
S.D. Pradhan
San Murugesan
Scott Ambler
Sanjeev Sharma
Steve Blais
Sunita Lodwig
Trivikrama Rao
Tushar Hazra
Vipul Kalamkar
Vivek Eshwarappa
Walied Askarzai
Warren Adkins
Yi-Chen Lan
Zahid Iqbal

Family

Thanks to my family for their support and good wishes: Asha (wife), Sonki Priyadarshini (daughter), Keshav Raja (son), Chinar (sister-in-law), and Benji (dog).

This book is dedicated to my wonderful neighbor, Janalee and Allen Heinemann, who succinctly abstracts humanity in all its joys and grace: *Worth Modeling!*

Finally, this work acknowledges all trademarks of the organizations whose names or tools have been used in this book. Specifically, I acknowledge the trademarks of the OMG (Object Management Group) who own the UML, StarUML (my favorite modeling tool), and Visio.

Author

Dr. Bhuvan Unhelkar (BE, MDBA, MSc, PhD; FACS, CBAP®) has extensive strategic and hands-on professional experience in the information and communication technologies (ICT) industry. He is an Associate Professor of IT (lead faculty) at the University of South Florida Sarasota-Manatee (USFSM) and is the founder and consultant at *MethodScience*.

Areas of expertise include:

- Business analysis and requirements modeling (use cases, BPMN, BABOK; helping organizations upskill and practice)
- Software engineering (UML, object modeling; includes undertaking large-scale software modeling exercises for solutions development)
- Agile processes (CAMS—practical application of composite Agile to real-life business challenges not limited to software projects)
- Corporate Agile development (upskilling teams and applying Agile techniques in practice)
- Quality assurance and testing (with focus on prevention rather than detection)
- Big Data strategies (BDFAB—emphasis on application of Big Data technologies and analytics to generate business value)
- Collaborative Web services (SOA, Cloud; upgrading enterprise architectures based on services, including developing analytics as a service)
- Mobile business and green IT (with the goal of creating and maintaining sustainable business operations)

His industry experience includes banking, finance, insurance, government, and telecommunications, where he develops and applies industry-specific process maps, business transformation approaches, capability enhancement, and quality strategies.

Dr. Unhelkar has authored numerous executive reports, journal articles, and 20 books with internationally reputed publishers including *Big Data Strategies for Agile Business* (CRC Press/Taylor & Francis Group, USA, 2017). Recent *Cutter* executive reports (Boston, USA) include *Psychology of Agile* (two parts), *Agile Business Analysis* (two parts), *Collaborative Business & Enterprise Agility, Avoiding Method Friction,* and *Agile in Practice: A Composite Approach.* He is also passionate about coaching senior executives; training, re-skilling, and mentoring IT professionals; forming centers of excellence; and creating assessment frameworks (SFIA-based) to support corporate change initiatives. Dr. Unhelkar is an engaging presenter delivering keynotes, training seminars, and workshops that combine real-life examples based on his experience, with audience participation and Q&A sessions. As a result, these industrial training courses, seminars, and workshops provide significant value to the participants and their sponsoring organizations as the training is based on practical experience and a hands-on approach, and accompanied by ROI metrics. Consistently highly ranked by participants, the seminars and workshops have been delivered globally to business executives and IT professionals, notably in Australia, the USA, Canada, the UK, China, India, Sri Lanka, New Zealand, and Singapore. Dr. Unhelkar is the winner of the Computerworld Object Developer Award (1995), Consensus IT Professional Award (2006), and IT Writer Award (2010). He also chaired the Business Analysis Specialism *Group* of the Australian Computer Society.

Dr. Unhelkar earned his PhD in the area of object orientation from the University of Technology, Sydney. His teaching career spans teaching at both the undergraduate and master's levels wherein he has designed and delivered courses including Global Information Systems, Agile Method Engineering, Object-Oriented Analysis and Design, Business Process Reengineering, and New Technology Alignment in Australia, USA, China, and India. Many courses have been designed and delivered online: for the Australian Computer Society's distance education program, the M.S. University of Baroda (India) Master's program, and, currently, Program Design with the UML and Mobile App Development at the University of South Florida Sarasota-Manatee, Sarasota, Florida. Earlier, at Western Sydney University, he supervised seven successful PhD candidates and published research papers and case studies. His current industrial research interests include Big Data and business value and business analysis in the context of Agile. Dr. Unhelkar holds a Certificate-IV in TAA and TAE and is a Certified Business Analysis Professional® (CBAP of the IIBA).

Professional affiliations include:

- Fellow of the Australian Computer Society (elected to this prestigious membership grade in 2002 for distinguished contribution to the field of information and communications technology), Australia
- Life member of the Computer Society of India (CSI), India
- Life member of Baroda Management Association (BMA), India
- Member of Society for Design and Process Science (SDPS), USA
- Rotarian (President) at Sarasota Sunrise Club, USA; past Rotary Club president in St. Ives, Sydney (Paul Harris Fellow; AG), Australia
- Discovery volunteer at New South Wales Parks and Wildlife, Australia
- Previous The Indus Enterpreuner (TiE) Mentor, Australia

Other CRC Books by the Same Author

Unhelkar, B., (2017), *Big Data Strategies for Agile Business* (CRC Press/Taylor & Francis Group/An Auerbach Book), Boca Raton, FL, USA.

Unhelkar, B., (2013), *The Art of Agile Practice: A Composite Approach for Projects and Organizations* (CRC Press/Taylor & Francis Group/an Auerbach Book), Boca Raton, FL, USA.

Unhelkar, B., (2011), *Green IT Strategies and Applications: Using Environmental Intelligence*, CRC Press (Taylor & Francis Group/an Auerbach Book), Boca Raton, FL, USA. Authored ISBN: 9781439837801

Unhelkar, B., (2009), *Mobile Enterprise Transition and Management*, (CRC Press/Taylor & Francis Group/ an Auerbach Book), Boca Raton, FL, USA.

Unhelkar, B., (1999), *After the Y2K Fireworks: Business and Technology Strategies*, CRC Press, Boca Raton, FL, USA.

Unique Features

With this textbook, professors will have:

- Fundamentals of object orientation and UML explained with practical examples
- Discussion questions at the end of each chapter to enable students to grasp the material quickly
- Team project case studies, with steps outlined at the end of each chapter, ensure consolidation of knowledge gained
- Complete presentation slides based on the material in this book
- Suite of problem statements to enable assigning different projects for multiple teaching semesters
- Suggested midterm and final quizzes as basis for consolidation and further quizzes

With this textbook, students will be easily able to:

- Learn the fundamentals of object orientation and UML and understand how they are applied in practice through a worked case study of a hospital management system
- Understand all UML 2.5 diagrams and segregate them based on their relevance in the creation of models of problem space (MOPS), models of solution space (MOSS), and models of architecture space (MOAS)
- Select and study in detail a subset of UML 2.5 diagrams depending on the interest of the reader—analysis, design, and architecture
- Understand the strengths and weaknesses of each diagram
- Learn from the common errors in modeling for each diagram
- Participate in practical discussion sessions and workshops based on the topics provided at the end of each chapter
- Understand the formats for midterm and final quizzes
- Locate practical references (books and websites) for UML

In this book, Dr. Unhelkar applies UML to critical societal functions. The book is replete with short, simple examples that explain the fundamentals of object-oriented software engineering and then explain the use of each of the UML diagrams and their relevance in practice. The presentation of common errors in modeling, discussion questions, team-based project work, and quizzes makes this book invaluable to readers. I think this book goes a long way toward helping to rectify the lack of modeling in teaching and practice.

—from the foreword by Scott Ambler

Chapter 1

Software Engineering Fundamentals with Object Orientation

Learning Objectives

- Learning software engineering and adopting it in practice
- Relating modeling in user requirements, software design, and development
- Understanding the relationship between programs, classes, data, and objects
- Establishing software engineering fundamentals with object orientation: classification, abstraction, encapsulation, association, inheritance, and polymorphism
- Undertaking a brief historical perspective on modeling
- Applying UML in visualizing, specifying, constructing, documenting, and maintaining software systems

This chapter introduces software engineering (SE) with the underlying basis of object orientation (OO). Starting with a discussion on how to learn and adopt SE, this chapter argues for the importance of modeling in good software design. Object and class are conceptually separated. The six fundamentals of OO discussed are classification, abstraction, inheritance, association, encapsulation, and polymorphism. A brief historical perspective on SE follows. The chapter concludes with a discussion on contemporary UML usage.

Introduction to Software Engineering

The goal of SE is to produce robust, high-quality software solutions that provide value to users. Achieving this goal requires the precision of engineering combined with the subtlety of art. Software projects also have diverse stakeholders with competing agendas, which adds to the complexity of managing people. SE is thus as much a branch of the social sciences as it is of engineering. A good software engineer continuously manages the delicate balance between the functioning of left and right brains.[1]

Initially, SE built and expanded on the existing and mature disciplines of engineering such as civil and mechanical engineering. The sequential steps of the earliest software development life cycle (SDLC) reflects the procedural approach of a civil engineer constructing a building: dig to create the basement, solidify the ground, erect the walls, and place the roof—all getting translated into identifying requirements, creating designs, coding, testing, and deploying. Mechanical engineering provides the backdrop for standardizing software components and assembling them to produce a software system.

These engineering characteristics continue to evolve as SE adapts to different types of developments. For example, the sequential life cycle of SE has now evolved into an iterative and incremental approach to software design. Component-based software development assembles large chunks of reusable software and services rather than handcrafting individual classes. Principles of usability are applied in designing mobile applications and Internet of Things (IoT) sensors. Agility brings in fundamentals of collaboration and visibility and, together with iterations and increments, is now the keyword for software development approaches. Agility provides immense value in software projects by drawing upon the "right-brained" traits of software developers.[2] For example, disciplined Agile development (DAD)[3] balances the artistic nuances of software development with the necessary engineering rigor. *The Art of Agile Practice*[4] further builds on the basics of agility to provide an organizational working style and a culture that provides value beyond software projects.

Software engineering, in its early days, comprised nothing but programming. Hard-earned practical lessons[5] within the business environment demonstrated the need for understanding and analyzing a problem and designing it carefully before programming. Software architectural practices (in the architectural space) ensure that the detailed solution design fits with the enterprise environment before it is implemented. Agile practices further extend the requirements of a system (in the problem space) iteratively and incrementally into a solution-level design (in the solution space). Such methodical analysis and design of software solution bodes well for its implementation quality and its ability to provide value to various shareholders. The need for formal standards for SE itself could not have been greater.

SE STANDARDS BODIES

Software engineering as a discipline is continuously acknowledged, monitored, and improved through various standards bodies. Some of the popular ones are Accreditation Board for Engineering and Technology (ABET),[6] Institute of Electrical and Electronics Engineers (IEEE) Computer Society,[7] Australian Computer Society (ACS),[8] Association for Computing Machinery (ACM),[9] and Software Engineering Body of Knowledge.[10]

Learning and Adopting Software Engineering

Software engineering encompasses functions, activities, and tasks, including development processes, project management, business analysis, requirements modeling, usability designs, operational performance, security, financial management, regulatory and compliance management, risk management, quality assurance, quality control, release management, and service management. Learning SE is therefore a complex process in itself that can start with learning the fundamentals of development through to the adoption of agility across project teams and the organization.

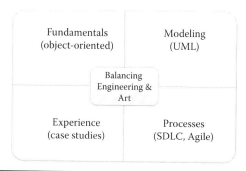

Figure 1.1 Learning and adopting SE.

A systematic approach to learning the aforementioned aspects of SE is necessary for success at both individual and organizational levels.

Figure 1.1 summarizes the approach to learning and adopting SE. The four important elements required to learn and adopt SE in practice are as follows:

- *Object-oriented fundamentals*: The fundamental concepts of object orientation, based on early programming languages such as Simula and Smalltalk provide a solid foundation for SE. These concepts are further expressed in languages like C++ and Java. Analytical languages such as Python and R and the corresponding development environments follow. All these SE technologies are better served with a strong conceptual understanding of OO fundamentals, as is attempted later in this chapter.

- *Modeling (UML standard)*: A modeling standard that enables the creation of standardized diagrams and associated specifications goes a long way in improving communication and increasing participation from all project stakeholders. Increased stakeholder participation improves the quality of the software, reduces errors, and encourages easy acceptance of the solution by users. The Unified Modeling Language (UML) provides this necessary standard. With the UML, diagrams and specifications are created, studied, reviewed, and modified by teams in a shared manner. These diagrams and models are easy to enter in a modeling tool, also called a computer-aided software engineering (CASE) tool, to enable a group of users, analysts, designers, and testers to work together. The UML can be considered a de facto standard for software modeling, and therefore it forms the crux of this book.

- *Process (SDLC, Agile)*: A process defines activities and phases and provides direction for software development. Such a software development life cycle provides significant guidance in the modeling effort undertaken by a team of designers and developers as they are able to understand the activities, tasks, roles, and deliverables of the entire project team in developing, integrating, and releasing a solution. Agility is a part of software development processes that intensely focuses on iterations and increments, collaboration, trust, and visibility. Processes are briefly discussed in Chapter 4.

- *Experience (case studies and team-based project work)*: SE fundamentals and their expression through UML are best understood through experiential learning. Experience in creating UML models, especially in a team environment, is a must for learning the art of SE. The examples in this book are based on a case study in hospital management systems (HMSs)—for a problem statement, see Appendix A. Experiential learning in groups is further expanded through a set of activities provided at the end of each chapter under the heading "Team Project Case Study."

Importance of Modeling

Software systems satisfy specific business purposes and functions. These business purposes are articulated by users. Users or their representatives are thus an integral part of the development process. Users state their needs, articulate the business scenarios, and often provide the vision for the product. The challenge is for these needs and requirements to be captured, modeled, and translated into an acceptable solution. Handling this challenge of developing a usable software that is acceptable to users is at the core of a software project's success.

Ideally, all SE projects start with an understanding of the key business objectives derived from the solution. SE projects then undertake requirements modeling and analysis. These activities help shed light on and model the needs and wants of users. Analysis is followed by the design of the software solution and eventual coding that is based on the available technical environment and capabilities of the organization. The activities within analysis and design are carried out in a highly iterative and incremental manner.

Design provides the bridge between analysis and coding. A good design is a smooth conduit that transforms requirements into implementation. Good software designers are aware of the analysis activities and the resultant requirements model and conversant with technologies (such as programming and databases) and limitations imposed by the organization's architecture.

Such models significantly enhance communications within and across development teams. This is so because these models represent requirements in the problem space, designs in the solution space, and constraints in the architectural space. Overall, models provide the project team with major opportunities to identify gaps, errors in understanding, technology mismatch, and changing user expectations. Models allow teams to do all they need to do before they start "coding." Coding, or programming, thus becomes almost the last and perhaps the least tiring activity of all in a well-organized and well-modeled software engineering project. Therefore, modeling and the ensuing communications are increasingly seen as one of the most important activity in producing quality and value in software solutions.

As shown in Figure 1.2, modeling in software engineering serves two major purposes: to help shed light on the existing business reality and to create a new business reality. The importance of modeling in SE is multifunctional: understanding existing systems, applications, and processes, followed by the creation of new processes, providing a basis for testing and enabling effective communications with all stakeholders.

Modeling enables a much better understanding of a problem and the solution *before* the solution is coded—thereby reducing unnecessary efforts and improving the quality of software.

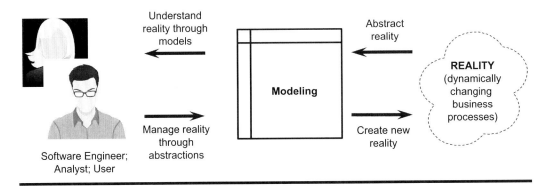

Figure 1.2   Importance of modeling in software engineering: Understand and create reality.

The maintenance and operational phases of a solution also benefit as models providing a reliable abstraction of the system that are easier to understand and change rather than directly changing the system.

THE UNIFIED MODELING LANGUAGE (UML)

The Unified Modeling Language (UML)[11] of the Object Management Group (OMG)[12] provides a standardized mechanism to model software systems. The UML can also help model the requirements of new systems and also help understand existing business processes and applications. The value of UML-based models comes from their ability to facilitate communication, discussion, documentation, and consideration of a number of "what-if" scenarios for large and complex software systems. UML is made up of 14 modeling constructs. These UML diagrams form the crux of discussions in most chapters in this book.

Software Engineering Fundamentals

Foundations for techniques and standardization in SE are based on the fundamentals of OO. The OO fundamentals provide strong theoretical foundations for the analysis, design, architecture, coding, and testing of software systems. These OO concepts result in software components and services that are versatile, changeable, reusable, and reliable. OO also helps in designing complex multimedia Web-enabled applications, mobile applications, service-oriented software applications, and Big Data analytical solutions. Programming (C++, Java), databases (SQL, Object, NoSQL), and business workflows are very well supported by OO fundamentals.

Programs, Classes, Objects, and Data

SE comprises some core terms. Figure 1.3 clarifies the four basic terms in SE. These are as follows:

- Programs—structured code specific to a programming language that reflect an algorithm. SE in the early days was synonymous with programming. Programs are written primarily to manipulate data according to the logic specified by users.
- Classes—specific styles of software programs that encapsulate data with functions (methods). Classes are object-oriented in nature. Classes are put together in different ways to produce systems. Figure 1.3 shows a class: clock. This class contains a description of a clock and its associated behavior.
- Data—instance-level representation of the business reality (characteristics) that is encoded and stored within databases. The aforementioned classes have attributes, and data represent the value contained within those attributes. Relational databases store data as records. Object-oriented databases store data and their functions together. Unstructured data (such as graphics, audio, and descriptive text) require special types of storage.
- Objects—instances of classes that comprise both data and the behavior associated with the data at runtime. Since objects are runtime entities based on the classes that define them, there can be a number of variations to objects for the same class. Figure 1.3 shows the number of instances of clocks derived from a class: clock.

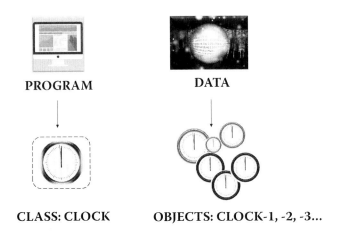

Figure 1.3   Programs, classes, objects, and data.

The Six Fundamentals (Cornerstone) of Software Engineering

Six fundamentals make up OO.[13] These fundamentals help in creating classes and programs that process and manipulate data and objects. As shown in Figure 1.4, at the core of SE are data. The six fundamentals of object-oriented SE revolve around data and extract value from them in various ways. Therefore, understanding these object-oriented fundamentals is at the crux of becoming a good software engineer. These object-oriented fundamentals are as follows:

- Classification (grouping)
- Abstraction (representing)
- Encapsulation (modularizing)

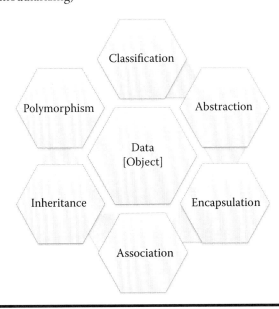

Figure 1.4   The six fundamentals (cornerstone) of software engineering.

- Association (relating)
- Inheritance (generalizing)
- Polymorphism (executing)

These object-oriented fundamentals are discussed in greater details in the following sections.

Classification (Grouping)

Classification is the starting point of OO. Good software engineers make sense of requirements by first identifying entities in the business space. Once these entities or potential objects are identified, they are *grouped* or classified. Classification is based on the requirements appearing in the problem space, and these requirements, in turn, are iteratively modified based on the classification.

For a given set of objects as shown in Figure 1.5, the butterfly and the crane are grouped under the label "bird," the cat and the frog under the label "animal," the hat and the clock under the label "thing," and so on. This classification is based on a group of objects that appear in the problem space. Changes in the requirements of the system in the problem space change the corresponding basis for classification. For example, if there are additional requirements for flying objects, then, in addition to the butterfly and the crane, the airplane is also included in that collection of objects, resulting in a different classification.

Abstraction (Representing)

Objects, which are real-world entities, need to be represented by a *template* that also defines their characteristics and behavior. Collections of classified objects are *abstracted* to classes. A class provides a detailed definition of all objects that can be instantiated from it. This is the basic level of abstraction.

Figure 1.5   Classification starts with meaningful groupings of objects.

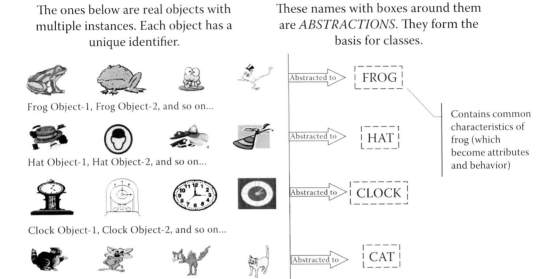

The ones below are real objects with multiple instances. Each object has a unique identifier.

Frog Object-1, Frog Object-2, and so on...

Hat Object-1, Hat Object-2, and so on...

Clock Object-1, Clock Object-2, and so on...

Cat Object-1, Cat Object-2, and so on...

These names with boxes around them are *ABSTRACTIONS*. They form the basis for classes.

Abstracted to → FROG

Abstracted to → HAT

Abstracted to → CLOCK

Abstracted to → CAT

Contains common characteristics of frog (which become attributes and behavior)

Good classification leads to creation of good abstractions.

Figure 1.6   First-level abstraction: Groups of objects are abstracted and represented by a class: *A class is an abstraction in itself.*

The numerous objects discussed under classification in the previous section are represented by a class. Few such classes are shown by their names within the rectangles in Figure 1.6, (e.g., Frog, Hat, Clock, and Cat). Note how none of these classes are the actual objects. Also note how the collection of objects on the left-hand side in Figure 1.6 is *not* a class.

Although a class is an abstraction representing a collection of objects, classes themselves are subject to further abstraction. This second level of abstraction is shown in Figure 1.7, wherein the classes Frog and Cat are abstracted to a higher-level class called *Animal*. Similarly, the Clock

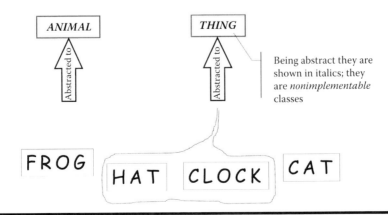

ANIMAL

THING

Abstracted to

Abstracted to

Being abstract they are shown in italics; they are *nonimplementable* classes

FROG   HAT   CLOCK   CAT

Figure 1.7   Second-level abstraction is where a meaningful group of *classes* is further abstracted to higher-level classes; thus, a class is abstracted to a higher class.

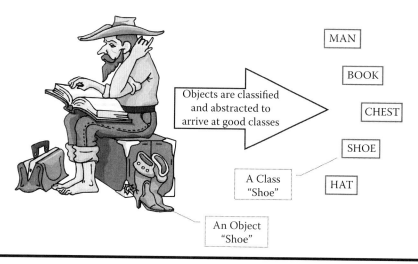

Figure 1.8 Classification and abstraction go together.

and Hat classes are abstracted to the class *Thing*. (Note: abstract classes are shown in italics because they cannot be instantiated. This is discussed further in Chapter 9.)

Classification and abstraction are not isolated activities. In fact, they are closely related, with one feeding into another. Classification and abstraction are iteratively applied in order to develop software models in practice.

As shown in Figure 1.8, if a problem statement deals with a man sitting on a trunk, there are numerous objects available through the man that must be classified *and* abstracted to classes. For example, man the "object" is abstracted to the class Man. This class Man now defines and represents *all* men objects. Furthermore, classes like Book and Shoe may find second-level abstraction, as discussed in Figure 1.7. This abstraction is available to define many other objects, not necessarily those shown in Figure 1.8.

Encapsulation (Modularizing)

As its name suggests, encapsulation is the fundamental of wrapping chunks of cohesive data with meaningful code. Encapsulation localizes data and prevents them from being directly exposed to the rest of the system. Encapsulation enhances quality and reuse because the data are only accessible through calls to the operations (methods or functions) of a class (discussed in detail in Chapters 8 and 11). Figure 1.9 shows a specific set of "data and code" that can be treated as "private" information belonging to a class.

With encapsulation, a programmer reusing a class doesn't need to know how a method is implemented in order to use it (invoke it). All that is required is knowledge of the class interface (heading and arguments) and how to call it. This is similar to calling a service. Service-oriented components have detailed documentation that help embed those services within new programs being written. The public (interface), or visible, part of the class is usually a subset of its methods or functions.

Encapsulation also facilitates easier debugging of code. This is because encapsulated code is localized. Errors can therefore be relatively easy to narrow down.

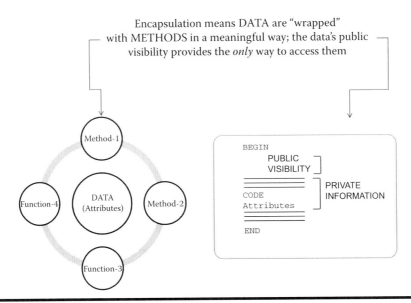

Encapsulation means DATA are "wrapped" with METHODS in a meaningful way; the data's public visibility provides the *only* way to access them

Figure 1.9 Encapsulation ensures data is not accessed directly. This localizes errors and protects data integrity while preventing a flow-on effect of one error on other parts of the system.

MODULARIZING SOFTWARE DEVELOPMENT

The development of a large and complex software solution starts with the development of smaller manageable and comprehensible subsystems. This modularity of solutions not only enhances quality but also helps in following an iterative and incremental development process. Responsibilities for development, estimates for development, and the location of errors and enhancements are much easier to achieve through modularity and encapsulation.

Association (Relating)

Objects are classified and abstracted into classes. Classes don't exist in isolation. They relate to other classes in multiple ways. The association relationship is a mechanism for two (more) classes to relate to each other. Figure 1.10, for example, shows the class Person associating with the class Clock in order to achieve the objective of, say, "find the time." There can be many additional associations between Person and Clock such as "changing the batteries of a clock," "buying a clock," or "setting the time."

Inheritance (Generalizing)

Classes in OO also relate to each other through inheritance. Inheritance results from classes being generalized into higher-level or abstracted classes. The second-level abstraction, shown in Figure 1.7, is the starting point of good OO hierarchies. A class can inherit the attributes, behavior, and relationships of another class. Inheritance enables the extensibility of design and reuse of code.

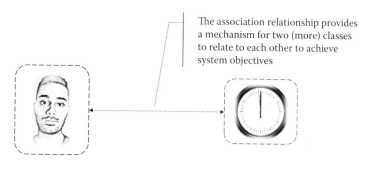

The association relationship provides a mechanism for two (more) classes to relate to each other to achieve system objectives

CLASS PERSON *ASSOCIATES WITH* CLASS CLOCK

Figure 1.10   Association.

When a suite of classes is abstracted to a higher level, it is called generalization; when a class is derived from an existing class, it is called specialization.

Figure 1.11 builds on the previously mentioned classification and abstraction example (Figures 1.5 and 1.7). The class Animal is inherited by Frog and Cat, resulting in specialization of the class *Animal*. The class *Bird* is similarly inherited by Crane with all its attributes and its relationships. Additionally, commonalities between *Bird* and Animal are generalized into a higher-level class called *Living*.

Polymorphism (Executing)

Polymorphism is the ability of an instantiated object (at runtime) to understand and interpret the message sent from a calling object. This interpretation of a message by an object depends on its own characteristics and definition.

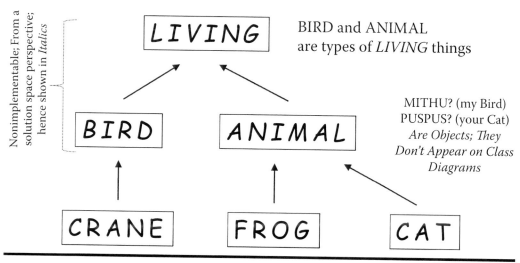

Figure 1.11   Inheritance enables generalization (through abstraction) and specialization.

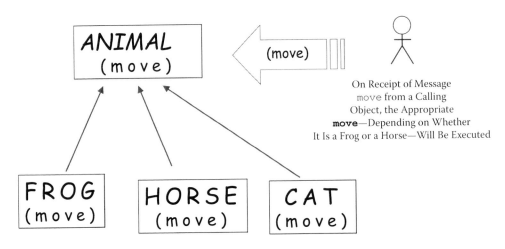

Advantage? CALLING object need not know what is Moved, so if
a *new* CAT object is added, the CALLING class doesn't change

Figure 1.12 Polymorphism.

Consider Figure 1.12, which shows an inheritance hierarchy wherein `Frog` and `Cat` are inherited from `Animal`. If a message `move` is sent to `Animal`, from which the object `Frog` is instantiated, then the frog executes its "move" in its own specialized way (with a "leap," for example). This leap is implemented underneath or within the `move` function for `Frog`.

Alternatively, if a `Horse` has been instantiated from `Animal`, then the code that implements the movement of a `Horse` is executed (a "gallop," for example). The two objects `Frog` and `Horse` have different ways of performing the same operation, `move`, when called.

The method names within the higher (generalized) and derived (specialized) classes need to be the same in order to facilitate polymorphism. Also note that polymorphism is a *runtime* characteristic of OO, compared with inheritance, which is a *structural* characteristic. Inheritance in design makes polymorphism at runtime possible.

One advantage of polymorphism is that the calling object (i.e., the object that is sending the message "move" to `Animal`) need *not* know which particular object at the receiving end is executing the "move" method. Another advantage of polymorphism is that when a new requirement for, say, a Cat arises in the model shown in Figure 1.12, the object sending the message "move" does not change. This reduces maintenance overhead and, in general, enhances code and design quality.

Software Engineering: A Historical Perspective

Evolution of Modeling

This section reviews a brief history of SE. Figure 1.13 shows the evolution of SE as a discipline: structured, data-based, object-class, component and services, mobile-Cloud-Agile, and Big Data.

SE started evolving in the 1960s when a language called Simula67 was developed at the Norwegian Computing Centre.[14] Simula67 was an object-based programming language that

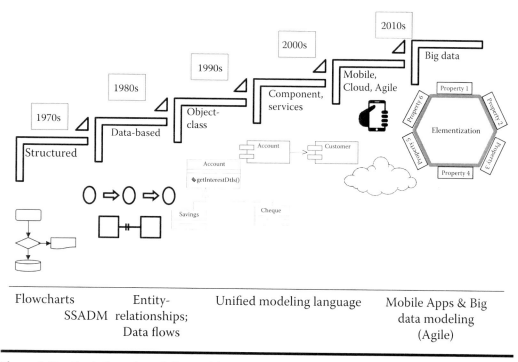

Figure 1.13 Evolution of modeling: A historical-futuristic perspective.

stored data and operations together, enabling tightly encapsulated and reusable code. Such code had higher quality and needed less time and effort. However, this programming effort did not follow a formal model or standard at a commercial level.

Simula was followed in the mid-1970s by Smalltalk at the Xerox Palo Alto Research Center (Xerox PARC)[15]. Smalltalk comprised a language and a programming environment wherein all its elements were implemented as an object. Smalltalk was the first complete and robust object-oriented language that was used in major industrial domains like defense and banking.

The 1970s also saw the arrival of COmmon Business Oriented Language (COBOL), which revolutionized commercial software development used in industries such as banking, airlines, and hospitals, to name a few. COBOL, however, was a procedural language that did not adhere to many object-oriented fundamentals such as encapsulation, inheritance, and polymorphism. The underlying data structures of COBOL were primarily supported by index sequential access method file structures. This was rapidly followed by relational structures.

Around the same time that Smalltalk started becoming popular in the 1980s, there also emerged a need to incorporate the concepts of objects in another commercially popular language called C. Structured system analysis and design method (SSADM)[16] became popular as an approach to modeling software solutions. C was augmented with object-oriented features leading up to C++, developed by Bjarne Stroustrup at AT&T, and Objective-C, developed by Brad Cox of Stepstone Corporation. Following on from the successes of these languages, and strongly influenced by Simula, the Eiffel language of Bertrand Meyer became available commercially in the early 1990s. In the mid-1990s, the Unified Modeling Language emerged as a standard for designing software solutions—from modeling objects and classes through to components and services.

Later, in the 2000s, mobile computing (including mobile apps) and Cloud computing emerged—based on the concept of offering and consuming "services." The architecture of software systems moved from being single system to a collaborative group of services, brought together from various sources at both design and runtime. The development and deployment of software solutions started shifting to the Cloud.

Since 2001, Agile-based project life cycles have revolutionized the way solutions are designed and deployed. The shift due to Agile is creating extensive models to collaborating with users. For example, visibility (based on sticking and tracking user stories on a wall) and collaboration (essentially through the daily stand-up meetings) are highly popular Agile techniques quite commonly applied in SE projects.

The current era of Big Data includes extensive analytics that are carried out on structured and unstructured data residing in NoSQL databases. Programming languages such as Python and R are in vogue. Sourcing of these data goes well beyond human entry and into the machine sensor and IoT space, and the display of the results from the analytics takes place in myriad ways, including and especially in handheld devices.

SOFTWARE MODELING HISTORY

Flowcharts were the initial attempt at modeling software, occasionally interspersed with coding sheets. The model-view-controller (MVC) pattern provided the initial basis for structuring a computer program. SSADM followed, with a focus on analysis as well as design, but it was still used for procedural approaches. The 1980s saw an explosion of relational databases and their modeling based on Chen's highly popular entity-relationship diagrams (ERDs) and data flow diagrams (DFDs). When languages like C++ and Java became popular together with object orientation, many modeling approaches came to the fore—eventually culminating in the UML. Modeling approaches are still evolving to incorporate software solutions for mobile applications (and IoT), those that deal with Cloud computing, and the use of Big Data analytics and services.

About the UML and Its Purpose

The UML is not the output of a single individual but, rather, a collective effort of numerous practitioners, methodologists, thinkers, and authors. The OMG facilitated this input and incorporated the results into a robust metamodel, resulting in a usable industry-standard modeling notation called the UML.

The UML was first proposed around 1995 as a combination of the three most popular methods (processes) of that time: Booch,[17] object modeling technique,[18] and Objectory.[19] Later, several other methods merged into UML, eventually resulting in the popular UML version 1.4. Around 2004, a partially formalized UML version 2.0 was released. This UML version comprised 13 official diagrams[20] and corresponding changes to the metamodel, leading to initiatives such as model-driven architecture (MDA). A decade later, UML 2.5, made up of 14 diagrams,[21] is considered the de facto modeling language for SE.

UML Usage

Figure 1.14 summarizes the purpose of the UML in modeling, developing, and maintaining software systems. There are five ways in which the UML is used in SE:

- Visualizing—this is the primary purpose of the UML as its notations and diagrams provide an industry standard mechanism for pictorial representation of requirements, processes, solution design, and architecture. These visuals are created using modeling CASE tools, which also enable team-based sharing of modeling work.
- Specifying—UML facilitates specification of modeling artifacts. For example, specifications for actors, use cases, classes, attributes, and operations provide additional details for visual notations. These specifications go a long way toward enhancing the quality of solutions since reviews of specifications help resolve many misunderstandings between the users and the developers.
- Constructing—UML is used for software construction because it enables code generation (e.g., C++, Java) depending on the CASE tool being used. However, this construction feature of the UML has limited application, mainly because once the code is generated, most practical projects work directly on modifying the code rather than the designs. Round-trip engineering was meant to help modify the designs based on updated code, but this feature is not as popular in practice as earlier thought.
- Documenting—with the help of UML, additional and detailed documentation for requirements, architecture, design, project plans, tests, and prototypes is provided to enhance specifications and visual representations.
- Maintaining—good UML models are a significant aid in ongoing maintenance of software systems. Models allow an easy view of an existing system, its architecture, and IT design. This allows programmers to identify the correct places within the system for changes and, more importantly, understand the effect of their changes on the rest of the system.

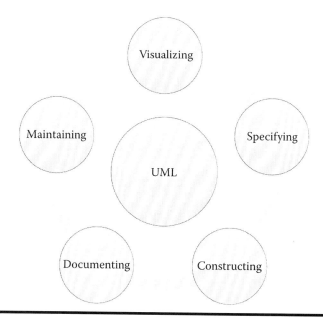

Figure 1.14   Purpose of Unified Modeling Language in SE.

Common Errors in Interpreting Software Engineering Fundamentals and How to Rectify Them

Common Error	Rectifying the Errors	Examples
Not being able to differentiate between a class and corresponding objects	Treat class as a shell or a template; object subscribes to that shell's definition.	Class = Person; Object = Sam, Mary, Ram.
Objects belong to a class, so they get treated as a subclass; objects get shown on a class diagram	Objects and classes cannot be shown on the same diagram because they are intrinsically different. Only subclasses derived from classes can be shown on a class diagram. Objects can be separately shown on object diagrams.	Class = Person; Subclass = Student; Objects belonging to Subclass Student = Sam, Zahid, Ram; Student "is a" Person can be shown on a class diagram (even though object Sam is also a person)
Data hiding vs. encapsulation	Don't write a method (function) to +set and +get every attribute; that is data hiding; instead, write meaningful operations that encapsulate multiple attributes and provide value to the calling classes.	For attribute Date, writing +setDate() and +getDate() is data hiding—which is not very helpful, but writing +getAge() is more meaningful and encapsulates date.
Inheritance vs. directional association	Be clear about the arrowheads (also see Chapter 9 on basic class relationships). Association is between two classes with no commonality; inheritance is between classes that have commonality.	Use directional association when customer accesses account; use inheritance when customer is a person.
Overclassification	Study the requirements before classification. Otherwise every object can end up as a class on its own.	Revisit Figure 1.5 to study how classification is happening.
Assuming UML is a method or a process for developing software	UML is a modeling standard; it does not specify the sequence in which models are to be developed.	A method makes use of UML. A method (or process) for developing software can specify the starting UML diagram to be used for (say) capturing requirements or developing an architecture and the ensuing diagrams.

Discussion Questions

1. Why is studying object-oriented fundamentals necessary in order to become a good software engineer?
2. What are key things to note in learning to become a good software engineer? *(hint – Figure 1.1)*
3. What is the purpose of modeling? Discuss with examples how modeling can help a project in practice. *(hint—Figure 1.2)*
4. How is a software development process different from software modeling? Explain how one helps the other in creating good-quality software? *(hint: process provides activities and steps; models provide software artifacts before they are programmed)*
5. What are the specific advantages of object-oriented software modeling? *(hint: compare with procedural approaches)*
6. List FIVE objects from your current surroundings. Create at least two classes from these five objects. With these examples, explain the difference between a class and an object. *(hint — Figures 1.3 and 1.6)*
7. Discuss the importance of classification as an OO fundamental?
8. Discuss how the OO fundamental of abstraction can be applied at two different levels? *(hint — from objects to classes, and from classes to classes)*
9. What is the difference between generalization and specialization in creating an inheritance hierarchy? Discuss with examples.
10. What is the difference between encapsulation and data hiding? Justify the extra effort required in encapsulation compared to data hiding.
11. What is the OO fundamental that is expressed only at runtime? Your answer should also describe the mandatory structural modeling requirements for that fundamental to be expressed.
12. What is the UML? Why is it considered invaluable for visualizing?

Team Project Case Study

1. Form groups of three to four students to work on a team project. Assign a case study (from the problem statements provided in Online Appendix A) to the team.
2. Read carefully the case study problem statement and have a discussion among team members on the case study.
3. REPHRASE the problem statement based on your group discussion. From this point onward, continue to focus on the deliverables of the project work. Continuous and sensible modification of your report document is required as part of this team project.
4. Consider the topics presented in this chapter in the context of the case study.
5. Explore and install a UML-based CASE tool that should be available to all project groups.
6. Students should "Create a Project" in their CASE tool. This usually means creating a project file or a workspace. Name the file appropriately as <studentgroupname>HMS-UML-Model***, for example. (Replace HMS by the acronym of your project.)
7. Experiment with the fundamentals of OO by creating a class diagram with inheritance and association.
8. Experiment with exporting and importing diagrams from the model files created in your modeling tool.
9. Share what you have learned from your diagrams with your group.

Endnotes

1. Sperry, R. (1982), "Some Effects of Disconnecting the Cerebral Hemispheres," *Science*, 217(4566). This theory essentially says that the left brain deals with precision, planning, calculations, and so on, whereas the right brain is associated with the artistic side of an individual. Notwithstanding this theory, software engineers need both these engineering and artistic aspects in producing software of value.
2. Unhelkar, B., *The Psychology of Agile: Fundamentals beyond the Manifesto,* Cutter Executive Report, Dec 2013, Agile Product & Project Management Practice, Cutter, Boston, USA. Vol 14, No 5.
3. http://www.disciplinedagiledelivery.com/ accessed May 7, 2017.
4. Unhelkar, B. (2013), *The Art of Agile Practice: A Composite Approach for Projects and Organizations,* CRC Press.
5. Glass, R. (1998), *Software Runaways*, Prentice Hall PTR.
6. www.abet.org/: global standard for programs in applied science, computing, engineering, and engineering technology.
7. www.computer.org/: membership organization dedicated to computer science and technology; accessed 19th October 2017.
8. www.acs.org.au The Australian Computer Society—Professional Association and peak body representing Australia's ICT sector.
9. www.acm.org/: Advancing Computing as a Science & Profession.
10. www.swebok.org—Software Engineering Body of Knowledge (https://www.computer.org/web/swebok).
11. www.uml.org/: All about UML from the Object Management Group OMG°.
12. www.omg.org/spec/UML/: official UML specifications by the OMG.
13. Extends earlier work with five fundamentals discussed in Unhelkar, B., (2005), *Practical Object Oriented Analysis*, Cengage (first published by Thomson Publishing), Australia, March 2005. ISBN 0-17-012298-0.
14. Nygaard, K. https://en.wikipedia.org/wiki/Kristen_Nygaard, accessed July 3, 2017.
15. Kay, A. https://en.wikipedia.org/wiki/Alan_Kay accessed July 3, 2017.
16. SSADM was produced for a UK government office concerned with the use of technology in government, from 1980 onward.
17. Booch, G. (1994), *Object-oriented Analysis and Design,* Benjamin/Cummings Publishing Company.
18. (Rumbaugh *et al.*,) James Rumbaugh, Michael Blaha, William Premerlani, Frederick Eddy, William Lorensen (1990), *Object-Oriented Modeling and Design*, Prentice Hall. ISBN 0-13-629841-9.
19. Jacobson, I., Christerson, M., Jonsson, P., and Overgaard, G. (1992), *Object-Oriented Software Engineering: A Use Case Driven Approach,* Addison-Wesley, ACM Press.
20. http://www.agilemodelling.com/essays/umlDiagrams.htm.
21. http://www.omg.org/spec/UML/2.5/: for documents associated with the latest specifications; accessed May 16, 2017.

Chapter 2

Review of 14 Unified Modeling Language Diagrams

Learning Objectives

- Briefly review all UML 2.5 diagrams: use case, activity, package, class, profile, sequence, communication, interaction overview, object, state machine, composite structure, component, deployment, and timing diagrams
- Study a simple example of each of the UML diagrams
- Understand the nature (static versus dynamic, structural versus behavioral) of UML diagrams to improve their use in practice
- Note the differences in the list of UML diagrams across versions

List and Nature of UML Diagrams

This chapter introduces all UML diagrams in version 2.5.[1] Understanding these UML diagrams is integral to SE. This is because these UML diagrams present a suite of modeling artifacts that are a globally accepted standard for SE. Knowledge and understanding of the diagrams provide the means and the language for software engineers to sketch and visualize their thoughts, as well as discuss, debate, question, communicate, and measure their work, particularly on a project team. Knowing UML and its underlying concepts is equivalent to learning most, if not all, of SE.

Note that all of these 14 UML diagrams are hardly ever used together by one person. Each diagram has a specific purpose in SE that needs to be understood by the modelers. The specific nature and purpose of a diagram dictates how and where it is used in modeling. For example, some diagrams provide an excellent way to understand the requirements and behavior of a system (e.g., use case and activity diagrams). Other diagrams provide a robust mechanism to model data storage (e.g., class diagrams). And yet another set of UML diagrams helps visualize the software architecture (e.g., component and deployment diagrams).

Further note that the UML only provides standards for modeling—that is, it creates these diagrams following certain standardized notations. The UML, however, does not dictate the sequence in which these diagrams can be produced. That sequencing is the responsibility of a software development process. Key aspects of a software development process are discussed separately in Chapter 4. Understanding the nature and purpose of the UML diagrams, as undertaken in this chapter, helps modelers better understand the sequence in which these diagrams can be produced and used. The iterative and incremental nature of new approaches to developing software (Agile) also benefits by proper understanding of these UML diagrams.

Table 2.1 lists all 14 UML diagrams. This table also has a brief description of these UML diagrams.[2] The rest of the chapter expands this list of diagrams and provides examples.

While these diagrams compose the toolbox of modeling techniques, they are not entirely independent of each other. Some of these diagrams have dependencies on each other that are important from both syntactic and semantic modeling perspectives. These diagrams, and the artifacts within them, enable visualizations of various aspects of a software system. The diagrams are further augmented by corresponding specifications and documentation.

Table 2.1   Table of 14 UML 2.5 Diagrams

UML Diagram	*Brief Description*
1. Use case diagram	Provides an overview of functionality of the system or business processes from a user perspective. The way in which a user "uses" the system is the starting point for creating a use case diagram.
2. Activity diagram	Models the flow anywhere in the system. In particular, the flow within a use case describing normal user interactions and the alternatives and exceptions is very well modeled by these activity diagrams.
3. Class diagram	Represents classes, their definitions, and relationships. Classes and entities from the problem space are also detailed technical entities in the solution space. The attributes and operations that define the classes are included within this class diagram. Relationships in a class diagram illustrate how classes interact, collaborate, and inherit from other classes. Classes can also represent relational tables, user interfaces, and controllers.
4. Sequence diagram	Models the interactions between objects based on their timelines. Objects can be specifically shown on these diagrams or they can be anonymous objects belonging to a class. The sequence of execution of messages between objects at runtime is well modeled by these diagrams, hence their name.

(Continued)

Table 2.1 (*Continued*) Table of 14 UML 2.5 Diagrams

UML Diagram	Brief Description
5. Interaction overview diagram	Presents an overview of the interactions within a system at a general, high level; it also enables an understanding of how UML diagrams (e.g., a sequence diagram) depend on and relate to each other.
6. Communication diagram	Shows how objects communicate (interact) between each other in the memory at runtime. These communication diagrams are similar to sequence diagrams in terms of their purpose; however, their representation is different.
7. Object diagram	Shows objects and their links in the memory at runtime. Therefore, these object diagrams also help visualize multiplicities in practice.
8. State machine diagram	Shows the runtime life cycle of an object in memory. Such a life cycle includes all the states of an object and the conditions under which the states change.
9. Composite structure diagram	Models the component or object behavior at runtime showing the layout, relationships, and instances of components during system execution
10. Component diagram	Models components and their relationships structurally. These components can include, for example, executables, linkable libraries, Web services, and mobile services. These diagrams add value to the architectural decision-making of the system.
11. Deployment diagram	Models the architecture of the hardware nodes and processors of the system and provides opportunities to show the nodes on which the software components will reside.
12. Package diagram	Represents the subsystems and areas of system organization. It can also model dependencies between packages and help separate business entities from user interfaces, databases, security, and administrative packages.
13. Timing diagram	Models the concept of time and the way in which the state of an object changes over time. Furthermore, these diagrams enable comparison between the states of multiple objects at the same time.
14. Profile Diagram	Enables the creation of extendible profiles that can be applied to elements inherited from the profiles. These diagrams add value by extending the standards in a controlled manner.

Nature and Basics of UML Diagrams

The nature of the UML diagrams is understood as follows (summarized in Figure 2.1):

- *Structural versus behavioral*—The structural aspect of a diagram illustrates the way a system is organized, whereas the behavioral aspect models the flow of the system. Structure, for example, shows how classes relate to each other in a class diagram. Behavior shows the way in which a user interacts with the system—through a use case or an activity diagram, for example.
- *Static versus dynamic*—The static versus dynamic aspect depicts the *time dependency* of the model. A diagram with no concept of time or movement is static, whereas one that shows changes in time (or even a snapshot in time) is considered dynamic.

The nature of UML diagrams mentioned previously is also not a watertight classification. Each diagram exhibits the aforementioned nature of UML diagrams—but some characteristics are very strongly exhibited and others may be nonexistent in those diagrams.

Brief Review of UML Diagrams

The following section is a brief review or "walkthrough" of the UML diagrams. The objective is to understand the nature, purpose, and "look and feel" of the diagrams. Each subsection also provides a basic example of the diagram. As mentioned earlier, not every diagram is important for every role within a software project. In Chapter 3 (see Table 3.2), there is a discussion on the relative importance of each diagram to different roles (such as a programmer, designer, or business analyst) within a software project.

Use Case Diagrams

A use case diagram is a model of the requirements of a system at a high level. Use case diagrams are primarily used to *visualize* use cases, corresponding sectors, and their interactions. The diagram itself is not a use case but rather a visual of actors and a group of related use cases. Visual

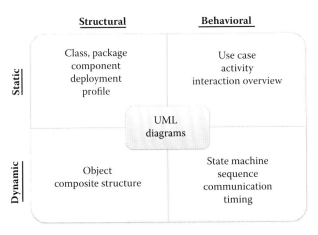

Figure 2.1 Understanding UML diagrams from a structural-behavioral and static-dynamic viewpoint.

models of use cases facilitate understanding the business processes and aid in communication with stakeholders. The specification and documentation of the use cases shown in the use case diagrams form the crux of requirements modeling.

Use case diagrams are *behavioral-static* in nature. This is because they help organize and evaluate the requirements of the system—in the problem space. The behavioral aspect of the requirements is not visible in the use case diagrams. Because the relationships between two use cases, or between actors and use cases, do not represent the concept of time, use case diagrams are categorized as static diagrams. Therefore, care should be taken to consider use case diagrams as depicting the flow or behavior of a system. The flow of a process is part of the textual documentation within a use case and the corresponding activity diagrams.

Use cases within use case diagrams cannot be decomposed in the same way that data flow diagrams (DFDs) are decomposed. There are no layers or levels of use case diagrams—they are all at the same level within the entire requirements model. The documentation of use cases is a rich source to identify business entities that eventually result in classes.

Figure 2.2 shows a simple use case diagram containing actors, use cases, and their relationships. Specifically, this diagram shows two actors: `ActorPatient` and `ActorStaff`. There are also two use cases called `ChecksDoctorAvailability` and `SchedulesConsultation` in the diagram. These actors and the use cases have associated documentation, which is not shown in the diagram. Also the lines connecting the actors to the use cases merely indicate an association or communication and not a dependency or a flow of information. In order to clarify the diagram further and make the intended process readable, it is always useful to provide additional annotation, descriptions, and notes.

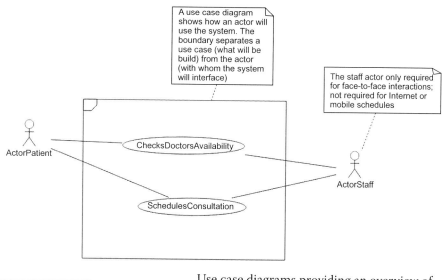

NATURE: *STATIC-BEHAVIORAL*

Use case diagrams providing an overview of the requirements through actors and use cases. Internal documentation of the use cases contains details of the interactions between actor and system.

Figure 2.2   Use case diagram.

Activity Diagrams

Activity diagrams model the flow, or process, in a system. Therefore, they are like flowcharts. This modeling of a flow can be done at the business process level, within a use case, and occasionally between use cases.

Activities are either at a detailed technical level or at a business level. Activity diagrams document the internal behavior within use cases, between use cases, or of the overall business. A higher-level activity diagram is used as a context diagram showing how various business processes are related.

Another important characteristic of activity diagrams is the ability to show dependency between activities. Activity diagrams also help in mapping the activities to corresponding actors within a system. Furthermore, because of their ability to show multiple threads (through forks and joins, as discussed in Chapter 7), they can also exhibit what happens *simultaneously* in the system. The multithreading modeling capabilities provided by activity diagrams are also helpful in modeling the problem space. Therefore, these diagrams provide an excellent mechanism to model business processes.

The nature of activity diagrams is considered to be behavioral. This is because these diagrams show activities and also the sequence in which these activities occur. However, activity diagrams do not show *when* exactly the activities occur. To that extent, activity diagrams are generic, behavioral flowcharts. They are therefore not considered dynamic diagrams (such as sequence diagrams). The nature of activity diagrams is thus *behavioral-static.*

Consider, for example, Figure 2.3, which shows a simple activity diagram from a hospital domain. `Patient` and `system` are shown as two partitions (called swimlanes in earlier versions of UML, discussed in detail in Chapter 7), in which a series of activities are taking place. The activity diagram shows how the `patient` enquires about the availability of the `doctor` in order to schedule a `consultation`.

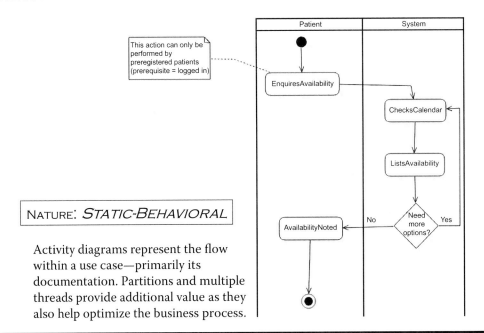

Figure 2.3   Activity diagrams.

Class Diagrams

Class diagrams are one of the most popular diagrams in SE. Class diagrams represent the key entities within the business as well as technical domain. Class diagrams are highly structural and static in nature, with no behavioral content. Class diagrams can show business-level classes, as well as technical classes derived from the implementation language (e.g., Java or C++ −). In addition to showing the classes, class diagrams also show the relationships between classes. The entire description of the classes (or entities, as they may be called in the problem space) and the relationships that they will have with each other is static. There is no dependency shown in this diagram and no concept of time. Notes and constraints (discussed during UML's extensibility mechanism in Chapter 10) show the dependency of the classes in a limited manner on a class diagram.

Figure 2.4 shows a simple class diagram with classes `Doctor`, `Patient`, `Surgeon`, and `Physician`. Furthermore, it shows an association relationship between `doctor` and `patient`, as well as an inheritance relationship to show derivations from the `Doctor` class. Detailed discussion on class diagrams is in Chapters 8, 9, and 11.

Sequence Diagrams

Sequence diagrams have been popular ever since Jacobson introduced them as a means of documenting the behavior within use cases. In earlier uses, sequence diagrams were also called scenario diagrams, because they represented, pictorially, a scenario (or an instance) within a use case. Because of their practical ability to show what is happening "inside" a use case, sequence diagrams are popular with both business analysts and system designers. Each step within a use case appears on the sequence diagram as a note or a narration.

Sequence diagrams represent the detailed interaction between actors and a system or between collaborating objects *within a given time block*. However, information as to what happened before

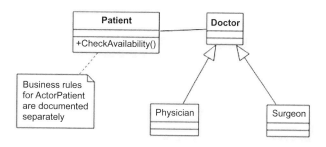

NATURE: *STATIC-STRUCTURAL*

Class diagrams model entities (i.e., classes at business and technical levels) and their relationships. Classes in these diagrams contain attributes and operations (which can be visible or hidden), relationships (inheritance, association), and multiplicities.

Figure 2.4   Class diagrams.

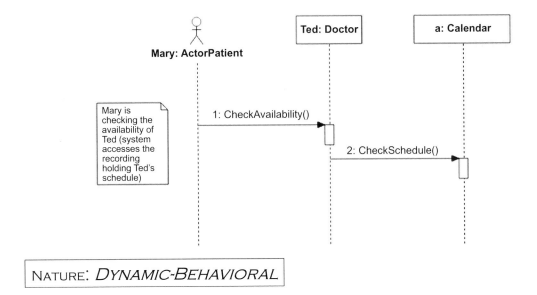

NATURE: *DYNAMIC-BEHAVIORAL*

Sequence diagrams show a single scenario of
interactions between objects and system (through
messages). The sequence of messages is important.
These diagrams may contain actors. Sequence diagrams
cannot show conditions ("if-then-else").

Figure 2.5   Sequence diagrams.

the interaction started and what happens after the time block stops is not shown in the sequence diagram. While messages shown in the sequence diagram can have preconditions and postconditions, these conditions are not directly visible in the diagram. Despite this limitation, the "time" appearing in the diagram is far more precise than in the activity diagram. Therefore, it is possible to show what happens between two messages and to ascertain what happens *as time progresses*. The sequence diagrams are thus considered dynamic-behavioral in nature.

Figure 2.5 shows a simple sequence diagram showing how an actor (`Ravi:Patient`) checks for the availability of a particular doctor (`Sue:Doctor`). The `Doctor` object, in turn, has to go to the `Calendar` object in order to check the availability of the doctor.

Interaction Overview Diagrams

Interaction overview diagrams, as their name suggests, provide a high-level overview of interactions happening within a system. Since those interactions are best depicted using sequence (or, alternatively, communication) diagrams, interaction overview diagrams contain a reference to sequence diagrams. An interaction overview diagram can depict an "if-then-else" situation. Therefore, interaction overview diagrams are closer to activity diagrams. An interaction overview diagram is considered to be *behavioral-static* in nature.

Figure 2.6 is a simple interaction overview diagram referencing two use cases: `ChecksDoctorAvailability` and `SchedulesConsultation`. Each of these references

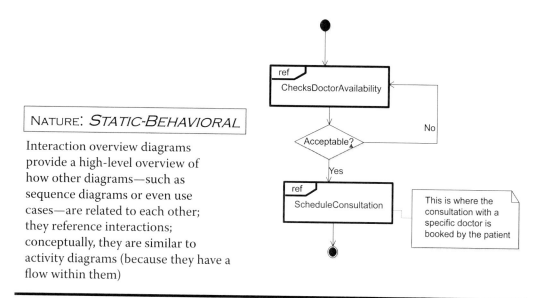

NATURE: *STATIC-BEHAVIORAL*

Interaction overview diagrams provide a high-level overview of how other diagrams—such as sequence diagrams or even use cases—are related to each other; they reference interactions; conceptually, they are similar to activity diagrams (because they have a flow within them)

Figure 2.6   Interaction overview diagram.

could also have been sequence diagrams. This diagram is able to show a high-level flow in the system, where the use cases and sequence diagrams are part of the "if-then-else" scenario. In Figure 2.6, this is shown by checking whether the availability of the doctor is acceptable. If not, the flow returns to the previous use case `ChecksDoctorAvailability`. If it is, the consultation is scheduled.

Communication Diagrams

A communication diagram shows a suite of collaborating objects, how they are related through their messages, and the sequence of those messages. A communication diagram shows information similar to that in a sequence diagram, but the manner in which it is shown is different. Still, for all practical purposes, the nature of the communication diagrams is *dynamic-behavioral*—the same as sequence diagrams and for the same reasons. Visually, a communication diagram may be considered a tool to show all the messages sent and received by an object. This information may be used to ascertain the load on an object at runtime.

Figure 2.7 shows a communication diagram. The actor (`Ravi:Patient`) checks for the availability of a particular doctor (`Sue:Doctor`) as was done in the sequence diagram shown in Figure 2.5. The `Doctor` object then goes to the `Calendar` object in order to check the availability of the doctor for the consultation. `1:CheckAvailability()` and `2:CheckSchedule()` methods have mandatory numbering (this number is optional in sequence diagrams). Because of their "techie" feel, they are used more in design than in analysis. Therefore, communication diagrams are not discussed further in this book. Instead, sequence diagrams are used to conduct all dynamic-behavioral modeling.

Object Diagrams

An object diagram shows, at a particular *point in time*, the *structure* of the various objects and their relationship to each other. Therefore, they are structural in nature. However, because object

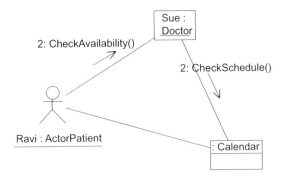

Communication diagrams are an alternative view to the sequence diagrams. These diagrams model interactions between objects and their links to each other. The sequencing of messages is depicted by numbers.

Figure 2.7 Communication diagram.

diagrams show the structure of runtime objects, modeling what is happening in the system at a particular point in time, they are also considered dynamic. However, this dynamicity is only a "snapshot" in the memory of the computer as the system is operated or a suite of links between multiple objects. The diagrams are *not* able to show any *change* in the system over time.

Thus, these diagrams are "suspended in time"—showing what happens in terms of relationships between objects either in the main memory or as a mechanism to express and discuss multiplicities on a whiteboard. Thus, the nature of an object diagram can be categorized as *dynamic-structural*.

Figure 2.8 shows an object diagram that links a doctor object called aDoctor, with three Patient instances: John, Mary, and Ravi. In Figure 2.4 (class diagram), the Doctor class is associated with the Patient class. An object diagram shows exactly how many patients are associated with a doctor.

In Figure 2.9, aDoctor is associated with John:Patient, Mary:Patient, and Ravi:Patient—because this particular doctor is dealing with three patients, perhaps during a session or a day. If another doctor were to deal with only two patients, then the object diagram would show those two patients. Note that for these two variations of object diagrams, the corresponding class diagram (Figure 2.4) remains the same.

State Machine Diagram

An object belonging to a class can be in various states, and so can an entire system. A state machine diagram (also called a state chart) indicates the various states in which an object or a use case or an entire system can be. As compared with an object diagram (which shows an "instance version" or "snapshot" of the system), a state machine diagram shows all possible states for an object.

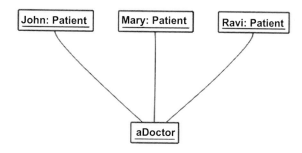

NATURE: DYNAMIC-STRUCTURAL

Object diagrams describe the various objects (*instances*) and how they relate to each other. The relationships are *links* in the memory. Being instance-level diagrams, they are ideal in depicting the multiplicities between classes.

Figure 2.8   Object diagram.

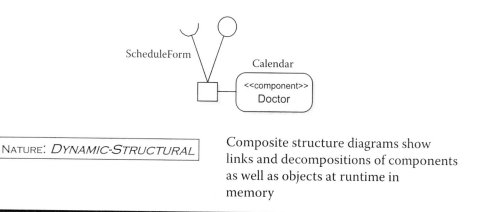

NATURE: *DYNAMIC-STRUCTURAL*

Composite structure diagrams show links and decompositions of components as well as objects at runtime in memory

Figure 2.9   Composite structure diagram.

The state machine diagram of the UML has the ability to represent time precisely and in a real-time fashion. "What happens at a certain point in time?" is a question that is answered by this diagram. Therefore, the nature of the state machine diagram is dynamic-behavioral. Because of this dynamic nature of state machine diagrams, they are ideal for modeling real-time systems. This diagram also shows the entire behavior of one object—depicting the life cycle of an object as the object changes its state in response to the messages it receives. As a result, this is a behavioral diagram, with hardly any structural content.

Figure 2.10 shows a state machine diagram depicting the states of a Doctor class (or an object of Doctor class). These states are Available, Booked, and Consulting. The diagram also shows the guard conditions, i.e., [AppointmentBooked], under which the transitions (the connecting lines between states) take place.

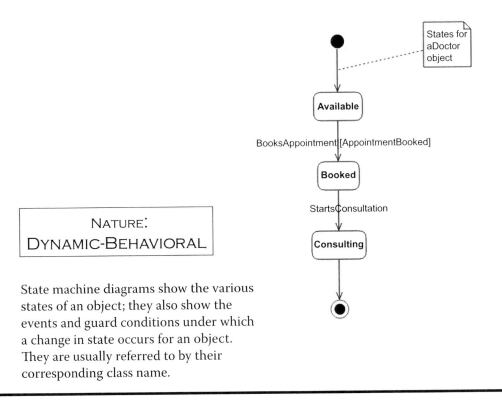

NATURE:
DYNAMIC-BEHAVIORAL

State machine diagrams show the various states of an object; they also show the events and guard conditions under which a change in state occurs for an object. They are usually referred to by their corresponding class name.

Figure 2.10   State machine diagram.

Composite Structure Diagrams

Composite structure diagrams are architectural in nature, fitting in well with the modeling requirements in the background space. Composite structure diagrams decompose an object or a component, at runtime, and show the various interfaces and realizations linked to that object, as shown in Figure 2.10. These diagrams show runtime scenarios in which the structure of the runtime components is revealed. As a result, their nature is dynamic-structural—similar to object diagrams.

Figure 2.10 shows a very simple composite structure diagram that depicts the runtime scenario of the Doctor component. The Doctor component is related to two other interfaces, ScheduleForm and Calendar. As will be obvious to requirements modelers, the Doctor component at runtime depends on the Calendar interface, which it uses to check the availability of the doctor. However, when it comes to displaying the information, it will be ScheduleForm that depends on the Doctor component for the information to display.

Component Diagrams

Component Diagrams are *static-structural* in nature. They show the structure of the system as it is implemented, but they do not show the behavior of the system in operation. Component diagrams also do not incorporate the concept of time, and therefore are not dynamic. Component diagrams only show where the classes and various other logical artifacts will eventually be realized

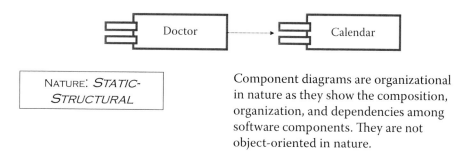

NATURE: *STATIC-STRUCTURAL*

Component diagrams are organizational in nature as they show the composition, organization, and dependencies among software components. They are not object-oriented in nature.

Figure 2.11   Component diagram.

(or coded) as final executables. A component diagram is thus a pictorial representation of the final executables and linked libraries that contain the code of the system.

Figure 2.11 shows a simple component diagram with two components: Doctor and Calendar. Furthermore, the diagram also shows the dependency of Doctor on Calendar. Note that at a technical level, components can also include COM+ objects, Enterprise Java bean executables, linked libraries of linked objects, and so on. Thus, a component becomes a physical representation of—mainly—a collection of classes. Components, like classes, can also reside in packages, and components also have interfaces.

Deployment Diagrams

Deployment diagrams are structural and static in nature. Unlike all other diagrams in the UML, deployment diagrams are the only "hardware" diagrams in UML. They show the organization of processing nodes to enable deployment of the software system. They also show the components that are executed on these nodes. Being a hardware diagram, the deployment diagram provides a valuable foundation for communicating hardware-related decisions. Deployment diagrams enable discussion of the operational requirements of a system including the ability of the system to handle speed and volume, location and security of the nodes, and the manner in which the executables are deployed across the network.

A limitation of deployment diagrams is that they do not have enough symbols to represent the various hardware nodes of a detailed system architecture. This results in a situation where various tool vendors and developers create a version of their own notations for deployment diagrams. There is thus a possibility of confusion in sharing and reading deployment diagrams.

Figure 2.12 shows a basic deployment diagram. It shows the existence of a Hospital Server machine or processor and two patient processors. Furthermore, the server is shown related to the printer, which is another physical device. A more sophisticated deployment diagram would contain additional devices such as a local area network (LAN), Internet, Cloud representation, firewalls, and database servers.

Package Diagrams

Package diagrams are static-structural in nature, providing an excellent means to organize the requirements in the problem space. Packages primarily represent a large and cohesive part of a system (a subsystem). From a modeling viewpoint, package diagrams are considered organizational

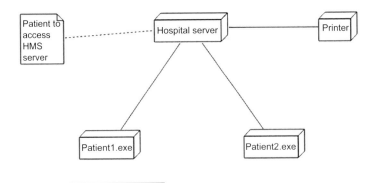

NATURE: *STATIC-STRUCTURAL*

A deployment diagram shows the manner in which a system will be deployed when in operation. These diagrams show processes and nodes in the physical design of a system. They are the only hardware diagram in the UML

Figure 2.12   Deployment diagram.

diagrams. A package is a collection of logically cohesive artifacts and diagrams of the UML. Package diagrams therefore only show the top view—a bird's-eye view—of the system organization. Package diagrams may also show dependencies between packages. However, dependencies in package diagrams are not mandatory and are not as important as the packages themselves. Because of their organizational role, package diagrams have no behavior associated with them.

Figure 2.13 shows a simple package diagram with the staff package dependent on the `Calendar` package. Note that `Staff` and `Calendar` are *not* classes but packages or subsystems containing detailed functional models relating to staff and calendar, respectively.

NATURE: *STATIC-STRUCTURAL*

Packages represent subsystems; They comprise large and cohesive collections of other UML diagrams. Package diagrams are organizational in nature and show packages and their dependencies.

Figure 2.13   Package diagram.

Timing Diagrams

Timing diagrams were introduced in the later versions of the UML (from UML 2.0 onwards). Their value is in comparing object states—in either the problem or the solution space. Timing diagrams are dynamic-behavioral in nature, depicting the states of an object and the state changes at precise points in time. These diagrams are derived from the timing diagrams used in engineering to show state changes to an object. While a similar purpose is achieved through state machine diagrams, timing diagrams show multiple objects and their corresponding states *at the same time.*

Figure 2.14 presents an example of a timing diagram showing two states for the Doctor object—operating and nonoperating. This timing diagram also shows the exact point at which the state change occurs and how long the object remains in the operating (On) state (in this case, it is shown by the constraint {80 minutes}) before returning to the nonoperating (Off) state. Timing diagrams are not as popular as other UML diagrams.

Profile Diagrams

The underlying metamodel of the UML allows it to be applied to various situations. One possible way to extend the UML to a project-specific application is the profile diagram. A profile definition can include UML elements as well as stereotypes, tags, and constraints. Such profiles are created for development-specific platforms such as .NET and J2EE. A profile can also be created for specific projects such as modeling business processes.

Consider, for example, Figure 2.15, which shows an example profile diagram inheriting a <<stereotype>> from a <<meta-class>>. The <<meta-class>> contains details that can be specialized using a profile. Such specialization enables restrictions and checks on the parameters and behavior of new classes that are based on a given meta-class. For example, a <<stereotype>> can restrict the new classes to single inheritance (as against a multiple-inheritance hierarchy). Such a restriction is based on the application of project-specific "profiles" created in the profile diagrams.

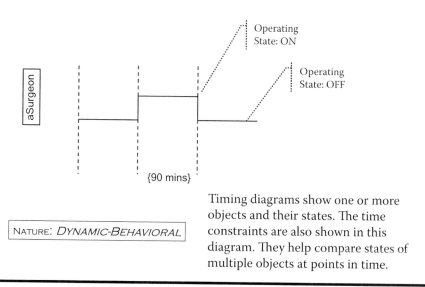

Timing diagrams show one or more objects and their states. The time constraints are also shown in this diagram. They help compare states of multiple objects at points in time.

Figure 2.14   Timing diagram.

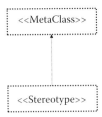

Profile diagrams enable extension of UML such as visualization of stereotypes (e.g., inheriting all the characteristics of a Meta-class as shown in this diagram)

Figure 2.15   Profile diagram.

Differences in List of UML Diagrams

Occasionally, trying to understand the exact list of UML diagrams is disconcerting because in almost all previous releases of the UML, authors and practitioners came up with their own slightly varying list of UML diagrams. For example, Booch et al.[3] in their earlier official UML user guide, listed only nine diagrams. Jacobson's earlier work, as well as that of Rosenberg and Scott,[4] lists robustness diagrams (a type of class diagram) separately, resulting in a total of ten diagrams. In UML 2.0 and beyond, package diagrams appear as separate diagrams, and the interaction overview, composite structure, and timing diagrams have been added to the list of UML diagrams. The communication diagrams used to be called collaboration diagrams and, together with sequence diagrams, are also referred to as implementation diagrams in the UML literature. Object diagrams are sometimes treated as independent diagrams in their own right, but they are not supported by CASE tools as independent diagrams.

A practical way to approach these diagrams is to understand their nature and how they are used. As discussed in the next chapter, these diagrams are best treated as a toolbox of techniques. As a result, they are used appropriate to the demands of the situation. CASE tools for modeling UML diagrams do a good job of providing a large number of the diagrams discussed in this chapter. However, not all diagrams are always provided, nor are they necessary for practical modeling work.

Common Errors in Understanding UML Diagrams and How to Rectify Them

Common Errors	*Rectifying the Errors*	*Examples*
Confusing use cases with use case diagrams	Note that use case diagrams provide a high-level overview of business requirements; the use cases themselves are documentation of the user-system interactions.	Figure 2.2 shows a use case diagram. The two ellipses within that diagram are the use cases `ChecksDoctorsAvailability` and `SchedulesConsultation`. Each of these use cases will have corresponding, detailed documentation. See Chapters 5 and 6 for more details on use cases and use case diagrams.
Using activity diagrams instead of interaction overview diagrams	Use activity diagrams primarily to model the user-system interactions documented within the use case. Interaction overview diagrams can be used to understand high-level dependencies between diagrams (such as sequence diagrams)	See Chapter 7 for examples of how activity and interaction overview diagrams are modeled.
Treating class diagrams as entirely technical	Class diagrams have many purposes within software development. These diagrams can be used to (a) model the business entities and create business domain models, (b) create solution models based on specific solution environments, and (c) model databases, especially relational databases, for storage.	See Chapter 8 for modeling business entities, Chapter 9 for creating basic class diagrams, and Chapter 11 for advanced concepts in class diagrams in the solution space.
Drawing both sequence and communication diagrams	While these two diagrams have their own identity, they provide similar information. Modelers can decide which of these two diagrams is most acceptable and then use that particular diagram throughout the project.	See Chapter 12 for a discussion on how to use sequence diagrams and read the note there on communication diagrams.
Treating object diagrams as class diagrams	Class diagrams are specifically structural diagrams that cover the entire organization of the system. Object diagrams are instance-level diagrams that only show a snapshot in time. Ensure objects are never shown in class diagrams.	A class "Student" in a class diagram contains many students—John, Ravi, and Mary, for example. None of these student objects can be shown in a class diagram. Objects need to be drawn separately in an object diagram.

Common Errors	Rectifying the Errors	Examples
Drawing a state machine diagram as a flowchart	States are unique to an object. These states are not the same as activities shown in an activity diagram. Ensure a list of states corresponding to an object (of a class) is created. Then apply the conditions that bring about a change to the states and then place them in a state machine diagram.	See Chapter 14 for examples of a state machine diagram—and note that this diagram does *not* have a flow of activities like the activity diagram.

Discussion Questions

1. Review the list of UML diagrams provided in Table 2.1. Discuss the nature of any two UML diagrams of your choice.
2. Which two UML diagrams would you consider most valuable in understanding the requirements of a user? Provide reasons with examples for your answer.
3. Which two UML diagrams would you consider as most confusing and hard to distinguish? Provide reasons with examples for your answer.
4. What is the relationship between sequence and communication diagrams?
5. Which UML diagrams are dynamic-behavioral in nature? Why?
6. A state machine diagram shows states of an object and not the object itself. Explain using an example.
7. An object diagram does not show states of an object. Discuss with example.
8. Compare a static-structural diagram with a dynamic-behavioral diagram of the UML. Your comparison must have examples.
9. Which UML diagrams are important from a solutions design point of view? Why? (*Hint: class diagrams, state machine diagrams*)
10. Which UML diagrams would you use to model system architecture?
11. Which UML diagram is the only hardware diagram? How do you see it being used in practice?

Team Project Case Study

1. Continue to work with your student group (it is important that the case study be worked through as a team project and not as an individual project because many nuances of the UML become apparent only when the models are created in a group by a team).
2. A UML-based modeling tool is downloaded by you (or made available to you in a lab). StarUML is a good option.
3. Experiment by replicating all the UML diagrams discussed in this chapter in your modeling tool. (*Note: some UML diagrams, such as timing diagrams, may not be supported by any modeling tool.*)

4. Experiment with the creation of a couple of diagrams in a *shared* mode—that is, two or more team members attempting to work on the same diagram at the same time. *(Note: the challenge here will be conflicts in the modeling files; revisit this exercise after discussions in Chapter 3 on package diagrams.)*

5. Continue to share your knowledge with your group by holding regular discussion meetings and workshops. *(Note: Chapter 4 briefly discusses Agility as a style of working. Its important that you follow the Agile working style—even though it is not discussed in great detail in this book. Holding regular meetings—preferably on a daily basis, but in this academic setting on a weekly basis—is integral to Agile working style.)*

Endnotes

1. http://www.omg.org/spec/UML/2.5/, accessed July 7, 2017.
2. Based on Unhelkar, B. (2005), *Verification and Validation for Quality of UML Models*, John Wiley and Sons, (Wiley Interscience), July 2005. ISBN: 0471727830.
3. Booch, G., Rumbaugh, J., and Jacobson, I. (1999), *The Unified Modeling Language User Guide*, Reading, Mass.: Addison-Wesley.
4. *Use Case Driven Object Modeling with UML: A Practical Approach*, Doug Rosenberg & Kendall Scott, 1999, Addison-Wesley Professional.

Chapter 3

Software Projects and Modeling Spaces: Package Diagrams

Learning Objectives

- Understand the diverse types of projects and organizations where UML can be used effectively
- Provide thoughts on UML usage in different project sizes (small, medium, large, and collaborative)
- Break down a project (decomposing) and organizing it into smaller, manageable parts (subsystems)
- Understand the three role-based modeling spaces: model of problem space (MOPS), model of solution space (MOSS), and model of architectural space (MOAS)
- Map relative importance of UML diagrams to corresponding modeling spaces and roles
- Use package diagram of UML to organize projects by representing subsystems as packages
- Understand namespaces and their use in UML

Understanding Different Types and Sizes of UML-Based Projects

Project Types and UML

This chapter starts with a discussion of the applicability of the UML to several types and sizes of projects. This discussion is important to avoid using the UML as a whole—but, instead, use it selectively and as appropriate for the given situation. The nature, type, and size of the software project dictates the situation for selective application of the UML. The versatility of UML allows it to be used in capturing requirements, modeling process flows, creating designs of software solutions, and developing architecture. This versatility of UML can also be a challenge in practice. Understanding the project situation and then carefully applying the relevant techniques of UML to the project is advisable.

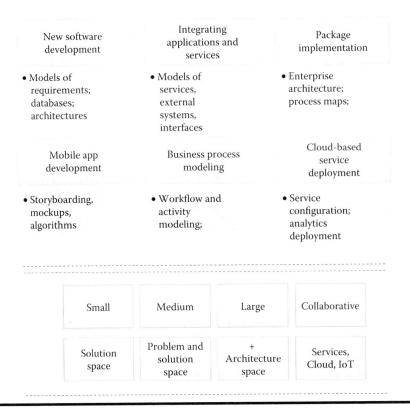

Figure 3.1 Various types and sizes of software projects and their use of UML.

The diverse types of projects using UML are summarized in Figure 3.1 and outlined below:

■ New software development projects—where systems are designed from scratch. Requirements for business applications can be modeled using the UML's use cases and activity diagrams. Solution architectures and design in these projects use class, sequence, and solution state diagrams.

■ Integrating applications and services projects—where newer systems are integrated with existing (typically legacy) systems. Interfaces for such systems require extra effort in modeling, most typically using class and sequence diagrams.

■ Package implementation projects—for example, implementation of a customer relationship management system (CRMS) or enterprise resource planning (ERP) systems. These projects use modeling techniques to specify the problem because the solution is already provided by the CRM package. Architectural diagrams of the UML (e.g., component and deployment) are also most helpful to ensure the solution fits the existing enterprise architecture (EA).

■ Mobile app development projects—where UML provides the basis for creating storyboards, relating them to mockups and enabling the modeling of algorithms for analytics and processing. However, the usability aspects of mobile interfaces are served only in a limited way by UML.

■ Business process modeling projects—where business workflows and related information are extensively modeled using the UML. Activity diagrams and BPMN are heavily used to model the processes of an organization. Occasionally package diagrams can be used to organize process modeling.

■ Cloud-based service development projects—where UML is used to model services and their interfaces. UML can also help in modeling the configuration of services and the way in which these services can be deployed in the Cloud.

Project Sizes and UML

The various sizes of projects[1] that can benefit from the UML are shown in Figure 3.1. This size classification, among other things, is based on rough guidelines of time, cost, and people. Considering the size of a project, however, helps in understanding the extent to which and the level at which the UML can be applied:

■ Small projects (5–15 people, 3–6 months, <$2 million) mainly use the UML in the solution space. For example, class, sequence, and state machine diagrams can be very handy and, at times, may be the only diagrams used by a couple of developers.

■ Medium projects (15–50 people, 6–12 months, $3–10 million) need more formality (ceremonies) than small projects in following development processes. These medium projects also create more sophisticated models—especially for the requirements—than small projects. These projects model detailed requirements with use cases and activity diagrams.

■ Large projects (50+ people, >1 year, >$10 million) not only have a need for modeling the requirements and solutions, but also have a regulatory need to do so. These projects use UML for modeling in the problem and solution spaces extensively. Also, the UML models in the architectural space play a major role in such projects.

■ Collaborative projects are typically outsourced projects[2] (50+ people, >1 year, $10 million). These projects benefit from enhanced accountability, traceability, and coordination when the UML is used. These collaborative projects can stretch over many departments and divisions of an organization and as separate development teams spread out globally. Typically, these are Cloud-based development and deployment projects. The distinct locations, time zones, and values of the teams that specify requirements and those that develop the solutions represent a major challenge—and UML can help with this challenge through standardized visual models, entering and sharing them in CASE tools or as teams, understanding and developing collaborative solutions, and tracking testing and delivery.

Organizing the Project
Identifying Business Objectives

UML becomes meaningful if the software project is properly organized. This is important regardless of the software development method being used (including Agile). Organization of a software project starts by understanding its key (primary) business objective (BO). Once this primary BO is ascertained, in terms of the "what, why, and how" of the system, that objective is systematically broken down. This decomposition of the objective reveals the key areas of the system, which are represented by packages. Clear documentation of the objectives provides a common understanding and means of communication for all stakeholders in the project. Breaking down (or decomposing) the BO serves a vital purpose in a project—that of prioritization.

BUSINESS OBJECTIVE FOR A HOSPITAL MANAGEMENT SYSTEM PROJECT

Business Objective:

- To provide electronic and mobile hospital management in an efficient way (WHAT)
- By developing and implementing a hospital management system (HOW)
- Resulting in excellent patient service and operational efficiency (WHY)

The WHAT in the preceding statement shows what the project is all about, the HOW describes the approach that is taken to achieve the objective, and the WHY gives the argument or reason for the project. Business objectives thus provide the basis for the entire project.

Dividing a Project into Smaller, Manageable Parts

Figure 3.2 shows how the business objective is divided into subparts. This decomposition is undertaken in workshop settings, with considerable input from domain experts and users of the system to arrive at acceptable performance criteria of the system. Based on multiple discussions with both business and technology stakeholders, the BO gets further divided into smaller parts or subject areas. Good business analysis skills, including the ability to conduct interviews and workshops, are most helpful here.

Prioritization of Requirements

The decomposed BOs (1, 2, and 3), listed in Table 3.1, provide the starting point for subsystems. Performance criteria also influence the nonfunctional requirements (NFRs discussed in Chapter

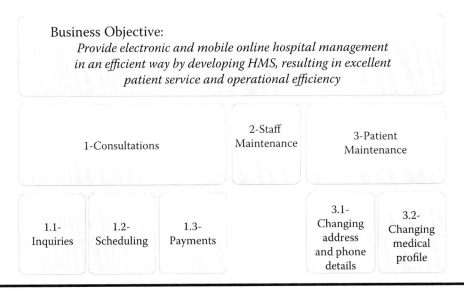

Figure 3.2 **Breaking down a project into subparts to enable controlled execution and monitoring of the project.**

Table 3.1   Applying Performance Criteria to Decompose Business Objectives

A Decomposed Business Objective	Performance Criteria (Examples)
Provide efficient response to basic interactions of patient with hospital.	Response time—less than 3 seconds online Response accuracy—99% Response cost—3 cents per transaction

1: Consultations
    1.1: Inquiries
    1.2: Scheduling
    1.3: Payments
	99% of all inquiry (informative) transactions and 100% of all scheduling and payment transactions should be accurate; anomalies to be automatically flagged and reported by the system.

2: Staff maintenance	Managing the details of hospital staff to occur on a daily basis; changing staff details securely by hospital's administrative staff; all changes must be auditable (with audit trails).

3: Patient maintenance
    3.1: Changing address and phone details, etc.
    3.2: Changing medical profiles
	99% of address changes/updates should be right the first time when undertaken by staff, 90% accuracy when by patients on their own devices; format flagging and redressing of inaccuracies.

20) of the system. These subsystems are represented as packages in the UML (packages are discussed in the next section).

Note that not all BOs result in packages. Some BOs may merge with other BOs, whereas others are decomposed into lower-level BOs. Once the high-level packages have been identified, they are prioritized. This prioritization process is carried out by project managers in a workshop environment with domain experts and business stakeholders. Agile projects use techniques like MoSCoW[3] and Delphi[4] to prioritize requirements.

The steps undertaken in the prioritization process typically undertaken by business analysts (BAs) are as follows:

- Break down BOs into lower-level objectives to evaluate, manage, and prioritize the solution development effort
- User representatives indicate their initial perceived importance of the BOs
- Domain experts provide input in terms of their perceived priorities of the BOs
- Consider and incorporate business (e.g., competition, compliance) and project risks (e.g., time, budget, resources) in the prioritization process
- Model the lower-level BOs as packages of the UML
- Iteratively undertake further prioritization by repeating the preceding steps
- Include the highest priority packages in the first iteration of the project
- Further lower-level objectives are candidates for use case diagrams (alternatively, in large systems, they become lower-level packages)
- User requirements within each package are modeled using use case and activity diagrams
- Designs are created using class, sequence, and state machine diagrams
- Repeat the preceding steps iteratively depending on the software development process

The Three Modeling Spaces in Software Engineering

Different areas of a software system need to be modeled. These areas are called modeling spaces. Each modeling space has roles that are responsible for carrying out modeling in that space. Roles within respective modeling spaces create as well as utilize the models.

This segregation of modeling spaces and corresponding responsibilities is crucial for the success of a software project. The analysis and design work in developing a software solution benefits from the segregation of responsibilities and use of the UML. Without such a delineation of modeling spaces, the use of UML can degenerate into incorrect or excessive modeling.

The modeling spaces as shown in Figure 3.3 are as follows:

1. The problem space
2. The solution space
3. The architectural space

Each modeling space is discussed in greater detail next.

Modeling of the Problem Space

The modeling in the problem space is meant to shed light on "what" the business problem of the user is. The problem space thus models the business requirement whose solution is yet to be developed. Main activities that take place in the problem space include investigating the business problem in detail, understanding the requirements, documenting them, analyzing them, optionally creating a conceptual prototype, and understanding the flow of the business process.

UML diagrams in the problem space explain the problem without going into the specifics of the solution. These UML diagrams are primarily a use case diagram and activity diagrams, followed by high-level use of class and sequence diagrams, and optionally state machine diagrams.

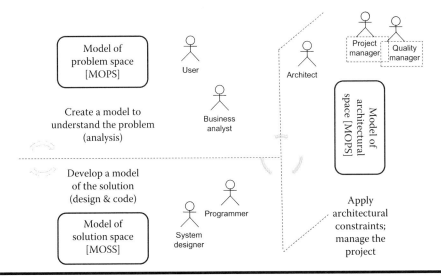

Figure 3.3 Software engineering uses three main modeling spaces and corresponding roles: model of problem space (in identifying the requirements and analyzing them), model of solution space (in creating the solution design), and model of architectural space (in applying constraints).

Key roles in creating the MOPS are the business analyst and the user. Apart from prototyping in the problem space, where some code may be written, there is no programming effort required in developing the MOPS.

Modeling of Solution Space

Figure 3.3 shows an MOSS that contains the design for the system. The solution space describes "how" the solution will be implemented to handle the problem described in the problem space. The creation of a solution model requires knowledge of the capabilities of the programming languages, corresponding databases, Web services, Web application solutions, and similar technical issues.

The MOSS contains solution-level designs expressed by technical or lower-level class diagrams. These design-level class diagrams contain the lowermost details, including attributes, types of attributes, their initial values, operations, and their signatures. With a parameter list and return values, sequence diagrams, together with their messages and protocols, are also used in MOSS. State machine diagrams and object diagrams can be used sparingly here. Key roles in the solution space are the system designer and the programmer, as shown in Figure 3.3.

Modeling of Architectural Space

The architectural space (also occasionally called the background space) deals with two major aspects of software development not covered by either the problem space or solution space: architecture and management. Figure 3.3 shows the architectural space in the third dimension—orthogonal to the problem and solution spaces.

Architectural models deal with a large amount of technical background work that must consider key issues of the architecture of the solution, existing architecture, technical environment of the organization, and the operational requirements of the system (e.g., stress, volume, and bandwidth needs of the system).

Architectural issues include aspects of reusability of programs, designs, services, and Cloud hosting. These activities require knowledge of how the organizational environment works and industrial knowledge of the availability of reusable architectures and designs. The MOAS presents organizational-level constraints by the architects and designers on both the problem and the solution models.

The architectural space uses the UML in modeling the deployment environment as well as in reusing both the architecture and the design. Therefore, deployment and component diagrams play an important role here. The component diagrams represent the executable chunks of code or libraries (e.g. .exe or.dll and service-oriented components), which are finally incorporated into the software solution. The UML domain also provides material, such as analysis patterns by Fowler (1997),[5] design patterns by the Gang of Four (Gamma et al., 1995),[6] cognitive patterns (Gardner et al., 1998),[7] and anti patterns (Brown et al., 1998[8]), that supports architectural work in MOAS.

Management in the background architectural space deals with the planning of the entire project and does not necessarily form part of the problem or the solution space. The project manager undertakes planning and resourcing the project hardware, software, and people, budgeting and performing cost-benefit analysis, tracking the project as it progresses as per the iteration plans, and providing the checkpoints that yield quality results for the roles in the problem and solution spaces. Thus, the quality manager is equally involved in the planning and execution of the project from a quality perspective.

Mapping UML to Modeling Spaces

With this understanding of the three modeling spaces, it is now easier to understand how each of the 14 UML diagrams can play a role in these different modeling spaces with varying degrees of importance and relevance. Some UML diagrams are more important and relevant in understanding problems and documenting and prioritizing requirements; other UML diagrams add more value in modeling the design in the solution space; whereas some UML diagrams can be used in modeling and applying architectural constraints as well as testing systems.

Table 3.2 summarizes the relative importance of each diagram in the three modeling spaces of problem, solution, and architecture. Additionally, this table also maps the UML diagrams to the major modeling roles within projects. Each diagram has a particular nuance that makes it relevant to a particular role within a software project. The UML is treated here as a toolbox of modeling notations and diagrams. Diagrams relevant to a role in a corresponding modeling space are then chosen from this toolbox.

Table 3.2 Importance of UML Diagrams to Respective Models (Maximum of 5 * for Utmost Importance to That Particular Space)

UML Diagrams	MOPS (Business Analyst)	MOSS (Designer)	MOAS (Architect)
Use case	*****	**	*
Activity	*****	**	*
Class	***	*****	**
Sequence	****	*****	*
Interaction overview	****	**	**
Communication	*	***	*
Object	*	*****	***
State machine	***	****	**
Composite structure	*	*****	****
Component	*	***	*****
Deployment	**	**	*****
Package	***	**	****
Timing	*	***	***
Profile	*	**	****

While project team members can work in any of these modeling spaces using any of the UML diagrams, good-quality models result from understanding the importance of the diagrams with respect to the roles played by the modelers and in each of the modeling spaces. Selecting the appropriate diagrams from this toolbox of UML techniques is a crucial step in good-quality SE.

A *subset* of the UML diagrams can be created in the problem, solution, and architectural spaces. UML diagrams that have received three or more "*" in each of the columns in Table 3.2 ideally form part of that particular modeling space. For example, the following diagrams are relevant in building the MOPS.

- Use case diagrams—used as a primary means to interact with users and in understanding their business problem. Hence, use case diagrams are ideal in the problem space.
- Activity diagrams—as sophisticated flowcharts, they can be used in the problem space to model flows and dependencies. Users and business analysts are particularly keen to use them to describe business workflows.
- Package diagrams—as a "grouping mechanism" for a subsystem, package diagrams are invaluable in the problem space, especially for project managers and project sponsors in organizing, evaluating, and scheduling projects.
- Class diagrams—represent the key business entities and their relationships and, as such, help create the "business domain model" in the problem space.
- Sequence diagrams—model the dynamic aspect of the requirements by showing interactions among business objects or interactions described directly by business users in the problem space.
- Interaction overview diagrams—provide an overview of dependencies between interaction diagrams, thereby enabling users and analysts to show relationships between sequences and use cases in the problem space.
- State machine diagrams—enable modeling of states of important business objects, providing a visual means of communicating the attribute values and their meanings in the problem space.

Similarly, Table 3.2 shows UML diagrams with three or more "*" to indicate their corresponding importance in MOSS and MOAS. These diagrams are as follows:

- Class diagrams—represent detailed designs and programming constructs; these diagrams can also model relational database tables.
- Sequence diagrams—in the solution space represent detailed technical models of interactions within a system; the objects in a sequence diagram in the solution space represent instances of entity, interface, controller, and database tables.
- Object diagrams—represent the multiplicities of class relationships in the memory.
- State machine diagrams—provide a more detailed, technical model of changes to the states of an object in the solution space; these diagrams also model the guard conditions and nesting to help design precise solutions.
- Composite structure diagrams—represent the runtime architecture of a group of objects and components, including their interfaces and realizations.
- Component diagrams—represent the structural as well as executable components; they provide excellent mechanisms to model the architecture of the solution.
- Deployment diagrams—represent the architectural organization of the hardware (nodes and links) of the solution.

- Timing diagrams—undertake detailed comparison of multiple states of more than one object in the solution space.
- Profile diagrams—create profiles that can be commonly applied across a system to ensure uniformity of constraints and, thereby, improvement of quality.

The preceding list of diagrams corresponding to the modeling spaces creates a subset of the UML that is relevant to a given modeling effort. Thus, apart from the type and size of project, the UML also needs to be selectively used by individuals within software projects. This selective use of the UML is important for success within SE. The extensive availability of modeling techniques within the UML can occasionally lead to the use of all modeling constructs by all roles—leading to chaos and lost value from modeling. Instead, selectively using the UML provides necessary value for a given role within the modeling space.

Package Diagrams

What Is a Package in UML?

A package in UML represents a logical collection of artifacts and models. Therefore, a package is going to contain classes, components, use cases, and all other related constructs belonging to that particular subsystem.

In the MOAS, a package can map to a component. Yet, in most practical modeling exercises it is better to treat it differently from a component. This is because a package, as discussed here, is not treated as an executable entity. Instead, it is treated as an organizational element representing a subsystem—as against, say, a Java package, which is an implementation entity.

A domain expert is always involved together with the architect and the project manager in creating and naming packages. Packages are named after the subsystems or large area of work they represent, using singular common nouns.

Once packages for the system are identified, they are then prioritized. After prioritization, the activity task list for the project is created. The assignment of priorities to the packages provides a basis for scheduling their development. Modeling and prioritization of packages and the modeling work within those packages are all carried out in iterations. These iterations can occur initially at two levels:

1. Iteration for the entire project.
2. Iteration for packages.

Increments are then superimposed on the iterations, with each business-level package representing an increment.

Creating Package Diagrams

Figure 3.4 shows the major notations of a package diagram: the notation of a package, the dependency relationship, and notes. A package diagram for a hospital management system is shown in Figure 3.5. In that package diagram, there are six business-level packages: Patient, Staff, Consultation, Surgery, Account, and Pharmacy (Note: they are NOT classes). Each of these packages is stereotyped as <<business>> (stereotypes are discussed separately under UML's extensibility mechanism in a later chapter).

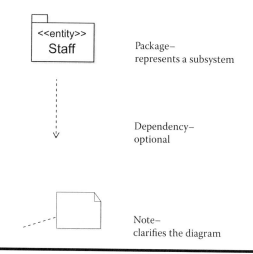

Figure 3.4   Major notations of a package diagram.

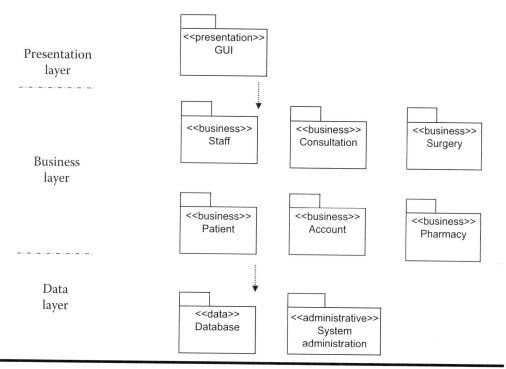

Figure 3.5   A package diagram for hospital management system with the three layered architecture of the system.

In addition to the business-level packages, there is the <<presentation>> graphical user interface (GUI) package that will contain all the user interfaces. This package contains the presentation layer of the system and the classes, class diagrams, and sequence diagrams that deal with the user interfaces. Note that *designing* (versus specifying) user interfaces is part of solution space modeling work.

Figure 3.5 shows the data layer represented by the Database package, which contains within itself all use cases and classes dealing with storage and retrieval of data. Similarly, the

<<administrative>> System Administration package deals with all administrative behavior of the system including backups, archiving storage, and maintenance functions. For example, the administration package contains details of login and password maintenance.

These packages are derived from the major subareas of work shown earlier in Table 3.1. They contain corresponding use cases, classes, sequence diagrams, and components. Figure 3.5 includes the dependency of GUI on Staff and that of Patient on Database packages. In the initial attempt at creating packages, it is not necessary to show the relationships between packages.

Namespaces

Packages provide namespaces for all modeling elements belonging to that package. Namespaces ensure that all modeling elements in a package have unique names. For example, a class Surgeon belonging to the package Staff is unique within that package. There is no other Surgeon within the Staff package. Consider now the need to use (or reference) the Surgeon class in the Patient package. There is no need to create a separate class Surgeon in the Patient package—because that will result in conflict between the two surgeons (one in Staff and another in Patient). UML modeling tools will prevent the creation of another class with the same name. In the preceding example, Staff:Surgeon can appear in the Patient package (implying that the Surgeon class comes from the Staff package). This example shows the importance of namespaces in UML-based modeling across multiple packages.

Strengths of Package Diagrams

Following are some of the strengths of package diagrams in practice:

- A package is an excellent organizational unit in modeling a system as it enables grouping of requirements and the subsequent work into manageable and coherent chunks (or subsystems).
- A package provides a container for all UML elements and diagrams that are used in modeling. Therefore, a package provides uniqueness through namespace for entities.
- Packages enable layering since it is possible to have packages within packages and thereby divide and better manage system development.
- Packages are used to organize work around multiple teams and people; thus, a package can be specifically assigned to a modeling and development team.
- Packages enable robust information architecture by grouping business models and understanding their dependencies.
- Packages, when appropriately stereotyped, provide an excellent high-level view of a system.
- Packages show dependencies between major areas of a system, thereby providing input as to which package should be developed first.
- Packages enable domain experts to indicate their criticality, thereby helping in prioritization.

Weaknesses of Package Diagrams

Following are some of the weaknesses of package diagrams in practice:

- Packages are unable to show technical details of the entities within them. Therefore, they are not easy to use in a technical sense.

- Packages are not object-oriented in nature, so many of the OO fundamentals (like inheritance and polymorphism) may not apply to packages.
- Occasionally, in practice, packages tend to get confused with classes.
- The dependencies between packages, in practice, can become circular dependencies. Strictly following the dependency rules and showing those dependencies on a package diagram can cause unnecessary confusion.

Common Errors in Organizing Project Packages and How to Rectify Them

Common Errors	Rectifying the Errors	Examples
Assuming all UML diagrams need to be used at once.	Consider the modeling spaces and the type/size of project; this will ensure you are able to select the right diagrams to create the models within the modeling spaces.	For example, use case and activity diagrams will be of value in creating the MOPS; but for a small project, class diagrams can be a good starting point. MOSS will use technical class diagrams and sequence diagrams.
Attempting a project without a clear BO	Ensure the BO is discussed more than once within the project team. Be prepared to revise the BO based on the initial iteration of modeling work.	Revisit Figure 3.2. Observe how the BO is clear in the what, how, and why of the project.
Business analyst using technical class diagrams	Use business case level classes that are <<entity>> classes.	For example, Patient, Doctor, Administrator, and Consultation are business-level classes. Classes from the language of implementation are technical classes.
Solution designers using use case diagrams as technical models	It is best to adopt use case diagrams to capture requirements. Although originally they were proposed as object-oriented, their greatest value stems from their ability to show requirements holistically at a high level.	Revisit the use case diagram shown in previous chapter (Figure 2.2) in the context of the discussion on modeling spaces (Figure 3.3). Note how a use case diagram is suitable for MOPS but not for MOSS.

Common Errors	Rectifying the Errors	Examples
Confusing packages with classes—mainly because in theory both packages and classes can have the same name.	Classes are within packages; therefore, classes can be prefixed by their namespace, which is in that package.	Class `Patient` is within package `Patient`. A patient class referred by another package will have Patient:Patient within that other package.
Having circular dependencies in package diagram	Avoid dependencies in business-level package diagrams.	See Figure 3.5 showing no dependencies. This figure treats packages as organizational elements only.
Not having stereotypes on packages	Add stereotypes (discussed in Chapter 10) to all packages.	`<<entity>> Patient`
Using namespace of a package within itself	A namespace is meaningful when a class is used in a different package.	Staff: `Surgeon` is not meaningful in `Surgeon`, but it is meaningful in `Patient`

Discussion Questions

1. Give a brief explanation of the different project types that can use UML. Argue for the relevance of your answer in practice.
2. How is UML used in small, medium, large, and collaborative project sizes? Compare any two project sizes in the context of UML usage.
3. What are the key characteristics of decomposing a project? Why is it important to decompose a project? What would happen if a project progressed without decomposition?
4. How would you organize your project? (*hint: discuss with example of a package diagram and Table 3.1*)
5. What is the importance of creating modeling spaces? (*hint: roles*)
6. List the two most important diagrams in each of the three modeling spaces. Argue with examples.
7. Compare and contrast the three different modeling spaces—especially in terms of the roles within those spaces.
8. Why are namespaces important in the modeling space?
9. What are the key strengths of package diagrams? Why?
10. What are the key weaknesses of package diagrams? Why?

Team Project Case Study

1. Identify the business objective (BO) of the case study system based on the problem statement (*revisit Appendix A for relevant problem statement*).
2. Undertake detailed discussion with team members in terms of the key performance areas of the system—then divide the BO into four to six key areas. (It is important at this stage of the study

that the requirements of the case study be understood in detail *in a team format*; if they are not, please undertake detailed rereading of the problem statement together with your team.)

3. Based on the reading and discussion, ascertain the type and size of your project. This is a generic understanding of the project that will help decide the level of UML usage within the project.

4. Identify and model decomposed subsystems of your project as packages.

5. Discuss the work that is to be undertaken in creating the MOPS, MOSS, and MOAS. Give each team member primary responsibility for each of these three modeling spaces.

6. Team members (for these short education projects) will also double up as key users, domain experts, architects, and project managers/Agile coach.

7. Collaboratively assign the roles to team members based on the three key roles presented in Table 3.2 (knowing that team members in this exercise will be doubling up for roles).

8. Create a high-level package diagram based on the requirements of the system. This package diagram will have only the packages from the business domain at this stage. Ensure there is at least ONE package PER STUDENT member of the team. Therefore, for a project group of four students, it is expected that you will have at least four packages. These packages will represent the major subject areas of your case study.

9. Add notes to the package diagram.

10. Enter the diagram in your modeling tool. Note how each package (owned by one person on the team) allows other team members to use it through namespaces.

Endnotes

1. Unhelkar, B., (2003), *Process Quality Assurance for UML-based Projects* Pearson Education (*Addison-Wesley*), Boston, 2003; (394 Pages + CD. Foreword by Vicki P. Rainey, Raytheon Corporation, USA). ISBN 9 780201-758214.

2. Unhelkar, B., *Sourcing Methods: Philosophy and Approach*, Cutter Executive Report, July, 2008, Vol 9., No 3, Sourcing and Vendor Relationship Practice.

3. MoSCoW—Must Should Could Won't—A Guide to the Business Analysis Body of Knowledge—BABOK—3rd Edition; www.theiiba.org.

4. Delphi—a method for estimation and forecasting based on inputs from experts. https://en.wikipedia.org/wiki/Delphi_method; accessed October 2017.

5. Fowler, Martin (1997), *Analysis Patterns: Reusable Object Models*, Reading, MA: Addison-Wesley, 1997.

6. Gamma, E., Helm, R., Johnson, R., and Vlissides, J. (1995), *Design Patterns: Elements of Reusable Object-Oriented Software*, Reading, MA: Addison-Wesley, 1995.

7. Gardner, K., Konitzer, K.R., Teegarden, B., Rush, A., and Crist, M., *Cognitive Patterns: Problem-Solving Frameworks for Object Technology*, CreateSpace Independent Publishing Platform, December 14, 2011.

8. William J. Brown, Raphael C. Malveau, Hays W. "Skip" McCormick, Thomas J. Mowbray, *AntiPatterns: Refactoring Software, Architectures, and Projects in Crisis*, April 1998, Wiley.

Chapter 4

The Software Development Life Cycle and Agility

Learning Objectives

- Understand the concepts of software development life cycles (SDLC) including waterfall and iterative, incremental, and parallel (IIP) life cycles
- Introduce Agile methods, disciplined Agile delivery (DAD), and Scrum
- Understand a process architecture and corresponding process elements: activities, tasks, roles, and deliverables
- Understand roles, ceremonies, and artifacts in Agile
- Write user stories and features
- Appreciate the role of the composite Agile method and strategy (CAMS)

Process in Developing Software

This chapter introduces software development processes. These processes (or methods—also called methodologies in the software literature) play an important part in the creation of good-quality software solutions. Developing the diagrams and models discussed here, putting together the ensuing programming constructs, creating database designs, and undertaking software testing—all require certain activities and tasks performed in a certain sequence by specific team members. A process forms the backbone of these activities in software development.

Thus, along with discussing the details of *what* gets produced (the artifacts—for example, a use case or a class diagram), it is equally important to discuss *how* to produce them (e.g., by identifying actors, analyzing use cases, and creating inheritance hierarchies in class diagrams). A software process (method) guides one on *how* to produce artifacts. A process also describes the roles (or people) *who* produce those artifacts (or deliverables).

Formality in developing software ameliorates randomness in development efforts and a lack of documentation and traceability. Processes provide the discipline necessary for a project team to collaboratively develop software solutions. Processes have a positive influence on eliciting user requirements, undertaking analysis, creating solution designs, programming code, and testing it.

Process-driven software development is based on rigorously defined activities and tasks that are also repeatable and measurable. Formal processes facilitate planning, analysis of requirements from multiple angles, design of high-quality software models by following standards and using team-based tools, and incorporation of quality through walkthroughs, inspections, and testing. As a result, such formal processes enhance quality and maximize user benefits.

UML and Process

One of the most common confusions in discussing UML-based analysis and design work is to presume that the UML itself is a process.[1] Although UML is an extremely significant part of a process, it is *not* a process. The UML is a set of notations and diagrams, standardized with an underlying metamodel and supported in practice by a modeling tool. UML provides the contents of the deliverables, whereas a process defines the activities and roles that produce the deliverables. Processes in software development have evolved to also incorporate the sociocultural factors (called "soft factors") in project management. Thus, team motivation, experience, collaboration, trust, and visibility are some of the factors incorporated into a process.

Figure 4.1 clarifies this difference between the UML and a "software process." The example software processes shown are the Unified Process, Agile, and CAMS. UML, which defines the contents of models, needs to be used within the confines of a software development process. In the absence of a process, the UML risks becoming a tool to produce substantial numbers of diagrams without cohesion that are of little value to software engineers.

Process Elements

The process discipline is complex. This is because a process considers myriad different hard and soft factors that impact development. Many software developers argue that processes restrict their creativity. Far from that, processes actually enable creativity with value. This is because processes ensure the effort made by architects, designers, developers, and testers will be well directed toward

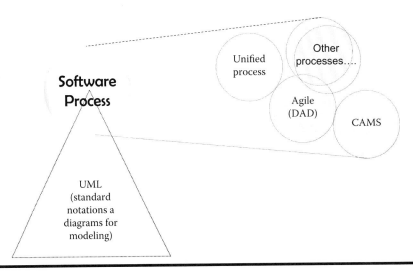

Figure 4.1   UML, processes, and quality. *Note: UML is NOT a process.*

the commonly agreed goals (business objectives) of a project. Processes also facilitate measures and metrics that indicate individual and team productivity and quality. Metrics and measurements in software projects also enable assignment of responsibilities and accountabilities.[2]

PROCESS DESCRIPTORS

There are several ways to describe a process. The following list indicates descriptors of a process:

- Identifier—a way to identify the process, e.g., name and a number (to indicate the revision number of the process).
- Purpose—indicates the purpose of the process, e.g., to produce new software, enable integration, support maintenance, or simply business process modeling.
- Owner—who owns the process or who is responsibility for maintaining, supporting, and updating the various elements of the process? Note that this is not the project or software owner but the personal specializing in and supporting the development process in a software project.
- User—who are the people/roles within the software project that will use the process. Obviously, there are multiple roles that apply the process to produce the deliverables assigned to them. A process enables these various users to work collaboratively and cohesively.
- Beneficiary—who will benefit from the outcomes of the process (e.g., the project manager and the business stakeholder).
- Artifacts/deliverables—definitions of what is produced by the process.
- Activities and tasks (or steps)—describe how a particular artifact or a suite of artifacts is produced; usually, these activities/tasks are grouped based on the role played by users in order to ease the execution of the process.
- Ceremony—the level or depth to which a process needs to be performed.
- Metrics and measurements—to help measure the progress of a process and its maturity (or repeatability).
- Related processes—list of other processes within the organization that support this process and are supported by it.

A large and complex software development process has an underlying architecture that shows how the various process elements are put together. Figure 4.2 shows the key elements that make up a process. These elements are put together in a process map. The process map forms the building blocks of a process. This process map is made up of activities, artifacts (deliverables), and roles. Tasks are associated with activities. While the deliverables describe *what* to produce, the activities and tasks show *how* to produce it, and the roles describe *who* produces it.

Each process map represents an area of work within the software project. Examples of process maps are project management, system architecture, system design, development, testing, quality assurance, and quality assurance.

Several such process maps are put together to make a software engineering process (SEP). As also shown in Figure 4.2, a SEP is based on a software development life cycle (SDLC). The life cycle provides the philosophical background for the construction of a process. Figure 4.2 shows

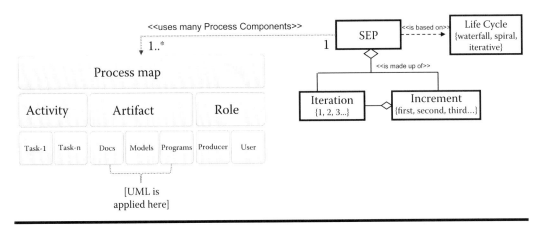

Figure 4.2 Key elements of a process.

how a SEP is made up of iterations and increments. The type and size of a project can dictate the way in which a SEP is instantiated in order to be applied to a specific software development project. Finally, Figure 4.2 shows at the bottom the place where UML is used to create models.

Software Development Life Cycles

Traditionally, software development is thought of as series of phases performed one after the other. As shown on the left-hand side in Figure 4.3, these phases are analysis, design, coding, testing, and deployment. This sequential approach is called the *waterfall*[3] SDLC. Just as water only flows from top to bottom in a sequential manner, so does software development. This life cycle is rigid—easier to manage and report but difficult to provide value. This is because this waterfall approach to software engineering does not factor in the inevitable changes in requirements.

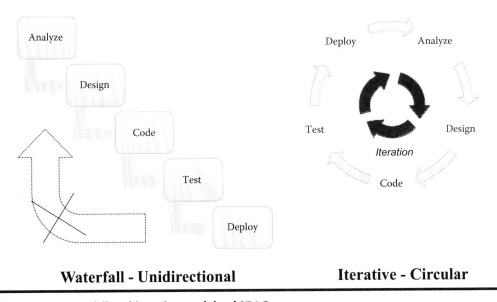

Figure 4.3 Waterfall and iterative models of SDLC.

Boehm (1986)[4] put together a spiral model of software development resulting in a more flexible approach. Development here is based on an ever-increasing spiral going through four major quadrants: evaluate, define, design, and code. The activities and tasks within the development phases are incrementally repeated through these quadrants. This approach enables the creation and prioritizing of requirements, developing those with highest priority first and gradually adding to their detail in subsequent iterations. As a result, deliverables are produced in smaller and manageable pieces, resulting in improved understanding of the system as it gets delivered. This method of delivering software is also friendly to users involved in the project as they begin to see the deliverables earlier than with the complete delivery of the system.

Iterative, Incremental, and Parallel Process in Software Development

The object-oriented approach to developing software makes it easier to incorporate iterations and increments within software development. This is because of the modularized (and encapsulated) nature of object-oriented software engineering. The right-hand side of Figure 4.3 shows a typical iteration that could be used in object-oriented development. While this iteration still comprises phases from the waterfall life cycle, the crucial difference is that those phases are repeated systematically and rapidly—forming the basis of what is known as an iterative, incremental, parallel (IPP) life cycle.

The iterations and increments shown in Figure 4.4 are the basis of most modern-day approaches to developing good software. In this iterative and incremental approach, no deliverable is produced in a single attempt. Instead, at least three iterations (repetitions) are undertaken before producing a deliverable. Figure 4.4 shows the three iterations undertaken to develop a package called Patient. This is followed by incrementally adding another package called Consulting, which would have its own three or more iterations. The three terms iteration, incremental, and parallel are further discussed next.

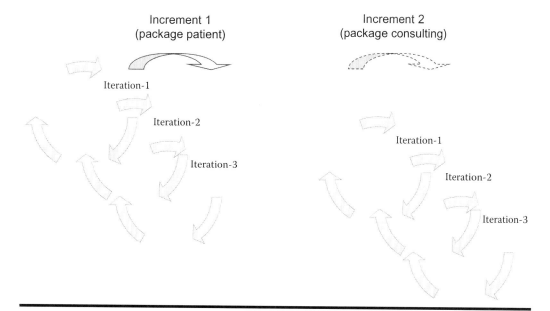

Figure 4.4   Iterations and increments.

Iterative

The iterative aspect of a process enables *repetition* of tasks. As a result, the deliverables are produced gradually. For example, when a use case is iterated, additional material is added to the description of the use case—such as alternative flows within the use case. The iterative approach encourages a *slow* and *steady* philosophy rather than hurrying and finishing up a deliverable in the first attempt. Deliverables are gradually matured by undertaking at least three iterations across multiple other deliverables. For example, while following an iterative process one might move from an initial use case to another use case in another diagram, then identify classes and draw a sequence diagram before coming back to the original use case and completing it.

Incremental

The incremental aspect of a process enables *adding* new elements and diagrams to an existing deliverable. An example is to add new packages to existing or developing packages. New requirements are thus discovered and modeled in an incremental fashion. This incremental aspect of the process enables the creation of parts of a system in as complete a manner as possible before proceeding with the development of additional parts of the system. The incremental aspect of a process often goes hand in hand with the iterative aspect. For example, while a new deliverable is incrementally added (a new use case), an existing deliverable is iteratively augmented during a later iteration (e.g., additional steps added to a use case).

Parallel

The previous two keywords (iteration, increment) describe the gradual development of artifacts in a software project. With object-oriented analysis and design, it is possible to produce two software artifacts *in parallel*. Thus, even if one package depends on another package, the development of the two packages can proceed in parallel. The only requirement in such parallel development is that the interfaces between the two packages must be formally defined and developed first. As long as the interfaces between the two packages do not change, developers are free to develop the internals of the two packages in parallel.

Time and Effort Distribution in Iterations

Figure 4.5 shows a typical distribution of time and effort in an IIP life cycle. It is worth understanding this distribution from the point of view of the project. Although iterations and increments are discussed as part of producing UML-based artifacts and deliverables, both of these concepts are intertwined with each other and apply at the project level. Figure 4.5 shows the time and effort expected to be spent in the three iterations at the highest project level.

- In the first iteration of a project, 15% of the time and effort is spent on rapidly modeling early parts of the requirements and prototypes. Activities that occur in a typical first iteration include: understanding the business objectives, creating initial use cases and use case diagrams, cost estimating based on the overall expected requirements of the project, project planning including resources, prototyping, and quality planning. As a result of this iteration, all project participants and stakeholders get a good feel for the project. Furthermore,

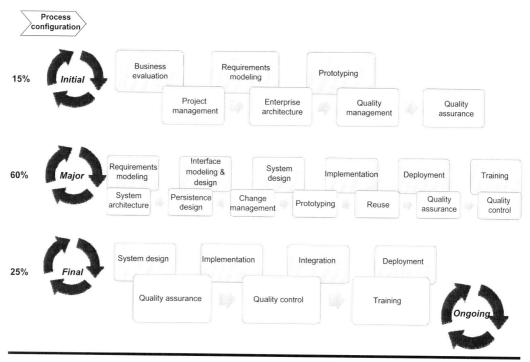

Figure 4.5 Mapping process maps to iterations.

this is also the iteration in which the identification and documentation of packages (incre-ments can be based on these packages, as discussed later in this chapter) take place. Most activities in the first iteration are undertaken in the problem and architectural spaces.

■ The second iteration, at the project level, consumes approximately 60% of the time and effort. It is a detailed iteration that undertakes the completion of requirements and applies the requirements model in creating the solution. Thus, most process maps are worked through in this iteration. Because of extensive work in the solution space, this iteration results in a major development of code and databases. The activities, thus, deal with the solution and architectural modeling spaces.

■ The third iteration, as shown in Figure 4.5, is the final iteration at the project level, con-suming 25% of the project's time and effort. In this iteration, the major focus is on testing the solution produced thus far at the project/system level. Extensive acceptance testing of the product is also undertaken here by end users. Activities related to performance testing, acceptance testing, and launching the system are accomplished during this iteration.

CAPABILITY MATURITY MODEL AND PROCESS MATURITY

The capability maturity model (CMM),[5] developed by the Software Engineering Institute (SEI) of Carnegie Mellon University, provides the most widely accepted benchmark for measuring and improving a software process. The CMM has evolved into an integrated maturity model called capability maturity model integration (CMMi). The importance of CMMi in this discussion is its potential to integrate the underlying structure of all process models—resulting in a framework to measure process maturity. The SEI mandates the following five levels of software process maturity:

- Initial—at this level of process maturity, the organization applies the process in an ad hoc manner.
- Repeatable—at this second level of maturity, the process elements (and process maps) are repeatable across the organization.
- Defined—at this third level of maturity every element of the process is properly defined. This means the "what," "how," "who," and supporting guidelines of "when" are all defined and formally documented.
- Measured—when the process elements mentioned in CMM level 3 can be measured in terms of their quality and contribution to the process, as well as the contribution of the process to the overall quality within the software development environment, the organization is said to be at level 4.
- Optimized—once something can be measured, the opportunity to improve on it becomes apparent. When the organization starts to fine-tune process elements, resulting in an optimization of activities and tasks, then the process discipline in the organization can be said to be fully matured. This is level-5 maturity.

Agile in Software Development

The Agile Manifesto

Agile methods provide a new paradigm for software development processes by focusing on "conversations." These are typically the ongoing conversations between users and developers. This Agile paradigm differs from the waterfall life cycle where requirements are documented and signed off on very formally and only thereafter can development begin.

Agile tends to be closer to an "art" (right-brained) than an "engineering" (left-brained) discipline (Unhelkar, 2013).[6] Therefore, Agile approaches are most suitable for undertaking SE which needs elements of art as much as engineering. The IIP life cycle discussed earlier is the basis for Agile software development approaches. Agility, as the name suggests, eschews large and bureaucratic documentation and enables programmers to produce functioning software in short life cycles. Agile methodological approaches are underpinned by the Agile Manifesto, which was signed by a group of 17 eminent developers and methodologists in February 2001[7] (see below).

AGILE MANIFESTO

We are uncovering better ways of developing software by doing it and helping others do it. We value:

- Individuals and interactions over processes and tools
- Working software over comprehensive documentation
- Customer collaboration over contract negotiations
- Responding to change over following a plan

The statements of the Agile manifesto contain significant *subjective* elements—hence the need for trust and collaboration in this approach. While arguing that the Agile movement is not anti-methodology, the Agile Manifesto signatories state, "We embrace modeling, but not merely to file some diagram in a dusty corporate repository. We embrace documentation, but not to waste reams of paper in never-maintained and rarely-used tomes. We plan, but recognize the limits of planning in a turbulent environment."[8]

Agile values aspire to minimal formality and planning. For example, individuals and their interactions are promoted through the "daily standup" meetings, and user stories are written and physically pasted on a wall. Similarly, working software is given high precedence over comprehensive documentation. Contracts fade in the background in light of high customer collaboration, and change is treated as a norm rather than an exception to a plan. These values have changed the traditional system engineering approaches—opening up possibilities of faster reaction to change as compared with the traditional SDLCs.

The popularity of Agile methods in engineering software systems development can be attributed to their promise to accommodate change and cater rapidly to the expectations of business (Unhelkar, 2013).[9] Agile approaches respond rapidly to changes (*adaptive*), rapidly iterate and test (*iterative*), comprise small "self-motivated" teams (*lightweight*) with different skill set (*cross-functional*).

The popularity of Agility also has its drawbacks as it lends itself to different interpretations. Therefore, it is important to understand what Agile means in the context of the work undertaken. In the context of systems engineering, Agile can be understood as a suite of software development methods (Ambler)[10] that are based around a manifesto, principles, and practice (Agile Manifesto, 2001[11,12]). This manifesto characterizes Agile as "a value statement not a concrete plan or process"[13]— thereby laying the foundation for extensive collaboration and iterations through the Agile values, priorities, and principles. Agile can also imply intense focus on delivery (DevOps, 2015),[14] closely accompanied by continuous testing and integration (Mistry, 2015).[15]

Scrum—An Agile Approach

Highly popular in the Agile space, Scrum is a lightweight process that employs iterative and incremental practices[16] (Scrum is a game mechanic derived from the sport of Rugby[17]). Scrum aims to get the entire project team together to set a shared and achievable goal. The team *sprints* toward this common goal. Collaborations and iterations ensure that the product is developed incrementally. Scrum projects are characterized by trust, simplicity, and courage—implemented through visual charting, daily standup meetings, and close collaboration.

Roles, Ceremonies, and Artifacts

An Agile method (typically Scrum) has the following elements: roles, ceremonies, and artifacts (shown in Figure 4.6). These Agile elements are put together dynamically in software development projects. However, these Agile elements can also be used in other nonsoftware initiatives in the organization. For example, business decision-making benefits by the application of Agile elements. A brief description of these three categories of Agile elements (roles, ceremonies, and artifacts) and the way they are used in software projects follows.

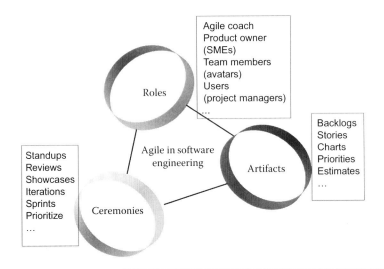

Figure 4.6   Three categories of Agile elements.

Roles

Agile methods have limited project roles (Figure 4.6). This is because Agile is results-oriented. Large numbers of roles with elaborate descriptions are not required in Agile. Typical Agile roles (and their specific terms in Scrum) are as follows:

■ Agile coach (Scrum master)—this role is that of a facilitator who encourages the team to reach its goals. The coach also protects the team from external pressures. An Agile coach is also a good team member—working to remove road blocks and show stoppers, thereby enabling the team to carry on without distractions. Note that hardly any "task management" is undertaken by this role as the Agile team is meant to be self-motivated. The Scrum master focuses on facilitation rather than management, versus a project manager who is involved in detailed planning, resourcing, and budgeting of the team. The Scrum master is typically an experienced software engineer who serves as an interface between the management and the Scrum team and manages the processes.

■ Product owner—this is the key business person for whose benefit the product is being developed. This person can also be the subject matter expert (SME), although in large projects the two roles (product owner and SME) are different. The SME in such large projects plays an advisory role. Users, also separately identified, are integral to the project—providing valuable input during development, testing, and deployment of the solution. The product owner in Scrum is the business representative on the project and is closely involved with prioritizing work (e.g., the packages mentioned in previous chapter) and managing the return on investment. The product owner is the stakeholders' representative who approves the changes to the product backlog. The product owner is in charge of obtaining the requirements and planning the releases (Cho, 2008).

■ Team members—these are the developers, coders, and testers. These are technical "hands-on" people who assume the responsibility of developing the product in close cooperation with the product owners and users. Occasionally, team members take on "avatars" to enable easier allocation of tasks across multiple or parallel iterations. A Scrum team usually consists of a cross-functional (i.e., from different functional areas of work) group of 5–10 people. A Scrum team structure is egalitarian, and the commitment of the team is to get the work done in a self-organized and self-managed manner. Thus, the Scrum team is responsible for planning its own work, tracking it, and taking full responsibility for outcomes.

■ Project manager—this is not an Agile role. However, most practical software development projects have this role and hence it is mentioned here. A project manager is an outward facing role addressing budgeting, schedules, and resources. The project manager also handles regulatory and compliance sign-off and stakeholder management. In small projects, the same individual may play the roles of both project manager and Agile coach.

Ceremonies

A set of Agile practices is described in Agile methods. A ceremony is the carrying out of an Agile practice (Figure 4.6). Daily standup meetings, iteration planning and estimation, iteration review, writing user stories, prioritization of features, showcasing a release, testing, and short, sharp sprints—these are all part of Agile project ceremonies. These ceremonies are embedded within the activities and tasks of an Agile iteration plan.

Scrum, for example, has a number of meetings such as the daily Scrum meeting, the sprint review meeting, the sprint planning meeting, the sprint retrospective meeting, and the Scrum of Scrum meeting.

■ The daily Scrum is a highly popular standup meeting that lasts about 15 minutes. All stakeholders attend this meeting (first thing in the morning), which is conducted around a "wall" with use stories pasted on them. Each stakeholder mentions precisely three things: what was achieved since the last meeting, what will be achieved by the next meeting, and any roadblocks. The coach makes rough notes and works to remove the roadblocks. The visibility of the work on a physical wall and the short and sharp focus of the meetings have made the daily standup meeting extremely popular and valuable.

■ The sprint review meeting is typically a half-day meeting that provides status updates to management and stakeholders. The planning meeting can last a day, in which the sprint team and the product owner decide on the outcomes to be achieved within that sprint—resulting in the product and sprint backlogs.

■ The sprint retrospective meeting discusses what went right and areas for correction in terms of the process being followed. This results in modifications to the way the team works in the next "sprint."

■ There is also an opportunity for a Scrum of Scrum meeting that brings together Scrum teams working on separate but related "sprints"—ensuring coordination and minimal overlaps while allowing the Scrum teams to scale up to a large number of team members on a large project.

Artifacts

Due to their focus on working code rather than documentation, Agile methods define minimalistic artifacts (or deliverables). Following is a discussion of Agile artifacts (stories, features, product backlogs, and charts):

User stories—User stories are a popular means of documenting the functional requirements of a system in an Agile project. The stories document a unit of functionality. Stories are an important artifact as they form the basis for discussion, collaboration, clarification, modifications,

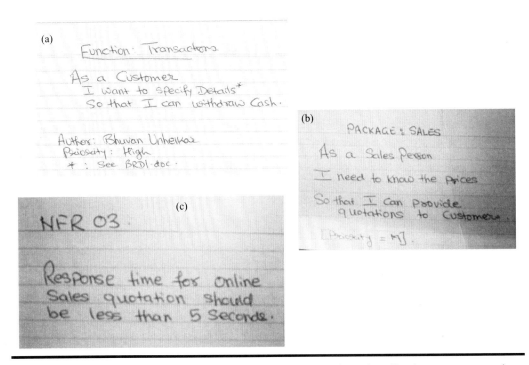

Figure 4.7 Examples of User Stories: (a) As a unit of desired functionality from Customer viewpoint and (b) from sales person viewpoint; (c) as a nonfunctional requirement (NFR) specifying performance (this is not a standard format for Use cases but is a practical way of having NFRs also placed on the project wall.

and tracking work in a visible manner. User stories are written at both informal (high level) and detailed levels. Figure 4.7 shows examples of stories. Priorities 4.7 (a) and (b) also indicate how priorities can be put up on the story card.

Features—Features are a list of requirements for a product. While the functional requirements can be documented with user stories, many nonfunctional requirements (NFRs, Chapter 20) cannot be written in that format. Lower-level, detailed features may occasionally be written on story cards, but not in a user story format (Figure 4.7). Cottmeyer and Stevens[18] describe features as "functional threads of working software that are independent of each other and can be scheduled and prioritized independently." Features, as high-level descriptions of functionality, can be scheduled independently; however, detailed features and NFRs may have many dependencies, requiring them to be treated as a group.

USER STORIES

A user story documents a conversation with a user.[19] Thus, stories are short high-level requirements artifacts. Mike Cohn[20] outlines the format for a user story as follows:

```
As a (role) I want (something) so that (benefit).
```

In composite Agile method and strategy (CAMS, discussed later in this chapter), user stories can be based on detailed use cases. Use cases provide the basis for a group of user stories. In turn, a user story can be an inspiration for a detailed use case document-ing the interaction between the user and the system. Stories are documented on a small 3×5-inch card and placed as part of the product backlog on the wall (Figure 4.7).

Story cards are also used to depict a unit of requirement that may not be functional. Thus, story cards are used to put up features on the wall. Examples of such features appearing on story cards are: Expected peak customers—3000 online customers per hour; browsers for online customers to include *IE* 8.0, and the latest version of *Safari* for mobile; and total customer records = 10 million (volume). Similarly, provisioning of services with the system can be put up as features on a story card. These stories will then not be stories but statements of requirements that are not from a specific user's viewpoint. These nonfunctional (or operational) requirements do not have a specific user. There can also be interface-related requirements, quality, and usability specifications and legal requirements that may not fall within a user story format. For the sake of visibility in an Agile project, it is worth placing these requirements on a story card and putting them up on visible charts (walls).

Charts

Product backlog—The product backlog artifact in Agile mainly comprises the prioritized func-tionalities (e.g., a list of user stories) that are scheduled for development. Product backlog also contains all other features (in addition to the user stories) that are prioritized by business value. The technology features and NFRs are prioritized by a combination of business and technology needs. A product backlog can be expanded into a combination of detailed requirements (depicting features to be developed) and a corresponding project task plan. Estimates (using techniques such as the planning poker) are applied to features usually to ascertain the time and effort required for development.

The *sprint backlog* contains information about the features and how to implement them in the current sprint. A product backlog is a superset of the sprint backlog; a sprint backlog contains the highest-priority features that are to be developed in that particular sprint. A sprint can be consid-ered a time-boxed iteration focusing on a list of goals. Team members also estimate the required time for completing each feature in the sprint backlog. A sprint lasts for about 2–4 weeks. Sprints get updated as the tasks are completed or as new tasks emerge.

The *sprint burn down chart* is a chart showing the remaining work in the sprint backlog on a daily basis. The entire Agile team has access to this chart.

Agile methods stress visibility in a project. Therefore, all requirements (features) and user stories are placed visibly on a large and visible chart that in turn, is put up on a wall. The stories on the charts are based on conversations with the user. They are essentially the "requirements" handled by business analysts together with users. As stories get developed, they physically move on the wall from the "to be done" section to "being done" and eventually "done" sections. Charts are organized in different ways depending on the needs of the project. For example, charts can be separately created for each iteration in an Agile project. Stories on charts can be annotated with priorities and estimates.

Disciplined Agile Development

Disciplined Agile development (DAD) is an agile process decision framework[21] that guides organi-zations in streamlining their information technology (IT) processes in a context-sensitive manner.

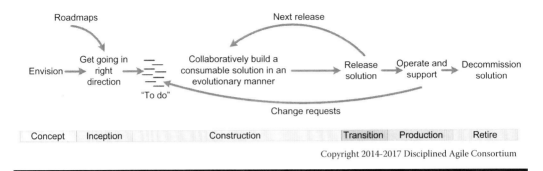

Figure 4.8   An Agile life cycle (from disciplined Agile consortium).[22]

Thus, the planning process elements, such as portfolio management, solutions delivery, and enterprise architecture, are brought together to work as a cohesive whole for the organization. While the DAD framework describes the activities to be addressed, these activities are undertaking based on an outline of corresponding tradeoffs. Thus, this DAD framework provides many choices—and users are free to make their choices in terms of process elements, provided they know the tradeoffs.

Figure 4.8[22] shows a high-level view of the system life cycle under DAD. The base of this product life cycle shows the major phases: concept, inception, construction, transition, production, and retire. The core phases of inception, construction, and transition make up the delivery portion of the product life cycle wherein the Agile practices play a major role. These phases, as shown in Figure 4.8, incrementally build a software product deliverable. Most systems iterate multiple times through the delivery life cycle.

Composite Agile Method and Strategy

The composite Agile method and strategy[23] (CAMS) brings together the planning and Agile aspects of software development processes in a balanced manner. CAMS is based on the premise that in large and collaborative projects, many elements of pure Agile approaches need to be complemented by formal, planned elements.

Figure 4.9 shows how CAMS embeds the principles and practices of Agile within formal (planned) methods in a software project. In addition to the synergy of planned and Agile software methods at the software level, CAMS is result of the merging of Agile principles and practices at *all* levels of the organization.

Agile, in CAMS, is not treated as an independent process that would replace the existing process being used by the organization, but rather a suite of practices or activities that need to be carried out within and across those existing processes. The result is a composite Agile method and strategy that uses the practices of Agile across the board. The CAMS process architecture shown in Figure 4.9 is an indication of how the waterfall (formal) life cycle can embed iterations within it. Figure 4.9 also shows how the Agile practices, drawn from a CAMS repository, can be used within iterations.

Thus, business space is given high significance in CAMS because it can dictate what can and cannot be specified in a requirement. The high-level business requirements and the enterprise architecture influence the solution design. A solution design in CAMS utilizes many practices of Agile directly. CAMS also advocates architectural frameworks in creating the MOAS that helps

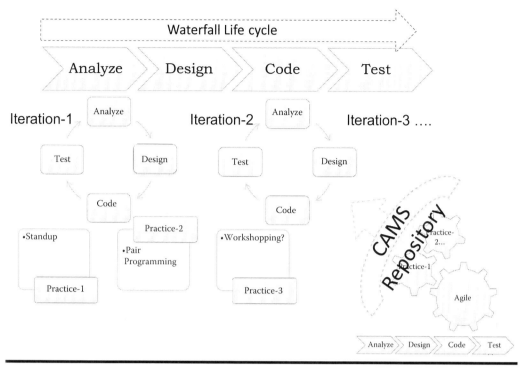

Figure 4.9 **Project level view of CAMS configuration (bringing together elements of waterfall, iterative-incremental, and Agile practices together).**

in strategic decision-making for the project. For example, in CAMS, the coach together with the team can decide on buying a component library, shifting toward Cloud- a Cloud architecture to make use of services (especially SaaS agreements), and incorporating a formal reuse strategy that goes beyond just code reuse.

Common Errors in SDLC and Agile Use and How to Rectify Them

Common Errors	Rectifying the Errors	Examples
Treating UML as a process	UML is a modeling standard; a process is an approach to create the model.	See Figure 4.1. Unified Process uses UML but is not UML itself.
Treating UML as a programming language	UML provides modeling standard; good-quality programming can result from it, but it is not a programming environment in itself.	For example, a naïve question is: Will UML replace XML? No, it won't because UML is not a direct programming language (although attempts through Executable UML are made to do so).

Common Errors	Rectifying the Errors	Examples
Not having a process	Create a basic set of activities, steps, roles, and deliverables. These steps will provide guidance on developing MOPS, MOSS, and MOAS.	Notice how in using UML the use case or sequence diagram gets drawn first; that is an internal, personal process. Formalize it.
Using Agile without discipline	Use DAD to understand the need for discipline; incorporate CAMS for balance.	Create a composite process map (Figures 4.8 and 4.9)
Confusing iterations with increments	Iterations repeat the same activity; increments produce new artifacts.	See Figure 4.4
Considering iterations without increments	Ensure new artifacts are incrementally produced.	See Figures 4.4 and 4.5
Considering CMM as a process	CMM is a way to understand the maturity of a process.	CMM can indicate whether an in-house version of UP is mature or not.
Presuming Agile means Scrum	Agile is a generic term; Scrum is specific.	Scrum, XP, Crystal, and DAD are all part of the Agile umbrella.
Using only Agile for large and collaborative projects	Large, collaborative projects need significant formality and documentation. Use CAMS.	Figure 4.9 explains the basics of how to use CAMS.

Discussion Questions

1. What is a process (method or methodology) and how is it different from modeling?
2. What is an SDLC? What are the four key elements that make up a process? Discuss with examples.
3. Discuss iterative, incremental, and parallel (IIP) aspects of a process. Explain, in particular, how an object-oriented approach to developing software enables parallel development to take place.
4. Explain, with reasons, whether you agree or disagree with the 15% (initial), 60% (major), and 25% (final) distribution of iterations (as shown in Figure 4.5).
5. Which of the Agile Manifesto statements do you agree with the most? Which of the Agile Manifesto statements do you disagree with the most? Argue with practical examples.
6. What is Agile? What is the difference between Agile and Scrum?
7. What is a role? Answer with examples.
8. How is an Agile coach different from a project manager? Also discuss why a project manager is still needed in practical projects.
9. What is a user story? Answer with an example. What is a product backlog? How is it related to a sprint backlog?
10. What is the importance of a daily standup meeting in an Agile project? Your answer must include key features of a daily standup meeting.
11. What is DAD? How does it help in developing quality software?

12. What is the importance, in practice, of CAMS (composite Agile method and strategy)?
13. How can Agile practices be used in gathering and modeling nonfunctional requirements?
14. Discuss, with examples, how you would use Agile practices in system architecture and system design.
15. Give an example of an Agile role, artifact, and ceremony. Explain how these Agile elements can be used in an iteration plan.
16. Why is the composite Agile method and strategy (CAMS) a more practical approach than a pure Agile approach? *(hint: scalability, balance, compliance, control, reporting)*
17. List two advantages and two challenges in modeling requirements with user stories in Agile. *(hint:* include challenges that go beyond the development of the system and into production)

Team Project Case Study

1. Consider the topics presented in this chapter in the context of the case study and have a discussion with your team members on the process to be used in our project.
2. Discuss the process maps (activities, deliverables, roles) you will need to create the deliverables (particularly the UML models) to be developed.
3. Create a high-level sketch of the major phases of your project; consider how this sketch can be further expanded into more details but following the iterative and incremental approach discussed in this chapter. Each phase is the basis for an iteration.
4. What are the likely major artifacts (deliverables) of your project? Create a list with an understanding that the list will be later updated to refine the artifacts.
5. What are the key roles within your project? List them within your project document; assign people to the roles.
6. Consider how Agile will fit in with your project—which parts of the Agile life cycle will you use and which parts will you not use? Why? Document it in your report document.
7. Attempt to write two use stories per student; this effort will be further improved upon after you have written use cases discussed later (Chapter 5).
8. Add one nonfunctional (feature, operational) user story per person (this activity can be iteratively performed after referring to Chapter 20 on NFRs).
9. Organize a workshop to discuss the activities and steps to be taken by your team to produce a MOPS, MOSS, and MOAS.
10. Explore how Agile practices can be used to overcome to challenges of a formal, planned approach to developing solutions.
11. Consider CAMS as a practical way to use Agile. Which formal/planned elements of an SDLC will you combine with Agile elements within your project? Discuss jointly and document half a page with your insights within your project report document.

Endnotes

1. Unhelkar, B., 2001, DeMystifying the UML. *Information Age,* publication of the Australian Computer Society, Oct 2001. pp 56–61; Unhelkar, B., 2005, "Demystifying the UML 2.0", Virtual Education across the Nation, Australian Computer Society series.

2. Based on *A Guide to the Project Management Body of Knowledge (PMBOK Guide) (5th ed.).* Project Management Institute, *2013.*

3. *Royce, Winston (1970), "Managing the Development of Large Software Systems" (PDF), Proceedings of IEEE WESCON, 26 (August): 1–9.*

4. Boehm, B.W. (1986), "A Spiral Model of Software Development and Enhancement," *ACS Software Engineering Notes,* 11(4), 14–24.

5. CMM—www.sei.cmu.edu. The Carnegie-Mellon University's Software Engineering Institute's site. This is the Institute responsible for the five levels of CMM—Capability Maturity Models.

6. Unhelkar, B. (2013), *The Art of Agile Practice: A Composite Approach for Projects and Organizations,* Boca Raton, FL, USA.: CRC Press/Taylor and Francis Group/an Auerbach Book. Authored ISBN 9781439851180.

7. The Agile Manifesto.

8. Fowler, M. and J. Highsmith, *Agile Manifesto,* Software Development, August 2001. http://www.sdmagazine.com/documents/s=844/sdm0108a/0108a.htm

9. (Unhelkar, 2013) *Art of Agile Practice.*

10. Ambler, S., The Object Primer 3rd Edition, *Agile Model Driven Development with UML* Cambridge University Press, 2004 ISBN#: 0-521-54018-6.

11. Manifesto for Agile Software Development 2001, http://agilemanifesto.org/; Viewed October 15, 2017.

12. Fowler, M. & Highsmith, J. 2001, *The Agile Manifesto,* Tech Web, viewed March 9, 2009, http://www.ddj.com/architect/184414755

13. (Coffin & Lane, 2007).

14. https://devops.com/devops-chat-state-devops-survey-2017-nigel-kersten-puppet/; viewed October 15, 2017.

15. Mistry, N., and Unhelkar, B. Composite Agile Method and Strategy: A balancing act. *Presented at the Agile Testing Leadership Conference 2015*, Sydney, Australia, August 21, 2015.

16. Schwaber & Beedle 2001.

17. http://www.methodsandtools.com/archive/Scrum1.gif—summarizes the Scrum life cycle succinctly.

18. (Mike Cottmeyer and Dennis Stevens, Rethinking the agile enterprise, July 2009) Cutter Executive Report, Boston, USA.

19. Stephen R. Palmer and John M. Felsing, 2001, *A Practical Guide to Feature-Driven Development,* Pearson Education, 2001, ISBN:0130676152.

20. Cohn, M., User Stories Applied: For Agile Software Development, Pearson Education, 2004.

21. The Disciplined Agile site. http://DisciplinedAgileDelivery.com.

22. https://disciplinedagileconsortium.org/resources/Documents/TheDAFramework.pdf.

23. (Unhelkar, 2013).

Chapter 5

Use Case Models-1:
Actors and Use Cases

Learning Objectives

- Identify actors and use cases in the problem space
- Represent actors and use cases with variations based on purpose
- Document actors and use cases in a structured format
- Analyze use cases to identify entity-level classes
- Clarify the difference between actors and classes (especially with the same names)
- Appreciate the strengths and weaknesses of use cases
- Relating use cases to acceptance testing

Use Case Modeling in the Problem Space

This chapter discusses use case modeling, which plays an important role in SE in the problem space. Use cases are based on users (actors) and their purpose (goals) in using the system. Use cases document the requirements from a user's perspective, hence their name. Use cases also help in modeling business processes.

Object-oriented SE with use cases was first introduced by Jacobson et al. (1992).[1] Since then, the popularity of use cases has grown to the point where they are now a popular way of capturing requirements in any type of project (including nonsoftware projects, e.g., business process improvements and service management). Mobile application development[2] and Big Data analytics[3] projects have also benefitted from use case–based modeling.

This chapter focuses only on the *identification* and *documentation* of actors and use cases in the problem space. The creation of use case diagrams based on actors and use cases identified here deserves separate discussion, which is carried out in the next chapter.

Actors

Use case modeling begins with the identification and documentation of users, or actors. The main purpose of developing a software solution is to provide for the needs of these users. The actor also indicates how the system will be used (hence the term use cases). Actors provide the core starting point for the rest of modeling, design, and development in a software project.

An actor is a role played by a person or a thing that is *external* to the software system. An actor (user of a system) interacts with the system in order to achieve business goals. An actor is:

- A role played by a typical user of the system (*note:* the actor is the role and not the actual person who is playing that role)
- A role that *initiates* an interaction with the system (such as a patient, who may not always interact with the system but whose presence invokes actions and responses)
- Time is considered an actor because time-triggered events initiate an interaction or a process within a system
- A role that derives benefit (achieves goals) from the system
- An "external system" with which the system under development will interact (such as a publicly available database or service)
- An external device with which the system under development will interact (such as a printer or handheld phone)
- Anything that sends a message to the system (such as an external entity)
- Anything that receives a message from the system (such as another system)
- Essentially anything that is outside the system

In addition, it is also worth noting the following about an actor:

- An actor may participate in multiple use cases because each actor is capable of initiating multiple processes within the system and have multiple goals to achieve from the system. An actor may serve as a starting point for interface modeling because an actor represents the interface of the system (interface modeling is discussed in Chapter 16). Finally, an actor may serve as the basis for good classes (however, an actor, as a business user itself, is not a class—this is explained later in this chapter).

As with everything else in an iterative and incremental life cycle, the first cut of actors is created from those users who will initiate a transaction with the system or who will derive some benefit from the system. While users are invariably actors, not all actors are human users. External systems and devices are also represented as actors. Since actors *interface* with the system, they are not *built*. Actors are what the developers are responsible for "interfacing with," whereas use cases, discussed later, represent that which is "implemented."

In the UML, an actor is represented by a "stick figure." Figure 5.1 shows this representation for `ActorPatient` for the hospital domain.

How to Find Actors?

Finding good actors is the first and most important activity during analysis in the problem space. Not paying enough attention to identifying, discussing, and documenting actors can lead to unacceptance of the solution by the users. Often a lack of understanding of actors causes rework, delays

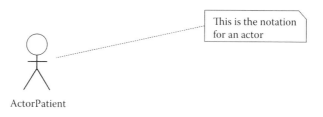

Figure 5.1 Notation for an actor.

in delivery of the solution, and overall dissatisfaction among users. On the contrary involvement of users at this early stage of modeling requirements assures their participation right through to the user acceptance testing stage.

During the initial iteration of use case modeling, a list of actors is created. Do *not* try to complete this list at the first attempt. Identification and documentation of use cases, drawing of activity diagrams, and subsequent identification of classes will invariably lead to the refinement of this actor list. Iteratively adding to the list of actors or modifying some of the actors is in accordance with the iterative and incremental (Agile) process.

Identification of potential actors and use cases happens in a workshop environment. The following are some of the questions that can be asked in a use case modeling workshop in order to arrive at a preliminary list of actors:

- Who will be the main and secondary users of the system?
- Who will be the primary beneficiaries of the interactions with the system?
- Who will be the primary initiators of interactions with the system?
- What external systems and devices will the system under development need to interface with?
- Is there a time-based process in the system?

A potential list of actors for the hospital management system (HMS) is shown in Figure 5.2. Note that there are three categories of actors in this diagram. They are the roles played by human actors interacting with the system, external systems, and devices. These actor categories have been roughly separated in Figure 5.2 for better understanding.

Actor Variations

In addition to the three groups of actors shown in Figure 5.2, there are also a number of variations in the types of actors that can appear in a system. In most practical analysis work, where business processes and workflows are modeled in the problem space, these actor variations do not have a major impact on the solution. Being aware of actor variations is beneficial in order to prevent potential confusion during modeling. Some of these variations are discussed next.

Primary versus Secondary Actors

The primary actors are those for whom the system exists. These are the main actors who benefit from the system—for example, a patient, a doctor, or a nurse in a HMS. The secondary actors are roles of *indirect* relevance in the HMS. For example, if a medical assistant is involved in processing a blood sample, but is not involved in the actual execution of any of the use cases, then she is

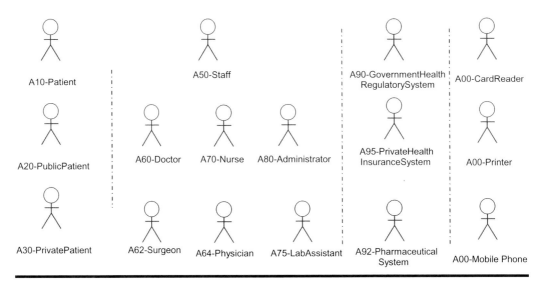

Figure 5.2   Potential list of actors for HMS.

an indirect actor. This variation of primary versus secondary actors depends on the perspective of the system. For example, if the system has use cases that deal directly with input of blood samples and test results, then the lab assistant will become a primary actor. A common example from the banking domain is that of a customer and a teller. Even if the customer, standing across the counter to withdraw cash, does not use the computer screen, she is still a primary actor. This is because the system exists for the purpose of this actor, and of course it is this actor that initiates the interaction.

Direct versus Indirect Actors

Direct actors are those who actually *use* the system. For example, an administrator *keying in* the details of a patient is a direct actor, whereas the patient, standing across the counter and providing her details, is an indirect actor. This is because the patient never gets to use the system directly. In the earlier example from the banking domain, the customer is an indirect actor, whereas the teller is a direct actor. Both direct and indirect actors are important and appear in use cases.

The understanding of whether an actor is primary or secondary, direct or indirect, is entirely dependent on the context of the actor's use of the system. For example, a patient that is indirect while standing across the counter would become a direct actor when accessing her details on the Internet. There is often no specific need to mention actors as primary/secondary or direct/indirect. This differentiation is for the understanding of the business modelers, but this differentiation may be mentioned in actor documentation when it helps clarify the modeling effort in the solution space.

Abstract versus Concrete Actors

The third variation among actors is abstract versus concrete actors. This actor variation is more important than the previous two and can be specifically shown in use case diagrams. The UML permits actors to be generalized. This means an actor can inherit the definition of another actor. For example, a "private patient" and a "public patient" may inherit all the characteristics of a

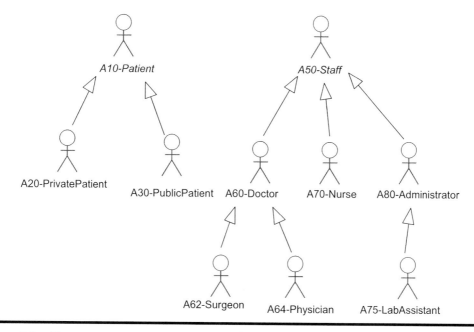

Figure 5.3 **Abstract versus concrete actors and a corresponding actor hierarchy in HMS.**

patient. As a result, the actor patient will become abstract and the private and public patients will become concrete actors. Abstract actors are at a common or higher level (generalized) in the model, from which concrete (specialized) actors are derived.

Generalization/specialization provides opportunities to reduce the complexity in use case diagrams. Abstract actors can model the common behavior of a system, such as staff logging into the system. Concrete actors model the specific behavior of the system, such as a doctor checking a consultation schedule on the calendar. Since a doctor inherits from staff, there is no need to separately model the log-in procedure for doctors if it has already been modeled for staff. Thus, a generalization of actors results in an actor hierarchy that reduces clutter and complexity in the use case diagram.

Actor hierarchies can be shown in a separate diagram. Figure 5.3 shows two separate hierarchies of actors: the patient hierarchy and the staff hierarchy. Nonhuman actors may not be shown in an actor hierarchy diagram unless they are related by inheritance. The relationship between abstract and concrete actors is that of inheritance (note the use of a formal inheritance arrow in the UML; these relationships are discussed in Chapter 6). Abstract actors A10-Patient and A50-Staff are shown in italics—as required for abstract entities in the UML.

Clarifying Actor-Class Confusion

Notice that the actor names have been prefixed with A10-, A20-, and so on. This numbering of actors, although not mandated by the UML, is a good way to group and document actors. Furthermore, prefixing actors with either the term "actor" or a simple numbering system helps avoid another potential confusion, that between an actor and a class.

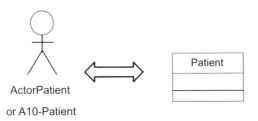

Figure 5.4 Distinguishing actors from classes.

Consider, for example, the actors Patient and Doctor. They appear to be straightforward roles played by users in a HMS. However, when the classes for the HMS are identified, the names for those classes tend to be the same as for actors.

Figure 5.4 shows the actor A10-Patient. This patient is the *user* of the system. The user will interact with the system and, as such, is *outside* the system. There are various attributes of the patient, such as his name, address, and medicare card number, that need to be stored in the system. The class that stores these details inside the system is likely to be called Patient as well. This Patient class is *not the same* as the actual user outside the system. In fact, the Patient class is designed and stored inside the system. It is important that this Patient class be differentiated from the Patient actor. A good way of creating this differentiation is by prefixing the actor names with the term "actor" or, as has been done here, with a simple numbering scheme. The prefix A10- for a patient refers to the actor, whereas a term without a prefix—such as Patient—refers to the class.

Actor Documentation

Having identified the list of actors, it is now important to document them. Although this documentation of actors is not mandatory, in practice it is always useful to document at least the main (or important) actors. This documentation improves understanding of the actors and is helpful in identifying use cases. Discussions with users and domain experts can also be stored in the actor documentation. Additionally, there are business rules and constraints specific to an actor that can be placed in actor documentation. Although modeling tools provide an opportunity to document actors, for some primary actors this can be done in a separate Word document and linked to the actor notation.

Documentation for an actor is not to be completed in a single attempt. First, the actor name and a brief description is provided. Then a few use cases corresponding to this actor are documented. As a result, more details of the actor are added to the actor documentation. The following template provides a starting point for actor documentation, followed by an example of actor documentation for the HMS.

Actor Thumbnail
<Name of the actor. Optionally, a number prefixes the name to facilitate grouping of actors. The prefix also differentiates the actor from a possible class with the same name.>

Actor Type and Stereotype
<Describes the type of actor. This can include whether it is a primary or secondary actor, person or external system or device, or if the actor is "abstract" or concrete. The type of actor may be described in general or it may be a formal stereotype.*>

Actor Description
<Short description of the actor and what he/she/it does. Together with the actor thumbnail, this might be the only thing documented for the actors in the first iteration.>

Actor Relationships
<Thumbnails of other relevant actors or use cases in the system with whom *this* actor is interacting. If there is an inheritance hierarchy, thumbnails of generalized/specialized actors can also be noted here.>

Interface Specifications
<Since, by definition, the actor has to interact with the system, we note here the details of the interface through which the actor performs this interaction. This will be a list of the numbers and names of GUI specifications related to this actor—including specifications of Web interfaces. For external systems and devices, it may be a description of the interface that may not be graphic.>

Author and History
<Original author and modifiers of this actor description>

Reference Material
<Relevant references, as well as sources from where material is inserted/available for *this* actor.>

Actor Documentation for "A10-Patient"

Figure 5.2 showed a potential list of actors for the HMS. One of the actors, A10-Patient, is documented here based on the actor template discussed earlier.

Actor Thumbnail
Actor: A10-Patient

Actor Type and Stereotype
This is an abstract actor representing all types of patients in the HMS.

Actor Description
The actor patient is the primary role interacting with the HMS in order to carry out all functions related to the patient. This actor will primarily use the system to update her details, check for the availability of doctors, schedule consultations with doctors, and seek follow-up advice. In order to carry out these functions, this actor will have to register herself, and also identify herself every time the system is accessed. This actor can be a private patient or a patient belonging to the public health system (a public patient). This private versus public distinction is made only during the registration process by the patient providing either her private insurance details or her Medicare details.

---

* Stereotypes are discussed in UML's extensibility mechanism in Chapter 10.

Actor Relationships
Two different types of concrete actors are derived from this actor:
A20-PublicPatient
A30-PrivatePatient
The actor will interface with the following use case (examples):
UC01-LogsIn
UC10-RegistersPatientDetails

Interface Specifications
UI010-LogIn*
UI020-PatientDetails
I900-GovernmentHealthCareSystem

Author and History
Colleen Berish

Reference Material
Government rules regarding patient registration in the hospital can be found on the government health regulatory system website.

Actor Documentation for "A60-Doctor"

What follows is another example of actor documentation for actor A60-Doctor for the HMS.

Actor Thumbnail
Actor: A60-Doctor

Actor Type and Stereotype
This actor represents the doctors in the HMS.

Actor Description
The actor doctor interacts with the HMS in order to carry out most medical as well as some administrative functions. These functions include checking bookings made by patients, updating diagnoses for patients, writing prescriptions, booking vacations, and providing follow-up advice to patients. The doctor is registered as a staff member and hence requires a valid login and password to access the system. The doctor is further specialized as a surgeon or a physician.

Actor Relationships
This actor inherits from A50-Staff.
This actor is specialized into: A62-Surgeon and A64-Physician.
The actor will interface with the following use cases (as shown in Figure 6.3 in Chapter 6):
UC14-CreatesPatientsMedicalProfile; UC16-UpdatesPatientsMedicalProfile
UC32-ExaminesPatient (as shown in 6.5 Chapter 6).

Interface Specifications
UI10-PatientRegistrationForm; I900-GovernmentHealthCareSystem

---

* All interface specifications mentioned in this chapter—here, in the actor specifications as well as in the use case specifications—are discussed at length in Chapter 16.

Author and History
Colleen Berish

Reference Material
Staff levels for doctors are specified in the "HMS Business Policies" document.

Use Cases
What Is a Use Case?

A use case documents a series of interactions of an actor with a system. This interaction is meant to provide some concrete, measurable results of value to the actor. Use cases describe *what* a system does, but they do *not* specify *how* the system does it. Furthermore, use cases not only document the interactions of the actor-system through a series of steps, they also add details like pre- and postconditions for the use case, user interface references, and alternative flows. A use case is represented by an ellipse in the system, as shown in Figure 5.5.

Use Case Variations

Use cases, like actors, can be of different types. For example, use cases can be at the business level (as is most common) or they can be at the system level. Use cases can also be abstract or concrete (this variation is discussed in the use-case-to-use-case relationship in Chapter 6).

Finding Use Cases

The initial list of actors is a good starting point for the identification of use cases. Use cases are best discovered in the same workshops in which actors are discovered. Actor documentation also leads to use case discovery. This is because actor documentation provides information on actor-to-use-case relationships. Use cases are sourced as follows:

- Interviews and discussions with users and domain experts in a workshop session
- Play-acting of various scenarios or "stories" told by users in terms of how they would use the system
- Identifying and documenting actors, leading to an understanding of their goals or purpose in using the system
- Revisiting the output of requirements analysis

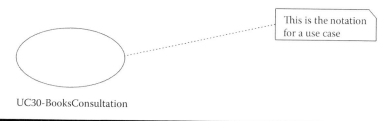

Figure 5.5   Notation for a use case.

- Formal and informal problem statements (such as presented in Appendix A)
- Executing existing systems (especially legacy applications), if available
- Investigating existing user documentation, if available
- Investigating existing "help" for the system, if available
- Researching the problem domain, especially on the Internet for relevant analysis models
- Researching and using published literature, such as *Analysis Patterns* (Fowler)

Use Case Documentation

A tentative list of use cases is created as they are discovered. Use cases are then documented iteratively. Since there is no specific format for use case documentation mandated by the OMG, there are many different formats in practice. Cockburn (2000) suggests the need for *two* templates: the first a "casual" low-ceremony format, the second a "fully dressed" format for high-ceremony projects. The practical approach is to come up with a use case format that is agreeable to all project members. This then forms the basis for all use case documentation.

Use Case Documentation Template

Use Case Thumbnail:
<This is the number and name of the use case and, optionally, a version number. The numbering may take the form UC10-, UC20-, where UC stands for use case and the numbering provides a common grouping mechanism, similar to the actors.>

Use Case Description:
<This is a short description of the use case. This description ranges from a brief "one liner" to a paragraph describing its purpose and usage. Sometimes, for a small, single-iteration project, this might be the only description of the use case.>

Stereotype and Package:
<Description of the stereotype and the package to which this use case belongs. This is optional information and may not always be documented, although it will be easily entered in a modeling tool.>

Actors:
<A list of the actors involved in this use case is documented here. >

Preconditions:
<Preconditions are the conditions that need to be satisfied before the execution described by the use case can commence.>

Postconditions:
<Postconditions are conditions that must be met at the end of a use case.>

Use Case Relationships:
<Thumbnails of other use cases that are included, extended, or inherited. These three use-case-to-use-case relationships are discussed in Chapter 6.>

Use Case Text (Basic Flow):

1.0 <description of step>

2.0 <description of step> (A1, E1, E2)

3.0 <description of step> (A2, E3)

≪include≫ <Thumbnail of use case(s) included>

≪extends≫ <Thumbnail of use case(s) extended>

Alternative Flow:

<A1—The optional descriptions here are alternative flows under conditions specified in the steps in the basic flow.>

Exceptions:

<E1 The optional descriptions here specify actions taken under "exception" conditions encountered during the basic flow of the use case. Technically, this can represent actions to be taken in case of an error.>

Constraints:

<Here are the documented special constraints or limitations that are relevant to the use case.>

User Interface Specifications:

<Number/s and name/s of UI specifications related to the use case, including Web screen specifications, as and when available. Note that these are not user interface designs but simply references to the likely screens/forms that will be used by the actor in interfacing with the system.>

Metrics (Complexity):

<Anything that needs to be measured that is related to the use cases will be put here—for example, complexity of the use case: simple/medium/complex. This information can be helpful in highly mature organizations, typically CMM level 4 and 5, where artifacts are measured for the purpose of optimization. Complexity may be based on the number of actors, relationships with other use cases, and even technical issues for each use case. However, the actual discussion on metrics is beyond the scope of this book.>

Priority:

<The importance of the functionality described by this use case: high/medium/low. This could be based on analysis and understanding of risks and importance of the use cases.>

Status:

<The state of completeness of the documentation of this use case: initial/major/final. This will indicate the level of maturity of the use case.>

Author & History:

<Original author and modifiers of this use case.>

Reference Material:

<Relevant references, as well as sources from where the use case has been derived. Any large documentation and material that does not form part of the "flow" in a use case (such as mathematical formulas, legal documents, and policy materials).>

Alternatively, a low-ceremony use case format will be a subset of the preceding detailed version and may contain just the following:

Use Case Thumbnail

Actors:

Use Case Description

Example: Use Cases in the Hospital Management System

Based on the templates for use case documentation, a few example use cases from the HMS are now described. A practical project will require substantially more use cases than described here. Also, initially the use cases described are in a low-ceremony format followed by examples of expanded high-ceremony documentation.

Brief Use Case Documentation for HMS

Use Case Thumbnail: UC10-RegistersPatient *(Figure 6.3 in Chapter 6)*

Actors: A10-Patient, A80-Administrator, A90-GovernmentHealthRegulatorySystem, A95-PrivateInsuranceProvider

Use Case Description
This use case deals with the registration of new patients in the HMS. These registration details include name, address, date of birth, and related details of the patient, his Medicare card and status, such as private or public patient. A10-Patient provides all the details and A80-Administrator enters them in the system. A90-GovernmentHealthRegulatorySystem is an interface to an external system, which is provided by the state department of health, to verify the Medicare card details of public patients. A95-PrivateInsuranceProvider is an interface to an external system for individual private health insurance companies, to verify the insurance details of private patients.

Use Case Thumbnail: UC12-MaintainsPatientDetails *(Figure 6.3 in Chapter 6)*

Actors: A10-Patient

Use Case Description
This use case describes how A10-Patient maintains selected personal details (such as address, phone, and status) using the system. These details are updated directly by the patient.

Use Case Thumbnail: UC14-CreatesPatientMedicalProfile *(Figure 6.3 in Chapter 6)*

Actors: A60-Doctor, A10-Patient, A80-Administrator

Use Case Description

This use case describes the creation of a medical profile (record) for a patient. This record is created by A60-Doctor, with input from A10-Patient. This profile contains details such as blood group, past illnesses, blood pressure, and x-ray records. The medical profile is created following the registration process. A80-Administrator helps create and verify the patient's details and is not required for profile maintenance.

Use Case Thumbnail: UC16-UpdatesPatientMedicalProfile *(Figure 6.3 in Chapter 6)*

Actors: A60-Doctor, A10-Patient

Use Case Description

This use case describes how the medical profile of a patient is updated. This modification is done by A60-Doctor with input from A10-Patient.

Use Case Thumbnail: UC22-MaintainsCalendar *(Figure 6.4 in Chapter 6)*

Actors: A50-Staff

Use Case Description

Any staff member of the hospital who has proper login authorization in the system can enter and change his/her calendar details. These calendar details include dates, vacation dates, days, times, and statuses (such as availability and booked for consultations and surgeries). Some cases, such as booking a vacation through the system, will require the authorization of the person's supervisor.

Use Case Thumbnail: UC30-BooksConsultation *(Figure 6.5 in Chapter 6)*

Actors: A10-Patient

Use Case Description

This use case describes the process by which A10-Patient is able to book a consultation with a doctor. This process requires that A10-Patient search for information on availabilities of doctors, relevant for particular ailments, on a particular day and time. The system provides alternatives, and the patient selects from those alternatives.

Use Case Thumbnail: UC36-ManagesConsultationSchedule *(Figure 6.5 in Chapter 6)*

Actors: A60-Doctor

Use Case Description

This use case describes how a doctor can view and change her consultation schedule. This management and updating of the consultation schedule by the doctors enable all other actors in the system to be aware of the availability of the doctor. The doctor can add, cancel, or modify scheduled procedures as necessary.*

Use Case Thumbnail: UC50-PaysBill *(Figure 6.6 in Chapter 6)*

Actors: A10-Patient

Use Case Description
This use case describes the process by which patients pay their medical bills. The basic procedure required to pay a bill is described here. This includes verification of the bill, corresponding procedure performed in the hospital, and the patient details. However, the actual method of payment is shown separately by other use cases that extend this use case.

Use Case Thumbnail: UC56-PaysBillOnInternet ≪extends≫ U50-PaysBill *(Figure 6.6 in Chapter 6)*

Actors: A10-Patient

Use Case Description
This use case extends use case UC50-PaysBill in that it describes the process of paying a bill online. Internet bill payment will require the patient to identify herself on the Internet, identify the bill that needs to be paid, and pay the bill using the Internet bill payment features such as "BPAY" (bill pay).

Use Case Thumbnail: UC57-CashChequePayment ≪extends≫ U50-PaysBill

Actors: A10-Patient, A00-Printer

Use Case Description
This use case extends use case UC50-PaysBill in that it describes the process of paying a bill by cash or cheque. This payment is expected to be across the counter at the hospital, although checks can also be posted by patients. A00-Printer will be used to print and post the receipts.

The following three use cases are additionally provided although they have not yet been modeled, i.e., they do not appear in any of the use case diagrams shown in Chapter 6. This practice is often encountered in the initial iterations because use case documentation leads to improvements in use case diagrams.

---

* In the HMS scenario, the consultation schedule is managed only by the physicians and not the surgeons because the physicians provide consultation, whereas surgeons perform operations. Therefore, Figure 6.5 (Consultation details) in Chapter 6 shows the actor as A64-Physician – a specialized A60-Doctor).

Use Case Thumbnail: UC52-IssuesBill

Actors: A50-Staff

Use Case Description

This use case describes the process of issuing a bill (or invoice) for hospital services. This bill is either posted to the patient or electronically sent to the patient or his health insurance company.

Use Case Thumbnail: UC62-ReordersMedicines

Actors: A75-LabAssistant, A50-Staff

Use Case Description

This use case describes the process for reordering medicines (drugs) in the laboratories and in the pharmaceutical section of the hospital. The actual ordering will require an authorized A50-Staff member together with help from A75-LabAssistant.

Use Case Thumbnail: UC60-ChecksInventory

Actors: A75-LabAssistant

Use Case Description

This use case describes the process for A75-LabAssistant to check the hospital's inventory of drugs. The lab assistant obtains the inventory level from the system and can then check the physical inventory to verify that the system is up to date. If the system's inventory does not match the physical inventory, then the lab assistant can adjust the system's inventory amount (with appropriate authorization).

Detailed Use Case Documentation for HMS

A few use cases from among those discussed earlier are selected for further detailed documentation. They are as follows:

- UC10-RegistersPatient
- UC22-MaintainsCalendar
- UC30-BooksConsultation
- UC50-PaysBill

The documentation for these four selected use cases is further visualized through activity diagrams (Chapter 7). The detailed use case documentation is also *not* completed in one attempt. Modelers should plan and expect to complete these documentations iteratively as they proceed through other parts of the analysis process, such as the creation of activity diagrams (Chapter 7) and identification of classes (Chapter 8). Although the documentation shown here is almost in its final form, this is not how it will appear in the first attempt at documenting use cases.

Use Case "RegistersPatient"

What follows is the documentation of use case "RegistersPatient." This example was shown in abbreviated form earlier. Here, it is documented using a detailed high-ceremony use case format.

Use Case Thumbnail: UC10-RegistersPatient

Use Case Description: This use case describes the process of registering a new patient in the hospital system. The patient must be registered and her details verified with the government health system before any of the hospital's services can be provided.

Stereotype and Package: ≪Patient≫

Preconditions: Patient must have not been already registered with the hospital.

Postconditions: Patient is registered in the hospital system.

Actors: A10-Patient; A80-Administrator; A90-GovernmentRegulatoryHealthSystem, A95-Private Health Insurance System

Use Case Relationships: Associated with actors: A10-Patient, A80-Administrator.

Basic Flow (Text):

1. A patient arrives at the hospital for some medical treatment.
2. The administrator asks the patient if she had been previously treated at this hospital.
3. Patient provides the answer (A1).
4. Administrator asks patient for her personal details such as name, address, telephone, date of birth, and emergency contact.
5. Patient provides details as requested.
6. Administrator enters details into system.
7. System verifies details (A2).
8. Administrator asks patient whether she is a public or private patient.
9. Patient provides the answer. [Public or Private][Public]

   9.1a Administrator asks public patient for Medicare number.
   9.2a Patient provides Medicare number.
   9.3a Administrator enters Medicare number into system.
   9.4a System verifies patient identity with the government health regulatory system (A3).

[Private]

   9.1b Administrator asks private patient for insurance details.
   9.2b Patient provides insurance details.
   9.3b Administrator enters insurance details (insurance company, patient's insurance number) into system.
   9.4b System verifies patient identity with private health insurance company system (A4).

10. System saves patient details.
11. System confirms patient registration.

Alternative Flow:
<A1 – If the patient has visited the hospital previously, the details are registered in the hospital's system. The administrator informs the patient of existing registration.>
<A2 – If insufficient or incorrect details have been provided, the patient is requested to provide the details again.>
<A3 – The patient cannot be verified in the government health regulatory system, so the administrator asks the patient for her Medicare card details again. If no verification is possible, the patient is conditionally registered as either a full fee–paying patient or one who will provide Medicare details later.>
<A4 – The patient cannot be verified in the private health insurance company's system, so the administrator asks the patient for the private health insurance details again. If no verification is possible, the patient is conditionally registered as either a full fee–paying patient and her details with the health insurance company are verified later.>

Exceptions: None.

Constraints: None.

User Interface Specifications: UI10-PatientRegistrationForm*

Metrics: Complex **Priority:** High **Status:** Major

Author and History: Vivek E.

Reference Material: Details of patient that are required by law are specified in the hospital's patient policy document available from the administration department. See <patientpolicy. doc>.†

Use Case "MaintainsCalendar"

Use Case Thumbnail: UC22-MaintainsCalendar

Use Case Description: This use case details the process of maintenance of personal calendars by the staff of the hospital.

Stereotype and Package: ≪Staff≫

Preconditions: Staff member should be valid and should have a valid login.

Postconditions: None.

Actors: A50-Staff.

---

* User interfaces are discussed in detail in Chapter 16. Here, in use case descriptions, they are simply mentioned.
† This is not a real reference to any document in this book. This reference is provided for readers to understand how a bulky document or document external to the use case is mentioned in the use case. Other common examples of references include, for example, legal documents and mathematical formulas.

Use Case Relationships: Associated with actors: A50-Staff (perhaps with other staff members)

Basic Flow (Text)

1. A staff member requests his personal calendar details from the system.
2. The system provides the personal calendar to the staff member.
3. The staff member enters his preferred working hours for the upcoming schedules available in the system.
4. The system validates the schedule with other staff members' schedules for possible conflicts (A1).
5. The system accepts the new schedule and updates the hospital master schedule.
6. The system displays a confirmation to the staff member.

Alternative Flow:
<A1 – The schedule entered conflicts with another staff member's schedule. The staff member is informed and asked to change his preferences.>

Exceptions: None.

Constraints: None.

User Interface Specifications: UI20-CalendarMaintenanceForm

Metrics: Simple   **Priority:** Low   **Status:** Major

Author & History: Janalee Heinemann

Reference Material: Details of patient required by law are specified in the hospital's patient policy document available from the administration department. See <patientpolicy. doc>.

Use Case "BooksConsultation"

Use Case Thumbnail: UC30-BooksConsultation

Use Case Description: This use case describes the process by which an outpatient is able to book a consultation session with a doctor (physician). This same use case is executed when the patient books the consultation online via the Internet portal – in which case the administrator is not involved.

Stereotype and Package: ≪Consultation≫

Preconditions: Patient is already registered in the system and has identified himself to the administrator.

Postconditions: Patient is given a date and time of consultation.

Actors: A10-Patient; A80-Administrator

Use Case Relationships: Associated with actors: A10-Patient, A80-Administrator

Basic Flow (Text)

1. Patient requests a consultation with a doctor via the administrator.
2. Administrator requests details of the patient's condition.
3. Patient describes her condition to the administrator.
4. Administrator enters condition into system.
5. System provides a list of doctors and their available consultation times for the specified condition.
   5.1 ≪include≫ UC24-ChecksCalendar
6. Patient selects a doctor and her preferred time (A1).
7. Administrator enters selected doctor and time into the system.
8. System schedules the consultation and updates doctor's personal calendar.
9. System confirms consultation time, room, and doctor.

Alternative Flow:
<A1> None of the offered times and doctors are acceptable to the patient, so the patient cancels her request.

Exceptions: None.

Constraints: None.

User Interface Specifications: UI30-ConsultationMaintenanceForm

Metrics: Simple   **Priority:** Low   **Status:** Major

Author & History: Allen Becker

Reference Material: Details of patient required by law are specified in the hospital's patient policy document available from the administration department. See <patientpolicy. doc>.

Use Case "PaysBill"

Use Case Thumbnail: UC50-PaysBill

Use Case Description: This use case describes payment of bills (or invoices) by the patient.

Stereotype and Package: ≪Account≫

Preconditions: Patient should be registered in the hospital system.

Postconditions: Bill is paid and system is updated.

Actors: A10-Patient

Use Case Relationships:
Associated with actors: A10-Patient (via Internet), A80-Administrator (over the counter)

Basic Flow (Text)

1. Patient receives bill for services performed by hospital.
2. Patient verifies charges on bill (A1).
3. Payment of bill can be made online by credit or debit card or by cash/check in person. The patient decides what type of payment she wants to make and proceeds to make the payment accordingly. Extended use case documentation can be referred to for the different payment methods.

Alternative Flow:
<A1 – If the bill has been misdirected or shows incorrect charges, the patient contacts the hospital's accounts department to correct the error.>

Exceptions:
<E1>

Constraints: None.

User Interface Specifications: UI50-BillPayInternetForm or a generic UI51-BillPayForm

Metrics: Simple   **Priority:** Low   **Status:** Major

Author & History: Andy Lyman

Reference Material: Details of patient required by law are specified in the hospital's patient policy document available from the administration department. See <patientpolicy. doc>.

Strengths and Weaknesses of Use Cases and Actors

Identification and documentation of actors and use cases in the problem space benefit by understanding their strengths and weaknesses. These strengths and weaknesses, discussed next, are for the use cases (and not for the use case diagrams, which are discussed in the next chapter).

Strengths of Use Cases

- Use cases directly relate to actors. Hence, they directly relate to the users of the system. This results in "buy-in" from the user community in the system.
- Use cases help the business analyst to document requirements in a commonly accepted format in the problem space of the project.
- The actor, through the use cases, specifies the suite of interactions with the system.
- Use cases capture the functional aspects of the system. More specifically, they capture the business processes carried out in the system. They are usually developed by domain experts and business analysts, resulting in the effective documentation of functionalities.
- Since use cases document the complete functionality of a system, no separate functional requirements document is needed (although additional operational and interface

requirements or additional details such as the referenced material may be available or placed in a separate document).

■ Use cases facilitate tracing of requirements. By providing well-organized documentation on the requirements, a use case provides a trace for a particular requirement throughout the system. This is especially helpful in creating and executing acceptance tests by users.

■ Use cases can help in the creation of prototypes. Developers can select a use case and produce a proof-of-concept prototype of the system that will validate system requirements.

■ Documentation of a use case provides a means for creating activity diagrams. The documentation of the flow within the use case can also be influenced and improved by the activity diagram(s) drawn for a use case.

■ Specifications and documentation of use cases also provide a rich source of information for the identification of business entities. These business entities can be put together in a suite of class diagrams—providing vital information in the model of the problem space.

■ Use cases can also provide a starting point for sequence diagrams—based on the scenarios (or instances of behavior) documented within a use case.

■ Use cases are the basis for test case development.

■ Use cases aid in requirement mapping: matching of a requirement to a software feature to the approved test case.

Weaknesses of Use Cases

■ Use case documentation is not standardized. This leads to confusion and debates on what makes up a good use case. Most projects proceed on the basis of a template (see previous discussion).

■ Use cases are not object-oriented in nature. Therefore, they are not an ideal mechanism to model design-level constructs in the solution space (where object orientation plays an important role).

■ Use cases do not have a granularity standard. Therefore, sometimes use cases are written as huge descriptive documents, resulting in the inability of modelers to capitalize on the reusable and organizational aspect of use case modeling. Alternatively, too brief a description will result in a large number of miniscule use cases—making them less comprehensible and manageable.

■ Use cases do not cover nonfunctional (operational) requirements, although they may allude to them. The operational aspect of the system (such as speed, security, volume, and performance) cannot be easily documented in a use case model but needs to be captured elsewhere in the requirements or solution design documentation.

■ Use cases do not provide a good basis for coding. Their documentation provides a foundation for subsequent modeling, but not for code generation.

Relating Use Cases to Packages

The discussion on packages (Chapter 3) outlined a mechanism to organize subsystems within projects. Understanding the organizational ability of packages is most helpful in creating and storing actors and their documentation. The modeling work discussed in this chapter needs to be undertaken within appropriate packages. For example, the actors identified as doctor and nurse will be modeled within the staff package. The patient actor will be placed in the patient package. When one actor from a package is to be used or referred to in another package, the namespaces described along with packages (Chapter 3) come in handy. For example, in the mentioned scenario, if a patient is to be referred to in the staff package, then it will appear as Patient:Patient within Staff. Alternatively, if a doctor is to be referred to in the patient package, that actor will appear as Staff:Doctor.

It is important to note that in iterative and incremental processes, it is expected that the discussions and modeling of actors, use cases, and use case diagrams will lead to the identification of new packages as well as refinement of existing packages. In fact, package names and descriptions should not be considered finalized until at least two use cases from each package are fully documented and deemed complete by the stakeholders.

Relating Use Cases to Functional Testing

The identification and creation of good test cases based on use cases are discussed in Chapter 19. Good use case documentation provides an excellent basis for writing good functional test cases and executing them. The text or steps within the basic and alternative flows of use cases can be treated as test cases or actions within a test case. Use cases, thus, provide a basis for user acceptance of the functionality of the system. In other words, if the software developed is able to satisfy the use cases, then it should be "accepted." This puts the onus of writing good use cases on the business analysts together with the user representatives on the project. The testing of the nonfunctional requirements needs additional considerations that go beyond use case testing.

In conclusion, note that:

■ The actors and use cases discussed and documented thus far are put together in use case diagrams (discussed in Chapter 6).
■ The documentation of use cases is related to the creation of activity diagrams (discussed in Chapter 7). Modeling those activity diagrams can help improve and update the documentation discussed in this chapter.
■ Documentation of use cases is a rich and primary source for entity classes in the business domain. Analyzing the use cases to arrive at these entity classes is discussed in Chapter 8.

Common Errors in Modeling Actors and Use Cases and How to Rectify Them

Common Errors	Rectifying the Errors	Examples
Treating all actors as humans	Consider nonhuman actors in MOPS.	• External systems • External devices (printers, smartphones) • Time
Not understanding that actors represent roles and not people	Separate real people from their roles.	Franki and Sam are people; they can play the role of a customer.

Common Errors	Rectifying the Errors	Examples
Not realizing that indirect actors can be primary beneficiaries	Study the primary beneficiaries of the system even if they do not interact directly with the system.	• Patient in a hospital bed • Customer standing across a counter
Unable to create an actor hierarchy	Study the requirement to identify commonalities.	See Figure 4.3
Unable to differentiate between an actor and corresponding class	Prefix actors to ensure they are differentiated from a class.	A10-Patient is an actor; patient is a class.
Misrepresenting a use case to be a use case diagram	Use cases are documentation of the flow; use case diagrams are discussed in the next chapter.	See Chapter 6 for use case diagrams.
Documenting a use case without an actor	Ensure a use case starts with an actor—and the objective/goal of the actor.	Nonhuman actors (such as time) are exceptions.
Too coarse or too fine granular use case documentation (e.g., a single use case running into 20 pages or more or, alternatively, one step of a use case being treated as an entire use case itself)	Be prepared to revise the documentation in a second iteration of requirements modeling to ensure it is not too long or short.	Refer to the brief and detailed documentation in this chapter. Ideally, a use case documentation is 3–5 pages.
Trying to complete the actor and use case documentation in one attempt	Ensure creation of an iterative and incremental plan to facilitate repetition.	See Figure 4.5 in previous chapter.

Discussion Questions

1. Who is an actor? List all variations of an actor with examples.
2. Why is time treated as an actor? Provide a situation where time is appropriately an actor.
3. Draw an actor hierarchy with at least five actors. Discuss the advantage of creating such a hierarchy.
4. What is the potential confusion between an actor and class? Explain how to avoid this confusion with an example.
5. Document an actor in detail.
6. Identify a list of five use cases.
7. Document one use case in brief.
8. Document one use case in detail (high ceremony) with flows and alternative flows.
9. Observe possible changes in the list of actors and of the use cases based on the aforementioned documentation of use cases.

10. Discuss one advantage and one limitation of actors and use cases; provide an example with your answers.
11. How is good use case documentation helpful in testing? What else is required besides the use case documentation to create good acceptance test cases?

Team Project Case Study

1. Hold a workshop to identify actors for the case study (four to five actors per package based on the packages identified in Chapter 3; this will result in four to five actors per student, as one student is the primary owner of one package, although all students in the team will work to produce the model).
2. Document the actors using the actor documentation template discussed in this chapter.
3. Apply the discussion in this module to identify use cases in the case study given to you. This identification of use cases requires you, the students, to "play act" the actors in your workshop setting. Query each actor as to how they are going to use the system in order to identify use cases.
4. Identify at least five use cases per package (for a team of 4 students, there will be a total of 20 use cases, which is not a big list for a project lasting around 15 weeks). Do note that this list includes use cases that are ≪included≫ and use cases that are ≪extended≫. (Inclusion and extension of use cases is discussed in detail in Chapter 6; hence, you will have to come back to this task list after you have worked through the team project in Chapter 6).
5. Initially, go to the Word document (where you are storing the project report) and document TWO use cases per package (per student) in that document.
6. The process of documenting these use cases will lead to a refinement of the actors, as expected.
7. Plan for documenting the remaining use cases, as per an iterative-incremental project plan: after the use case diagrams are drawn (Chapter 6), activity diagrams are modeled (Chapter 7), and an initial list of classes is identified (Chapter 8).
8. Make a note of how use case documentation can be helpful in acceptance testing (revisit this note after studying Chapter 19 on testing).

Endnotes

1. Jacobson, I., Christerson, M., Jonsson, P., and Overgaard, G. (1992), *Object-Oriented Software Engineering: A Use Case Driven Approach*, Addison-Wesley, ACM Press.
2. Unhelkar, B. (2009), *Mobile Enterprise Transition and Management*, Boca Raton, FL, USA: Taylor & Francis (Auerbach Publications), 393 pages, ISBN: 978-1-4200-7827-5.
3. Unhelkar, B. (2017), *Big Data Strategies for Agile Business*, Boca Raton, FL, USA (CRC Press/Taylor & Francis Group/an Auerbach Book).

Chapter 6

Use Case Models-2: Use Case Diagrams and Requirements Modeling

Learning Objectives

- Model requirements in the problem space with use cases
- Create use case diagrams with actors, use cases, and relationships
- Study the three relationships in a use case diagram: include, extends, inherits
- Understand the importance of system boundaries in use case diagrams
- Add notes in use case diagrams to improve their readability
- Understand the strengths and weaknesses of use case diagrams

Use Case Diagrams

This chapter discusses use case diagrams. Extending the discussion in the previous chapter, this chapter demonstrates how to place actors and use cases in a visual format.

Use case diagrams provide a comprehensive visual overview of the requirements of a system in the problem space. Fowler (2003)[1] calls them a "graphical table of contents" of the use cases. Use case diagrams contain actors, use cases, their relationships, and notes. Use case diagrams are ideal for engaging users and ensuring their participation in modeling requirements.

As mentioned in the previous chapter, use case diagrams show, through actors, where the users fit in the overall solution and how they will use the system. Use case modeling workshops usually have increased participation from users in the software development process and result in an overall increase in their satisfaction from solutions. Good software engineers are therefore keen to understand and draw use case diagrams to ensure their efforts are directed toward fulfilling user needs.

Notations of a Use Case Diagram

Figure 6.1 shows the notations in a use case diagram. They are actor, use case, relations, boundary, and notes. These are discussed in greater detail next.

Boundary

The system boundary is an important notation in a use case diagram. The system boundary, shown by a rectangular box in Figure 6.1, separates actors from use cases. The actors are all *outside* of the boundary and the use cases are all *inside*. Although the boundary line is optional in the UML standard, it is advisable to draw it whenever possible. If the modeling tool does not support the drawing of a boundary, creating a visual arrangement by keeping the use cases all together in the middle of the diagram surrounded by actors is a good option for the aesthetic quality of a use case diagram.

Notes

Notes add semantic and aesthetic value to a use case diagram (as it does to all other diagrams in the UML). Notes are shown with a corner-cut rectangle (also known as a dog-eared rectangle) in Figure 6.1. Notes in use case diagrams can be used to explain the use case relationships (discussion follows), provide additional information on actors, and highlight the importance of certain use cases.

Actor

Actors, as discussed in previous chapters, represent the roles played by system users. Actors can also represent an interface to another system or an external device. Actors are represented by stick

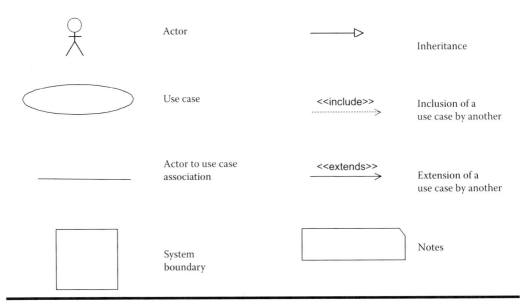

Figure 6.1   Major notations in a use case diagram.

figures, as shown in Figure 6.1. Since an actor is *outside* the system boundary, it is only interfaced with, not built. Actors and their documentation were discussed in the previous chapter.

Use Case

The use case, discussed in the previous chapter, is shown visually by an ellipse, as shown in Figure 6.1. A use case represents a cohesive set of interactions between the actor and the system. Pictorially a use case simply *represents* the interaction but does not *show* it in the diagram. The documentation of a use case contains the details of the interaction. Use cases and their documentation were discussed in the previous chapter.

Relationships

Relationships in a use case diagram are a powerful mechanism to organize and reuse requirements. There are three main types of relationships in use case diagrams:

1. Actor to actor—This is the generalization relationship and represented by the inheritance arrow in Figure 6.1. This relationship was also discussed in the previous chapter (notably Figure 5.3).
2. Actor to use case—The relationship between an actor and a use case is called an association, also occasionally called "communication" because it represents a communication between the actor and the system. This association is represented by a straight line in Figure 6.1. The association is an interface through which an actor interacts with the system. Occasionally, an association line may have an arrowhead (not shown in Figure 6.1), representing the actor initiating the use case. This direction on the association relationship is only shown if absolutely necessary.
3. Use case to use case—There are three specific relationships permitted between two use cases in a use case diagram. They are the *include, extends*, and *inherits* relationships, as shown by the three arrows and appropriate stereotypes on them in Figure 6.1. These relationships deserve a detailed discussion, which follows

Use Case Relationships

Figure 6.2 shows a sample use case diagram. This diagram is meant to highlight the three relationships between use cases. Note that in Figure 6.2, the actor to UsecaseA relationship is simply shown as a line (association), as discussed earlier. That relationship is an actor-to-use-case relationship and needs to be noted as separate from the discussion on use-case-to-use-case relationships.

Include

When a part of the behavior documented within a use case is likely to be reused by other parts of a system, it is advisable to factor out that common behavior and show it as an independent use case. This newly created use case can then be "included" in the original use case from which it was factored out. The newly created use case also becomes available to other use cases in the system. The relationship between two such use cases is that of *includes*, and the arrowhead on this relationship points from the including use case to the use case being included. In Figure 6.2, UsecaseA is

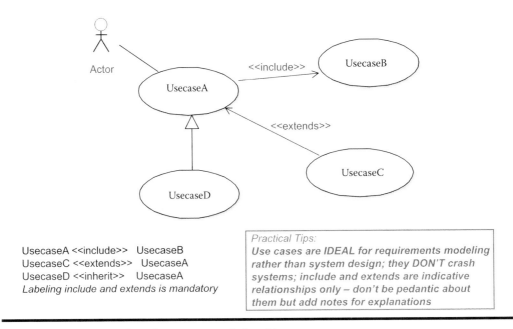

UsecaseA <<include>> UsecaseB
UsecaseC <<extends>> UsecaseA
UsecaseD <<inherit>> UsecaseA
Labeling include and extends is mandatory

Practical Tips:
Use cases are IDEAL for requirements modeling
rather than system design; they DON'T crash
systems; include and extends are indicative
relationships only – don't be pedantic about
them but add notes for explanations

Figure 6.2   UML notations for use case relationships.

shown including UsecaseB. Hence the arrow points from UsecaseA to UsecaseB with the stereotype <<include>> written on the relationship.

Extends

When a use case extends or specializes the behavior of another use case, the relationship is "extends." This extension may be undertaken in order to add functionality to an existing use case. The extension can also superimpose a new special type of behavior on an existing behavior. The extends relationship may also describe an anomalous situation or an exception, beyond that provided in the base use case (Henderson-Sellers and Unhelkar, 2000).[2] The extending use case may thus be thought of as representing an "option." In the "extends" relationship between two use cases, the arrowhead points to the use case that is being extended. UsecaseC in Figure 6.2 shows how it extends UsecaseA. The arrow is pointing from UsecaseC to UsecaseA, and the word <<extends>> is stereotyped on the relationship.

Inherits (Generalize)

"Inherits," also known as generalization, literally means a use case implements the behavior described by another higher-level abstract use case. While an abstract use case contains a generalized description of how an actor will use the system, the corresponding concrete use case, which is inherited from the generalized use case, will describe the actual steps in the identification of the user. Unless a use case has been correctly documented as an abstract use case, the generalization relationship will tend to confuse rather than prove valuable (Henderson-Sellers and Unhelkar, 2000).[2] This is because inheritance is meant to represent one behavior (that described by the abstract use case) being replaced by another (that described by the concrete use case). Cockburn (2000) also notes that there isn't actually an agreed semantics for generalization/specialization (i.e., subtyping) when applied to use cases. In the absence of a formal internal structure for the documentation of use cases, it is difficult to ascertain which bits and parts of the abstract use case are being "overridden" or replaced by the concrete use case.

PRACTICAL USE-CASE-TO-USE-CASE RELATIONSHIPS

In practice, the two primary use-case-to-use-case relationships `include` and `extends` are sufficient to model almost all requirements in the problem space, obviating the need to use the `generalization` relationship. In practice, however, the "`include`" and the "`extends`" relationships can also be confusing. Both relationships are subject to interpretation. It is advisable to annotate use case diagrams with notes to clarify the intended meanings behind the relationships used. For most practical purposes, though, the "`include`" relationship will suffice together with notes.

Naming a Use Case Diagram

The effort in identifying, naming, and diagramming actors and use cases needs to be complemented by proper naming of the use case diagrams. There is no mandated standard in the UML for naming a use case diagram. However, creating and naming a use case diagram is important in organizing the requirements and conveying the meaning behind the diagram, including its many actors and use cases. A use case diagram should be named to represent a "subject area" of the system. For example, all use cases that deal with maintaining details of a patient can be put together in a "Patient Maintenance" use case diagram. Subject areas will emerge and be refined as the requirements modeling exercise continues in an iterative and incremental manner. Therefore, requirement modelers should be prepared to refine and update the initial names they give to a use case diagram.

Use Case Diagrams for Hospital Management System

Revisiting the actors and use cases identified and documented in the previous chapter leads to a number of subject areas with the HMS that can be modeled in detail through use case diagrams. These potential use case diagrams are as follows:

"Patient Maintenance" use case diagram
"Calendar Maintenance" use case diagram
"Consultation Details" use case diagram
"Accounting" use case diagram
"Surgery Details" use case diagram
"Inventory and Reordering" use case diagram
"User Administration" use case diagram

The first four of these diagrams listed are shown next as examples.

"Patient Maintenance" Use Case Diagram

Figure 6.3 shows a typical use case diagram that represents the patient maintenance module of the HMS. Although deceptively simple, this use case diagram carries substantial

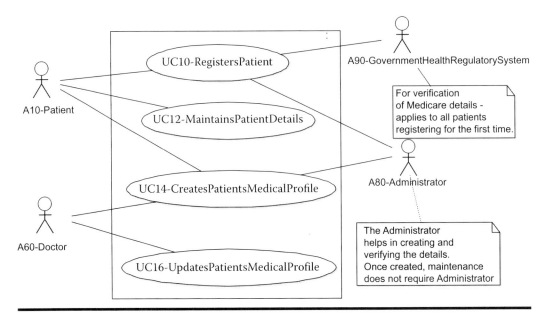

Figure 6.3 Patient maintenance "use case diagram."

information from the problem space. First of all, it shows the users of the system in the roles of Patient, Doctor, and Administrator. The use case diagram also shows an actor called GovernmentHealthRegulatorySystem, which in this case is an external system.

Considering a typical patient maintenance system, the Administrator interacts with the system in various ways, one of which is when he deals with all aspects of creating a patient's medical profile. This interaction is represented by a use case called "CreatesPatientsMedicalProfile." The line that connects the actor Administrator to the use case "CreatesPatientsMedicalProfile" is an association relationship showing the interaction of the administrator with the system during the process of maintaining the patient's details.

The creation of a patient's medical profile is a use case represented by another ellipse. As mentioned in Chapter 5, the documentation of these use cases is not visible in the diagram but is hidden inside the use case or created separately, i.e., using Word and linked to this use case symbol.

The Patient Maintenance use case diagram also has a use case, RegistersPatient, which has multiple actors interacting with it. The specification of the RegistersPatient use case may, optionally, contain pre- and postconditions. One of the preconditions might be that whenever any new patient is registered, his Medicare details are verified by passing the message to the GovernmentHealthRegulatorySystem. The appearance of this "interface actor" representing another system is quite common even in the problem space, and especially so in large and legacy integration projects. In these projects, the system being built will interface with legacy systems, external agencies, and databases.

"Calendar Maintenance" Use Case Diagram

Figure 6.4 shows a use case diagram that represents the Calendar Maintenance module of the hospital management system. The use case diagram gives a high-level picture of the activities involving calendar maintenance. The main actor involved in this module is the hospital staff. This actor is associated

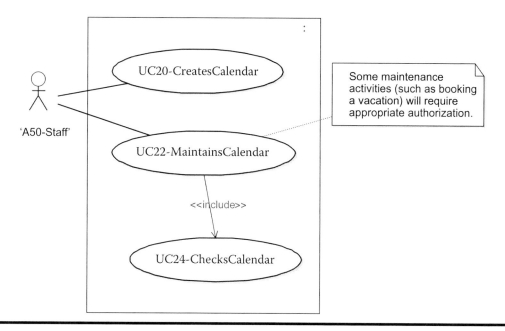

Figure 6.4 Calendar maintenance "use case diagram."

with the `CreatesCalendar` and `MaintainsCalendar` use cases. The special note attached to the `MaintainsCalendar` use case indicates the authority required by the staff accessing this module. The use case `ChecksCalendar` performs the tasks related to checking the calendar for the availability of consultation times, for example. This module is used by the `MaintainsCalendar` use case for its complete operation and hence is shown as an `include` relationship.

"Consultation Details" Use Case Diagram

Figure 6.5 shows a use case diagram for the Patient Consultation module of the hospital management system. The actors involved in this module are the physician and patient. The patient is associated with the `BooksConsultation` use case. The `ChecksCalendar` use case, as first seen in the previous diagram, is referenced in this module by the `BooksConsultation` as an include relationship. This ensures the proper functioning of the `BooksConsultation` use case.

Note that use cases are not restricted to a single use case diagram and can be included in another use case diagram for reusability. The physician and the patient interact with the `ExaminesPatient` use case, indicating that both actors are required for the functioning of this module. The physician is also associated with other use cases such as `OrdersTests`, `WritesPrescription`, and `ManagesConsultationSchedule`, which deal with other miscellaneous tasks related to the patient examination.

"Accounting" Use Case Diagram

Figure 6.6 shows a use case diagram that represents the working of the Accounting module of the HMS. The actors involved in this module are the `Patient`, `PrivatePatient`, `CardReader`, and `Printer`. Once the patient receives the bill, he starts the payment process.

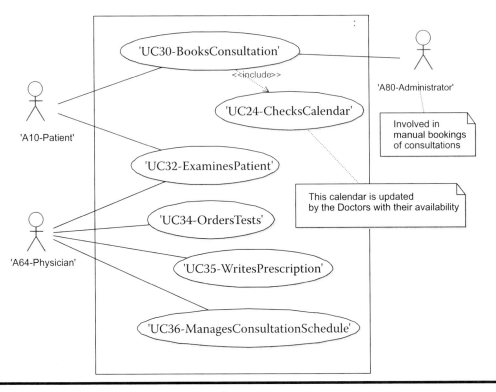

Figure 6.5   Consultation details "use case diagram."

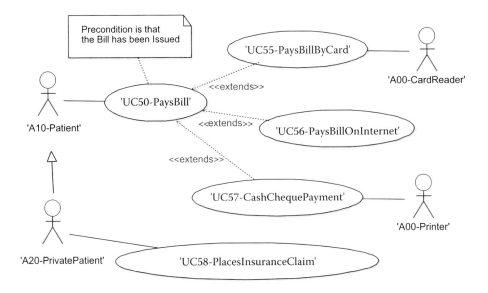

Note: In this use case diagram, the system boundary has not been drawn. However, observe how the use cases are all grouped together in the center of the diagram and the actors are on the outside. This improves the aesthetics of the use case diagram.

Figure 6.6   Accounting "use case diagram."

This is indicated as the precondition of the `PaysBill` use case. The `PrivatePatient`, apart from performing all the tasks associated with the normal `Patient`, also interacts with the `PlacesInsuranceClaims` use case. This is represented as the generalization between the `Patient` and the `PrivatePatient` actor (note the arrow shape).

The use cases `PaysBillByCard` and `PaysBillOnInternet` form the two methods of paying the bill and, hence, extend the `PaysBill` use case. In the case of `PaysBillByCard`, the use of the external system `CardReader` is shown as an actor interacting with the use case. Where the bill is paid by cash or cheque, the CashChequePayment use case becomes active and the receipt is printed via the external system `Printer,` also shown as an actor.

Strengths and Weaknesses of Use Case Diagrams

Strengths of Use Case Diagrams

What follows are some of the strengths of use case diagrams in practice. Awareness of these strengths at the start of a requirements modeling exercise is most helpful in improving the quality of the model of the problem space (MOPS):

- Use case diagrams model the communication between actors and a system and provide a summary view of system usage and behavior. This summary view provides an immediate understanding of the overall requirements—and then readers can drill down to specific actors and use cases of interest.
- Use case diagrams can organize requirements by showing the intended behavior of a system. They are helpful in identifying the core requirements of the system, as well as their variants. A walkthrough of these requirements in a use case diagram can help shed light on and improve those requirements early in the life cycle of a software development project.
- Use case diagrams can effectively summarize the interactions needed between users (actors) and a system that will provide value to business.
- Use case diagrams show graphically the opportunities for reuse of use cases; this reuse is at the requirements level and is modeled within a use case diagram through include and extends mechanisms.
- Use case diagrams can aid in dividing a large system into multiple modules. Each module can itself be represented by a use case diagram. (Note, however, that there are no levels within a use case diagram.)
- The boundary feature of use case diagrams helps in isolating the internal and the external elements of a system—with the actors all being outside and the use cases inside the system.
- Evaluating and prioritizing requirements: use case diagrams can be used to evaluate the requirements. With the help of use case diagrams, it is possible to ascertain a set of business processes that represent some significant and central functionality that can be categorized as a high-priority job. The remaining business processes (or functionalities) may take less precedence over the significant ones.
- Facilitating project estimation: use case diagrams can be used to estimate project size and complexity as they show the context in which a use case exists and relates to other use cases and actors. For example, use cases involving an easy user interface and requiring minimal database interaction could be classified as an easy task. On the other hand, a complex use case involving an intricate user interface and multiple database interactions can be classified as a complex task and assign the highest value in the time scale.

Weaknesses of Use Case Diagrams

Following are some of the weaknesses of use case diagrams in practice. Awareness of these weaknesses at the start of a requirements modeling exercise is also very helpful in improving the quality of the MOPS:

- Similar to use cases, the use case diagrams are not object-oriented and do not provide any active application of the concept of object orientation to the development of the solution.
- Imprecise relationships: The relationships between two use cases shown in a use case diagram (i.e., <<include>>, <<extends>>, and <<inherits>>) do not have rigorous definitions within the UML. These relationships provide a generic description of how use cases relate to each other. Practical software projects do not use these relationships as rigorously defined but, rather, as indicative of the connections between two use cases. Notes are needed to provide value to the relationships.
- Granularity in use case diagrams is a matter of aesthetics. A use case diagram can easily lose its aesthetic quality by either having too many or too few use cases. Furthermore, a system can have different levels of granularity and, hence, create complexity in terms of creating, reading, and understanding the use case diagram.
- Use case diagrams do not show any flow or dependencies in the system. They only provide a high-level picture of the system and have no features to represent the sequence of actions and alternative actions.

Common Errors in Use Case Diagrams and How to Rectify Them

Common Errors	Rectifying the Errors	Examples
Assuming that there is only one use case diagram for the system	The system's requirements view should be expressed with multiple use case diagrams. Each use case diagram represents a key subject area of the system.	See Figures 6.3 through 6.5.
One use case can appear in only one use case diagram	Use cases can appear in multiple use case diagrams depending on the needs of the system. Multiple appearances of use cases in use case diagrams show their use in different contexts.	UC24-ChecksCalendar use case appears in "Calendar Maintenance" and "Consultation Details" use case diagrams
One actor can appear in only one use case diagram	An actor can be shown in different use case diagrams to represent different ways in which the actor achieves goals by using the system	"A10_Patient" appears in multiple use case diagrams in this chapter.

Common Errors	Rectifying the Errors	Examples
An actor-use case combination is limited to only one package.	A package is only an organizational entity. Actors and use cases can come from different packages and appear in many packages.	Use namespace (discussed in a previous chapter) to identify the source of an actor or use case package.
One can code directly from use cases.	Use cases are no longer object-oriented in nature; they are excellent for capturing requirements, but their models are fuzzy and not as precise as, say, class diagrams.	Not recommended.
They are treated as data flow diagrams (DFD)	They look like a DFD but they do not show a flow of data like a DFD does.	There is no "if-then-else" or any layering in use case diagrams.
Every communication between actors and use cases needs to be represented in the use case diagram.	If this is attempted, the use case diagrams can look like a spider's web. Actors should be abstracted and the diagrams annotated in order to create an aesthetically good diagram.	See Figure 6.6, where the private patient is derived from the patient—and in that way, the clutter in the diagram is reduced.
Use case diagrams are treated as deliverables	More than 50% of the work in use case modeling deals with documenting use cases and not drawing use case diagrams.	This is why use case diagrams are called "visual tables of contents" of requirements.
Showing an inheritance relationship between an actor and use case	Only communication line representing an association relationship is possible between actor and use cases.	Revisit the relationships shown in Figure 6.2.
Showing an <<inherits>> or <<includes>> between an actor and a use case	These are only use-case-to-use-case relationships.	Revisit the relationships shown in Figure 6.2.

Discussion Questions

1. How is a use case diagram different from a use case?
2. Is it possible to draw a use case diagram without writing a use case? Answer with reasons.
3. Provide an example for each of the three relationships on a use case diagram: actor–actor, actor–use case, and use case–use case with examples.
4. Why is a use case diagram called a visual table of contents for requirements? Agree or disagree with this statement by providing arguments.

5. What is the importance of the system boundary in a use case diagram?
6. What is the element in a use case diagram that is "interfaced" with and what is the element that is "built"?
7. Why should there be a separate actor hierarchy drawn in the modeling tool at all? Discuss its advantages.
8. What is the relevance of writing <<include>>, <<extends>>, and <<inherits>> for the use case relationship? Give an example for each one.
9. List and provide examples of the three use-case-to-use-case relationships.
10. What is the importance of notes in a use case diagram?
11. What are the two key strengths of a use case diagram?
12. What are the two key weaknesses of a use case diagram?

Team Project Case Study

1. Place the actors and use cases identified in the previous chapter in a use case diagram using your modeling tool.
2. These use case diagrams will be within each package in the modeling tool.
3. Name the use case diagrams appropriately to represent the subject area for that diagram.
4. Since actors and use cases can appear in various diagrams, it is expected that there will be more than one use case diagram per package. Therefore, there can be a total of 8 to 10 use case diagrams for the project.
5. Be sure to use both <<include>> and <<extend>> relationships in the use case diagrams.
6. Be sure to have at least one nonhuman actor in at least one use case diagram.
7. Ensure you have shown the system boundary in at least one use case diagram.
8. Stereotype the actors and use cases appearing in the use case diagram.
9. It is normal to find additional actors and use cases at this stage. Document any additional actors and use cases using appropriate templates.
10. Create a separate diagram showing the actor hierarchies within the modeling tool (this will be a diagram similar to Figure 5.2 in the previous chapter).
11. Provide relevant stereotypes for the use cases (initially they will all be <<entity>>. (Stereotypes are discussed in detail in Chapter 10; therefore, you will have to come back to these diagrams to update them with stereotypes.)
12. Add detailed notes on ALL use case diagrams, providing additional explanations about the diagram. Make sure that there are no inconsistencies among the members of the group.

Endnotes

1. Fowler, Martin (2003), *UML Distilled*, 3rd Edition, Addison-Wesley, USA.
2. Henderson-Sellers, B., and Unhelkar, B. (2000), *OPEN Modelling with the UML*, Addison-Wesley, UK.

Chapter 7

Activity Diagrams, Interaction Overview Diagrams, and Business Process Models

Learning Objectives

- Understand the importance and complexities of process models
- Learn UML notations for activity diagrams
- Create activity diagrams with activities, partitions, multithreads, and decision points
- Relate activity diagrams to use case documentation
- Learn UML notations for interaction overview diagrams
- Create interaction overview diagram
- Learn Business Process Model and Notation (BPMN)
- Use BPMN to create process models

Introduction

The discussion in this chapter focuses on process modeling. These processes are documented within use cases; they are also business processes comprising many use cases. Process modeling starts with the documentation of use cases (as discussed in Chapter 5) and their modeling in a use case diagram (Chapter 6). In this chapter, the focus is on visual modeling of the use case documentation using activity diagrams. The activity diagrams of the UML have a rich suite of notations and guidelines, making them ideal for modeling any kind of process within a system or business. Business Process Model and Notation (BPMN) is another rich suite of notations that can be used for process modeling. BPMN is owned by the Object Management Group (OMG) but is not a part of the UML. However, the richness of its notations and semantics means it can be used for modeling large and complex business processes. In addition to the activity diagram and BPMN, this chapter also discusses the interaction overview diagram (IOD) of the UML. The IOD is conceptually similar to an activity diagram (because it also has a flow); however, the IOD provides opportunities to model the interactions at a high level as compared to the detailed models created by activity diagrams.

SEPARATING BUSINESS PROCESSES FROM SOFTWARE DEVELOPMENT PROCESSES

An important word of caution here: the process modeling discussed in this chapter is based on business processes and use cases. The software development life cycle (SDLC) and Agile processes discussed in Chapter 4 are dimensionally different as they focus on the approach to developing a software solution. Thus, those processes support solution development, whereas the processes in this chapter are the actual business processes that describe how to perform a particular business function.

Activity Diagrams

Activity diagrams of the UML are meant to show any flow, or process, in the system. This makes them capable of modeling the following:

- Business processes or workflows within the organization that describe how the business functions are carried out
- The flow within a use case by creating a visual map of the documentation of that use case
- Dependencies between use cases by using the activity notation to represent a use case (although this requirement is better served by the interaction overview diagram)
- The navigation of a mobile app (storyboard) by representing the mobile screens as activities within the activity diagram

Since the activity diagram shows the processes like a flowchart, it is far more readable from the user's viewpoint than the use case diagram. As a result, users find this an attractive way to discuss their requirements, but at a lower level than with use case diagrams. Furthermore, since activity diagrams represent process flows, they can be used to model the existing business processes as well as the new (envisioned) business processes. This modeling of processes enables comparison between current and new processes, identifies gaps between them, and creates a systematic opportunity to transition the gap in those processes.

Notations of Activity Diagrams

The UML notations used to create activity diagrams include activities, transitions, start and end points, synchronization points, decision points, and guard conditions. Figure 7.1 shows these activity diagram notations.

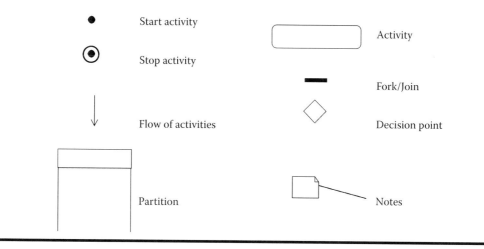

Figure 7.1   **Notations of an activity diagram.**

The start activity and stop activity are shown with their corresponding notations in Figure 7.1. Syntactically it is necessary to have only one start activity in the activity diagram; however, multiple stop activities are allowed. The stop activity is optional, though. All activities other than the start and stop activities are represented by the rounded rectangle, marked "activity" in Figure 7.1.

The dependency between activities, and their flow (similar to a flowchart), is shown by an arrow marked "Flow of Activities" in Figure 7.1. Activity diagrams also have a decision point similar to that in a flowchart. The decision point enables branching of the activities based on specified conditions. Notes are also a part of activity diagrams, and should be liberally used to explain diagrams.

While an activity diagram has the look and feel of a flowchart (see Figure 7.2, discussed in detail in the next section), it is more than a flowchart. One key difference is the activity diagram's ability to show partitions. Partitions, also known as swimlanes in previous versions of the UML, indicate "lanes" in which the activities are performed by actors. The actor that performs the activities is shown as a label on top of the partition. Activity diagrams are usually drawn top-down, but they can also be drawn going left to right depending on the modeling tool being used. The arrangement of the actor and its label is not dictated by the UML—hence modelers can use their judgment to improve the aesthetics of their activity models.

An activity diagram can also have synchronization (sync) points that are either a fork or a join. A sync point is indicated by the horizontal bar in Figure 7.1. The sync point indicates the start and stop of *parallel* activities—that is, activities that don't depend on each other but that need to be performed simultaneously.

Naming an Activity Diagram

An activity diagram is usually named after the use case whose flow is being modeled. A "verb like" name similar to the use case is appropriate for the activity diagram, e.g., "*Books*Consultation." Some activity diagrams in the system may model activities belonging to multiple use cases. In these cases, the appropriate behavioral names covering multiple use cases should be provided.

Activity Diagrams for Hospital Management System

A good way to understand the modeling of activity diagrams is to use the running example of the HMS. In this section, four specific activity diagrams corresponding to the four use cases that were documented in Chapter 5 are discussed. These activity diagrams, based on those four use cases, are as follows:

- RegistersPatient activity diagram
- MaintainsCalendar activity diagram
- BooksConsultation activity diagram
- PaysBill activity diagram

Each activity diagram shows a specific nuance of process modeling. Each activity diagram is further discussed next.

"RegistersPatient" Activity Diagram

Figure 7.2 shows the activity diagram that represents the process of registering patient details. This diagram starts with a pseudo start activity, followed by the activity AnnounceArrival.

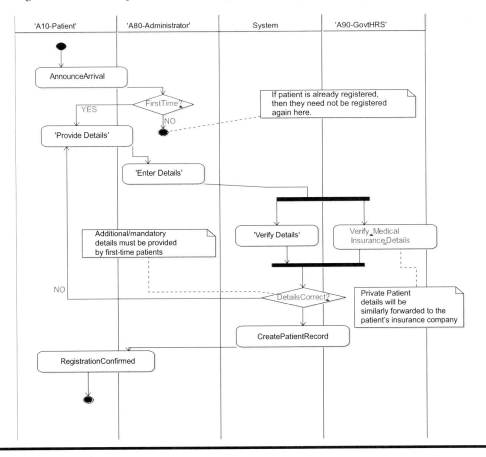

Figure 7.2   RegistersPatient activity diagram.

On completion of this activity, the flow within this activity diagram reaches a decision point. The decision point checks whether the patient is visiting the hospital for the first time. A patient not coming for first time is shown by the activity diagram as entering the pseudo `stop` state as that patient's details are present in the system. A `patient` visiting for the first time starts the activity of `ProvideDetails`. The process control then transfers to the `EnterDetails` activity in the `Administrator` partition. The flow then reaches the sync point where activities are split into two threads. The `Verify/Details` in the system partition checks for the correctness of the details entered and the `VerifyMedicalInsuranceDetails` in the `GovtHRS` partition verifies the patient's medical insurance details.

If these two activities are conducted sequentially (one after the other), the processing time will take much longer than if the activities are conducted in parallel. The two activities occurring in parallel join back at the next sync point. The time taken by each of these two activities conducted in parallel can be different. For example, `VerifyDetails` may take only 30 seconds, but `VerifyMedicalInsuranceDetails` may take a few minutes. When both these activities, with different time frames, are complete, then the next activity can start. Completion of both these activities at a point in time is shown by the horizontal joining bar. This forking and joining of an activity diagram facilitates the optimization of workflows and enhancement of quality.

Once the details of the patient are verified as correct, the patient record is created in the `CreatePatientRecord` activity. Alternatively, the flow is redirected to the `ProvideDetails` activity. The registration of the new patient record is confirmed in the `RegistrationConfirmed` activity, which then concludes at the pseudo stop state.

"MaintainsCalendar" Activity Diagram

Figure 7.3 shows the activity diagram that represents the process of maintaining the calendar details. This diagram starts with the pseudo `start` activity, followed by the activity `RequestPersonalCalendar` in the staff partition. Control is then transferred to the `ProvidesPersonalCalendar` activity in the system partition. The activity of `EnterPreferredDetails` follows in which the staff enters his preferred working times. These details are verified in the `ValidatePreferredRosterDetails` activity and control reaches the decision point.

In the case of a conflicting calendar, the control is passed to the `ProvideCalendar OptionsToStaff` activity, which follows the `EnterPreferredDetails` activity for another set of validation. If the requested roster details do not conflict with the existing schedule, the details are accepted in the `AcceptDetails` activity. The accepted details are updated in the calendar in the `UpdateCalendar` activity in the system partition. The new calendar details are confirmed in the `RegistrationConfirmed` activity, which then concludes at the pseudo `stop` state.

"BooksConsultation" Activity Diagram

Figure 7.4 shows the activity diagram that represents the process of booking a consultation. This diagram starts with the pseudo `start` activity, followed by the activity `SpecifiesInitialDetailsForConsultation` in the `Patient` partition. The special note attached to this activity states that the details need to be selected from the list of services

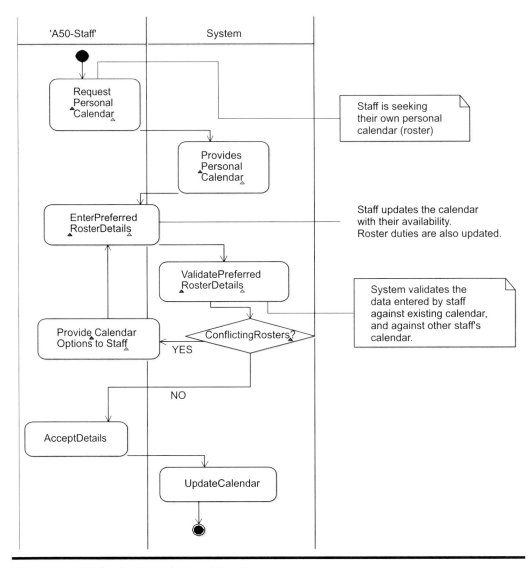

Figure 7.3 "MaintainsCalendar" activity diagram.

provided. The list of physicians is provided in the `ProvidesListOfPhysician` activity in the system partition.

The patient then selects the physician in the `SelectsPhysician` activity. The system then provides the available consultation times for the selected physician in the `ProvidesAv ailableConsultationDay&Times` activity. The patient then selects the date and time in `SelectsDay&Time`, which is updated in the `UpdateCalendar` activity.

The consultation could be brief or detailed. This variation is not easy to depict using the activity diagram notations—hence it is shown in a special note. The confirmation is viewed in the `ViewConfirmation` activity, which then concludes at the `stop` state.

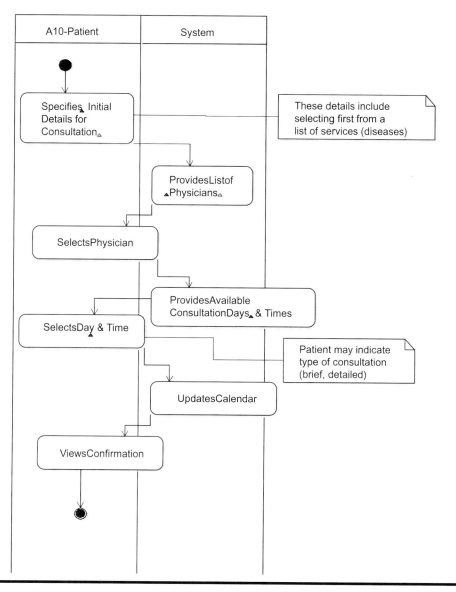

Figure 7.4 **"BooksConsultation" activity diagram.**

"PaysBill" Activity Diagram

Figure 7.5 shows the activity diagram that represents the process of paying a bill by a patient. This diagram starts with the pseudo `start` activity, followed by the activity `ReceivesBill` in the `Patient` partition, in which the patient receives a bill for all services. The bill is verified against all the consultations in the `VerifiesBillAgainstConsultation` activity, and then the control passes to the decision point `Valid`. If the details are valid, the `PaysBill` activity starts and later concludes at the `stop` state. If there are errors in the bill, the control is transferred to the `ReportError` activity, which again is concluded at the pseudo `stop` state.

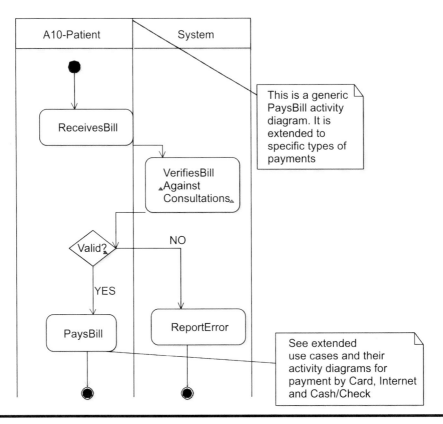

Figure 7.5 "PaysBill" activity diagram.

Strengths and Weaknesses of Activity Diagrams

Strengths of Activity Diagrams

What follows are some of the strengths of activity diagrams. An understanding of these strengths is helpful in conducting workshops and modeling process flows in practice:

- Activity diagrams model the flow within a use case (or a number of use cases). They complement use case documentation by showing a visual representation of the *internals* of a use case and result in improved use case documentation.
- Activity diagrams show the flow of a process and are ideal for documenting use cases and system flows in practice. This allows requirements to be modeled in great detail in the problem space.
- Activity diagrams can show multiple flows that occur simultaneously within a system by using sync points (forks and joins). This is a major strength of activity diagrams over traditional flowcharts as these techniques help in optimizing workflows.
- Activity diagrams can show decisions that occur and the alternative paths with the help of decision points. The ability to show multiple paths ("if-then-else") is most helpful in modeling processes (as compared with use case diagrams, which do not have a decision point).
- Partitions show a clear mapping between the actors and the activities they undertake. This mapping helps in categorizing, assigning, documenting, and testing the activities as well as assigning them to the actors.

- Activity diagrams act as a bridge between use cases and sequence diagrams. This enables the text-based documentation of the use cases to be shown pictorially in activity diagrams. At the same time, activity diagrams enable a high-level view of what is shown in detail, at the object level, on a sequence diagram (sequence diagrams are a topic of Chapter 12).
- The use of notes on the activity diagrams enables easier reading and understanding of the diagrams for users with no technical background. Explanations of the activities, their dependencies, and the decisions points all provide excellent user-level documentation. Therefore, activity diagrams are used when training users new to a system.
- Activity diagrams are easily understood by people new to UML. Therefore, it is often easier to start a requirements modeling workshop with an activity diagram, especially if users participating in workshops are new to the concept of modeling.
- Activity diagrams can provide documentation on the use of a system. Therefore, they can be inserted in user manuals and help files, with the judicious use of explanatory notes.
- Activity diagrams can also be used in business process engineering, in which the existing business processes are first documented using these diagrams and then reengineered for optimization.

Activity diagrams are also used in documenting software development processes (although that use is outside the scope of discussion in this chapter).

Weaknesses of Activity Diagrams

What follows are some of the weaknesses of activity diagrams. An understanding of these weaknesses is also helpful in conducting workshops and modeling process flows in practice:

- Activity diagrams have minimal structural characteristics, and they do not provide direct information on how a system or requirements are organized and prioritized.
- Activity diagrams do not give a complete picture of a system when they are used to model use case behavior; thus, unlike use case diagrams, activity diagrams do not show the full requirements of a system at a glance.
- Activity diagrams depict flow, and therefore they should be used only when there is a need to show dependencies between activities. Activity diagrams are not ideal for organizing and managing requirements.
- Activity diagrams that document large and complex use cases can quickly become very complicated and lose their value. Several smaller activity diagrams are needed to model the flow of complex use cases.
- Activity diagrams have been confused with state machine diagrams in earlier versions of UML—perhaps because there were similar notations in those earlier UML versions. For example, it was common to confuse an activity with a state. Inexperienced modelers can still make the same mistake, and care should be taken to differentiate between an activity and a state.
- Activity diagrams have been confused with data flow diagrams (DFDs). The two are different in that activity diagrams focus on the business workflow and DFDs focus on the flow of data. DFDs also have levels, but activity diagrams do not.
- Different types of processes cannot be shown in a single activity diagram because the scope of an activity diagram is a singular use case or a business process. In such cases, multiple activity diagrams are required with notes linking them with each other.

■ Although activity diagrams can be used in the solution space, unless a system is multi threaded and multitasked, they don't add great value in this space.

■ Modelers are prone to assume that the activity flow within an activity diagram includes a timeline; however, because activity diagrams do not display time, they are not considered dynamic.

Interaction Overview Diagram

Interaction overview diagrams (IODs), as their name suggests, provide a high-level overview of the interactions happening within a system. Therefore, these diagrams show dependencies and flows between use cases. As discussed later in Chapter 12, sequence diagrams also depict interactions, but at a detailed, object level. IODs contain references to the corresponding sequence diagrams. Thus, one IOD can contain references to multiple sequence diagrams and also show the dependencies between those sequence diagrams. IODs can also reference other diagrams such as the activity diagram or a use case and provide an overview of how these other diagrams are related to each other. Because of their ability to show "if-then-else" scenarios, these IODs have a similar look and feel to activity diagrams.

Notations of an Interaction Overview Diagram

IODs are created with the UML notations shown in Figure 7.6. Some of these notations are similar to those of an activity diagram. This is because the interaction overview also represents a flow—albeit at a higher overview level and not at the activity level. The reference notation in an IOD provides the ability to reference another use case or sequence diagram. The start and stop states, decision points, flow, sync points, and notes in IODs are similar to those of activity diagrams.

Naming an Interaction Overview Diagram

Since IODs can show the "if-then-else" situation between use cases, they are "flowcharts" of use cases. They should be named similarly to the use case diagrams that were discussed in Chapter 6. Two examples of IODs for the HMS are discussed next.

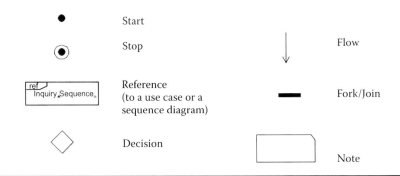

Figure 7.6   Notations of an interaction overview diagram.

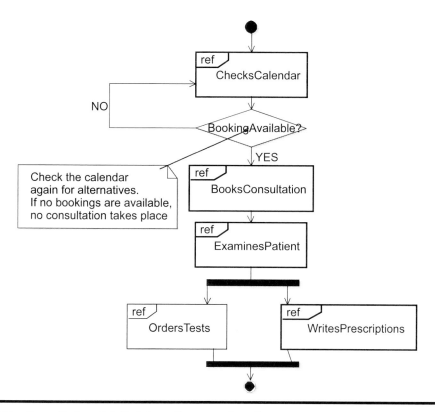

Figure 7.7   **Consultation details interaction overview diagram.**

Interaction Overview for "Consultation Details"

Figure 7.7 shows an IOD for the process of booking and providing consultations. The use case diagram corresponding to this IOD was shown earlier in Chapter 6. This interaction starts when the calendar is checked for availability of booking as represented by CationsCalendar in Figure 7.7. If booking is not available, the ChecksCalendar sequence or use case is executed again. If booking is available, then the BooksConsultation use case is executed, followed by ExaminesPatient. Finally, there is an opportunity for two parallel process referenced in the diagram by OrdersTests and WritesPrescriptions. When both of these processes are completed, the consultation process ends.

Interaction Overview for "Accounting"

Figure 7.8 shows another example of an IOD for the HMS. In this diagram, the first reference is PaysBill, which describes the common part of the process of bill payment. After that, the process checks how the bill will be paid. For each of the three alternatives of Card, BPAY, and CashCheque, there are three corresponding references. They are PaysBillByCard, PaysBillOnInternet (representing BPAY on the Internet), and CashChequePayment, respectively. These are references to use cases described in Chapters 5 and 6. After the bill payment is completed, it is verified whether or not the patient is private. If the patient is private, then there is another reference to a use case called PlacesInsuranceClaim; otherwise the process ends.

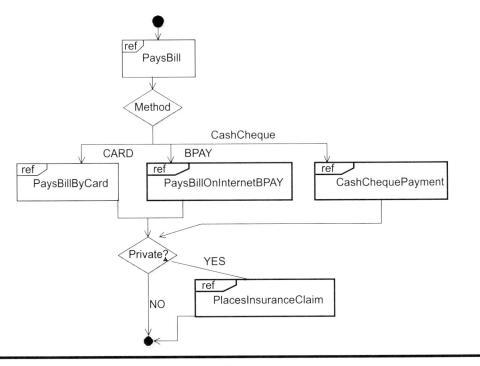

Figure 7.8   Accounting interaction overview diagram.

Strengths and Weaknesses of Interaction Overview Diagrams

Strengths of Interaction Overview Diagrams

What follows are some of the strengths of IODs in practice. Awareness of these strengths by modelers is most helpful in improving the quality of the model of the problem space (MOPS):

- The primary strength of IODs is they are able to show the dependencies between various sequences within a system. IODs provide strength to the modeling effort in the problem space by enabling the display of conditions and multiple threads in the diagrams.
- Being similar to activity diagrams, IODs show the normal and alternative flows of sequences within a system through a combination of flowchart and references to sequence diagram mechanisms.

Weaknesses of Interaction Overview Diagrams

- What follows are some of the weaknesses of IODs. Awareness of these strengths by modelers is most helpful in improving the quality of the MOPS: IODs may have weaknesses similar to those of activity diagrams. IODs may not be able to show "instance" level modeling and should not be used for that purpose.
- Being an overview diagram, the IOD should be used sparingly. Excessive modeling with IODs can lead to confusion between those and activity diagrams.

- IODs are precisely that—overview diagrams. These diagrams are not closely linked to the other diagrams they reference. As a result, there isn't a good syntax and semantic check possible for these diagrams during the quality assurance exercise.
- Referencing to other diagrams within IODs is not clearly understood in practice. There is the possibility of confusion as to what is being referenced (sequence diagram, communication diagram, or a use case) within the IOD.

Business Process Modeling

Business processes are an integral part of modern businesses. Business processes have inputs, process those inputs, and produce outputs. Business processes provide value to a user. Therefore, any good software design needs to start with a process model. Activity and interaction overview diagrams of the UML are useful in modeling business processes. Business processes make use of software systems during their execution.

Business process modeling is usually undertaken with a recognized suite of notations derived from a framework. In practice, Business process modeling also requires the use of a modeling tool that will enable a team of modelers to work together. Occasionally, Business process modeling also represents the "management" of business processes—and includes modeling, indexing, documenting, storage, retrieval, and removal of a suite of processes within an organization.

Several techniques can be used to model a business process. Some of the well-known techniques are listed in Table 7.1.

Business process modeling is an in-depth visualization of a process before designing its solution. Such modeling can be used not only to create a new process but also to understand and improve existing processes. The complexity and importance of business processes led to the formation of a rich suite of notations—the Business Process Model and Notation (BPMN). Business process modeling has been used as a basis for the overall organizational structure that can be moved from a hierarchical inward-facing structure to a process-based organizational structure. Business processes can be both external facing (by providing value to an external stakeholder) and internal to the organization (by satisfying the needs of an internal stakeholder).

While early attempts at business process modeling focused on modeling a single process and improving it from a time and cost perspective, increasingly business process modeling is moving toward modeling a collaborative suite of processes that are likely to provide value to a stakeholder based on multiple, cross-functional processes. Modeling collaborative processes end to end as the "customer interacts" provides much higher value to stakeholders than the silo-centric (standalone) view.

Examples of business processes (that are identified as use cases) that are primarily external facing include "customer withdraws cash," "passenger checks in for a flight," and "patient admitted to a hospital." On the other hand, examples of business processes that are internal facing include "end-of-day cash-in and cash-out from a bank branch," "scheduling of flights," and "reorder antibiotics." These examples include many different aspects of a business coming into play. For example, in each case, a primary stakeholder gains value, and many other stakeholders are involved in providing that value. Each process also needs extensive support with technologies including software systems, mobile devices, and security/privacy.

Table 7.1 Common BPM Techniques and Their Brief Explanation

BPM Technique	Brief Explanation
Flowcharts	Provide a basic flow of a business process from start to finish with alternative subprocesses in between.
Functional block diagrams	Provide a high-level view of a large and complex business process (or a suite of business processes).
PERT and Gantt charts	Provide precise routing of one or more business processes with opportunities to optimize on time and costs associated with the processes.
Data flow diagrams	Provide a more technical view of a business process that is primarily based on the way in which key data elements of the process change as the process is executed
Use case diagrams (UML)	Provide an important view of a business process that is based on actors, use cases, their relationships, and a system boundary
Activity diagrams (UML)	Based on (and similar to) flowcharts, activity diagrams provide an excellent basis for modeling business processes by mapping activities to actors within a partition and optimizing processes through multithreads.
Business Process Model and Notation (BPMN)	Rich suite of notations that create business process models that can be embedded in standardized case tools, shared, and optimized.
Business Process Modeling Language (BPML)	A modeling language based on BPMN and supported by modeling tools.

The following figures show some important aspects of BPMN, including their flow and connecting notations (Figure 7.9) and their grouping objects (Figure 7.10).

- Events—happen during the course of a business process and are made up of start, intermediate, and end stages.
- Activities—generic term for what the business does; made up of process, subprocess, and tasks.
- Gateways—control divergence and convergence in business flow; include branching, forking, merging, and joining
- Sequence flow—denotes the order of activities
- Message flow—denotes the flow of messages between two entities (such as pools) or directly to an object within a pool

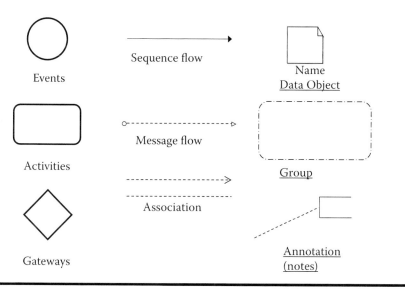

Figure 7.9   BPMN notation.

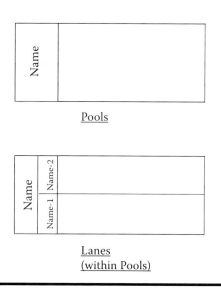

Figure 7.10   BPMN – grouping with pods and lanes.

- Association—used to associate information and artifacts
- Data object—denotes the Object within the process flow
- Group—a mechanism to treat multiple activities together
- Annotation (notes)—are explanatory labels or comments on any artifact on the process model to provide further explanation

Figures 7.11 and 7.12 show examples of BPMN-based process models (insurance example)

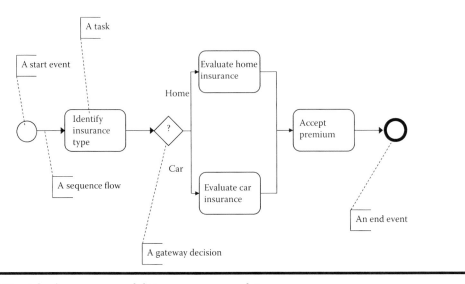

Figure 7.11   A basic process model (Insurance example).

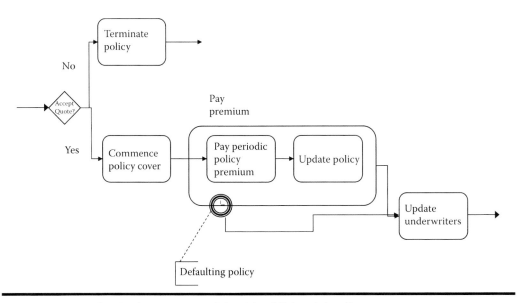

Figure 7.12   Another basic process model (with additional details).

Common Errors in Activity Diagrams, Interaction Overview Diagrams, and Business Process Models and How to Rectify Them

Common Errors	Rectifying the Errors	Examples
Drawing activity diagram independent of use cases	Ensure a continuous cross-reference between activity diagrams and use case documentation.	Study Figures 7.2 through 7.5 and their corresponding use cases in Chapter 5. The mapping between the use cases and these activity diagrams is important.
Not having proper start and stop activities	Ensure one start activity and as many stop activities as needed.	Figure 7.5, like Figures 7.2 through 7.4, has one start activity but more than one stop activity.
Having a fork (sync point) but not having a join (sync point)	Ensure all forks have a join and vice versa.	Figure 7.2 on the right-hand side has a fork *and* a join. Every fork should ideally have a join.
Unsure of where to place activities that seem to belong to multiple actors	Place the activity in the partition belonging to the main actor who owns that activity.	In Figure 7.2, the activities belonging to the patient are AnnounceArrival and ProvideDetails; these are mainly within the patient partition, but the administrator is also involved in their execution.
Assuming system to be an actor	While a system is not an actor, there is usually a partition for the system.	Figure 7.2 has a partition corresponding to system. This partition contains all activities that are responses of the system to an action by an actor from the other partitions.
Confusing activity diagrams with use case diagrams	Activity diagrams have flow and decision points.	Study the examples in this chapter and compare them with the use case diagrams in Chapter 6.
Confusing activity diagrams and interaction overview diagrams	IOD are at a higher overview level	Figure 7.7, ConsultationDetails IOD, has references to "ChecksCalendar" and "BooksConsultation" use cases.

Discussion Questions

1. Does an activity diagram represent a use case diagram or a use case? Explain with examples.
2. What is the purpose of a partition in an activity diagram?
3. Draw a simple activity diagram, like a flowchart, based on a use case (e.g., like the one documented in Chapter 5).
4. Draw a detailed activity diagram that shows partitions, multithreads, and decision points.
5. How do multiple threads help optimize workflows? Discuss with examples.
6. Draw a simple interaction overview diagram (IOD) for any system (note: the boxed references within the IOD can represent an entire use case or a sequence diagram).
7. Add notes to your activity and IOD.
8. What is BPMN? How can it help in process modeling efforts?
9. Consider how you would represent the activity diagram you have drawn using BPMN.
10. What is the difference between a business process and a software development process?

Team Project Case Study

1. Identify TWO use cases from EACH package you are working on.
2. Revisit and study the flow within the use case, including alternative flows and exceptions.
3. Draw an activity diagram for a use case based on the flow of the use case appearing in its documentation. Repeat for another use case.
4. Ensure each activity diagram has carefully created partitions including the system partition.
5. You should thus have TWO activity diagrams per package corresponding to the two use cases.
6. You may have an additional activity diagram that covers two or more use cases. That is not mandatory, but if it happens, it is acceptable. However, depending on your modeling tool, such a diagram may not get linked to a use case.
7. Add notes to your activity diagrams to further explain the diagrams.
8. Show multiple threads, running in parallel, in any one of the activity diagrams in your system.
9. Draw ONE interaction overview diagram within each package. This IOD will represent the high-levels interactions among use cases, activity diagrams, or sequence diagrams. (Since we have yet to discuss sequence diagrams, you will have to come back to update the IODs after the discussion on sequence diagrams in Chapter 12).

Chapter 8

Class Models-1: Classes and Business Entities

Learning Objectives

- Separate classes in problem space from those in solution space
- Identify classes by analyzing use case documentation
- Differentiate between objects and classes based on object orientation fundamentals
- Name and define classes
- Name and define attributes and operations
- Apply visibility (private, public) to attributes and operations
- Study the strengths and weaknesses of classes

Understanding Business Entities, Classes, and Objects

This chapter starts with an understanding of the business entities within the problem domain. Any business element is potentially an entity that can be modeled. For example, a customer and an account are business entities in the banking domain that can be modeled as classes.

This chapter focuses on classes representing business entities. These classes are used in creating the model of the problem space (MOPS). Business classes are based on the vocabulary of the business domain. Use cases provide a rich source for this vocabulary. Use cases are functional descriptions in the problem space of how users will use the system. Classes are derived by analyzing use case documentation. Classes evolve into detailed design, where they are complemented by implementation-level artifacts such as programs, databases, and user interfaces. These business-level classes evolve seamlessly into technical classes in the model of the solution space (MOSS). This seamless evolution of classes is possible in object-oriented software engineering (as compared with early, procedural approaches to software development).

Classes and Business Entities

Classes and objects were introduced in Chapter 1. These terms represent distinct modeling constructs. However, the terms "object" and "class" are used interchangeably in object orientation, leading to potential confusion. Modelers need to be very clear about the difference between objects and classes. A succinct way to understand this difference is to note that:

Objects are instances of a class.

Alternatively:

A class is a template for objects.

Another helpful statement is:

A class is not a collection of objects (as occasionally mentioned in the literature). Instead, a *class is an abstraction of all existing and new objects with similar characteristics.*

Consider, for example, Figure 8.1, which shows a dog object. Note that it shows a *specific* dog that might be playing in *your* backyard. *That* dog is an object. At the same time, there could be another dog that is sleeping in *my* kennel. That is *another* object. Together they make two dog objects. At a given time, there can be a large collection of dog objects that might be of interest, wherein *each* dog object will have his unique identifier and might be exhibiting a unique state and behavior.

When there is a need to describe and define the characteristics of these dogs, it would be impossible to do so individually. There is a need to have an *abstract* description of what defines all dogs. A class provides a detailed description of that abstraction, and potentially unlimited numbers of objects can subscribe to that class definition.

Objects are instantiated from classes and are defined by their identity, state, and behavior. These terms are explained next.

■ *Identity*: The identity is a unique identifier of an object. For example, a student can be identified by a Student-ID and a clock by a Clock-ID. Note there can be multiple objects with the same attribute *values*. For example, any two students in a school may take exactly the same subjects to study, attend the same class, and participate in the same projects. In fact, they may even have the same first and last name, yet they can be differentiated by their identifications such as a student ID, which has to be unique. Similarly, many clocks with the same color, price, and time may be stored in a warehouse, but they can all be differentiated by an Item-Number.

- "DOG" in general is a CLASS.
- *My* DOG is an OBJECT.
- Dog named *Benji* is an OBJECT.
- *The* DOG is an OBJECT.
- "DOGS"—representing a group of dogs is *NOT* a class, but a collection of objects

Figure 8.1   Classes and objects.

■ *State*: The state of an object is based on the current (usually dynamic) values of its attributes. For example, a student may have a numerical value in her `Fees-paid` attribute denoting a Paid state, whereas another student may have a `Fees-paid` attribute value of "0," resulting in an `Unpaid` state. For the clock example, the values of the attribute `Time` can be quite different for the clocks in usage.

■ *Behavior*: Objects collaborate with each other through communication. This communication is primarily the sending and receiving of messages, and it results in state changes to objects. The behavior of the overall system is affected through the behavior of collaborating objects. `Student` objects can send and receive messages to and from `Course` objects. As a result, the student objects can be in the state `registered` or `withdrawn`. Similarly, a `Clock` can send messages by striking the hour, or it may need to receive a key to wind it up.

The aforementioned three descriptors of a large number of objects are *defined* in a class. Note how a class name represents the entire class definition. Note also that a class name is not a unique identifier. Compared to this, an object must have an identity and should be unique.

Identifying and Naming Classes

An important part of analysis in the problem space is the identification and documentation of classes. What follows are the various sources from which classes are identified in the initial iteration in the business domain (problem space):

■ Use case documentation. Analyzing the *nouns* in the use case documentation provides an excellent starting point for the identification of classes. Proper nouns are converted to common nouns and all plural nouns should become singular.

■ Any other documentation available in the problem space, such as user manuals (if it is an existing system) and formal or informal problem statements (such as the one provided in Appendix A).

■ Discussions with domain experts can provide immediate access to a list of business entities that are potential classes.

■ Prototypes of any kind (conceptual, technical) can provide a valuable list of potential classes.

■ Revisiting the activity diagrams and the sequence diagrams (iteratively, that is, more than once) provides information on potential classes through the behavior modeled in these diagrams.

Class Identification by Use Case Analysis

Class identification is a formal process. The workshop for use case identification and analysis is extended to identify business-level classes. Inspecting the use case documentation is the starting point for identifying business entities in the problem space. The descriptions of interactions between the actor and system, as documented within the use cases as well as other descriptions in the problem space, reveal many entity classes. This initial attempt at identifying the nouns (occasionally called "noun analysis") provides a preliminary list of classes. During design, this list of classes gets modified with additional classes from the solution space. For example, the implementation language provides numerous classes that are now required to enable detailed design and coding. The already existing entity classes are also further refined in detail during design—with additional attributes and operations.

Identifying classes from use cases needs to consider the following:

- Careful inspection (analysis) of use cases reveals a list of nouns as mentioned earlier.
- Inspecting any other description of the business scenario (e.g., the problem statement) also reveals a list of nouns.
- The nouns identified previously form a preliminary list of candidate classes in the problem space.
- At this initial stage, these nouns are a combination of objects and classes.
- Proper nouns are usually objects; common nouns are usually classes. Convert these proper nouns into corresponding common nouns for appropriate class representation.
- Convert all plural nouns in the preliminary list of classes to singular nouns (e.g., patient*s* to patient). This is because a singular common noun is the ideal way to name a class.
- Make a note of the fact that many nouns identified in the list of classes are potentially attributes within a class, rather than a class (this is discussed later in this chapter).

Keep in mind the iterative and incremental nature of the process; therefore, this list of classes (and, potentially, attributes) will not be completed in the first attempt. This list of classes continues to be modified iteratively as the analysis proceeds with the creation of other diagrams and models in the system.

Most practical analysis and design work indicates it is impossible to identify and document all classes in one attempt. Incremental development of classes means first identifying and listing the classes, entering them into a modeling tool, adding some attributes, and then modeling with other UML diagrams before coming back to update the list of classes and their respective definitions.

As a result of these activities, when the modeling work moves from the problem space to the solution space, the list of business-level classes is relatively stable. Design activities reexamine these analysis-level classes, but if the analysis is carried out properly and formally (especially with user participation), then design activities have sufficient time to focus on implementation-level constructs for those classes.

Class Identification by Sequence Diagrams

In addition to conducting a noun analysis of use case descriptions, classes can also be discovered by creating and analyzing detailed design-level sequence diagrams. A detailed discussion on sequence diagrams is carried out in Chapter 12. Sequence diagrams provide clues for undiscovered classes because stepping through the execution of a sequence of messages reveals missing classes within that sequence. Sequence diagrams also reveal methods (or operations) required for existing classes. This is true especially in the solution space where designers draw the sequence diagrams in great detail, showing all *messages* and *objects* required to complete a particular sequence. Sequence diagrams during design go beyond the simple analysis-level sequence diagrams and show the details of implementation. Therefore, objects depicted in sequence diagrams during design contain—in addition to the objects from the problem space—numerous solution-level objects that represent controller, user interface, and database objects. Each of these objects belong to a class in the class diagrams (further discussed in Chapter 12).

Naming a Class as a Business Entity

The naming of a class can play an important part in understanding the purpose of the class. Properly named classes improve the readability of class diagrams. The semantic and aesthetic quality of class diagrams is enhanced by the proper naming of classes. The class names in a project can conform to a style guide. This guide can be a combination of available and published style guides (such as that put together by Ambler*), internal project standards, and styles made available in implementation languages and databases. For most analysis and early design, though, classes are created and named by analysts and designers per their project style guide.

Classes are usually named with singular common nouns. This noun is a single (or joint) keyword that represents the core responsibility of the class. Analysis of use cases and problem definitions may occasionally reveal objects (e.g., *this* student or *a* student) rather than classes. These objects may appear as a collection (e.g., "class of students" or "list of accounts"). Such descriptions need to be converted into a suitable singular common noun—like "Student" or "Account"—for class representation. Consider an example where a problem statement describes how John, Ravi, and Mary are taking a particular course in English literature in college. A good class name that represents these students will be:

STUDENT

Note how, based on the previous discussion, the following names for a class will be considered inappropriate:

RAVI (because this is a proper noun)
or
STUDENTS (because this is a plural noun);

What follows are suggestions for naming and representing classes and their definitions:

- Class names are bold and centered when placed in a class model (e.g., patient)
- Class names for abstract classes are bold, italic, and centered (e.g., *Person*)
- Stereotypes should be represented in plain font enclosed in guillemets (angled quotes), which are placed above the class name and centered
- Class names begin with an uppercase letter
- Classes are named as singular common nouns
- Joint class names (composed of more than one word) should have the second word in capital (e.g., PrivatePatient)

During design in the solution space, there are additional classes derived from the language or a library or service for implementation. In that case, the naming standards used by the vendor of that library or service will impact the standards used by the project team. Therefore, it is quite likely that a detailed design level class diagram in the solution space will be made up of more than one style of class name; however, the less variation in class naming, the better the readability and quality of the UML diagrams.

Analyzing the "RegistersPatient" Use Case to Identify Classes/Business Entities

Consider the following use case reproduced from Chapter 5. The relevant *nouns* have been under-lined to highlight the fact that these are potential classes based on this use case. In practice, this list will be refined and updated based on similar analyses of other use cases, as well as other sources of classes mentioned earlier.

---

* Scott Ambler provides excellent online UML style guide for each UML diagram. http://www.agilemodeling. com/style/; accessed October 19, 2017.

Use Case Thumbnail: UC10-RegistersPatient

Use Case Description: This use case describes the process of registering a new patient in the hospital system. The patient must be registered and the details verified with the government health regulatory system before any of the hospital's services can be provided.

Stereotype and Package: ≪Patient≫

Preconditions: Patient must have not been already registered in the hospital system.

Postconditions: Patient is registered in the hospital system.

Actors:

A10-Patient; A80-Administrator; A90-GovernmentHealthRegulatory System, A95-PrivateHealthInsuranceSystem

Use Case Relationships:

Associated with actors: A10-Patient, A80-Administrator.

Basic Flow (Text):

1. A patient arrives at the hospital for some medical treatment.
2. The administrator asks the patient if he/she had been previously treated at this hospital.
3. Patient provides the answer (A1).
4. Administrator asks patient for his personal details such as name, address, telephone, date of birth, and emergency contact.
5. Patient provides details as requested.
6. Administrator enters details into system.
7. System verifies details (A2).
8. Administrator asks patient whether he is a public or private patient.
9. Patient provides the answer. [public or private]
   [Public]
   9.1a Administrator asks public patient for Medicare number.
   9.2a Patient provides Medicare number.
   9.3a Administrator enters Medicare number into system.
   9.4a System verifies patient identity with government health regulatory system. (A3)
   [Private]
   9.1b Administrator asks private patient for insurance details.
   9.2b Patient provides insurance details.
   9.3b Administrator enters insurance details (insurance company, patient's insurance number) into system.
   9.4b System verifies patient identity with private health insurance company system. (A4)
10. System stores patient details.
11. System confirms patient registration.

Alternative Flow:

<A1 – If the patient has previously visited the hospital, he will have been registered in the hospital's system. The administrator informs the patient of <u>existing registration</u>.>

<A2 – If <u>details</u> are insufficient or incorrect, the patient is asked to provide the details again.>

<A3 – The patient cannot be verified with the government health regulatory system, so the administrator asks the patient for the Medicare card details again. If no verification is possible, the patient is <u>conditionally registered</u> as either a <u>full fee paying patient</u> or will provide Medicare details later.>

<A4 – The patient cannot be verified with the private health insurance company's system, so the administrator asks the patient for the private health insurance details again. If no verification is possible, the patient is <u>conditionally registered</u> as either a <u>full fee paying patient</u> and his details with the health insurance company are to be verified later.≫

Exceptions:
None.

Constraints: None.

User Interface Specifications: UI-PatientRegistrationForm

Metrics: Complex **Priority:** High **Status:** Major

Author & History: Anand K.

Reference Material: Details of patient that are required by law are specified in the hospital's patient policy document available from the administration department. See <PatientPolicy.doc>.*

---

* This is only an example reference to a document. This reference is provided so readers can understand how a bulky document or document external to the use case is mentioned in the use case. Other common examples of references include, for example, legal documents and mathematical formulas.

The following *nouns* are identified from analyzing the preceding use case (singular common nouns are listed).

```
Patient
Administrator
Registered (same as Registration, Existing Registration)
Government health system (same as GovernmentHealthRegulatorySystem)
Insurance company (same as PrivateHealthInsuranceSystem)
Hospital
Medical treatment
Personal details (same as Details)
Name
Address
```

```
Telephone
Date of birth
Emergency contact
System
Medicare number
Insurance details
Patient's insurance number
Identity
Conditionally registered
Full fee paying patient
```

Note that although system appears as a noun, it is not modeled as a class. A system is a combination of classes and components and is not a class on its own. Exceptions to this statement may occur in the solution space.

Class Definitions

Initial business-level classes are stereotyped as ≪entity≫ (stereotypes are discussed in Chapter 10). This is because they all represent business entities in the problem space. Attributes and responsibilities are added to arrive at a more complete definition for business-level classes. During design in the solution space, additional database- and language-level classes are introduced in the class diagrams to enable implementation.

Class Documentation Template

Classes are defined by documenting them—which takes place after an initial list of classes has been identified. This separate documentation of classes can help in getting the class description and responsibilities right. This activity is followed by entering the classes in a modeling tool. What follows is a class documentation template.

Class Element	Corresponding Description
≪Stereotype≫ last name	<A one-word name for the class; the name is prefixed by an optional stereotype. Stereotypes were discussed in UML's extensibility mechanism in Chapter 10. Classes typically have entity, interface, and controller stereotypes of which ≪entity≫ is the only stereotype of importance during analysis.>
Description	<A brief description of the class that will help readers understand what this class represents.>
Relationship	<A list of other classes and the type of relationships they have with this class. This list may not be available initially but can later be ascertained from the class diagrams or use case documentation.>
Attributes	<A list of all attributes of a class. These are the characteristics that describe the class. As discussed later in this chapter, attributes are also nouns but with no behavior of their own.>

Class Element	Corresponding Description
Responsibilities	<These are the responsibilities of this class. Responsibilities can be plain English statements; hence they can be documented using this class template. The responsibilities can be ascertained iteratively in discussions and workshops. Eventually, responsibilities will be translated into a combination of attributes and behavior and placed in the class specifications. Responsibilities can also be ascertained by reviewing activity and sequence diagrams.>
Business rules	<Special business rules and constraints that are not easily listed under responsibilities that apply to the class.>
Complexity	<Simple/medium/complex. The complexity of a class is a detailed topic of discussion requiring an understanding of the metrics that deal with such complexities—for example, number of associations and depth of inheritance. Complexity may be mentioned here from the point of view of business and later refined when more understanding about the class is gained.>

Documenting the Patient Class

Class Element	Corresponding Description
≪Stereotype≫ Class Name	≪entity≫ Patient
Description	This class represents the details of a patient in the hospital management system.
Relationship	This class relates to the doctor, consultation, and diagnosis classes.
Attributes	Name, address, phone, email, emergency contacts.
Responsibilities	To know and manage all details of the patient. To relate patient to consultation.
Business rules	Patients without either private or government medical support still need to be entered and treated. But their process needs to be separately considered.
Complexity	Medium

A patient class from the HMS can be documented based on the preceding template as follows.

Class Notation in UML

Classes are represented by a rectangle in the UML, as shown in Figure 8.2. This rectangle is divided into three parts (compartments): name, attributes, and operations. However, it is not mandatory to show all three parts of the class. Occasionally, as in early requirements analysis, only the class name will appear on the class diagram—without its attributes and operations.

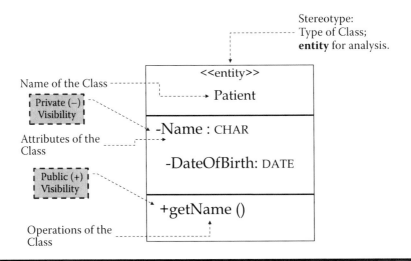

Figure 8.2   Representation of a class (notation).

In modeling tools, a class is defined and entered using the three compartments of the class that are described as follows:

- *Name* of the class—which is usually a singular common noun. This is shown as `Patient` in Figure 8.1. Note, even if there were many patients in the system, the class that represents all those patients would be `Patient` and not `Patients`. Name is written in the first compartment of a class.
- *Attributes*. This is a list of attributes representing the characteristics of the class. They could also have their own stereotypes and visibilities (discussed later). Figure 8.1 shows `Name` and `DateOfBirth` as two common attributes of a `Patient`. Attributes are written in the second compartment of a class.
- *Operations*. During business analysis, these operations also represent the behavior of the class. Operations are known as methods or functions as far as the problem space is concerned. `getName()` is the operation shown for the `Patient` class in Figure 8.1. Operations are written in the third compartment of a class.

Class Attributes

Attributes are the things that describe a class. Attributes are also nouns derived from analyzing requirements—therefore, attributes can be confused with classes. The reason for this confusion is that attributes *can be* potential classes. When an attribute exhibits behavior *of its own*, it is a likely candidate to become a class. When a class does not exhibit behavior of its own, it is likely to become an attribute of another class.

For example, if class `Patient` has attribute `Name`, and if the only thing that needs to be done with `Name` is add or change it, then it can comfortably remain an attribute of the `Patient` class. If, however, `Name` needs sorting, sequencing, and several operations that are specific to it, then keeping `Name` as an attribute of class `Patient` will unnecessarily clutter the `Patient` class. In such cases, it is advisable to show `Name` as a separate class related to the `Patient` class.

Class Operations (Methods)

Operations (also called methods and, at times, functions of a class) are the implementation of the behavior of a class. Operations enable a class to carry out its responsibilities. During analysis, classes are assigned responsibilities that they have to fulfill; responsibilities indicate how a class should behave and operations to implement that behavior.

For example, the `Patient` class documented earlier has the responsibility of knowing the details of a patient. The class `Patient` is also responsible for maintaining the patient details. These responsibilities require the class to behave in a certain way—that is, it should be able to create, collect, manage, and provide patient details to other classes. The overall responsibilities of the class Patient start getting decomposed into many smaller operations, one of which is `getName()`. A class can have multiple responsibilities. Each responsibility can determine the modeling of corresponding operations that help the class fulfill that responsibility.

For example, a `Doctor` class has numerous operations like `speak()`, `consult()`, `operate()`, and `apply for vacation()`. The context of the system provides the analyst with the opportunity to describe appropriate responsibilities for the class. If the `Doctor` class is made responsible for `consultation`, then the operation (method) dealing with `applying for a vacation()` is not relevant.

Naming Conventions for Attributes and Operations

Attributes and operation names within classes are written left justified and in a plain font. Attribute naming conventions mostly follow the class naming convention. Abstract attributes are shown in italics. Attribute names usually start with a capital letter; operation names, however, can start with a lowercase letter. Names with multiple words should not have spaces between words, and each word within should be capitalized, e.g., `DateOfBirth`

Similar to the earlier discussion on class names, naming conventions for attributes and operations can vary based on the language of implementation, project specifications, and guidelines. For example, while an attribute name starts with a capital letter during analysis, in most designs and code, these names start with a lowercase: dateOfBirth is closer to Java code than DateOfBirth. Regardless of what the actual convention and standard is, as long as all members of the project are following the same convention and standard, the quality of the models in problem and solution spaces will be enhanced.

Visibilities on a Class

The attributes and operations that define a class have an important additional feature called visibility. Visibility indicates access control for those attributes and operations and is an important criterion for good-quality designs. Access control applies to both attributes and operations.

Visibilities for attributes and operations for the class Patient are shown in Figure 8.2.

The UML symbols for access control are as follows:

+	Public access
#	Protected access
−	Private access

A minus (−) visibility indicates that a particular attribute or operation is private. This means the attribute or operation cannot be seen or accessed by other classes within the system. The − sign in front of `Name` and `DateOfBirth` in Figure 8.2 indicates this private visibility for those attributes.

A plus (+) visibility indicates public operations or attributes that can be accessed by the rest of the system. This is shown as a + sign in front of the `getName()` operation.

Occasionally, and if permitted by the language of implementation, attributes and operations can also have protected visibility, shown by a # (not shown in Figure 8.2). Protected attributes and operations mean that they can be seen by the inheriting classes but not by any other classes in the system.

Keeping the attributes "private" and operations "public" ensures that the attributes of a class cannot be changed by operations from other classes directly. This is the concept of encapsulation, which improves the quality of design and code because it localizes all changes to within the class.

While encapsulation implies attributes are private and operations start as public, it is permissible to modify these visibilities depending on the requirements of the class. For example, a particular attribute that deals with counting the total number of patients (+PatientCount) may be made public so that other classes (i.e., their runtime objects) can access this attribute directly. Accessibility is discussed in greater detail in Chapter 11 (Figures 11.13 for attributes and Figures11.16 for operations).

Designing a Class in the Solution Space

Figure 8.3 shows details of the `Patient` class with greater details in design in the solution space. In this `Patient` class, the attributes and operations (methods) are more detailed than in an analysis-level class definition, shown in Figure 8.2. The attributes have additional attribute types that specify what data type the attribute will be, e.g., "CHAR" indicates the attribute will be made of CHARacters. Additionally, the attribute "SNO" (which may be considered as representing a serial number for a patient) has an initial value of 0. Likewise, for attributes, the operations have data types that indicate the type of the return value.

The attributes with the "−" (minus) denote they are a private member of a class and are accessible only by methods of class `Patient`. The "+" (plus) in front of operations `getName()`

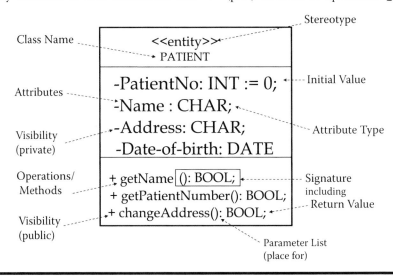

Figure 8.3   A class in design has greater details in its three parts.

and `getSerialNumber()` indicates they can be accessed by other classes in the system. The "BOOL" after the colon are the return types for the operations, which can either be "void" or a pointer.

By designing a program around entities (such as a patient entity) that have their own set of data and operations encapsulating those data, rather than using built-in data structures, the program becomes increasingly independent of implementation details. This "localizes" code and improves both quality and maintenance.

What follows is Code Example 8.1, which maps the `Patient` class shown in Figure 8.3 to its corresponding code (this is a pseudo-code and not in a specific language; PatientDB is assumed to be the patient database). This code example demonstrates a mapping between what is modeled as a class and how it translates into code. Note that additional details such as return values are discussed later in Chapter 11 in advanced class diagrams in design.

CODE EXAMPLE 8.1

```
class Patient
{
 // private attributes
 private int PatientNo;
 private String Name;
 private String Address;
 private Date DateOfBirth;

 // public methods
 public boolean getName(String PatientName)
 {
 // code here
 return false;
 }
 public boolean getPatientNumber()
 {
 //code here
 return false;
 }
 public boolean changeAddress(String NewAddress)
 {
 this.Address = NewAddress;
 return true;
 }

 public int saveChanges()
 {
 int ReturnValue;
 PatientDB db = new PatientDB();
 // pass the current values of the attributes of the "this" Patient
 // the next line calls a database module to save the details of
"this" Patient to the DB.
 // Return Values will identify success or reasons for failure.
 ReturnValue = db.saveDetails(PatientNo, Name, Address,
DateOfBirth);
 // generally, if ReturnValue is not 0 then there was an error.
```

```
 // It is upto the calling class to deal with this in an appropriate
manner.
 // e.g. notify the user that there was an error, log to error log,
etc.
 return ReturnValue;
 }
}

class PatientDB

{
 public int saveDetails(int p, String n, String a, Date d)
 {
 return -1;
 }
}
class Date
{

 }
```

Class Identification in Design (MOSS)

During design in the solution space, additional design-level classes are needed that make the ≪entity≫ classes implementable. For example, a "Patient" class identified during analysis in the problem space is not sufficiently detailed to be implemented. This is because this class Patient needs additional attributes and operations to fully implement its responsibilities. Additional classes from the language of implementation are also required to display and store the details of the objects belonging to this class. This is accomplished by two design-level classes, namely, "Patient_Form" and "Patient_Table," respectively.

A design-level class diagram has almost two or three times the number of classes identified in analysis. Developing the model of solution space (MOSS) requires the designer to continuously ask:

> "How do I implement this class?" In other words, "What additional attributes, operations, and classes do I need to implement this entity class?"

The answer to this question takes the designer to the sources of the design-level classes required in modeling the solution space. Some of these sources of classes in design are as follows:

■ Language of implementation—each development language has its own set of built-in classes that are provided to the designer to use. Most development languages such as .NET and Java have a large set of classes that are commonly used: Date, Integer, String, Char, and Currency, for example.
■ Forms and interfaces—including GUI, printers, and handheld devices that enable a user to access the system.
■ Databases in design—class diagrams are often mapped into relational database schemas during implementation. However, relational databases have some limitations that require adding extra classes to provide a closer match between the class diagram and the database schema, such as associative classes/tables.

- Design patterns—provide a rich source of well-organized classes that enhance the quality and speed of the solution. This is because design patterns contain an entire structure (pattern) of a recurring suite of classes that can be adapted to a solution.
- Prototypes—creation of prototypes in the solution space reveals design-level classes. Some design approaches evolve the prototypes into final solutions.

The need for different *types* of classes leads designers to classify classes further. Extensibility mechanisms of the UML are discussed in Chapter 10. These mechanisms help in the classification of classes and help in adding value to the overall UML models.

Strengths and Weaknesses of Classes

Strengths of Classes

What follows are some of the strengths of classes in UML.

- Classes capture everything about an entity that is needed to fully implement it in a system. Through the use of attributes, all the descriptive information about an entity is captured; likewise, through the use of operations, all of the behaviors of an entity are captured.
- The use of private visibility for attributes and public visibility for operations provides an excellent means for applying encapsulation, which is an important fundamental in good software engineering.
- Classes can be mapped to tables in a relational database for implementation by using the class's attributes as the fields in the table.
- The operations or methods in a class directly relate to the messages shown on sequence diagrams. This is further discussed in the cross-diagram dependencies between classes and sequence diagrams in Chapter 12.

Weaknesses of Classes

What follows are some of the weaknesses of classes in UML.

- Classes and attributes are similar, which may lead to confusion with modelers as one can become the other, depending on the context.
- Classes in the problem space needs to be related to their corresponding implementation in the solution space—not always easy to do as there is no one-to-one mapping.
- Using classes to model tables in a relational database does not conform to the principles of good object-oriented design, such as inheritance and encapsulation.
- Classes provide very little indication of the number of objects that will be instantiated and how those objects will behave in the memory.

Common Errors in Classes and Business Entities and How to Rectify Them

Common Errors	Rectifying the Errors	Examples
Confusion between classes and objects	Focus on classes as modeling entities (design) and objects as runtime entities.	Patient is a class and Mary is an object; Mary is instantiated from the Patient class. Designing a class focuses on Patient but utilizes the behavior of Mary the patient (and many other such patient objects).
Treating a collection of objects as a class	Objects help in defining classes but they are not part of class design. Objects are real-life instances that appear in computing memory at runtime.	Many patients together (e.g., Mary, Ravi, and John) will still not make a class. They are all a collection or group of objects. Their common characteristics and behavior is abstracted and defined within a class Patient.
Not differentiating between class and attributes	Entities with their own independent behavior are candidates for good classes; classes that don't have their own behavior are candidates for attributes in other classes.	FirstName is a common noun; it can be considered as a candidate for a class. However, it does not have specific behavior associated with it. Therefore, it should be made an attribute within another relevant class (e.g., Person)
Using (+) public visibility on all attributes	Most attributes are private (−). This is because these attributes need not be accessed by any other class in the system (other than the class they belong to); exceptions are global attributes.	See Figure 8.3. All attributes in the class Patient there are private (−). Should any other class need values within these attributes, they need to call the corresponding operations.
Using (−) private visibility on all operations	Operations are the services provided by the class. These services need to be visible and available to the rest of the classes in the system. Hence they should be mostly public (+). Exceptions are some internal services within a class that are used only by that class.	See Figure 8.3. All operations in this class are public (+). That means these operations are visible to the rest of the system. These operations can be called upon by any other class in the system to perform a certain function.

Discussion Questions

1. What is the difference between a class in problem space and the same class in solution space? (*hint: classes in the problem space are business entities; they don't have implementation details*).
2. Why should classes be named by a singular common noun? Discuss, in particular, why the class name is singular even though that class represents a collection of objects?
3. Discuss how a class represents a collection of objects but a class is NOT a collection of objects?
4. Differentiate between objects and classes. Include the object identifier and its states as part of your answer.
5. What are the three key parts of the definition of a class? Answer with an example.
6. Differentiate between attributes and classes. What is the similarity between them? What is the difference between them? Answer with examples.
7. Which types of classes identified in the initial list of classes become attributes? Answer with examples.
8. What is visibility? What are the different types of visibilities and where are they applied?
9. Why is (−) private visibility appropriate for attributes? Is there an exception to this situation? Answer with examples.
10. All operations of a class cannot be (−) private. Why? Explain with examples.
11. What are the two key strengths of classes in modeling?
12. What are the two key weaknesses of classes in modeling?

Team Project Case Study

1. Work in teams to identify classes from the descriptions of the use cases you created in previous modules. This will require you to READ and ANALYZE both the use cases and the problem statement for your system. *Reminder: Although package-wise project work is specified throughout, it is for convenience only. In reality, all modeling work is a common TEAM work and placed in one common model file.*
2. List AT LEAST 10 entity classes PER PACKAGE from the preceding analysis. Note that the analysis of the first use case will reveal more entity classes (say five), and the subsequent analysis of use cases will reveal fewer classes. So for a team of four students, the total ENTITY classes will be 40.
3. Enter all your entity classes in your modeling tool. *Note: It is highly likely that you have not identified all the classes at this stage. When you conduct abstraction and create additional hierarchies of your classes, you will discover and invent many more entity and other classes.*
4. Fully document the entity classes by correctly naming them (singular common noun), stereotyping them (≪entity≫), and indicating whether they are abstract. *Note: Because of the iterative and incremental nature of the process, these class definitions will be refined later in subsequent iterations.*
5. Each entity class during analysis is expected to contain AT LEAST 8 to 10 attributes and a similar number of operations. In practice, more attributes and operations than merely 10 are required to implement a class. Ensure you have entered these attributes and operations in the business class diagram.
6. Provide private (−) visibility for all attributes and public (+) for relevant operations.

7. Extend two entity classes from each package to a detailed design. (Note: As we are following an iterative and incremental process for modeling and developing the solution, it is natural for you to make a first attempt at design here; then, after you have completed studies of Chapters 9 and 11, you can come back to update these design-level classes.)

8. Make provision for implementation-level classes to your solution design. (Since we are not actually implementing the solution, this will be a theoretical exercise; however, it is possible to list some implementation-level classes if you are familiar with a programming language.)

9. Make sure that there are no conflicts among the group's classes and their attributes and operations.

Chapter 9

Class Model-2:
Basic Class Diagram

Learning Objectives

- Learn the UML notations for a basic class diagram
- Develop basic class diagrams using entity classes (business entities)
- Apply relationships to the basic class diagrams (inheritance, association, and aggregation)
- Add multiplicities on basic class diagrams as a means to capture business rules
- Add design-level details to class diagrams in the solution space
- Study the strengths and weaknesses of basic class diagrams

Class Diagrams

This chapter discusses the creation of a basic class diagram. Classes in practice are not standalone entities—rather, they continuously interact with each other. That is how an object-oriented software system is formed. A group of such collaborating classes appears in a class diagram. Thus, class diagrams are made up of classes, their attributes and operations, class-to-class relationships, stereotypes, multiplicities, and notes.

Notations of Class Diagrams

Figure 9.1 shows the major notations that make up a class diagram. Some of these notations were discussed in Chapter 8 when defining a class. The rectangle with three compartments, shown in Figure 9.1, represents a class (classes `Patient` and `Doctor`, in this case). This is followed by the two basic relationships between classes, inheritance and association, shown in Figure 9.2. The third one, called aggregation, is a special case of association, also shown on Figure 9.2. These relationships are discussed in greater detail next, followed by discussions on the remaining notations in a class diagram.

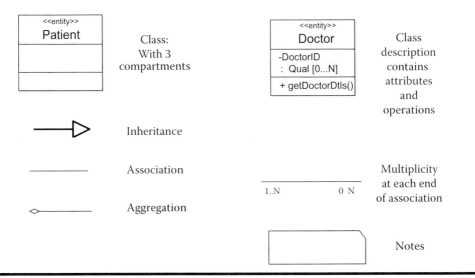

Figure 9.1 Major notations of a class diagram.

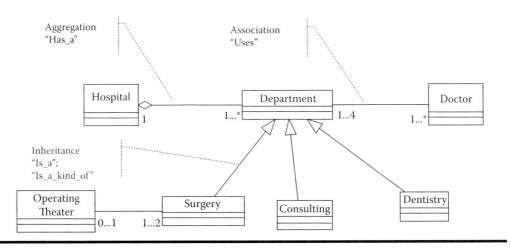

Figure 9.2 Relationships on a class diagram.

Inheritance Relationship in a Class Diagram

Inheritance is an important relationship between two classes. This relationship is specific to an object-oriented approach (versus to a procedural approach) to developing software solutions. Inheritance implies that the attributes, operations, and relationships of a higher-level class (super-class) are inherited by—made available to—a lower-level class (subclass). Thus, the lower-level classes are "kind of" higher-level classes.

Figure 9.3 shows this inheritance relationship between Department and the three special types of departments: Surgery, Consulting, and Dentistry. These three special types of department are a "kind of" generic Department. Attributes and operations that are common to these three departments will be modeled in the common Department class.

Searching for commonality in the attributes and operations of a group of classes and placing them in a common or generic class is called generalization. As shown in Figure 9.4, moving up the

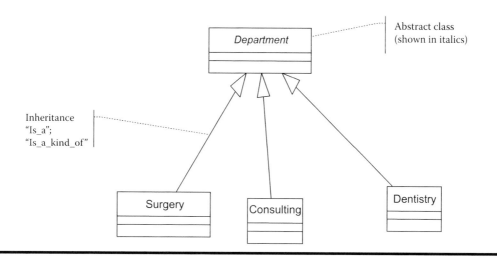

Figure 9.3   The inheritance relationship.

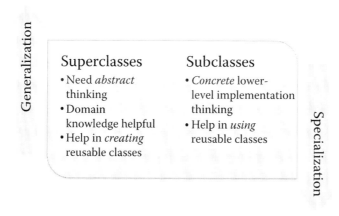

Figure 9.4   Generalization versus specialization.

inheritance hierarchy requires domain knowledge and abstract thinking. When classes are derived based on existing classes into special classes, it is called specialization.

As also shown in Figure 9.4, specialization requires concrete thinking—moving toward implementation. These higher-lower level classes are also known as super-sub, parent-child, or base-derived classes. In the UML, if the super class is "abstract" (that is, noninstantiable or, in other words, does not become an object) then it is shown in italics. Department in Figure 9.3 is such an abstract class.

Association Relationship in a Class Diagram

Association relationships between two classes can be categorized as "uses"—because they represent one class using another class in some way. An association is the most basic and the most common relationship between two peer classes in object-oriented designs.

Figure 9.5 shows two classes, `Department` and `Doctor`, associated with each other. Both `Department` and `Doctor` classes "use" each other. Most associating classes are cohesive—that

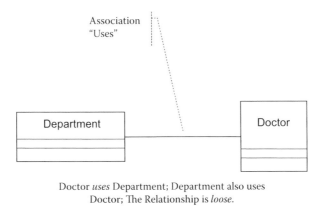

Figure 9.5 Association relationship on class diagrams.

is, they work together to achieve a goal in the system. For example, a `Patient` superclass (with subclasses `PublicPatient`, `PrivatePatient`) directly associates with a `Surgeon` class (subclass of `Doctor`) to engage in relevant behavior.

Aggregation Relationship in a Class Diagram

The association relationship indicates a relatively loose relationship between two classes. This loose relationship means the objects belonging to these associated classes can exist independently of each other. However, if the relationship between two associated classes is tight, then it is represented by aggregation. Aggregation is thus a special form of association.

Figure 9.6 shows the "has a" relationship where a `Hospital` *has* `Departments`. Aggregation represents one class *containing* another class. For example, a Hospital has Department*s*. Aggregation also represents *composition*—that is, one class *made up of* another class or classes. For example, a `Room` is *made up of* `Walls` (the classes that compose the room) and the relationship between them is one of aggregation. The "senior" level aggregated class (Hospital or Room in the aforementioned examples) in the aggregation relationship has a diamond on its right-hand side.

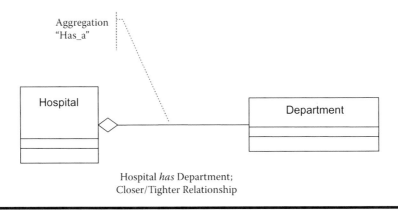

Figure 9.6 Aggregation relationship in class diagram.

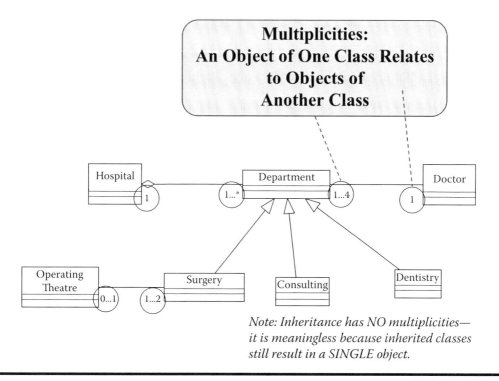

Figure 9.7 Multiplicities in class diagrams.

Multiplicities in Class Diagrams

An association relationship between two classes can also carry information on the number of object (instance) counts at each end of the association. This object count is called multiplicity. Multiplicities indicate the *number* of objects of one class related to an object of another class. Thus, multiplicities make sense when two classes are in association or aggregation. Examples of such relationships are shown in Figure 9.7 between Hospital-Department (aggregation), Department-Doctor and OperatingTheatre-Surgery (associations).

Multiplicities also indicate the rules of the business. For example, if a Department can have many Doctors but a Doctor must have one and only one Department, then the multiplicities in the Department–Doctor association relationship will be 1 and *, respectively.

> *Note that there can be NO multiplicities between two classes having an inheritance relationship. Understanding this concept helps in further clarifying these relationships.*

Further note how, in the case of aggregation, a multiplicity in the higher-level class (the aggregator class), although not syntactically wrong, has limited minimal semantic meaning. Consider, for example, a Room and Wall relationship. A Room is made up of four Walls. Although the multiplicity on the wall side of the relationship is four, there is no opportunity to show a multiplicity of more than one on the Room side of this aggregation relationship. Since the "aggregator" has to be present for the aggregate objects to exist, giving the aggregator or "senior" class a multiplicity is usually redundant.

Class Diagrams for Hospital Management System

What follows are examples of some class diagrams in the HMS. These diagrams highlight important characteristics of design-level class diagrams, as compared with analysis class diagrams. In practice, many more classes are expected in these class diagrams, and the definitions of each class are more detailed than shown here.

The following four class diagrams are presented here for the HMS:

- `Patient Details` class diagram
- `Staff Details` class diagram
- `Consultation` class diagram
- `Accounting` class diagram

"Patient Details" Class Diagram

Figure 9.8 shows the Patient Details class diagram with various classes, their relationships, and multiplicities. The `Person` class is an abstract class representing all persons in the system. The `Person` class is made up of attributes `FirstName`, `LastName`, and `DateOfBirth`. The class `Person` also has operations `createPerson()`, `changePerson()`, `calculateAge()`, and `getPerson()`. Additional attributes like `Address` and `Phone Numbers` can belong to the class `Person` are separated into independent classes : `Address` and `Phone`. These classes have the attributes and behavior of their own, as seen in Figure 9.8. Therefore, the class `Person` aggregates the classes `Address` and `Phone`.

Patient inherits from the class `Person`, which aggregates with `Address` and `Phone`. These are all entity classes. The class `Patient` is made up of attributes `PatientID`, `MedicareCard`, and `EmergencyContact`. The class `Patient` also has the operation `getPatientDetails()`, which is responsible for providing patients' details to any other class in the system. In addition to its own attributes and operations, the class `Patient` has all the attributes, operations, and relationships of the class `Person`. `PrivatePatient` and `PublicPatient` inherit from the `Patient` class. Finally, the notes provide an additional explanation about the class `PublicPatient`.

`Patient _ Details _ Form` is a boundary class that is associated with `Patient`, taking its details and displaying them on the screen. `Patient _ Details _ Form` has all the necessary fields used in displaying data as attributes and the methods to display and receive data. Figure 9.8 shows only one example method `+display()`, whereas in practice there are many more methods for the class `Patient _ Details _ Form` to be fully implemented.

The `Patient _ Details _ Form` class also shows a boundary stereotype (stereotypes are discussed in detail in Chapter 10) because this class is a user interface that is at the boundary of the system and the actor. `Patient` also is associated with `Patient _ Table`, which is a <<table>> stereotyped class. This table stereotype indicates that the `Patient _ Table` represents a database table responsible for storing and retrieving data related to `Patient`. The `Patient _ Table` class has all attributes needed to store `Patient's` details and the database related functions such as create, read, update, and delete. Only the create() function is shown in Figure 9.8. Table classes are discussed in detail in Chapter 13.

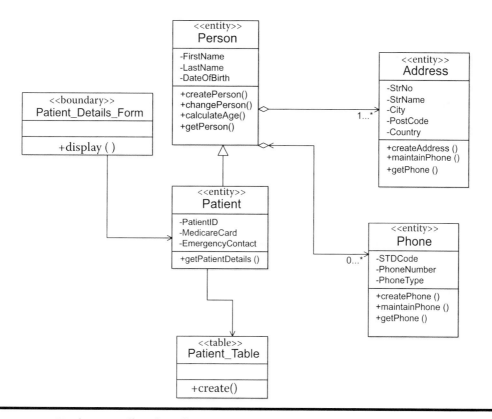

Figure 9.8 "Patient Details" class diagram.

"Staff Details" Class Diagram

Figure 9.9 shows the Staff Details class diagram in design. As with all design-level class diagrams, this diagram shows not only all the entity classes that are used in processing information but also the classes that are responsible for interacting with the user and the classes that represent databases. Once again, in practice, it is not feasible and not aesthetically pleasing to show all classes required in the design in one class diagram. Hence, small parts of the design are shown in each class diagram.

The class Staff is a superclass that contains attributes and operations that are common to all classes that inherit from it. The class Staff is specialized into three subclasses: Administrator, Nurse, and Doctor. The class Doctor is further specialized into Surgeon and Physician classes. Thus, Doctor is both a subclass of Staff (inheriting attributes and operations from it) and a superclass for Surgeon and Physician (which inherit attributes and operations from Doctor). The class Nurse has an attribute type that describes the type of nurse, as seen in the note attached to it. It may be possible to "convert" this attribute Type into three subclasses for Nurse for each type listed in the note, if attributes and operations are found to justify this measure.

Details of the doctor and nurse are stored in the corresponding table classes: Doctor _ Table and Nurse _ Table. These table classes have the minimal create(), read(), update(), and delete() functions described in the previous section. A separate table to store the higher-level Staff class may be required but is not mandatory (this mapping of classes to corresponding tables is also discussed in Chapter 13). The HMS _ Login _ Form—a boundary class—provides the system with the ability to display and receive information from the ActorStaff.

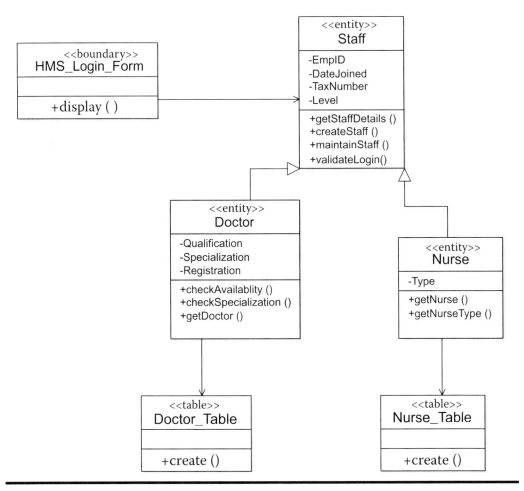

Figure 9.9 "Staff Details" class diagram.

"Consultation Details" Class Diagram

Figure 9.10 shows the Consultation Details class diagram for the HMS. The class `Consultation` is central to this diagram because all other classes are associated with it. For example, `Patient` and `Physician` have no direct association—their relationship is created through a `Consultation`. All these entity classes are shown in the figure with their corresponding <<entity>> stereotypes. Both a `Physician` and a `Patient` can participate in many `Consultations`, as shown by the multiplicities on the `Consultation` class side of their associations. A `Consultation` must, however, have one `Physician` and one `Patient`. A `Prescription`, however, can only be given for one `Consultation`, although a `Consultation` does not have to have a `Prescription`, or it can have many. The class `Consultation` also has data types added to the attributes, as indicated by the note. Attribute types can provide some additional explanations in a class diagram, for example, the attribute `Booked` is of the type Boolean. Boolean denotes that this attribute would contain a "Yes" or "No" value rather than a text or numeric value.

This diagram also shows the <<control>> class called `ConsultationManager`. This control class facilitates the robustness of design by separating the view from the business model of the

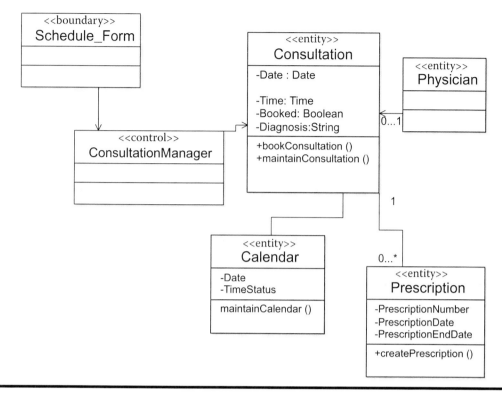

Figure 9.10 "Consultation Details" class diagram.

system. The view of the system is represented by the boundary class Schedule _ Form. This Schedule _ Form is used by any actor that is interested in using the scheduling functionality of the system—including creating and modifying schedules based on the calendar. Note that the prescription class is shown associated with the Consultation class, but it may not play a part in the Schedule _ Form display and receive functions.

"Accounting" Class Diagram

Figure 9.11 details the Accounting Class diagram for the HMS. The Bill class represents the invoice that a patient receives for medical services rendered. A Payment is made against a Bill, representing an association relationship. Note that a Bill can have one to many payments made on it, as shown by the multiplicity "1..*". On the Payment side of this association, a patient might choose to pay his/her bill in several installments.

The Payment class is specialized into payment types BPay, Cheque, and CreditCard that inherit the same attributes and operations from their parent class and have their own unique attributes and operations as shown. A fourth type of payment, by cash, is described in the note. Because no attributes or operations are needed for a cash payment (other than those already in Payment class), this type of payment is not extracted into an additional subclass, as has been done with BPay, Cheque, and CreditCard.

Figure 9.11 is a small part of the design for accounting details. It shows the Bill and the Payment classes, which are both entity classes, associated with the Payment _ Form.

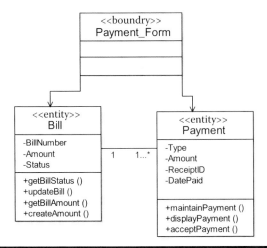

Figure 9.11 "Accounting" class diagram.

One would expect the screen that shows the Payment details to a user (typically a patient) to contain details of the Bill and enable receiving the Payment. This diagram also shows the relationship between Bill and Payment. This association relationship, with multiplicities, is between two entity classes that send and receive information related to the bill and the payment.

Strengths of Class Diagrams

Strengths and Advantages of Class Diagrams

What follows are some of the strengths of basic class diagrams discussed in this chapter.

- Basic class diagrams are an excellent structural representation of the system, allowing the modeler to capture all of the important entities in the problem space.
- Class diagrams show relationships between classes, thereby enabling coupling and highlighting opportunities for cohesion.
- Class relationships demonstrate dependencies between classes that enable understanding of the sequence in which messages are sent between their corresponding objects.
- Class diagrams encourage reusability, especially through the inheritance relationship, which in turn improves system quality and efficiency.
- Multiplicities shown in class diagrams provide information on business rules.
- Multiplicities provide valuable information on database modeling.
- Class diagrams in design provide a modeling construct that is closest to coding.
- UML tools can generate class templates or "shells" from class diagrams, with attributes and operations as a "first cut" of the code.
- Multiplicities in a class diagram aid in the creation of a relational database schema by showing which tables require foreign keys to create the relation (i.e., classes with many [*] relationships will require a foreign key when mapped to a table).

Weaknesses of Class Diagrams

What follows are some of the weaknesses of class diagrams:

- Class diagrams do not show any dynamic/behavioral information and thus do not display any concept of time. They cannot show an "if-then-else" scenario, which makes them extremely weak in representing the dynamics of a system.
- The aggregation relationship, and variations of it (such as composition, not discussed in this text), is unclear and has led to numerous debates and interpretations.
- A class may also represent a role, or it may simply be a type within the problem domain. This precise difference between what is exactly represented by a class is not clear by looking at the class itself.
- Inappropriate level of usage. A developer should use the advanced class diagram, with extra implementation classes and full signatures, at the solution level, whereas a business analyst should remain at the business entity level and only show <<entity>> classes in these diagrams.
- Attempting code generation from a class diagram without adequate preparation can lead to confusion and errors.
- A lack of granularity considerations (in terms of size of a class) can create an unwieldy design as classes can be too big or too small.

Common Errors in Basic Class Diagram and How to Rectify Them

Common Errors	Rectifying the Errors	Examples
Using inheritance instead of association	Ensure a semantic relationship with commonalities for inheritance; otherwise relate the two classes through inheritance.	"Car is a vehicle" has meaningful commonalities—an inheritance relationship; but a car and a driver will be an association relationship. Note: a customer "has an" account and the relationship is association.
Paying too much attention to association versus aggregation	Start with an association relationship by default. Move it to aggregation only if the relationship is so close that objects from one class are tightly integrated with objects from another class.	Room "has" walls is an aggregation because if the room is removed, the walls are also removed; if unsure of such closeness, use association.
Not identifying superclasses up front	Additional effort and experience is required to identify super- and abstract classes upfront.	Identifying a car is relatively easy versus identifying a vehicle class. This is because car is most probably described in the use cases; vehicle class is an invention of the designer.

Common Errors	*Rectifying the Errors*	*Examples*
Not adding multiplicities in association	As much as possible, add multiplicities to association relationships.	When unsure, add "*" or "N" to indicate unknown multiplicities.
Adding multiplicities to inheritance relationships	Inheritance implies one class *is a* type of another class. The object instantiated from this inheritance relationship is a single object. Therefore, multiplicities make no sense here.	Consider "car is a vehicle." When this class design is instantiated, the single object that is created has the definition of both a car and a vehicle. Therefore, there is no multiplicity (number of objects of one class in relationship with number of objects of another class) in a car—vehicle inheritance relationship.
Showing a concrete class in italics	Only abstract classes are shown in italics. This is to ensure that abstract classes are not instantiated.	In "car is a vehicle" relationship, only a car object is instantiated. A vehicle object is shown in italics because instantiating a vehicle (without knowing whether it is a car or any other object) is meaningless and should be prevented.

Discussion Questions

1. What are the major elements that make up a class diagram?
2. Explain the two main relationships in a class diagram with examples. (It is mandatory to create a sketch of a class diagram to answer this question.)
3. Consider the possibility of NOT having the aggregation relationship in UML. What would be the impact of not having aggregation in class diagrams?
4. What are the formal relationships between classes that represent "uses," "made up of," and "kind of?"
5. What is the importance of multiplicity in a class diagram? Answer by showing multiplicities in a sketch of a class diagram.
6. For which relationship in a class diagram do multiplicities not make sense? Why? Answer with an example.
7. What are the two key strengths of a class diagram?
8. What are the two key weaknesses of a class diagram?

Team Project Case Study

1. Place the classes identified in the previous chapter into TWO class diagrams per package.
2. Review the attributes and operations entered in those classes once again—after placing the classes in corresponding class diagrams.

3. Ensure the <<association>>, <<inheritance>>, and <<aggregation>> relationships are shown in the class diagrams for each of the packages.
4. Show the required multiplicities in the class diagrams—for all <<association>> and <<aggregation>> relationships.
5. Add NOTES on all your class diagrams to provide clarifications on any aspect of your classes.
6. Add design-level classes (forms, tables, and controls). Note that this is an iterative exercise, and you will come back to these classes after completing study of advanced class designs in Chapter 11.
7. Since you are creating these classes as a TEAM, some classes will overlap with each other (i.e., a class in one package may be required by classes in another package). Make sure that there are no conflicts among the classes.
8. Keep in mind that the details entered in each class, as well as the classes themselves, are likely to change once we iterate through other diagrams.

Chapter 10

UML's Extensibility Mechanisms: Notes, Stereotypes, Constraints, and Tags

Learning Objectives

- Understand UML's extensibility mechanisms: Notes, stereotypes, constraints, and tags
- Discuss user-defined and abstract classes in object-oriented designs
- Assigning stereotypes to attributes and operations
- Use a profile diagram as a means to extending stereotypes
- Appreciate the advantages and limitations of extensibility mechanisms in software engineering

UML's Extensibility Mechanisms

UML has a wide-ranging applicability in various projects types and sizes (Chapter 3). In addition to the standardized UML diagrams, UML also comes with an ability to extend itself. This extensibility of UML makes it versatile. However, extensions to the UML should be carefully understood and commonly agreed to. This chapter discusses UML's extensibility mechanisms, which are as follows:

- Notes—can be used to add further value to UML diagrams by providing explanations that cannot be captured directly by notations in the diagrams
- Stereotypes—are a mechanism to classify anything and everything in UML that facilitates comprehension of the many diagrams and models
- Constraints—are restrictions applied to models that help enhance the model quality
- Tags on models—are identifiers on models used to tag them with predefined properties

These UML extensibility mechanisms are of value in all diagrams. These mechanisms also play a crucial role in classifying, organizing, and providing additional information about the diagrams. This obviously has a bearing on the quality of the diagrams drawn and the ability of the diagrams to express the underlying semantics. What follows is a discussion on each of these extensibility mechanisms.

Notes

Notes provide an excellent descriptive means of clarifying UML diagrams. Notes also provide further explanations of the dependencies between elements of a UML diagram. The Notes mechanism is very helpful, especially in structural static diagrams, where it is difficult to show dependencies. Notes are represented by a rectangle with a bent corner and are linked to any other "things" in the diagram.

Notes in a UML diagram are similar to comments in a well-written program. A few lines of comments in program source code go a long way toward explaining the rationale behind a difficult or complex piece of code. Similarly, judicious Notes on a UML diagram can provide a lot of information and explanation that will help the reader of the diagram understand the deeper and implied meanings behind the diagram.

Notes can contain, for example, textual comments but may also contain graphics, detailed descriptions, links to web pages, and references to other documents. Furthermore, Notes themselves can be stereotyped (discussed next) in order to facilitate their grouping. This grouping or stereotyping of Notes depends on their purpose and the way they are used. For example, Notes may be used to comment on an actor–use case relationship in a use case diagram in the problem space. Alternatively, Notes can explain a multiplicity rule in the solution space.

Figure 10.1a shows a note that has a text comment in it capable of providing additional explanations wherever it is used. This note is also stereotyped as ≪comment≫ (versus a note being used to explain a dependency between two uses cases). Figure 10.1b shows another example of a note that describes how the actor Patient behaves differently once it is an InternetPatient. A third example in Figure 10.1c of the note relates to a use case and an actor—both have a precondition that needs to be satisfied and is expressed visibly by the note. These examples demonstrate how users can explain things that might otherwise be difficult to clarify or may be subject to misinterpretation.

Stereotypes

Stereotypes are used to classify almost every UML element. While they are mostly optional, they help in understanding the diagrams by providing a high-level grouping for elements in the diagram. Thus, by just referring to a stereotype, it is possible to understand whether a particular element in a diagram is technical or business, a hardware device or software, or whether it belongs to a team of designers or business analysts.

Furthermore, such grouping also helps in communicating the purpose of the UML element. As shown in Figure 10.2, the symbol used for specifying stereotypes is a double arrowhead: ≪ ≫ (also called guillemots). These double arrowheads are used to classify some example elements of the UML as follows:

- Use cases (≪functional≫, other possibilities being ≪technical≫)
- Classes (≪entity≫, versus, say, ≪boundary≫ or ≪controller≫)
- Node, being stereotyped as ≪device≫

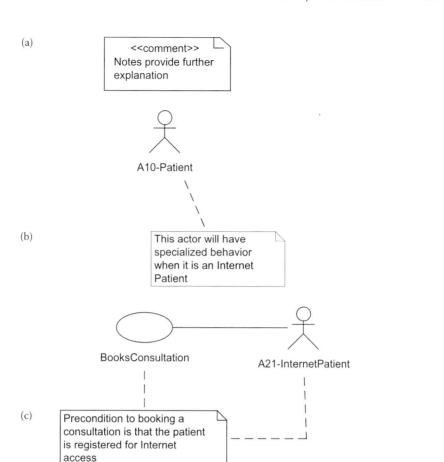

Figure 10.1   Examples of use of Notes in UML: (a) Standalone note, (b) Note attached to an element on a diagram, and (c) Note attached to multiple elements on a diagram.

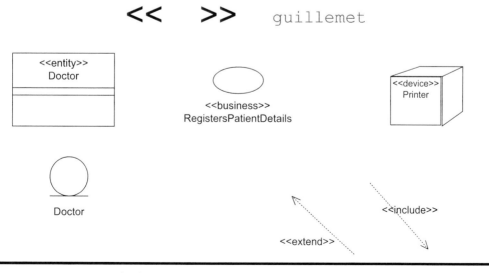

Figure 10.2   Stereotypes in the UML.

Note that while the aforementioned stereotypes are suggested and commonly used for classes, stereotypes for other UML elements can be quite different from these stereotypes. For example, use cases may have stereotypes that classify or group them based on whether they are for business or the system. In the case of use cases, therefore, ≪functional≫ and ≪technical≫ stereotypes are more relevant.

While stereotypes can be applied to various elements of the UML (such as use cases, components, and relationships), understanding them in the context of classes is important in creating good designs. Classes are not standalone entities. Systems are made up of a larger number of classes. These classes are of different types and have different attributes and behavior, and systems are built by bringing together these different types of classes. The different types of classes are grouped under "stereotypes." Thus, stereotypes are high-level classifiers. They are also called a "metatype" as they specify "types of types." This is because most UML elements, such as a class, represent a "type" for objects. There are five major stereotypes that commonly appear in class diagrams in the solution space (Figure 10.3). They are:

- Entity or business type classes,
- Boundary or interface type classes,
- Control,
- Table or persistence type classes, and
- Utility (not shown in the diagram) or supporting type classes.

While the first row of classes is stereotyped using the ≪ ≫ notation, the second row in Figure 10.3 represents the same stereotyped classes using different icons for each of those stereotypes (instead of the guillemots ≪ ≫). The icons representing the stereotypes in Figure 10.3 belong to a particular modeling tool provider. While the use of icons to represent stereotyped classes in a class diagram improves its readability, it can also create challenges because of variations in the standard.

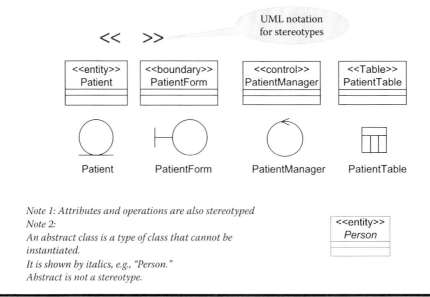

Figure 10.3   Using stereotypes for classes in solution space.

A designer has to understand the icons, in addition to knowing the UML stereotypes, to read a class diagram that uses icons.

UML's extensibility further allows designers to create additional stereotypes, as required, to further classify classes in design. Additional stereotypes should be created carefully and judiciously, as overuse of stereotypes can create more confusion than the additional stereotypes were attempting to reduce in the first place.

Some stereotypes are mandatory—such as the ≪include≫ and ≪extend≫ stereotypes for use-case-to-use-case relationships. In other cases, the stereotypes for the relationships are implicit in the symbol or icon used to represent that relationship. Stereotypes for class relationships are only represented by icons, and the extensibility of these relationships is limited. For example, the ≪inheritance≫ stereotype in a class-to-class relationship need not be labeled. The arrowhead representing the inheritance relationship between two classes makes that relationship unique and clear even without the stereotype label of ≪inheritance≫.

Entity Class

≪entity≫ represents the basic class stereotype that describes a business entity, e.g., a patient or an invoice. Entity classes make up the main set of business classes and thus are the first classes to be discovered during the analysis phase. In fact, an analysis-level class diagram is almost always comprised only of entity classes. However, sometimes additional entity classes are needed and are added to the design class diagram.

Boundary Class

≪boundary≫ is a stereotype to indicate that the class is an interface (i.e., a boundary between the system and the user). Boundary classes are commonly screens, forms, and Web pages. Boundary classes also provide interfaces to external systems and devices. Therefore, system-to-system data interfaces (e.g., an electronic data interchange interface between two banks) are part of these stereotypes.

Designing user interface classes of this stereotype require application of all usability concepts. Finally, note that printing classes are also considered interface or boundary classes. The terms interface and boundary are used interchangeably here.

Control Class

≪control≫ is a stereotype of a class that is used to link entity classes to boundary (interface) classes, in order to reduce class coupling. Control classes are temporary classes and manage a set of interactions, their sequences, and timings in a system and then disappear. A control class is typically provided between a set of classes to ensure these classes are "loosely coupled." This means the control classes ensure the entity classes do not directly associate (link) to the boundary classes. This loose coupling is helpful for creating a flexible design, so changes to one part of the system do not affect the rest of the system. This enables the boundary class to be changed independently of the entity class and vice versa—resulting in a concept of robustness. Robustness in class diagrams is discussed later in Chapter 15.

Table Classes

≪table≫ is a stereotype of a class that represents a table of a database. Using ≪table≫ stereotyped classes provides the ability to transform an object-oriented class diagram into a relational database schema. A set of ≪entity≫ classes in a class diagram are mapped to a corresponding set of ≪table≫ classes in a database class diagram (Chapter 13). It is often necessary to add additional table classes to accommodate the limitations of a relational database.

Utility Classes

≪utility≫ classes are classes provided by the development environment. They are typically classes that provide utility functions that are generic and applicable across many situations. For example, classes that provide basic data management functions, date, time management, and currency conversion are part of ≪utility≫ classes.

User-Defined Classes

User-defined classes are created by system designers. Although they do not have a standardized or dedicated stereotype, they are worth mentioning in this discussion of the classification of classes. The user-defined classes (and types) can be incorporated into object-oriented designs similar to those provided by the language of implementation. Attributes can be declared as belonging to these user-defined classes. User-defined classes form an objected-oriented environment of their own. Users of these classes need to know exactly what their definitions are—making the task of modeling and documenting them extremely important.

Abstract Classes

Abstract classes are an important "type" of class. However, they do not have a stereotype of their own. Instead, when a class is abstract, its name is written in italics. Abstract classes in object-oriented designs exist for the following reasons.

As discussed in OO fundamentals, classes can be abstracted to higher-level classes and then related to each other through an inheritance relationship. This leads to two (or more) sets of classes in each inheritance hierarchy. The class at a higher level of abstraction can be "instantiated" into objects. Consider, for example, the class `Patient` inheriting from the class `Person`. Although the class `Person` is at a higher level of abstraction than the class `Patient`, Person can still be instantiated.

However, it is possible, based on the specific design, that instantiating a class `Person`, without its being either a patient (or a doctor, for that matter) may not make sense. An instance of only the class `Person` may be incomplete from the system's viewpoint. A designer then specifically indicates that such a class is an "abstract" class. Abstract classes, shown in italics in class diagrams, indicate that there can be no object in a system belonging to that class; objects can only be instantiated from classes derived from the abstract class.

Interfaces, Roles, and Types

Many elements in the UML are similar to classes but are not exactly classes. These are called interfaces, roles, and types. Together with classes, these elements can be referred to as a class, interface, role, type (CIRT). Interfaces can be understood as classes that contain a subset of another class's operations; however, an interface does not implement operations. Roles represent the way in which classes appear to different parts of a system. For example, a `Patient` class can appear in a different role when associating with an accounting system as compared with when getting admitted to the hospital. Informally, types can be considered classes without operations.

Stereotypes for Attributes and Operations

In addition to classifying classes, UML also allows modelers to stereotype logically grouped attributes and operations in a class. Thus, the attributes and operations of a class can have their own specific stereotypes.

Attribute Stereotypes

What follows are some examples of stereotypes that can be used for attributes (note: these stereotypes are practical examples, and designers are encouraged to create their own stereotypes for attributes that are relevant):

> ≪business≫ may be the stereotype for all attributes that deal with the business logic of a class, ≪counter≫ may be the stereotype for all attributes that are used in counting or summing or listing objects, ≪global≫ may be the stereotype for all attributes that are global to a system.

Operation Types

A class, in practice, has numerous operations. The number of operations can range from 5 to 25 or more, depending on what the class is trying to implement. Stereotypes can be used to help us classify or group operations. Based on Lippman (1991)[1] operations can be categorized into the four types: manager, implementer, access, and helper. Operations belonging to these types can be stereotyped accordingly: ≪manager≫, ≪implementer≫, ≪access≫, and ≪helping≫.

Manager Operations

One subset of operations of any class provides functions that help manage the class itself. These operations include, for example, initialization, creation, destruction, and memory management and can be called manager operations. Other examples of manager operations are constructors and destructors, which carry out the creation and destruction of *objects* of a class.

Implementer Operations

The subset of operations of a class that provide the capabilities of implementing the class are called implementer operations. These operations are the prevailing ones identified in analysis and are carried through into design. Implementer functions perform most of the detailed implementations inside an operation identified during analysis. An example would be an operation that schedules a doctor for an appointment. If any traceability is wanted or necessary, these are the operations that are traced through design.

Access Operations

Classes also have a need to store and retrieve data. The subset of operations that deals with this part of a class's responsibility are called access functions. They implement the concept of information hiding by providing read and write access to the attributes of the class (commonly called "get" and "set" operations).

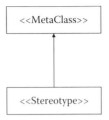

Figure 10.4   Profile diagram as an extensibility mechanism.

Helping Operations

Helping operations carry out the secondary functions of a class so the primary functions are carried out successfully. Helping functions are not generally intended for the user of a class. Therefore, they are likely to be private functions that are not part of the public interface of the class. They are usually invoked and used by other operations of the class. As with class stereotypes, care should be taken not to go overboard with stereotyping attributes and operations.

Profile Diagram

Profile diagrams were introduced in UML 2.0 but first appeared in the "official" taxonomy of UML diagrams in UML 2.2. The profile diagram is an extension mechanism that provides additional understanding and clarity to the "typing" mechanism in UML. Thus, profile diagrams enable the extension of existing constructs that are specific to a particular domain, platform, or method. New constraints that are specific to a profile can be added to a metamodel. Figure 10.4 shows an example Profile diagram. In this diagram, the ≪stereotype≫ (which is a higher-level classifier) is itself derived from the profile of a ≪MetaClass≫.

A profile, along with its customized metamodel definition, is applied to a package. Depending on the tools being used for modeling and deployment, profiles can be dynamically applied to or retracted from a model. Profiles can also be dynamically combined so that multiple profiles are applied at the same time to the same model.

Constraints

A constraint is an additional rule that a modeler can assign to a UML diagram in order to lend special significance to either an element in the UML diagram or to the entire diagram. For example, Figure 10.5a shows a constraint imposed on the relationship between Patient and Doctor—it limits the relationship through the {examined by} constraint. This constraint states that the Patient cannot be related to the Doctor in any other way (e.g., when the Patient is paying the bill).

Tagged Value

Tagged value can be "tagged" to a modeling element that enables the modeler to create new properties for the existing modeling elements in the UML. A tag will apply to all instances of a modeling

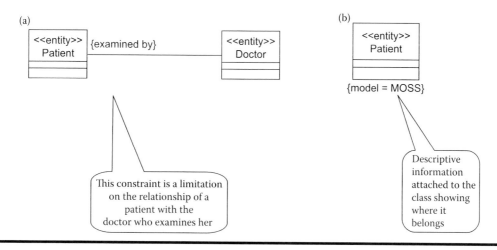

Figure 10.5 Examples of (a) constraints and (b) tags in UML.

element and not to a particular instance. This allows the UML to be extended to suit the specific modeling scenario. Figure 10.5b shows a {model=MOSS} to indicate a project management type of tagged value that indicates that all objects belonging to this class will be part of the model of the solution space (MOSS). Another example for, say, the `ElectronicPayment` class can be {Amount >= $10} to indicate that this tag applies to all instances of `ElectronicPayment` and that the `Amount` must be greater than $10.

Common Errors in UML's Extensibility Mechanisms and How to Rectify Them

Common Errors	Rectifying the Errors	Examples
Ignoring Notes on UML diagrams	Notes play a vital role in explaining nuances within UML diagrams; when in doubt, use Notes.	See most of the example diagrams in Chapter 2. They are annotated with Notes of explanation.
Considering Notes only as a description	Notes can be stereotypes—as descriptive, technical, conditional, and so on; Notes can be used as a rich source of extensibility by stereotyping.	See the earlier discussion in this chapter on stereotyping Notes.
Not being able to differentiate between stereotypes and types	Types are closest to classes—types are created based on classification (discussed as an OO fundamental in Chapter 1); stereotypes are further classification of these types.	A group of business classes includes person, doctor, and patient. All of these are stereotyped as «entity».

Common Errors	Rectifying the Errors	Examples
Assuming stereotypes are only for classes	Standardized UML stereotypes are primarily provided for classes; however, stereotypes can be user defined and used to classify any element within the UML.	For example, ≪business≫ and ≪technical≫ can be one way of stereotyping use cases; stereotypes can also be for relationships: e.g., ≪include≫ and ≪extends≫; also check discussion in this chapter on stereotyping attributes and operations.
Inability to differentiate between UML-provided stereotypes and user-defined stereotypes	≪entity≫ and ≪control≫ are standardized stereotypes for classes; ≪association≫ and ≪aggregation≫ are stereotypes for class-to-class relationships; however, additional user-defined stereotypes can also be created based on common agreement among project team members.	Check the standardized UML stereotypes for classes, e.g., ≪entity≫, ≪boundary≫ (or ≪interface≫), and so on. Note that despite these classifications, additional stereotypes can be created by the project team.
Inability to understand that abstract classes need not (and should not) be instantiated	Abstract classes are precisely that—higher-level abstractions of a group of classes exhibiting similar characteristics. They need not and should not be instantiated. Use the mechanisms provided by the development language to ensure an abstract class is not instantiated.	See the discussion on abstract classes; for example, *Person class*—(shown in italics to represent an abstract class) need not be instantiated because Person on its own doesn't make sense (unless it is either a doctor or a patient).

Discussion Questions

1. Why are Notes important in UML diagrams? Discuss with an example where a diagram is difficult to interpret without Notes.
2. What is a stereotype? Why is it called an extensibility mechanism? Explain how a stereotype helps design quality.
3. What are the UML-specific stereotypes for (a) classes? (b) class-to-class relationships? How would you differentiate them from user-defined stereotypes?
4. Discuss how profile diagrams can support the purpose of stereotypes?
5. What is an abstract class? What are the important considerations around not instantiating an abstract class?
6. What is a user-defined class? How does a user-defined class extend the development environment?
7. Provide an example of constraints and tags for a class and for a use case.

Team Project Case Study

1. Revisit the modeling work done thus far within each of the packages for your case study.
2. Inspect each modeling element in the context of the discussion in this chapter on extensibility mechanisms.
3. Apply relevant stereotypes for all elements within your model where relevant (e.g., use cases and activity diagrams in MOPS and classes in MOSS).
4. Make a note of the fact that these stereotypes will be further applied by you to the new elements you discover and models you create as you progress through the case study.
5. Revisit all models you have created thus far and inspect them taking the Notes into consideration; are there sufficient Notes on the diagrams that provide subtle and obvious explanations to the reader?
6. Add detailed Notes to ALL diagrams, providing additional explanations.
7. Add constraints and tags to a use case diagram and to a class diagram—within each package.
8. Make a note of the discussion on abstract classes, user-defined classes, and stereotypes for attributes and operations; you will revisit these discussions when new solution-level classes, attributes, and operations are discussed in the next chapter.

Endnote

1. Lippman, S., 1991, *C++ Primer*, Reading, MA: Addison-Wesley.

Class Model-3: Advanced Class Designs

Learning Objectives

- Learn the additional UML notations for a class diagram in solution space
- Define advanced design-level classes
- Separate runtime objects from their corresponding classes
- Create advanced class diagrams in solution space
- Incorporate advanced class-to-class relationships in the solution space
- Use object diagrams to interpret multiplicities on a class-to-class relationship
- Map a class diagram to corresponding pseudo-code

Introduction

This chapter extends the concepts developed in Chapter 8 (classes) and Chapter 9 (initial class designs). The discussions in this chapter are on advanced classes and class diagrams modeled in the solution space (MOSS). These class diagrams in the solution space contain more details than the classes specified during analysis in the problem space (MOPS). Classes from the software implementation environment are added to these advanced class diagrams, and class-to-class relationships are further refined in this stage of design. Such refinement of relationships includes firming up multiplicities, specializing aggregation, realizing classes, and defining in detail attributes and operations. Object diagrams of the UML are also used here in the solution space to visualize multiplicities.

Understanding Class Relationships

Notations on an Advanced Class Diagram in the Solution Space

Figure 11.1 shows the UML notations that are used in creating an advanced class diagram in the solution space. These notations are an extension of the class notations discussed in Chapter 9 and are described next.

- Class—as shown in Figure 11.1, a class is the basic notation in a class diagram. A class is made up of three compartments—name, attributes, and operations. However, in design, additional information on each class includes stereotypes, attribute types, and operation signatures provided (discussed earlier in Chapters 8 and 10).
- Multiplicity—as shown in Figure 11.1, multiplicity is depicted at each end of an association relationship to indicate the number of objects of one class required in a relationship with one object of another class. This information is part of the business rules shown in class diagrams.
- Notes—help clarify the class diagrams (Figure 11.1). Notes should be extensively used in all class diagrams (discussed in Chapter 10).
- Relationships—are the various class-to-class relationships (Figure 11.1). In order, they are: inheritance, association, aggregation, composition, realization, interface, and dependency.

Class-to-Class Relationships

Class-to-class relationships can be placed into two separate groups: basic and advanced relationships. Basic relationships between classes are typically used by a business analyst in creating a business-level class diagram in the problem space (discussed in Chapter 9). The basic relationships can have advanced features in the solution space.

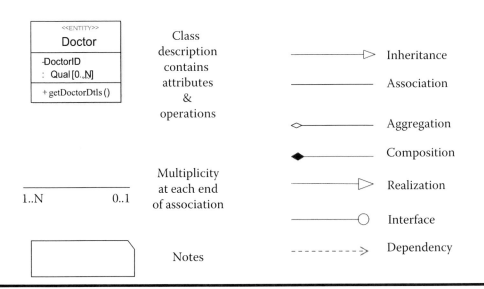

Figure 11.1   Notations of a class diagram in solution space.

These basic relationships between classes are association and inheritance. To recap the discussion in Chapter 9 (Figure 9.2), Department and Doctor have an association, because Doctor belongs to a Department. Department is also inherited by three other classes: Surgery, Consulting, and Pharmacy. These are three specialized departments inherited from Department. Surgery class is also associated with Operating Theater. An association relationship can be specialized to aggregation. Since a Hospital is made up of departments, the association relationship between them can be made into an aggregation relationship. During design, these relationships contain additional details required for implementation—hence they are called advanced relationships in design.

Advanced Relationships in a Class Diagram in Design

Figure 11.2 shows an advanced class diagram in design. The association relationships between the classes ConsultationBookingForm, ConsultationManager, and Department are similar to the aforementioned basic association relationship. The Department class in Figure 11.2 shows two interfaces: DepartmentDoctor and DepartmentAvailability. Each interface represents a subset of the operations of the Department class. Interfaces in class diagrams do not implement the operations.

The dashed arrow with the closed arrowhead, going from DepartmentDoctor to AssignDoctor, represents realization, and the ConsultationBookingForm shows dependency on the interface DepartmentAvailability. The inheritance relationships that specialize the Department class are straightforward. Thus, this diagram essentially introduces two additional relationships (realization and dependency) and the interface notations.

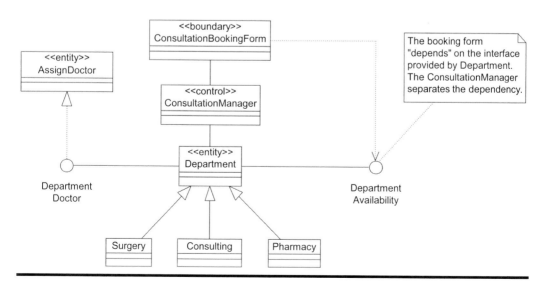

Figure 11.2 Advanced relationships in a class diagram in design.

Association Relationship in Design

The association relationship between two classes was shown in Chapter 9 (Figure 9.5). Association, represented by a straight line, indicates a bidirectional connection between classes. At runtime, this relationship translates into a link between objects of the associated classes. For example, an association between the `Department` and `Doctor` classes implies that objects in the `Department` class are connected to objects in the `Doctor` class at runtime. This connection is for objects of one class using the services of objects from the other class or vice versa (i.e., making themselves available for use).

Associations get implemented through attributes in class definitions. For example, in the association relationship between `Doctor` class and `Department` class, `Department` is declared in `Doctor`. This is shown in the pseudo-code in Code Example 11.1. In that example, the class `Department`, which is associated with the `Doctor` class, is declared as `DEPARTMENT *dept;` notice how, in the code for class `Doctor`, the rest of the attributes, namely `INT *PatientID`, `CHAR *name`, and `DATE Date-of-birth`, all belong to data types provided by the language of implementation (natives). `DEPARTMENT`, however, is a data type created by the system designer (user-defined type).

Code Example 11.2 shows the effect of a bidirectional association on `Department` and `Doctor` classes. The `Department` declares `CHAR *DeptName`. `Department` also has an operation `+getDeptName()`. On the right-hand side of this code example there is a declaration of `DEPARTMENT`. However, notice here how `Doctor` uses `Department`. This is achieved by the call from `Doctor` to `Department` as follows:

```
aDept.getDeptName()
```

When the aforementioned piece of code is executed in `Doctor`, the doctor object gets the name of the department from the `Department` object. Further notice that the actual code to fetch the department name is written in `Department` and only used in `Doctor`.

The converse of the foregoing is also true. `Department` can also use the `Doctor` class. This usage is shown with the `aDoctor.getDocID()` call in `Department` class and the coding of the corresponding operation in the `Doctor` class.

CODE EXAMPLE 11.1: FOR ASSOCIATION RELATIONSHIP: IN DOCTOR CLASS FOR ASSOCIATION RELATIONSHIP WITH DEPARTMENT

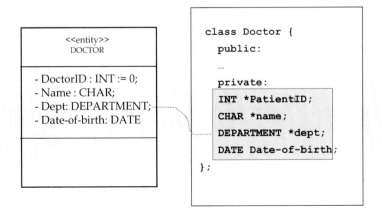

**CODE EXAMPLE 11.2: FOR BIDIRECTIONAL ASSOCIATION
RELATIONSHIP IN BOTH DEPARTMENT AND DOCTOR CLASSES
FOR BIDIRECTIONAL ASSOCIATION RELATIONSHIP**

```
class Department {          class Doctor {
 private:                    public:
  INT *DeptID;                DEPARTMENT *aDept;
  CHAR *DeptName;            aDept.getDeptName();
 public:                     +getDocID(){---
  DOCTOR *aDoctor;             -code to get DocID --};
  aDoctor.getDocID();        private:
                             INT *DoctorID;
  +getDeptName() {           CHAR *Name;
   -code to get DeptName --};  CHAR  Address;
 };                           DATE Date-Joined;
                             };
```

The preceding examples demonstrate bidirectional association. However, associations can be implemented in various ways other than those shown in Code Examples 11.1 and 11.2. For example, operation arguments and return classes can also denote an association relationship between classes. Such relationships in design are established through a calling operation with the called class specified in the parameter list (argument) or the return class (parameter list and return classes are discussed later in this chapter under operation signatures).

The straight line drawn to represent the previously mentioned bidirectional association does not give any indication of its direction. Sometimes the direction of association—also known as the navigation of the association—may be relevant to the design. This is important, for example, when the designer specifies that one class of the association calls another class but not vice versa. A directional association can be shown with an open arrowhead on the association line.

Dependency Relationship in Design

A directional association, discussed in the previous section, indicates a dependency relationship between two classes. This dependency implies that the objects of a class (called the client class) depend on the objects of another class (called the supplier class). During design, a dependency relationship is drawn as a dashed arrow as shown in Figure 11.3. In this figure, the class `Schedule` is shown as being dependent on the class `Doctor`. In other words, changes to objects belonging to class `Doctor` immediately affect objects belonging to the class `Schedule`.

However, any changes in the state and behavior of objects in the class `Schedule` will not influence the objects belonging to the class `Doctor`. The actions resulting from a dependency relationship can be summarized as follows:

■ Objects of the client class change their state as a result of changes in the state of the supplier class.
■ Operations of the client class create objects of the supplier class.

CODE EXAMPLE 11.3: FOR DEPENDENCY RELATIONSHIP

```
class Schedule {
  public:
  DOCTOR aDoctor;
  private:
  CALENDAR calendar;
};
```

```
class Doctor {
  public:

  private:
  INT *DoctorID;
  CHAR *name;
  CHAR  address;
  DATE Date-Joined;
};
```

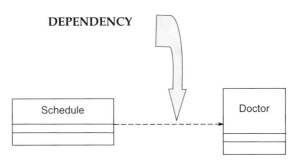

DEPENDENCY

Schedule here depends on Doctor;
changes to Doctor object will affect the Schedule object,
but not the other way around.

Figure 11.3   Dependency relationship in design.

- The operations of the client class have signatures whose return class or arguments are instances of (or references to) the supplier class.

Interface and Realization Relationship in Design

A class or a component (components are discussed in Chapter 17) can be complex with numerous attributes and operations. When a class is complex, and when it is used by another class, the complexity only increases. During design, a complex class provides a small part of its public operations as a "subset" for use by other classes. This subset of operations can be considered an "interface." Such an interface (or a suite of interfaces) represents a specific and cohesive set of functionalities of the class. This functionality can then be called upon by the consumer classes to seek the services of the classes that provide the interfaces.

Consider, for example, Figure 11.4, which shows the relationship between two classes, `PatientForm` and `Patient`, through an interface. The `class  Patient` is a substantial

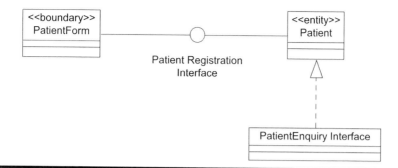

Figure 11.4   Relating two classes through interface.

class and, at the design level, contains numerous operations. However, not all of these `Patient` operations are important when it comes to `PatientForm`. Therefore, when `PatientForm` has to use `Patient`, it will not directly use the `Patient` class but rather one of its interfaces. To achieve this, `Patient` provides an interface called `PatientRegistrationInterface`, which can be used by `PatientForm`, versus the entire `Patient` class. As seen in the example in Figure 11.4, interfaces facilitate the provision of a subset of the public operations of a class to other classes in the system.

Interfaces are also classes, albeit without the details of the operation implementation and without all the attributes. Interfaces can thus be represented by a class. `PatientRegistrationInterface` provides a subset of operations belonging to the Patient class, which provide the template for the operations with the actual implementation—or realization—of the interface that is in the Patient class.

An interface, as its name suggests, is only the "front end" of the class with no underlying implementation details. Therefore, every interface needs to be realized by its corresponding implementation. This scenario requires that the two classes be related by a realization relationship. The realization relationship in design indicates which particular class realizes the interface.

Aggregation Relationship in Design

An aggregation relationship is a specialized form of association. In aggregation, classes are related more closely to each other than in an association relationship. Aggregation can be described as a whole–part relationship wherein an entity is "made up of" or "composed of" other entities, or classes. Therefore, aggregation is also known as a part-of or containment relationship. The UML standard notation for aggregation is a line (similar to association) with a diamond next to the "senior" (or container or aggregator) class in the relationship.

Figure 9.6 (Chapter 9) shows aggregation or "has a" relationship between Hospital and Department classes. That diagram reads "Hospital has Departments" with the diamond of the aggregation on the side of the Hospital. This implies that Hospital *is made up* of departments. Technically, in the solution space, this aggregation means the Hospital object is composed of Department objects. Code Example11.4 shows how aggregation is implemented in Java. Department objects are *a part of* the hospital object and that the lifetime of department objects in a sequence diagram (discussed in Chapter 12) is dependent on the lifetime of the hospital object.

"By Reference" implies only a reference (or pointer) to the object (e.g., Department). Therefore, it is possible for other objects to point to the same Doctor object.

Note: Association is also implemented "By Reference"

By reference

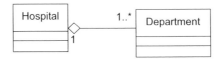

Figure 11.5 **"By reference" aggregation relationship in design.**

Implementing the Relationships: By References and By Value

There are two ways in which association and aggregation relationships are implemented: "by reference" and "by value." Figures 11.5 and 11.6 show these two approaches, respectively.

A hollow diamond (Figure 11.5) indicates that although the "main" (or higher) class is made up of objects from the "other" class, it can still exist independently during execution. This is so because it had its own attributes whose values are sufficient for its existence.

A solid or filled diamond (Figure 11.6) indicates composition, which means that the main class is made up entirely of objects in the other class and cannot exist independently.

Thus, if a `Hospital` object has to associate with a corresponding `Department` object, then the `Hospital` object can "refer" to a `Department` object. This is the use of a "pointer" that points to the `Department` object. Alternatively, the Hospital object can use a copy of the `Department` object. In cases where a copy of the `Department` object is created, the aggregation relationship is "by value." Since a copy of the `Department` object has been created, the original object continues to exist as is. Additional copies of `Department` can be created and used by other objects in the system. The multiple "by value" copies of `Department` has a potential for confusion as various objects that try to use `Department` try and update their own copies of `Department`. During execution, the `Department` object may be updated from multiple sources—leading to synchronization issues.

When "by reference" is used to implement the relationship between the two classes, the `Hospital` object does not make a copy of `Department` but rather points to or references the `Department`. As a result, the `Department` object is unique in the system. Other objects that need the `Department` object reference it rather than make a copy of it.

In implementing "by value," a copy of the aggregate parts (e.g., Department) is made. The "contained" Department is not shared by other objects in the system

By Value

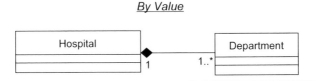

Figure 11.6 **"By value" aggregation relationship in design.**

The comparison between the two approaches to implementation can be summarized as follows:

■ In "by value," the Hospital and Department objects are "closely" stuck. This means when the Hospital object is created, the Departments are created within it; similarly, when the Hospital object is destroyed (deleted), it has to delete the Department objects. Also, when a Hospital object is moved from memory location A to B, so should the Department object be moved from related location A to B.
■ With "by reference," Hospital and Department are related through a reference only. This means that when Hospital is moved from memory location A to B, the Department object need not necessarily be moved and the Hospital object can continue to reference it.

CODE EXAMPLE 11.4: FOR AGGREGATION RELATIONSHIP IN JAVA

```
class Department
{
  int DeptID;
  String DeptName;
  int[] AllDoctors;
  int HospitalID;
  public String getDeptName()
  {
    //code to get DeptName
  }
  public int getHospitalID()
  {
  }  public String getHospitalName()
  {
  }
  public int getDoctors(Doctor DoctorArray[])
  {
  }
}class Hospital
{
  int HospitalID;
  String HospitalName;
  Department[] AllDepartments;
  Address HospitalAddress;
  public String getHospitalName()
  {
  }
  public int getDepts(Department DepartmentArray[])
  {
    //get list of departments in the hospital
  }
}
```

Parameter Visibility

An object can be passed as a parameter, through the operation signature, to other objects. The extent to which such an object is visible to other objects in the system has a bearing on the design of the relationship between the classes.

Objects can have the following visibilities in design:

■ Global visibility enables an object, at runtime, to be visible to all objects in the system; this may translate into an association.
■ Class visibility—makes the object visible only to the class or other objects and operations in the class; this also makes the two classes representing the two objects related by association.
■ Function visibility—keeps the object visible and available only to a given function or operation; this translates to aggregation in a class-to-class relationship.
■ Field (or parameter) visibility—enables the object to be visible only as a field within the list of parameters.

Depending on the implementation language, a programmer can choose options to make a parameter object visible to parts (or all) of the system.

Multiplicities and Object Diagrams

Multiplicities in Design

Multiplicities indicate the number of instances (i.e., objects) of a class that will participate in an association or an aggregation relationship. Multiplicities are shown as numbers on either side of an association relationship indicating the range of objects that will be involved in this relationship at runtime.

Multiplicities are initially specified during analysis. These multiplicities result from the business rules that have been specified in the use cases. Estimates of multiplicities made during analysis are further updated and refined during design. For a good design, it is advisable to specify multiplicities on all association and aggregation relationships. This is because, in addition to specifying the business rules, multiplicities are also used later, during database design, to develop <<table>> classes and their relationships. Since multiplicities are an important influence on the database designs, they are again separately discussed in Chapter 13.

Chapter 9 (Figure 9.7) discussed multiplicity specification in a class diagram. Multiplicities can be interpreted as follows:

■ One hospital object has to have one department, but it can have many departments.
■ A department must have one, and only one, hospital.
■ A department must have one doctor, but it can have many doctors.
■ A doctor must belong to one department but may belong to as many as four departments.
■ A surgical department may not have any operating theaters but can have only one specific operating theater.
■ An operating theater must have a surgical department attached to it and can serve up to two surgical departments.

Object Diagrams Interpreting Multiplicities

Note that there are numerous "optionalities" in specifying multiplicities. For example, when a multiplicity of 0.1 is specified, it indicates that, at runtime, there may be no or one object associated at that end of the association. Therefore, by looking at multiplicities, one cannot always ascertain the exact number of objects that will be linked with an object of another class. An object

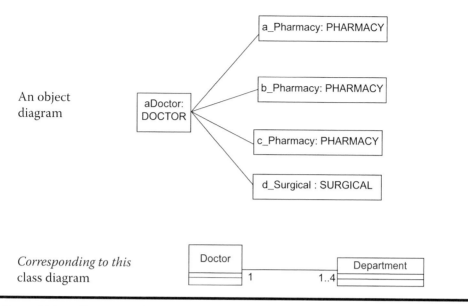

Figure 11.7 Object diagrams to interpret multiplicities.

diagram can be drawn to show, visually, the number of objects that may be linked to another object at runtime.

Figure 11.7 shows an object diagram corresponding to the simple class diagram in the same figure. The multiplicities in the Doctor—Department association on that class diagram are translated to the object diagram through physical objects and their links. Figure 11.7 shows aDoctor object belonging to class DOCTOR and four other department objects belonging to their corresponding DEPARMENT classes (or the derivatives of DEPARTMENT classes). This diagram depicts a runtime scenario for the Doctor–Department relationship.

Note that whenever multiplicities specify optionality (or range, as in this case 1.4), then one object diagram is not sufficient to display their entire range. For example, in some other execution of the system, only two or three Department objects will be linked to aDoctor. There is no need to draw an object diagram for every possible multiplicity. Instead, draw an object diagram only when the relationship is complex and important and requires visual representation. Furthermore, at runtime, checks are required to ascertain the number of objects and the links that exist. These checks could be achieved through special operations in those classes to verify the existence of links corresponding to the multiplicities. Finally, when links between objects are shown, their visibilities (as discussed earlier) are also refined.

Collection Class and Multiplicities

As discussed thus far, a multiplicity of more than one indicates a range of numerous objects instantiated for that class. For example, if class Patient has a multiplicity of more than one, then there are numerous Patient objects instantiated from that class. Analysis of the use cases that describe the behavior of the Patient class reveals functions—technically operations—that are also of two categories:

■ One set of operations deals with *an individual* Patient object. These are all the operations associated with the behavior of a single patient, such as createPatient(), calculateAge(), getDiagnosis(), or changeDetails().

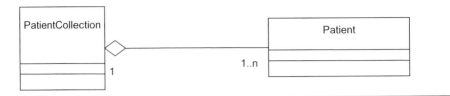

Figure 11.8 A collection class.

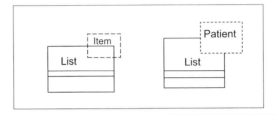

Figure 11.9 A parameterized class for designing a multiplicity of one or more.

■ Another set of operations deals with *a group* or *collection* of Patient objects. These include operations that enable storage, retrieval, sorting, and manipulation of a group of Patients. Examples of such operations are `listPatientByName()` and `totalPatients()`. These operations do not apply to an individual `Patient` object and therefore they should not be placed in a `Patient` class.

Operations that apply to a collection of objects point to the need for a "container" or Collection class. Such a Collection class is shown in Figure 11.8 as `PatientCollection` class. A container or Collection class is one whose instance merely points to a list or an array of objects belonging to another class. Collection classes are modeled on the container classes available in the development environment (language of implementation). Examples of such container classes include `sets`, `arrays`, `lists`, `dictionaries`, `stacks`, and `queues`.

Container classes are often modeled as parameterized classes in the UML. This is shown in Figure 11.9, where the list class has an Item representing a collection. This Item is replaced by Patient when modeling the collection scenario using the UML.

Inheritance and Polymorphism in Design

Inheritance (discussed in Figure 9.3 in Chapter 9) relationship implies one class shares the structure and behavior of another class. A subclass inherits from a superclass three specific elements: attributes, operations, and relationships. A practical inheritance hierarchy is usually three deep. Code Example 11.5 reflects "surgery extends department." The inheritance relationship shown in this code example also enables class reuse.

Incorporating Polymorphism in Design

Polymorphism is one of the fundamentals of software engineering (Chapter 1). Polymorphic behavior implies, at runtime, the same message has different behavioral effects. The calling object sends that same message to the called object. The called object receiving the message, however, can

CODE EXAMPLE 11.5: FOR INHERITANCE RELATIONSHIP

```
public class Department {
   public void setDeptDtls() {   };
   public void changeDeptDtls() {   };

   private char DeptID;
   private double Capacity;
   }
-----------------------------------------
public class Surgery extends Department {
   public Surgical (); {
   }
   public void operate(); {  }
   public void bookOperation (); {  }
   public void releaseTheatre(); {  }

   private char Name;
   private int NoOfRoom;
   }
-----------------------------------------
```

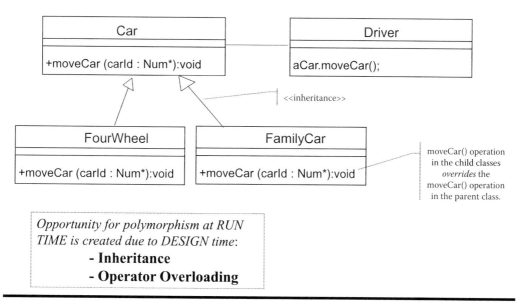

Figure 11.10   Polymorphism (through method or operator overloading).

belong to one of the many inheriting classes. Thus, the received message gets executed in different ways—depending on the receiving object that has been instantiated.

Figure 11.10 shows polymorphism through a simple example. In this example, the class Car is inherited by two types of cars: FourWheel and FamilyCar. Car is the superclass that contains a method (operation) +moveCar(). This operation is a dummy operation that is "overloaded" by the +moveCar operations in the FourWheel and FamilyCar classes. The effect of this design can be seen in Code Example 11.6.

CODE EXAMPLE 11.6: SIMPLE CODE EXAMPLE FOR POLYMORPHISM

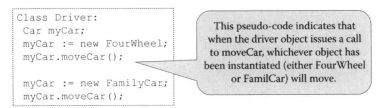

```
Class Driver:
  Car myCar;
  myCar := new FourWheel;
  myCar.moveCar();

  myCar := new FamilCar;
  myCar.moveCar();
```

This pseudo-code indicates that when the driver object issues a call to moveCar, whichever object has been instantiated (either FourWheel or FamilCar) will move.

Figure 11.11 shows another example for polymorphism and operation overloading. In this example, the +getName (P _ ID : Num*):void operation is overloaded by the inheriting classes Patient and Doctor. The sample Code Example 11.7, corresponding to Figure 11.11, further explains how a polymorphic object executes any object's operation (method) based on the object receiving the message.

CODE EXAMPLE 11.7: ANOTHER SAMPLE CODE EXAMPLE IMPLEMENTING POLYMORPHISM USING JAVA BASED ON FIGURE 11.11

```
/**** sample code for Polymorphism
Purpose: A simple program that shows the usage of Polymorphism in
Object Oriented Java.
Author:
Last Updated: 05/01/17
File Name: PolyMorphic.java
*/
class Person //this is the Super class
{
public void getName()
{
System.out.println("This is super class");
}
}
class Doctor extends Person //Sub-class of the Person
{
public void getName() //Inherited Method which overridees the
getName() of Person
{
System.out.println("This is sub-class Doctor");
}
}
class Patient extends Person //another sub class of the Person class
{
public void getName() //Inherited Method which also overrides the
getName() of Person
{
System.out.println("this is sub-class Patient");
}
}
/*
```

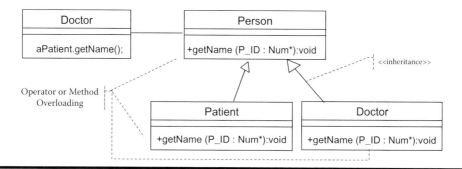

Figure 11.11   Another example of polymorphism and operation overloading.

This example demonstrates the advantage of the polymorphism that runs the getName() method based on the type of Person—either Doctor or Patient. The polymorphic aspect of design appears in Code Example 11.8, wherein the ExecuteObject method of the Execute object is the argument of the type Person. Since the Person is a superclass, it can execute the getName () method of any subclasse at runtime. This arrangement eliminates the need for an IF-THEN-ELSE condition to decide which of the two getName () methods (belonging to either Doctor or Patient) needs to be executed.

CODE EXAMPLE 11.8: SAMPLE CODE EXAMPLE TO EXECUTE POLYMORPHISM

```
*/
class Execute
{
public void ExecuteObject(Person p) // This is where the polymorphic
object is passed as a parameter!
{
p.getName();
}
}
class PolyMorphic // this is to execute the polymorphic class
{
public static void main(String args[])
{
Execute e = new Execute(); //Polymorphic class
Doctor aDoctor = new Doctor();
e.ExecuteObject(aDoctor); //executes Doctor's method
Patient aPatient = new Patient();
e.ExecuteObject(aPatient); //executes Patient's method
}
}
```

Multiple Inheritance

Figure 11.12 illustrates inheritance wherein a class has inherited from two superclasses. This is known as multiple inheritance. In the given example, the class Doctor inherits from Person as well as Staff. The relationship shown in this figure implies that attributes and operations from

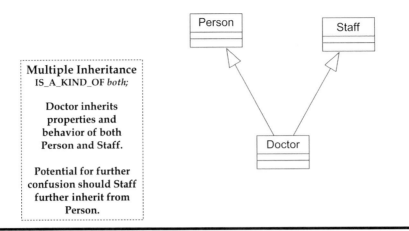

Figure 11.12 Multiple inheritance.

both higher-level classes are inherited. Multiple inheritance is to be used with caution as it is not supported by many object-oriented languages.

However, multiple inheritance is available in C++ and has its own uses in some implementations. For example, a Windows class could inherit from both a `Scrollbar` and a `RadialButton` class. Multiple inheritance should be used with caution because it can result in conflicts between attributes and operations inherited from the two (or more) superclasses.

Incorporating Errors and Exceptions in Design

Incorporating error detection and error handling is an important activity in good design. Error handling is the mechanism to detect errors in objects at runtime. Error handling also specifies the action to be taken by objects when errors occur. Examples of errors in objects include a wrong list of parameters, erroneous values within parameters, or inappropriate return values. While errors usually occur due to a wrong call from the calling object, it is still important in a good design that the receiving objects deal with the errors in a graceful way. In the absence of such error handling facilities, the system "crashes" and the user is left with no control or redress.

Good error handling in design incorporates handling an error by an object other than the object in which the error has occurred. This improves the quality of design, as usually the impact of an error in an object at runtime is not always known across the system. Most implementation languages provide built-in error handling features that support a robust design.

Separate error monitoring objects may continue to send test operations that verify and validate the integrity of the object. These "test objects" continue to monitor the state of the main object by sending test messages and checking its state after the message has been acted upon.

Simple Code Example 11.9 shows incorporating error handling in a `Patient` class of the HMS (note this is a pseudo-code example not specific to a programming language). This example shows what happens when a `schedule` is obtained by the `patient` object. This schedule is based on an index (from 1 to 10, as only 10 schedules are allowed in this example). When the index goes out of range, an error occurs. Instead of "crashing" the system, this error handling mechanism displays an error "index out of range."

CODE EXAMPLE 11.9: FOR ERROR HANDLING

```
Class Patient {
Public:
Class RangeError { int badIndex; }
Schedule getSchedule {int index} const;
};
Schedule::getSchedule (int index) const {
        If (index < 0 || index > 10) //only 10 schedules allowed
            Throw RangeError (index); //error is thrown
        Return contents[index];
}
Void useSchedule() {
    Try {
    Patient aPatient = new Patient;
    Schedule s = aPatient.getSchedule(11);
     }
     Catch (const Schedule::ErrorRange&) {
        cout << "Index out of range. Wrong index is " index;
    }
}
```

Exceptions are used only in "exceptional" situations that are not anticipated. Therefore, exceptions are not ordinary error situations that can be handled by an "if-then-else" logic within the classes. Exceptions are incorporated in class designs to handle situations where there is an error that is not planned for and not understood by the classes. Errors in the algorithms or logic of the program itself are not exceptions. However, these erroneous algorithms "throw" exceptions when executed and error handling is the mechanism to "catch" or handle the unanticipated errors.

Attribute Identification, Naming, and Definition

An attribute is the name of a property of a class. Every class has attributes that express some of its properties. Attributes are similar to classes in many respects but are not the same. For example, the procedure to identify attributes is the same as that of classes—noun analysis. Attributes, unlike classes however, do not have behavior of their own. This lack of behavior, in fact, is one of the criteria for determining why an attribute is an attribute and not a class. Figure 11.13 shows the details of how attributes are defined and displayed during design in the solution space.

Examples of attributes for the Person class are LastName, FirstName, and DateOfBirth

In UML, every attribute has a name and a type. The type can be any data type, class, or interface that is in the model.

Naming Attributes

Like a class, attributes are also named as singular common nouns. A style guide that dictates the naming conventions for attributes is advisable. For example, a common standard for naming attributes is to start them with a capital letter. Also, if two or more words must be joined for an attribute name, they should be put together with each subword starting in capital. No underscores are used.

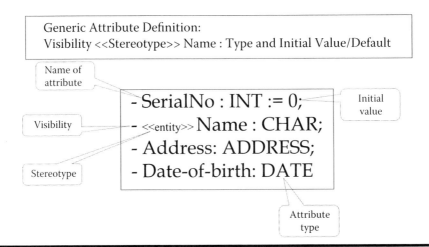

Figure 11.13 **Defining and displaying attributes in design (showing visibility, types, and initial values).**

Discovering Attributes

Many attributes are discovered by analyzing the flow of events within use case documentation. As a first cut, nouns that are not good candidates for becoming a class can become an attribute. Additional attributes are discovered when the class is defined. Domain experts also provide good attributes. The discovery and refinement of attributes in classes is an iterative and incremental process throughout both the analysis and design phases. Additionally, during design, attributes are provided with greater details to enable the corresponding class to be implemented.

Attribute (Data) Types

Attributes are further defined in design by declaring the data type. The data type is listed after the attribute name followed by a colon (:), as seen in Figure 11.14. There are three types of data types:

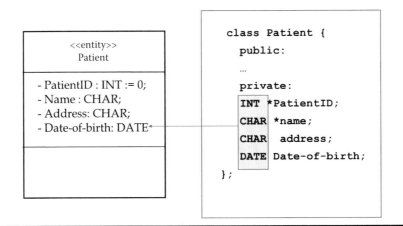

Figure 11.14 **Attribute types and classes provided by implementation language.**

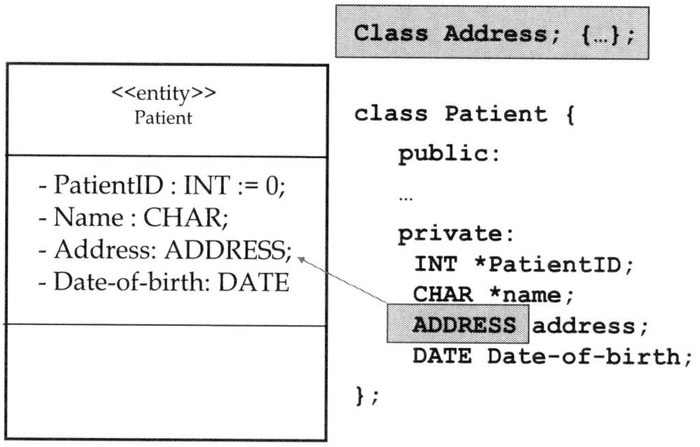

```
                              Class Address; {…};

    <<entity>>               class Patient {
      Patient                   public:

    - PatientID : INT := 0;        …
    - Name : CHAR;              private:
    - Address: ADDRESS;           INT *PatientID;
    - Date-of-birth: DATE         CHAR *name;
                                  ADDRESS address;
                                  DATE Date-of-birth;

                              };
```

Figure 11.15   Attribute types and classes created by developers and designers.

- Data types provided by the development language, e.g., INT (for integers) and CHAR (for characters).
- User-defined data types, e.g., Color, which may describe the color of a car.
- User-defined classes, e.g., a Patient object will have an attribute called Address, which is itself a class (Figure 11.15).

The "user-defined" types provide a "pseudo" language that allows the designer to extend the language to use for coding the system. Some development languages provide more data types than others; for example, a Date data type might not be predefined in some languages, which necessitates its creation during coding. The choice of development language should not affect the design of classes as the data type can always be user-defined during coding if it is not already predefined in a particular language.

Attribute Values

While attributes are the "definition" of the data items within a class, attribute values are the "actual" values of the data items. For example:

- Attribute is lastName
- Attribute value is "Potter"
- Another attribute value is "Sharma" and so on…

Attribute values are also helpful in providing the *state* of and object; for example, in an Account class, if the *value* of the attribute dateClosed is 0, the *state* of corresponding Account object is *closed*. Also, if the dateClosed attribute contains a real date, then the *state* of the Account object is *closed* (more details of state can be found in the discussion on state machine diagrams in Chapter 14).

Common Errors in Designing Attributes

Attributes are similar to classes. This similarity is the reason for some common errors in designing attributes. The common errors in attribute designs include:

- Naming a class as an attribute, e.g., making Address an attribute of Patient, whereas Address is more suited as a class in its own right

- Naming an operation as an attribute, e.g., `getName` is a bad name for an attribute as it implies an action and not a characteristic of a class
- Naming an attribute value as an attribute, e.g., `Sam` is the value of an attribute called Name but is not an attribute itself
- Not initializing attributes when required, e.g., `DateOfBirth` is an attribute of patient class that should be initialized as "00/00/00." A counter and should be initialized (i.e., should be `PatientCount:= 0`)
- Not providing appropriate visibility—attributes should have a private visibility by default, although occasionally global attributes may have public visibility. Not providing visibility or providing inappropriate visibility is a design error.
- Giving the wrong attribute type for an attribute, e.g., `AccountBalance: CHAR`; attribute type for account balance should be a CURRENCY or DOUBLE.
- Not providing attribute stereotypes when required. Stereotype is a grouping mechanism in UML, and if there is a large number of attributes in a class, it is always a good idea to group them by their stereotypes. Common stereotype examples for attributes are <<entity>>, <<business>>, <<date>>, <<counter>>, and so on.

Operation Identification, Naming, and Signature

Figure 11.16 shows the details of an operation in a solution space.

Understanding an Operation in a Class

An operation in a class enables the class to execute its responsibilities. They are the actions that can be performed by the objects instantiated from that class.

Examples of operations include:

- Checking validity of accounts, customers
- Create, read, update, and delete (CRUD) operations from databases

– Shown in the third compartment of a class

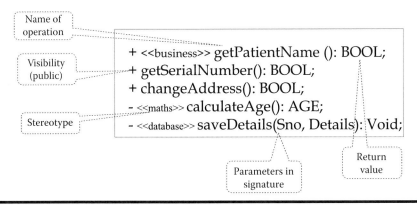

Figure 11.16 Defining and displaying operations in design.

■ Performing internal calculations to produce results called from outside

Operations in a class also provide the mechanism to implement encapsulation. Operations provide internal and external services that can be called by other objects. In other words, a class has all of the operations it needs to provide information to other objects that ask for that information. For example, if an object asks a `Person` object for the age of the person, the `Person` object will calculate the age itself from the `dateOfBirth` attribute and `today-sDate` to provide the answer. By applying the fundamental of encapsulation, the `Person` object does not allow any other object in the system to access its attribute (`dateOfBirth` in this example).

Naming Operations

Operations are the interfaces to a class for other objects in the system. For this reason, operations should be named to indicate their outcome, not the steps behind the operation. This is because the steps within an operation can change as the class itself is developed and refined further. This necessitates renaming the operation and modifying any other class it interfaces with – if the operation is named for what it does, rather than what it provides.

The following examples illustrate the principle behind naming an operation:

■ `getBalance()`—this is a well-named operation because it indicates the outcome from the "calling class" viewpoint.
■ `calculateBalance()`—poorly named because it indicates that the balance must be calculated, whereas there can be many ways to arrive at the balance. This name represents the implementation decision. Note, however, that if `calculateBalance()` is used by another operation *within* the class, then such a name for an operation is quite acceptable.

Understanding Operation Signatures

Operations provide the behavior of a system. These behaviors are initially identified and documented in use cases. However, during design, the operation "signature" includes greater details, so that the operation can be implemented. Therefore, during design, the operation definitions are expanded to include the list of arguments (also called parameters), their data types, and the return value data type of the operation.

For example, an operation within a Patient class could be fully defined as `getAge(int PatientID): int`, which means that the operation is sent the patient ID (which is an integer), and returns an integer, which is the patient's age. (Note that the Patient class itself would contain the necessary attribute `DateOfBirth`, which is used to calculate the age—this is encapsulation.) During analysis, it is optional to include the signature; however, during design, the signature is mandatory.

The signature of an operation can also indicate a relationship. If the class in an operation argument (or return from an operation) is a fundamental class (e.g., a string), then that relationship is not shown in a diagram. For other classes, the relationship typically is displayed on one or more class diagrams. Operations may be combined or split into a class and additional operations added to the class to implement it.

Common Errors in Modeling Advance Class Designs and How to Rectify Them

Common Errors	Rectifying the Errors	Examples
Not completing attribute details in design	Ensure each attribute is formally defined with its type, visibility, and initial value.	See code Example 11.1. –DoctorID : INT = 0;
Not having full operation signatures	Ensure operations have parameter list, visibility, and return values.	See Figure 11.16
Designing solution-level class diagrams directly from the basic class designs	Ensure sequence and state machine designs are drawn as part of the process of developing models before moving to system design.	Revisit Chapter 4 on processes, Chapter 12 on sequence diagrams, and Chapter 14 on SMDs
Overuse of multiple inheritance	Avoid multiple inheritance where possible at least in the problem space (entities)	Figure 11.12 is only provided as an example to understand multiple inheritance; it is not recommended.
Exploring polymorphism without good inheritance design	Carefully created inheritance hierarchies with proper operator overloading is required for polymorphism.	Study Figure 11.10
Confusing by reference and by value	By reference is where the same data are pointed to (referenced) by multiple sources; by value is where a copy of the data is made before processing.	Study Figures 11.5 and 11.6.

Discussion Questions

1. List and discuss two key differences between class diagrams in analysis and those in design. Use examples in your discussions.
2. Identify the ASSOCIATION relationships between any two entity classes of your choice. Write pseudo-code to demonstrate your understanding of that association (*hint: see Code Examples 11.1 and 11.2*).
3. Apply multiplicities to either end of any association relationship. Draw an object diagram to show multiplicities in an association relationship.
4. Create an inheritance hierarchy in an example class diagram. Include an abstract class in your inheritance hierarchy. Write pseudo-code to explain this inheritance in design.
5. What is multiple inheritance? Discuss its limitations and merits in practice.

6. Create a polymorphic class diagram of your choice in design. Demonstrate your understanding of it through pseudo-code.

7. Explain why polymorphism is a runtime characteristic of object-oriented designs. Also describe the structural design necessity to ensure polymorphism at runtime.

8. Add an aggregation relationship to the class diagram used in creating a polymorphic design.

9. What is the difference between "by reference" and "by value"? Discuss with examples.

10. What is a parameterized class? Answer with an example.

11. How are attributes fully defined in design? Explain with examples.

12. How are operations defined in design? Explain with examples.

13. What is an operation signature? Explain the importance of having another class within an operation signature?

14. How are exceptions different from alternative flows? Discuss with examples.

Team Project Case Study

1. Identify and document *additional* design-level classes (such as database classes and classes from your possible language of implementation) that extend your original class design. Assume at least TWICE the number of additional classes for implementation. *Note: You will identify new classes as you conduct abstraction and create additional hierarchies.*

2. Fully DEFINE all the entity classes in design by identifying and fully defining their attributes and operations as discussed in this chapter. Enter and update the details in your modeling CASE tool.

3. Each class at design time is expected to contain AT LEAST 8 attributes and 10 operations. In practice, more attributes and operations than merely 10 are required to implement a class.

4. Ensure that ALL attributes are FULLY defined. That means all attributes must have visibility, name, attribute type, and initial values (where appropriate).

5. Ensure ALL operations have signatures (containing parameters and return values) and visibility. Note that classes should be created/entered in the space for class diagrams in your CASE tool—although the actual class diagrams will result only after the class relationships are discussed in the next chapter).

6. Generate pseudo-code for your class diagram in the modeling tool you are using (all modeling tools enable code generation—use a language of your choice if necessary to enable code generation).

7. Consider some of the advanced design features discussed in this chapter (polymorphism, multiple inheritance), and enhance your class diagram with those features.

Chapter 12

Interaction Modeling with Sequence Diagrams

Learning Objectives

- Understand interaction modeling with sequence diagrams
- Create basic sequence diagrams in the problem space
- Create advanced sequence diagrams in the solution space
- Show the creation and destruction of objects in sequence diagrams
- Understand the focus of control in a sequence diagram
- Enhance and enrich class diagrams with sequence diagrams
- Study the advantages and limitations of sequence diagrams

Interaction Modeling

This chapter presents sequence diagrams as the key mechanism to model interactions, which are real-time exchanges of messages between objects. Modeling these interactions is an important part of understanding the dynamics of a system. This is because interaction models of the UML are based on "time." The interaction diagrams form the basis of dynamic modeling as compared with the static structural models (such as class diagrams).

The two interaction models in UML are the sequence diagram and the communication diagram (also known as a collaboration diagram in the earlier versions of the UML). Sequence diagrams model the sequence of messages between collaborating objects in a system. Communication diagrams serve the same purpose as sequence diagrams but are visually different (see Figure 2.7 in Chapter 2).

About Sequence Diagrams

Sequence diagrams in analysis (problem space) model the behavior of the system from the actor's (user's) viewpoint. Thus, sequence diagrams are a good "whiteboard" technique to capture the various usage scenarios described by users.

Design-level sequence diagrams are more detailed, showing objects collaborating with each other in a given sequence. Design-level sequence diagrams also contain messages in detail, the sequence of those messages, a parameter list within messages, and the return values of the messages. The diagrams help the modelers visualize the objects and the messages that are passed between the objects. They represent a scenario or *example* in the system.

Modeling with sequence diagrams starts with objects. Since the objects are based on classes, sequence diagrams have a close nexus with class diagrams. Therefore, creating the dynamic sequence diagrams enhances and upgrades the structural class diagrams. Understanding this cross-diagram modeling and enhancement is important for successful use of UML in software engineering. The class-sequence diagram dependencies demonstrate that the UML is not an assorted collection of many diagrams; instead, there is a close dependency between many diagrams based on a metamodel.

Sequence diagrams show the behavior of objects and actors. As a result, the concept of time, as well as dependencies between objects, appears in sequence diagrams. This, in turn, enables sequence diagrams to show "what happens" in the system.

The entire dynamic modeling with sequence diagrams is, however, within a given time frame. Thus, sequence diagrams show a "snapshot" of events. They are not to be used to model end-to-end messaging (which is the purview of use case and activity diagrams).

Sequence Diagrams in Detail

Notations on a Sequence Diagram

Figure 12.1 shows the key notations of a sequence diagram. These notations include the following: actor, object, timeline, focus of control, message, self-message, return message, asynchronous message, object destruction, steps (in a sequence), and notes. Many of these notations are optional as their usage depends on the modeling space. For example, "focus of control" and "return message" may not be used in model of problem space (MOPS). However, these notations carry important meaning in the model of solution space (MOSS) and therefore are used extensively there. On the other hand, the actor (:Patient in Figure 12.1) represents a role played by a user (part of a use case). This actor is helpful in modeling a scenario from a use case in the MOPS—but not of much value in MOSS.

In Figure 12.1 is an example of an aPatient object belonging to class Patient. Sometimes the object is shown on its own in a sequence diagram—that not shown as belonging to a corresponding class. However, each object in design needs to be linked with a corresponding class. At other times, class names appear in a sequence diagram without an object, e.g., :Patient. In that case, :Patient is assumed to be an anonymous object belonging to the class Patient. Whatever the mode of expression in a sequence diagram, it still shows only instance-level objects and not classes.

The next notation in Figure 12.1 is a dashed line coming down from the object to indicate the timeline of that object. The timeline represents the sequence of messages in terms of time for that object.

Occasionally, the timeline coming down from the object is thickened. This thickening of the timeline indicates that the particular object has the "focus of control" during the message interaction. Focus of control is specifically required in design to indicate which particular object is in charge or active in a given sequence. The focus of control also indicates how long the message sent from an object is active and waiting for a response to be completed (this is clarified later in the chapter).

A message represents communication between objects. The notation for a message on the sequence diagram is shown on the right-hand side in Figure 12.1. Messages in a sequence diagram

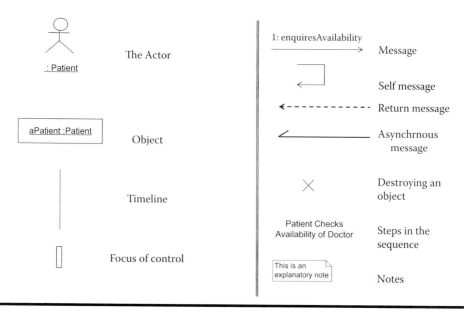

Figure 12.1 Notations of a sequence diagram.

go from one object timeline to another. This message flow results in a call to the method on the receiving object. Messages are usually shown going left to right. Occasionally messages can also go from right to left—depending on which method is activated in a class. Note that the object receiving the message to act has the arrowhead of the message.

While messages are usually sent from one object timeline to another, they may also be sent by an object to itself. In that case, a self-message notation, as shown next in Figure 12.1, is used.

Figure 12.1 next shows a return message, represented by a dashed arrow, to indicate that the response to a message is provided. This response complements the original message. Pairing a message and its return message is usually modeled in the solution space.

Asynchronous messages indicate the sending object does not have to wait for the response from the receiving object before proceeding with the next message in the sequence. A half arrowhead shows an asynchronous message (Figure 12.1).

A normal message arrow is used to show creation of object. But there is occasionally a need to show the destruction (deletion) of objects. This is shown by an "X" (Figure 12.1) at the end of the timeline of the object being deleted. This notation indicates the object is removed from the memory.

Documentation related to messages can be provided on the left-hand side (sidebar) of the sequence diagram (labeled "steps" in Figure 12.1) and notes used liberally in sequence diagrams to provide explanations.

The Sequence diagrams tend to be technical and far more detailed in design. For example, the format of a message in a sequence diagram in design is as follows:

sequence-number sequence-iteration: message(arguments): return-value

A message in a sequence diagram corresponding to the preceding format will be as follows:
`1: getSchedule(DoctorID, Schedule): void`
Alternatively, a schedule can be returned by a message as follows:
`1: getSchedule(DoctorID): Schedule`

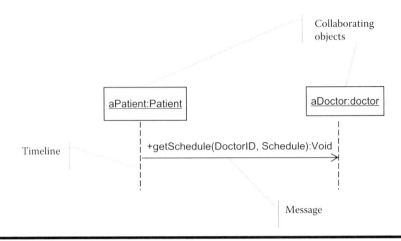

Figure 12.2   Basics of a sequence diagram.

Creating a Basic Sequence Diagram

Figure 12.2 shows the very basics of a sequence diagram. These are:

- Collaborating objects—these objects send and receive messages that result in achieving a particular system behavior. The two collaborating objects shown here are `aPatient:Patient` and `aDoctor:Doctor`.
- The message is shown as being sent by the `aPatient` to the `aDoctor` object—and the message is `+getSchedule(DoctorID, Schedule):Void`. This message, sent by `aPatient`, also has a parameter list that includes the `DoctorID`, and the `Schedule` is received by the `aPatient` object from the `aDoctor`.
- The timeline indicates the progress of time in the interactions between the objects and, therefore, the sequence in which the messages are sent and received by the collaborating objects.

Relating Sequence Diagrams to Class Diagrams

Sequence diagrams are not drawn in isolation. Sequence diagrams update and enrich the class diagrams drawn earlier in the design process. There is an interdependency between class and sequence diagrams. Each diagram adds value to the other diagram. It is therefore essential to understand this close mapping between the two diagrams.

The fundamentals of this mapping of sequence diagram to class diagram are demonstrated in Figure 12.3. In Figure 12.3a, a part of the sequence diagram is shown with an object `aPatient:Patient`. The class corresponding to this object is shown on the right-hand side of the diagram: class `Patient`. Thus, for a sequence diagram to be semantically meaningful, it is essential to map the objects in that sequence diagram to the corresponding classes in the class diagram. Most UML modeling tools would facilitate this mapping by displaying a list of classes corresponding to an object in a sequence diagram and offering the designer a choice of classes to select. If a class corresponding to the object created in the sequence diagram does not exist, then the modeling tool facilitates creation of that class.

Thus, a sequence diagram also becomes a mechanism to identify missing classes. There can be multiple sequence diagrams corresponding to a class diagram. This is because sequence diagrams

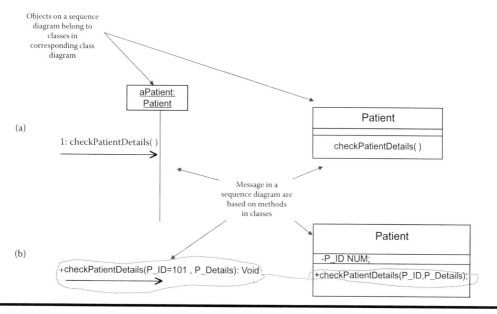

Figure 12.3   Relating sequence diagrams to class diagrams.

only visualize one particular sequence (a snapshot), whereas class diagrams show the classes that handle all possible sequences.

Figure 12.3b also shows a message received by the `aPatient` object as follows:

$$+checkPatientDetails(P\_ID=101 \, , \, P\_Details): Void$$

The method corresponding to the preceding message is also shown in the class on the right-hand side of Figure 12.3b. This mapping indicates that the messages shown in the sequence diagram need a corresponding method in the class diagram. Furthermore, since the object receiving the message (`aPatient`) should be capable of understanding the message, there is a need to have the corresponding method in the class corresponding to the object [i.e., Patient class must have a `checkPatientDetails()` method designed and coded in it].

Thus, a message (appearing in sequence diagrams) can be considered an instance of a method (appearing in class diagrams). Despite the closeness of the mapping between the two diagrams discussed here, sequence diagrams do not have a one-to-one relationship with class diagrams or use cases. One sequence diagram is likely to cut across many class diagrams. And many sequence diagrams may update a class diagram.

Advancing Sequence Diagrams from Analysis to Design

During analysis, a sequence diagram can be used to represent the interactions documented in the use case. Therefore, the initial sequence diagrams in analysis may be drawn with only two objects: the actor and the system, as shown in Figure 12.4a. Any additional objects during analysis are permitted in a sequence diagram but are not mandatory. Such a sequence diagram represents the "actor – system" interaction format used in documenting use cases.

Figure 12.4b shows how design-level sequence diagrams cannot have a system as an object receiving the message. Instead, it is necessary to specify "which part of the system" is responsible for

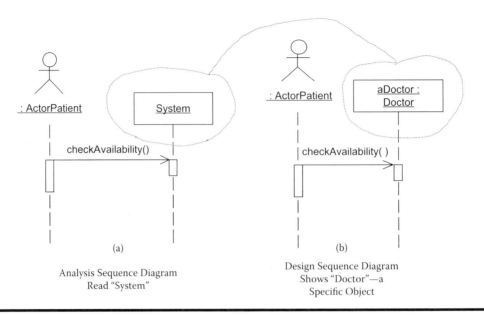

(a)

Analysis Sequence Diagram
Read "System"

(b)

Design Sequence Diagram
Shows "Doctor"—a
Specific Object

Figure 12.4 Advancing the sequence diagrams from analysis to design: (a) Analysis level Sequence Diagram shows the entire System as an object; (b) design level sequence diagram specifies an object within the System—in this case aDoctor:Doctor.

receiving and then sending messages—shown by `aDoctor:Doctor` in Figure 12.4. Note that it need not be just a single `aDoctor` object receiving the message—there can be a collaboration of objects receiving messages, processing and sending them back, as part of a detailed sequence.

Understanding Focus of Control and Return Message

Figure 12.5 shows an important aspect of sequence diagrams that is specific in the solution space. Here, the Patient object is shown sending a message—`getSchedule()`—to the Doctor object. However, the timeline underneath the Patient object is thickened after that message. This means that the `aPatient` object is now "in control" of the interactions.

The second message sent by the `aPatient` object is `getAvailable()`. Despite this second message being sent by `aPatient`, the control still remains with `aPatient`. This means that the system will wait for `aPatient` to complete its sequence of messages and relinquish its control before messages from other objects can be sent or received.

The second message, `getAvailable()`, is also paired with its response—`availability`—shown by the dotted returning arrow. This is the return message arrow. It is not mandatory to have this return shown because in most cases the message itself implies a return value inside. Also, when there is a focus of control on the timeline, it is implied that the focus remains until the calling object has received a meaningful return value.

For example, in the case of the sequence diagram in Figure 12.5, the `getSchedule()` message has many other messages in the system that help produce the required outcome for `getSchedule()`. One example of such messages is the `getAvailable()` message. At the end of all these messages, `getSchedule()` receives a meaningful answer—either in its list of parameters or in the return value in its signature. It is only after the completion of the entire sequence of messages that the focus of control on the `aPatient` object is released, and the timeline returns to normal.

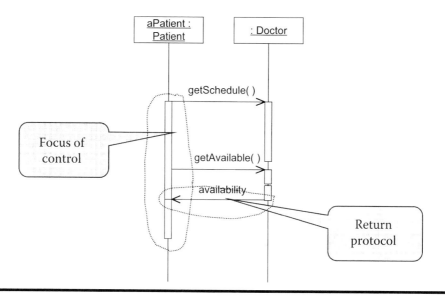

Figure 12.5   Understanding focus of control and return message.

Creating and Destroying an Object

Figure 12.6 demonstrates the modeling of two other important functions in a sequence diagram in design—the creation and destruction of an object. In Figure 12.6, the creation of an object is shown by the message arrows pointing directly to the object (as against the timeline of the object). The message arrow pointing to the object implies that the object's timeline has started—in other words, the object has come into being in the system at that point in time (the object is created). Another example of object creation (a constructor in C++) is shown when :PatientForm creates aPatient. In this second example of the constructor, the object that creates aPatient is also shown; it is the boundary object :PatientForm.

The other important notation demonstrated in Figure 12.6 is the destructor. This is the "X" shown at the end of the timeline for both the aPatient object and the :PatientForm object. The destructor is indicating the deletion of the object from the memory. It is important to delete objects during system execution because otherwise objects left in the system without purpose could continue to use up memory and potentially corrupt the system.

Sequence Diagrams in Hospital Management System

Sequence Diagrams in the Problem Space

This section shows four sequence diagrams. These sequence diagrams model a snapshot of the requirements. Therefore, these sequence diagrams add value in the problem space.

The sequence diagram corresponding to the "RegistersPatient" use case is shown in Figure 12.7. In this sequence diagram, the :ActorPatient announces his arrival to the administrator. This message (interaction) is between the two actors—ActorPatient and Administrator. This interaction is happening outside the system as the message is not send to an object within the system. The patient provides details (identification and insurance). These details are provided to the System using an interface by the Administrator.

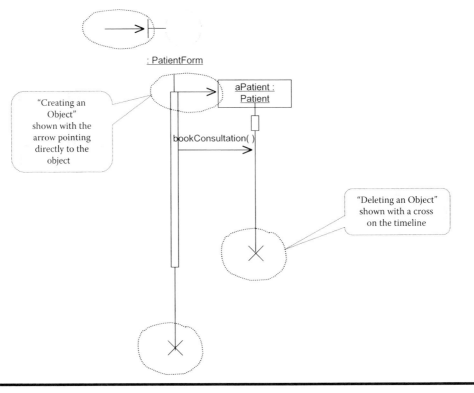

Figure 12.6   Creating and destroying an object.

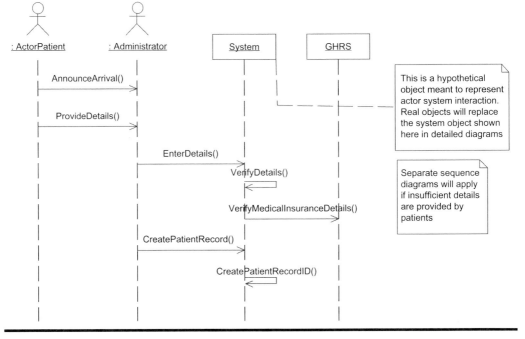

Figure 12.7   "Registering a Patient" sequence diagram.

The class System exists only in this problem space analysis-level sequence diagram. In solution design, there is no system class and, hence, no corresponding object. In design, however, many objects belonging to specific classes will replace the system.

This System object (hypothetical) sends a message to the system (itself) to validate and verify the patient details. Additional verifications are also carried out by the GHRS(Governm entHealthRegulationSystem) class, via an interface, for the medical insurance details. On verification and validation of patient details, another self-message is sent by the system to CreatePatientRecordID(). Subsequently, a PatientRecordID is generated by the system, which provides a basis for all communications with the patient.

Figure 12.8 shows the Updating a Calendar sequence initiated by the Staff actor through aInterface object by sending a message ShowCalendar(). The aInterface object, in turn, sends a message out to the Calendar object and retrieves the details of the calendar. The actor Staff then enters his preferred roster details using the aInterface object. A validation check is send to the Calendar object. This process starts two self-messages: ValidateRosterDetails() and UpdateCalendar(). On completion of all validations, the actor Staff accepts the roster details.

Figure 12.9 shows the Booking a Consultation sequence diagram. The actor Patient starts the sequence of messages by SpecifyInitialConsultationDetails() message, which is sent to the aInterface object. This message results in a list of physicians provided by the Physician object to the actor Patient via the aInterface. The patient makes a choice of physician from the list provided. The Calendar object then provides a list of available dates and times for the selected physician. The patient then makes a choice of date and time, and a message is sent to the Calendar object to update the calendar. The actor Patient confirms his booking.

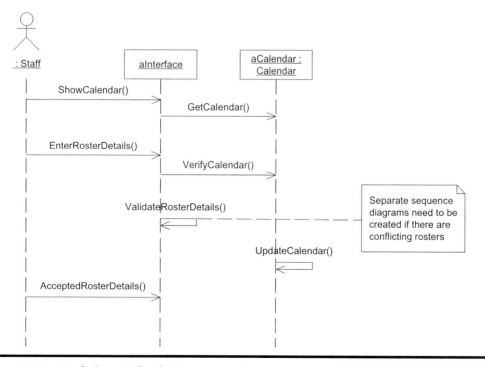

Figure 12.8 "Updating a Calendar" sequence diagram.

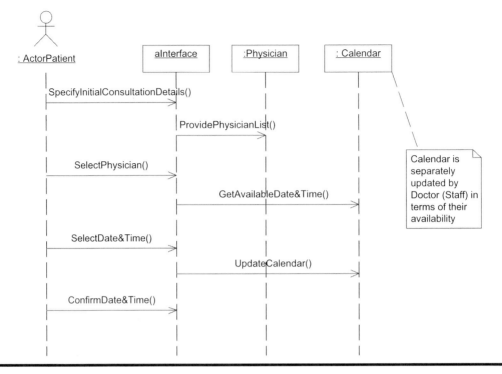

Figure 12.9 Sequence diagram for "Booking a Consultation."

Figure 12.10 shows the Paying a Bill sequence diagram. The actor Patient initiates the sequence of events by requesting the display of the payment details. On receiving a reply from BPay the actor Patient verifies the BPay statement. The patient then proceeds to make payment for the payment statement received. This event sends out a message from the BPay object to the Bill object to update the record for the corresponding billing reference number. The Bill object generates a receipt for the amount paid. The BPay object confirms the receipt with the actor Patient.

Design-Level Sequence Diagrams in the Solution Space

Figure 12.11 shows an advanced sequence diagram drawn in the solution space. This diagram is drawn by designers to model the detailed interactions between various *types* of objects, represented by various stereotypes (Chapter 10). Figure 12.11 shows <<boundary>> and <<table>> classes in addition to the <<entity>> classes (note that the term class used here implies objects belonging to the class). Each of these stereotypes are shown with corresponding icons in Figure 12.11.

In Figure 12.11, the :PatientForm boundary object sends a message bookConsultation() to aPatient:Patient. In order to book the consultation, the aPatient object sends a message to the :Doctor object called getSchedule(). While the parameters on getSchedule(DoctorID, Schedule*) are not shown in the diagram, they are passed by aPatient to :Doctor. :Doctor, in turn, sends a message getDoctorRoster() to the <<table>> object called :DoctorTable. :Doctor then also sends a message getPatient-Record() to :PatientTable. Once these details have been retrieved from the table object by the :Doctor object, the aPatient object sends another message to :Doctor to get the

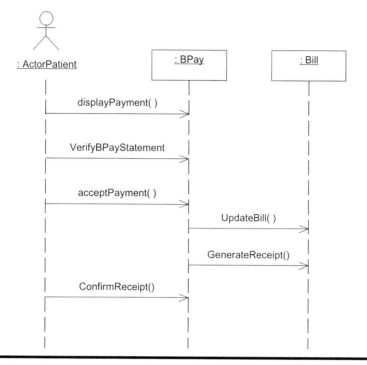

Figure 12.10 **"Paying a Bill" sequence diagram.**

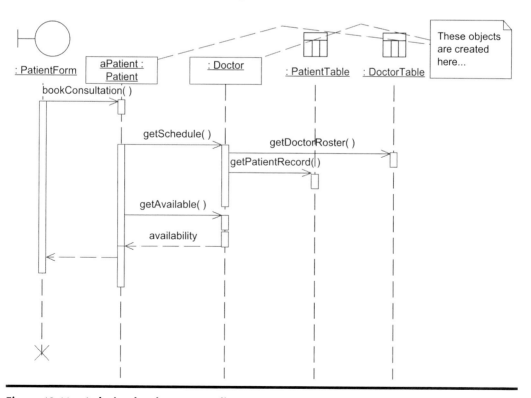

Figure 12.11 **A design-level sequence diagram.**

availability of the doctor—getAvailable(). In the case of this message, a return message indicating availability is also shown in the diagram. The :PatientForm is then deleted from the memory.

Registering a Patient Sequence Diagram in Design

Figure 12.12 describes the sequence of events for registering a patient. Upon receiving a request to register a new patient, the <<control>> object :TransactionManager creates a <<boundary>> object :PatientRegistrationInterface through the message Display(). The details of the new patient are entered into this form and saved, which sends a message to :TransactionManager, which creates a new instance of a patient object from the patient class with the message updatePatient(). :TransactionManager further sends a message to the <<control>> object :DatabaseManager, which requests getPatientDetails() from the patient object and then saves the details in the :PatientTable through the message savePatientRecord(). Once this sequence is complete, the objects :PatientRegistrationInterface, :Patient, and :PatientTable are destroyed. Note that "destruction" of an object only implies its removal from the memory during execution. The "X" in the sequence diagram does not mean a complete erasure of the object from the storage facility (database) of the system.

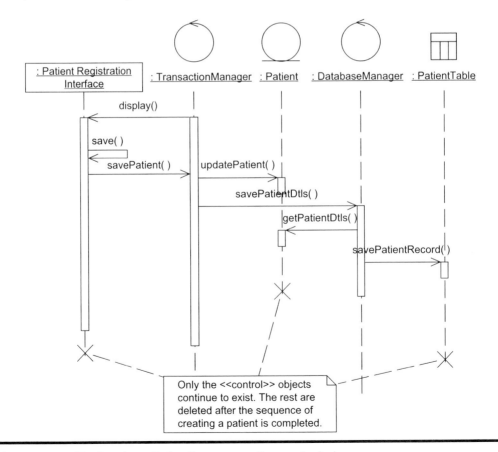

Figure 12.12   "Registering a Patient" sequence diagram in design.

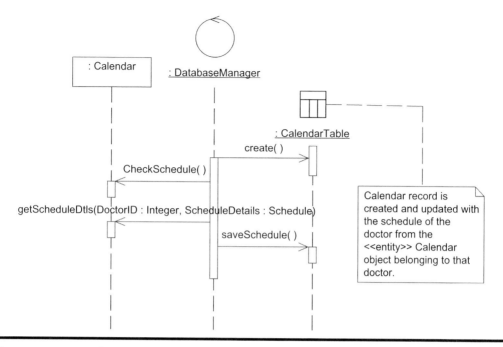

Figure 12.13 **"Updating a Calendar" sequence diagram in design.**

Updating a Calendar Sequence Diagram in Design

In Figure 12.13 the sequence for updating a calendar is detailed. The <<control>> object :DatabaseManager first creates :CalendarTable by sending a message create() to it. :DatabaseManager sends a second message checkSchedule() to :Calendar <<entity>> object. If the schedule is found to be the right one (e.g., for the right doctor), then a second message getScheduleDtls(), with the necessary parameters, is sent to :Calendar. The schedule is saved in :CalendarTable by the message from :DatabaseManager saveSchedule().

"Changing Booking Times" Sequence Diagram in Design

Figure 12.14 describes the sequence of events for changing a booking time for a consultation. The details of the new booking time are entered into the :ConsultationBookingForm and submitted, which sends the message changeConsultation() to the consultation <<entity>> object, aConsulation. aConsultation sends two messages from here to two booking objects: the first to 10amBooking, telling it to deleteBooking() (destroy itself), and the second to 4pmBooking to createBooking(). Once this is done, aConsultation sends a self-message to update the consultation booking.

"Paying a Bill" Sequence Diagram in Design

In Figure 12.15, the sequence for paying a bill is described. First, the <<control>> object :PaymentManager creates the <<boundary>> object :PaymentForm through the message createPaymentForm(). :PaymentManager then populates the form by getting the appropriate details from :Patient and sends displayPaymentForm() to the form. When

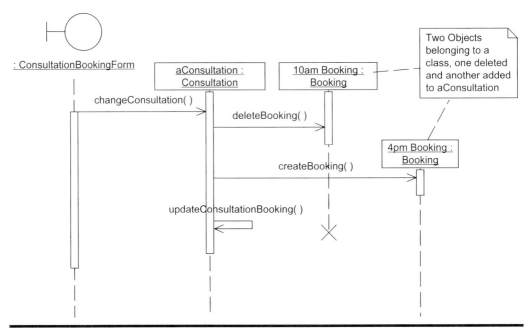

Figure 12.14 "Changing Booking Times for a Consultation" sequence diagram in design.

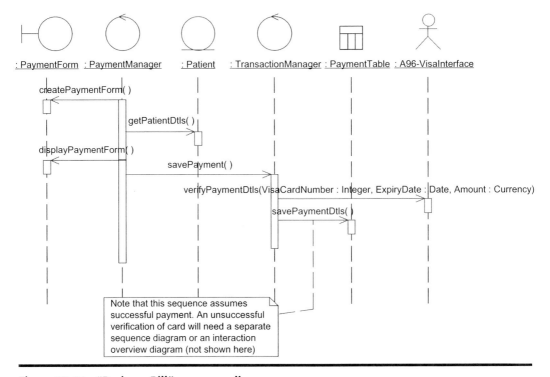

Figure 12.15 "Paying a Bill" sequence diagram.

the payment details are submitted in this form, `:PaymentManager` sends a `savePayment()` message to `:TransactionManager`, which interfaces with the external actor `:A96-VisaInterface` in order to verify the credit card transaction. Since this sequence only describes a successful payment, the next message is sent by `:TransactionManager` to save the payment details in the `:PaymentTable` <<table>> object.

COMMUNICATION DIAGRAMS

The communication diagram also shows objects, their interactions and links to each other. The information in a communication diagram is similar to the information displayed in a sequence diagram. Hence, they are only briefly alluded to here. Experimentation with communication diagrams should be done after sequence diagrams have been created. In some modeling tools, a sequence diagram can be converted into a communication diagram by pressing of a button. This demonstrates the closeness of these two UML diagrams. Hence, communication diagrams are not discussed any further in this book.

Strengths and Weaknesses of Sequence Diagrams

What follows are the strengths of a sequence diagram in modeling:

1. Sequence diagrams can pictorially show what a user describes as "an example." They provide a mechanism to build storyboards or scenarios from these examples. Hence, they can also be a good starting point for mobile app development.
2. Sequence diagrams show a sequence of messages passed between collaborating objects within a given time period. The sequencing information is most helpful in design as it shows preconditions.
3. They provide an ideal "snapshot" of what happens in a time period in the system.
4. Sequence diagrams enable identification of missing objects, which can be added as classes in a class diagram.
5. Sequence diagrams enable identification of missing operations within a class, which can be added in a class diagram.
6. Being an "instance diagram," a sequence diagram is capable of showing multiple objects belonging to the same class in a diagram. For example, a sequence diagram can contain two or more patient objects (`aPatient` and `bPatient`) belonging to the class `Patient`. (Notice how it is not possible to show these two patient objects belonging to the same class on a class diagram.)
7. Sequence diagrams can show the same message being passed between two or more objects more than once. For example, if the `aPatient` object sends a message called `checkAvailability` to `aDoctor`, then, after a few more messages, the same message `checkAvailability` can be sent to `aDoctor` again. The ability of the sequence diagrams to display multiple objects, multiple messages, and messages passed to the same objects shows some of the dynamic strengths of the diagram.
8. Mapping between sequence diagrams and class diagrams enhances the quality of class diagrams. This is because stepping through a sequence diagram can reveal (a) missing classes and (b) missing methods within classes.
9. Methods with their signatures are a rich source of detailed design-level information to designers and programmers on how to design messages (operations).
10. Showing object destruction helps ensure object deletion during execution (and thereby reduce memory clutter).

What follows are the weaknesses of a sequence diagram in practice:

1. A sequence diagram, being a snapshot between two timeframes, is in a way an "incomplete" diagram. It is not meant to show a complete process or flow, as is documented within a use case or an activity diagram, from start to stop. Therefore, such diagrams cannot (and should not) be used for complete process documentation.
2. It is difficult to show an "if-then-else" or a "for-next" condition in sequence diagrams. Therefore, a sequence diagram should not be used to depict such scenarios.
3. A sequence diagram is able to represent only a single flow or thread within a process. Multiple threads require multiple sequence diagrams for appropriate modeling. However, there is no relationship *between* two sequence diagrams. This weakness of sequence diagrams is overcome by interaction overview diagrams, which can show multiple threads as well as "if-then-else" scenarios encompassing many sequence diagrams.
4. Attempting to complete an entire sequence in a sequence diagram can lead to an unwieldy and confusing sequence diagram. Only an appropriate (important and/or complex) subset of a detailed sequence should be modeled per sequence diagram.
5. The number of sequence diagrams required in a given design is not clearly known. It depends on the experience of the designer as to when to stop developing them. Theoretically numerous sequence diagrams can be drawn within a given design.
6. The way in which system designers use these diagrams (technical level) is different from the way business analysts use them (business process level). Inappropriate type of usage of these diagrams can be counter productive in practice.

Common Errors in Interaction Modeling with Sequence Diagrams and How to Rectify Them

Common Errors	*Rectifying the Errors*	*Examples*
Not mapping object in a sequence diagram to a class in a class diagram	Ensure each object in the sequence diagram has a corresponding class in the class diagram—when the design is complete.	`aPatient` in sequence diagram should belong to `patient` in class diagram.
Not mapping a message in a sequence diagram to a method in a class	Ensure that a method in the sequence diagram has a corresponding message (operation function) in the class diagram.	`+enquiresavailability()` message in a sequence diagram should correspond to the same method in a class (`Doctor` in this case) in the class diagram.
Pointing the message arrow to a sending object (and not receiving object)	The message arrowhead points to the object that has to take action—and not the object making the request.	If `aPatient` object is checking the availability of `aDoctor`, then the arrowhead on the message `+enquireavailability()` will point to `Doctor` and not `aPatient`.

Common Errors	Rectifying the Errors	Examples
Using message arrow to indicate return message	Forward-moving message arrow is thick and return arrow is dashed.	Figure 12.5 shows the return protocol (or return value of a message—availability in this case) with a dashed arrow; this availability is not a fresh message but a value returned to the calling object; this returning value should not be shown with a thick (normal) arrow but, rather, with a dashed arrow.
Attempting to show if-then-else scenario	Sequence diagrams are snapshots in time. They cannot show conditions.	All sequence diagrams in this chapter have no if-then-else Figure 12.1 showing the major notations of a sequence diagram also has no provision for a condition to be shown in this diagram.
Not understanding focus of control	Ensure focus of control is used only when a message continues to remain in focus (in control) for a period of time and for a suite of subsequent messages.	Figure 12.5 shows the focus of control. This focus of control starts with the getSchedule() message and remains beyond the return value of availability. This model indicates that the messages in a group are all together and maintain control of the system till that group is executed.
Not understanding object destruction in memory	Objects need to be properly removed from the memory; otherwise, they will keep accruing "garbage" with every execution of the system.	Figure 12.6 shows the deletion (removal, destruction) of aPatient from the main memory at the end of execution of that suite of messages. This is shown by an "X" at the end of the timeline for aPatient. Note how :PatientForm is deleted after the aPatient has been deleted from the memory.

Discussion Questions

1. Explain the characteristics of "interactions" in interaction modeling. Further, discuss how interaction modeling is different from static, structural modeling.
2. How do you think sequence diagrams was named that way
3. What are the similarities between sequence and collaboration diagrams? *(hint: visit the review of all UML diagrams in Chapter 2)*
4. Why are sequence diagrams "incomplete"?

5. Sequence diagrams can show "multiple threads" of execution—true or false? Elaborate your answer.
6. Why is it important to show the creation and destruction of objects? What will happen if an object is not formally destroyed at the end of a sequence?
7. What is a focus of control in a sequence diagram?
8. How does "self-messaging" work in a sequence diagram? Discuss with example.
9. What is a "return message" in a sequence diagram? How is it shown? Your answer must include the pairing of messages in a sequence diagram.
10. Consider a `messageXYZ()` sent by `ObjectA` to `ObjectB`. Which of the two objects will have the code to execute the `messageXYZ()`? Why?
11. What are the strengths of sequence diagrams? Explain specific scenarios?
12. How can sequence diagrams enrich class diagrams? What are the potential problems with doing so?
13. Demonstrate with an example how an object in a sequence diagram maps to a class in a class diagram.
14. Demonstrate with an example how a message in a sequence diagram maps to a method (operation) in a class diagram.

Team Project Case Study

1. Draw a sequence diagram in the problem space corresponding to a use case within a package of your case study. Ensure you have included one actor and three to five objects in your sequence diagram. Give your sequence diagram a sensible name.
2. Repeat the preceding item for a use case from each of the other packages within the model.
3. Further ensure that your objects in the sequence diagram are linked to their corresponding classes drawn in the class diagram. If suitable classes don't exist in the class diagram, add them to the class diagrams (this is an exercise in identifying missing classes through sequence diagrams).
4. Also ensure that the messages in your sequence diagrams are NOT typed up but, rather, are based on corresponding methods in the classes. This is an exercise in identifying missing methods in classes.
5. Ensure a self-message appears in a sequence diagram.
6. Add relevant notes and text to the sequence diagrams.
7. Draw ONE *additional* detailed design-level sequence diagram within EACH package for your system.
8. Each sequence diagram has 7 ± 2 objects in it; ensure the diagram has all the important design-level objects such as entity, user interface or boundary, controller, and database tables. Some of these design-level objects will get further clarified when their corresponding classes are discussed later in Chapter 13 (database classes) and Chapter 16 (GUI classes). Therefore, be prepared to return to these sequence diagrams and update them with all the different types of classes required in design.
9. Each sequence diagram can typically contain 6–10 messages. Ensure your sequence diagrams have sufficient messages to clearly and successfully carry out a "sequence" of events.
10. Demonstrate clearly in your design-level sequence diagrams your understanding of "focus of control." You may do this by providing documentation for an operation that has focus on control in the diagram.

11. Add explanatory Notes to your design-level sequence diagrams to clarify the diagrams further.
12. As discussed earlier, when you draw sequence diagrams, the corresponding class diagrams get updated. It is natural that in the process of drawing sequence diagrams, you will discover (a) additional methods and (b) additional classes. The updates are in terms of their attributes and operation signatures, as well as the discovery of new classes. Ensure that your corresponding class diagrams have been updated.

Chapter 13

Database Modeling with Class and Sequence Diagrams

Learning Objectives

- Understand and incorporate database persistence in software solutions
- Study the differences between relational and object-oriented databases
- Map class diagrams to relational data storage structures
- Map class relationships to databases
- Incorporate multiplicities of the association relationship in database designs
- Use sequence diagrams to model database updates and retrievals

Introduction to Persistence

This chapter discusses persistence in software engineering. Persistence deals with the continued existence of an object beyond a single execution of the system. Objects in the memory of a computer are transient—they exist only during the execution of a system. Persistence enables the storage of objects at the end of the execution cycle and subsequent retrieval when a fresh instance of system execution begins.

Further, note that only objects are persistent, not classes. While UML literature tends to use the terms "object persistence" and "persistent classes" interchangeably, both terms mean persistence of objects and not that of classes. Persistence requires careful considerations in designing databases and incorporating them in software solutions. Two popular storage mechanisms—relational and object-oriented databases—are considered in this chapter.

The object-oriented classes in design need to map to the relational storage structures that are non-object-oriented in nature. The traditional, procedural approach kept data and processes separate. Therefore, in a procedural approach storage implied storing and retrieval of only the data. Persistence in object-oriented approaches implies storing of data, functions, and relationships because object-oriented designs encapsulate data (objects) and functions together. Relational storage technologies are not amenable to storing objects together with their functions. Mapping an object-oriented system to relational tables is one of the interesting challenges of software persistence design—forming part of the discussion in this chapter.

STEREOTYPES FOR PERSISTENCE

Most <<entity>> stereotyped objects have a need to exist even after the system is shut down—so as to be available for use next time around. This is persistence. Making <<entity>> classes directly persistent does not lead to a flexible design. Therefore, the onus of persistence is assigned to another category of classes that are stereotyped as <<table>>. <<table>> classes and their mapping to the <<entity>> classes is of significant interest in this discussion.

While a persistent object exists beyond the execution of the system, a transient object vanishes when the system is shut down and is recreated when the system is executed again. Most <<boundary>> and <<control>> objects are transient, and there is no need to save these types of objects.

Persistence Mechanisms—Databases

Data Storage Mechanisms

Persistence can take various shapes and forms. What follows are some techniques for making objects persistent:

- Storing in a simple flat file. Such storage can contain the data that are used by the system but is not intelligent and does not offer a way to search within the data.
- Storing in an indexed sequence access mechanism file or database that organizes data through indexes that can be used for searching specific data records and updating them.
- Storing in a relational database, which is most appropriate for business data that can be easily formatted into rows and columns, thereby lending themselves to search.
- Storing in an object-oriented database, which are more appropriate for unformatted or scientific information.
- Storing in a NoSQL database, which can handle large, unstructured documents and machine data that can also be optionally searched.

Saving and retrieving data is as challenging as the intricacies of business logic. Database design is a complex task requiring specialist database design skills. System engineers appreciate how classes map to relational structures in database designs.

Object-Oriented Databases

Object-oriented databases are based on the object-oriented fundamentals and concepts discussed in Chapter 1. Being object-oriented in nature, object-oriented databases are able to store objects together with their attribute values, operations, and relationships. With object-oriented databases the object structures in the memory during execution can be directly stored "as is" in the database. Binary large objects (BLOBs) and complex unstructured data (e.g., video and audio) can also be stored in these databases without the need for conversion to any other format.

In addition to the data, object-oriented databases also store relationships like inheritance, association, and aggregation directly in the database. The mapping of persistent objects to an object-oriented database is simple (compared to a relational database) because the underlying fundamentals of the software application and the corresponding storage mechanism are the same.

This ability of object-oriented databases to directly store objects "as they are" is helpful in designing software systems based on object-oriented fundamentals. This is because BLOBs (especially complex objects like audio and map BLOBs) do not conform to the format of "rows and columns" as used in relational databases. As a result, objects need to be stored as they are and not "decomposed" into rows and columns (discussed later).

Storing objects in object-oriented databases is easy and flexible. The flexibility of storing objects in object-oriented databases is important. Consider, for example, a simple hierarchy of Patient inheriting from Person. There is a need to store a Patient object in the object-oriented database, and later the same Person object has the Patient attributes attached to it, making it a Patient object.

Thus, in object-oriented designs, different objects may be instantiated based on different parts of an inheritance hierarchy. This required extensibility of objects, depending on the class definitions, is handled relatively easily by object-oriented databases compared with relational databases. Object-oriented databases also support encapsulation, which helps hide the data and implementation from external entities. They also support the concept of object IDs, which uniquely identify an object.

NoSQL Database

There are two unique aspects of NoSQL: first, it does not follow the traditional row-column format of a structured query language (SQL), (relational) database but is able to handle unstructured data. Second, the underlying technology enables large-scale data handling. Combined with the large volume and velocity, NoSQL databases handle a highly complicated and federated database structure that spans organizational boundaries and usually resides in the Cloud. The federated database structure of NoSQL databases is also understood as a distributed database architecture.

The ability of NoSQL databases to accommodate a lack of data structure creates opportunities for business processes to make use of unstructured data "as is." Since the business reality (external to the software system) does not have a schema, the natural representation of that reality within NoSQL databases makes it possible to generate new and unique insights. For example, a NosQL database (e.g., MongoDB) can store an unstructured email or feedback on a social media site and enable its analysis to generate insights. Ample storage space, distributed architecture, and high processing power Hadoop distributed file systems (HDFSs) make this possible.

For example, in a NoSQL database, the customer-account relationship is not just an association relationship. The account is a collection (aggregate) of the many accounts belonging to a customer. Thus, an array of accounts is embedded within each customer. This NoSQL storage is not amenable to rows and columns. The structure of each instance of the aggregate can change. This change is easily reflected in the NoSQL storage mechanism (as compared with the nonintuitive row-column structure).

Relational Databases

In spite of the potential advantages of object-oriented and NoSQL databases for object-oriented designs, most commercial business applications still use relational databases. The storage and retrieval of data in these relational databases is done by means of SQL. Relational databases provide ideal and mature mechanisms to store, retrieve, and manage data that are structured and can be placed in rows and columns. Relational technologies have proved reliable in most commercial business settings.

Although relational databases offer several advantages, some issues accompany their use. As mentioned earlier, data stored in tables are structurally different from objects. This requires "translation" of classes to tables, which are conceptually and structurally different. The capability of storing data and behavior in a class cannot be directly transferred to a table because relational tables can only store data. The mechanism to handle class relationships is also fundamentally different. Additionally, mapping of inheritance hierarchies is not straightforward. These factors make the mapping of object-oriented designs to relational structures a difficult task.

The maturity and availability of relational technology and their prevalent use in most commercial organizations means object-oriented software designs still have to interface with backend relational applications. In such cases, where backend relational technology is employed, objects are split ("decomposed") and stored as rows in tables.

Most UML-based modeling tools enable the architect to mark the classes as persistent, either by using the stereotype facility or as additional information in the class specifications. These persistent classes can then be used by the UML modeling tools to create an initial relational database schema from the class diagrams. Conceptually, a class without its operations is a relational table. Hence, a class diagram with <<table>> classes does the work of the entities in an entity relationship (E-R) diagram.

Modeling tools can automate the mapping of classes to tables. Despite this automation, it is essential for a designer to understand the entire mapping process and limitations of interfacing these two different object-oriented and relational technologies.

The following section details various aspects of mapping objects to relational databases and discusses various alternatives.

Using Relational Databases in Object-Oriented Designs

As mentioned previously, most business systems use a backend relational database. If the software system is designed using OO principles, but the database used for persistence is relational, there is a need to map an object-oriented design to the relational database. This mapping is discussed in the following sections.

Challenge of Storing Objects in Relational Tables

An object, as part of a system that is executing, is a single coherent entity. Storing objects as rows within a table requires a certain "translation," and therefore, there is conflict involved in storing objects as rows. Figure 13.1 shows objects called `Car1` and `Car2`. At the bottom of Figure 13.1 are the various tables that can be used to store the Car objects. If a Car object is stored directly as an object or as a row in a single table, then there is not much translation required of the object. In practice, a Car object is unlikely to be a small object with a few attributes. Practically, a Car object is made up of numerous attributes and behaviors and requires more than one table to store the related data. The various possible tables that store parts of the Car object are shown as

`Car_Body_Table, Car_Wheel_Table, and Car_Engine_Table.`

This setup requires a mapping algorithm where the attributes of objects Car1 and Car2 are saved in the columns of the respective tables. Basically, the important attributes of the Car class

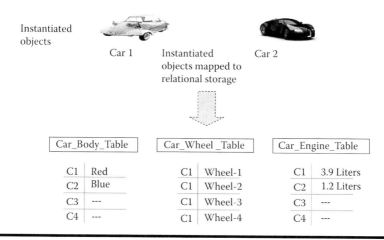

Figure 13.1   Storing objects in relational databases compromises OO principles, but it is practical.

have become a table, which helps in building a normalized relational database. The process of storing objects in a relational database is "… like having to disassemble a car each night rather than just putting it in the garage."[1]

The key challenge is that objects cannot be directly written to or read from relational databases. While the objects have data (also understood as attribute values that result in states of the objects) and behavior (again, understood as operations or methods of the classes), relational databases are only capable of storing data. The objects are connected by direct references (object IDs) while the relational database connects tables through keys. The goal of using a relational database is to normalize and reduce redundant information; the objective of objects is to model the real world, which involves a large amount of redundancy. These differences make the task of mapping difficult.

Still, the reasons for the mapping are as follows:

To start with, where a car object has many wheels, it cannot be mapped directly to a relational table but instead requires two tables that are related: one for the car itself, the other for the wheels. In another case, a wheel may represent a complex structure (a user-defined type), which then needs to be stored as a separate database table in order to store its complete structure. In the case of multiple objects, the respective Car objects (e.g., Car 1 and Car 2) are represented as rows within the corresponding tables. These rows are accessed using their keys or indexes. These keys, such as carID in the figure, are used to connect or relate the tables.

Subsequently, when the Car object is required by the system, it has to be "hand coded" by the programmer. This hand-coded module is responsible for integrating the different parts like wheel, body, and engine back to the Car object. This involves reading the tables related to car based on a common identifier (such as carID), assimilating whatever has been read from the tables, and putting it together in a Car object.

Mapping OO Classes to Relational Tables

The simplest form of mapping would be a one-to-one mapping, as shown in Figure 13.2. In this case, all the attributes of a class would be converted to the columns of a table. Each instance of the class Person (the person objects) is stored as a row in the table. For example, consider the class

- Class:

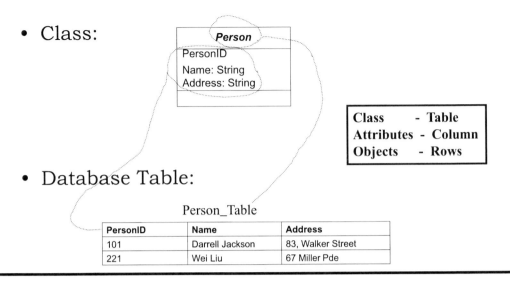

Class	- Table
Attributes	**- Column**
Objects	**- Rows**

- Database Table:

Person_Table

PersonID	Name	Address
101	Darrell Jackson	83, Walker Street
221	Wei Liu	67 Miller Pde

Figure 13.2   Mapping classes to database tables.

`Person`, which has two attributes: `Name` and `Address`. When mapping it to a table there are two columns—one for each attribute. The additional column `PersonID` in the table is created to maintain the uniqueness of each row and help create relationships between various parts of the object, as discussed later. Since relational databases use the concept of keys (primary key) to uniquely identify a row (in this case an object), there is a need to create such keys for each table so that classes can be mapped.

Basic Persistence Functions (CRUD)

There are four basic functions that enable an object to be persistent, as shown in Figure 13.3. These four functions operating on an object stored in a database are as follows:

- Create—used in creating an object
- Read—used in searching for an object (record) from storage based on a criterion (key)
- Update—used in searching and updating objects (records)
- Delete—used in locating and removing a persistent object (record)

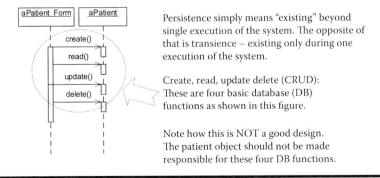

Persistence simply means "existing" beyond single execution of the system. The opposite of that is transience – existing only during one execution of the system.

Create, read, update delete (CRUD): These are four basic database (DB) functions as shown in this figure.

Note how this is NOT a good design. The patient object should not be made responsible for these four DB functions.

Figure 13.3   Understanding object persistence (storage and retrieval).

These basic persistent functions are together known as CRUD functions. Figure 13.3, which is a simple sequence diagram, shows how a <<boundary>> object—aPatientForm—performs the CRUD operations on another object belonging to the Patient class.

These four operations are not always performed in the sequence in which they are shown in Figure 13.3. In practice, they are rarely executed together in the shown sequence. Furthermore, they are also not the only operations performed on the receiving object. Instead, there are many business functions that may be intermingled with these CRUD operations.

Thus, object persistence not only needs to consider issues related to the CRUD operations, but also how the CRUD operations mix with other business operations, and why and how they can be sensibly separated. This separation of the business functions from the database-specific functions is discussed next.

Robustness in Persistence Design

Separating Persistence Operations from Business Logic

The simple sequence diagram in Figure 13.4 shows the Car object receiving messages from another object in the system: the Driver object. Both Driver and Car are <<entity>> objects that deal with the behavior of the system. Note how the Driver sends two separate "types" of messages: Drive() and Save(). The corresponding <<entity>> Car class shown in Figure 13.4 is shown with both these functions in its third compartment—making it capable of receiving both messages.

Now consider the difference between these two "types" of messages. The Drive() message deals with the business behavior of the receiving object, whereas the Save() message deals with the persistence of the receiving object. These two message types highlight one of the major issues associated in persistence design: separation of application-specific behavior from database-specific behavior.

Placement of the Save() method is a part of this issue—should the persistent class Car contain Save(), the database-specific method, or should it be moved elsewhere? In other words, should the Car class contain behavior to interface with the database (e.g., code that generates

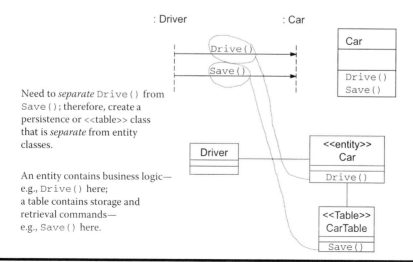

Figure 13.4   The need to separate object persistence (storage) from behavior.

SQL to do reads/writes from/to the database)? Having both these types of operations in the same class is obviously not good design as this conflicts with one of the principles of good OO design—cohesion.

A cohesive design will ensure that the two classes that are responsible for these messages are separate but related to each other: the Car class dealing with the business behavior of the system and another class responsible for the CRUD functionalities. This has been modeled in the simplified class diagram shown in Figure 13.4 with the <<entity>> Car and the <<table>> CarTable classes. The separation of the Drive() and Save() functions received by the Car object are now mapped to the two classes in Figure 13.4.

Robustness in Design Keeping Relational Storage and Objects Separate

Separating persistent functions from business functions is an important step in good persistence design. However, there is also a need to consider the additional principle of robustness in this design (discussed in greater detail in Chapter 15). Application of the principle of robustness, in the context of object persistence, is discussed here using Figure 13.5.

Figure 13.5 considers the previous example of object persistence, shown in Figure 13.4, in further detail. The process of storing an object is described in Figure 13.5 by using a sequence diagram. In this figure, the object persistence is separated from the object behavior. This separation is achieved by introducing one more class introduced between the Car and the CarTable classes: the TransactionManager class. This TransactionManager is the control class that will now be the intermediary between the Car and the CarTable classes, routing the CRUD operations. This class that provides the interface to the database is the "control" class, as described under the robustness principles. This control class appears between the objects and the corresponding relational table structure.

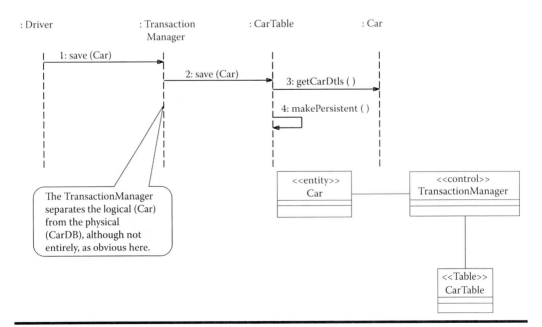

Figure 13.5   Incorporating robustness in object persistence.

This design ensures that the application will remain totally separate from the database, offering advantages in terms of flexibility, and reduced of an effect of changes in application on the database and of any changes in the database on the application. There is, however, a performance overhead because more logic has to be traversed and translations performed at runtime.

Figure 13.5 has two entity classes: Car and Driver. They, in turn, are associated with the control class TransactionManager, which provides the bridging between the entity classes (Car) and the database classes (CarTable). The CarTable would store the details of the Car in table form. Whenever there is a need for the Car class to be stored, the control class TransactionManager communicates with the CarTable class and performs the required operation. In this design, the entity class only contains the business logic and all backend logic is stored separately. Whenever there is a change in the backend, those backend classes and the control class TransactionManager need to be recoded.

Inheritance Relationship and Relational Tables

Figure 13.6 shows a typical inheritance relationship in an object-oriented design. The two classes, Patient and Doctor, inherit from the Person class. Mapping of this inheritance hierarchy to relational tables can provide several options. This is because there are multiple ways to map classes participating in an inheritance hierarchy to relational tables. These options are shown in Figure 13.7.

The easiest way is to map all the attributes from the parent class, as well as subclasses, to the columns of a single huge table. This is as shown in Figure 13.7a.

Even though it seems to be the easiest solution, various other factors should be considered that affect system performance. The problem with this option is that it can lead to wasted space and expensive operations. For example, a Doctor object is stored, and the columns that deal with the

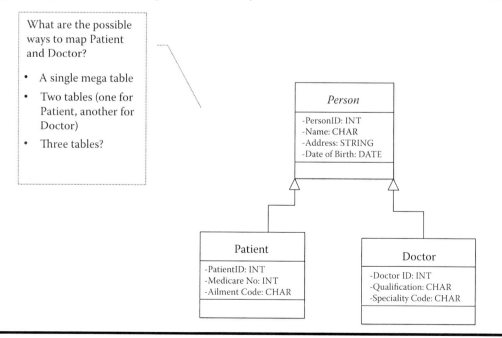

Figure 13.6 Mapping inheritance hierarchies.

13.7 a

PERSON_TABLE

PersonType	PersonID	Name	Address	MedicareNo	Ailmentcode	Qualification
P	P001	Mark	Parrramatta	13254678	PC2003	
D	D001	Bala	Strathfield			M.B.B.S
P	P020	Mariana	Campbelltown	15487962	AS5006	
D	D023	Fiona	Redfern			F.R.C.S

13.7 b

PATIENT_TABLE

PatientID	Name	Address	MedicareNo	Ailmentcode
P001	Mark	Parramatta	13254678	PC2003
P020	Mariana	Campbelltown	15487962	AS5006

DOCTOR_TABLE

DoctorID	Name	Address	Qualification
D001	Bala	Strathfield	M.B.B.S
D023	Fiona	Redfern	F.R.C.S

13.7 c

PERSON_TABLE

PersonID	Name	Address
P001	Mark	Parrramatta
D001	Bala	Strathfield
P020	Mariana	Campbelltown
D023	Fiona	Redfern

PATIENT_TABLE

PersonID	PatientID	MedicareNo	Ailmentcode
P001	IP2001	13254678	PC2003
P020	OP2003	15487962	AS5006

DOCTOR_TABLE

PersonID	DoctorID	Qualification
D001	DP3005	M.B.B.S
D023	DS2334	F.R.C.S

Figure 13.7 **(a) Single mega table design. (b) Two table design. (c) Three-table design.**

attributes specific to the Patient objects would be blank (e.g., Medicare number). Similarly, when a Patient object is stored in this particular table, it would leave the columns specific to Doctor (e.g., Qualification) blank—or NULL in relational terminology. This problem is compounded if the levels of inheritance hierarchies is deep. Furthermore, if too many classes are mapped to a single table, then there is a high traffic of objects requiring persistence operations. Such a mapping can lead to locks and conflicts with the stored objects and potential degrading of system performance.

Another design alternative would be to create tables for all the child classes and append the parent class attributes to it. This is shown in Figure 13.7b. This would get rid of NULL columns as discussed in the previous approach. For example, the hierarchy shown in Figure 13.6 could be mapped to two tables as shown in Figure 13.7b. These two tables are Patient_Table and Doctor_Table. Each of these two tables has its own attributes along with the attributes of the parent class, Person. This solution is easy to understand when there is only a one-deep inheritance hierarchy; however, it becomes more challenging for multiple levels of inheritance and multiple types of access.

The third option of mapping the inherited classes to relational tables is to create separate tables for parent as well as child classes. These tables are then linked using the primary key of the table representing the parent class, although, alternatively, keys from the child classes can be used in the parent class, which results in increased redundancy and is not a good option. A good solution is to add the primary key of the parent class to the child class. This procedure leads to the table structure shown in Figure 13.7c. Herein, the PersonID has also been added to the Patient_Table and the Doctor_Table.

Mapping Associations in Relational Tables

Consider the object-oriented design in Figure 13.8 showing an association and one aggregation relationship. When mapping such classes to relational tables, consider criteria like performance, maintainability, and consistency of the database. While retrieving data from tables there should be minimal join dependencies, and the query should minimize the data transfer to optimize performance.

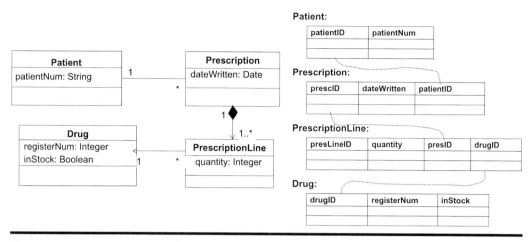

Figure 13.8   Mapping associations to tables.

While mapping such relations, the general rule followed is that the associating class is converted into a table and the attributes of the associated class are appended. To reduce the data redundancy, the class with the "many" multiplicities is taken as the associating class. This is because in relational databases, associations are implemented through a common column that is generally the key of the associated object. Further it should be emphasized that, although in the class diagram an association is bidirectional, implementing it in a relational database makes it unidirectional. This rule is kept in mind when mapping a simple association.

The `Patient` class is converted into a `Patient` table and the `Prescripion` class is converted in a `Prescription` table. The association relationship is mapped by adding the key from the Patient table to the Prescription table. Although such association mapping is straightforward, there are challenges when the multiplicities change. For instance, if the multiplicity is "many" on both sides, the mapping results in three tables instead of two. This is further explained in the next section.

Multiplicities, Association Class, and Link Table

Multiplicities play an important role in database design. Mapping an association to a database depends on the multiplicities.

Consider, for example, Figure 13.9a. This figure shows an association between `Doctor` and `Patient` classes. The business rule, based on these multiplicities, indicates that a doctor is allowed to handle 3 patients at a time but cannot handle more than 10 patients. Conversely, a patient has to have one doctor but may have up to four doctors looking after him/her. When there are many-to-many multiplicities, the challenge that faces database designers is that of placing the KEY for the relationship. Should the `PatientID` be placed in `DOCTOR_TABLE`, or `DoctorID` in `PATIENT_TABLE`? In this mapping, each class is first translated to a table in the relational database and a new table is created to map the association—the reason being that in relational databases, an association having many-to-many multiplicities cannot be directly implemented.

The association here is through an additional table and not directly implemented between the tables corresponding to the mapped classes. This new table will have the keys from both associated classes. This table is known as a link (or association) table, because the only purpose of this table is to link the other two tables.

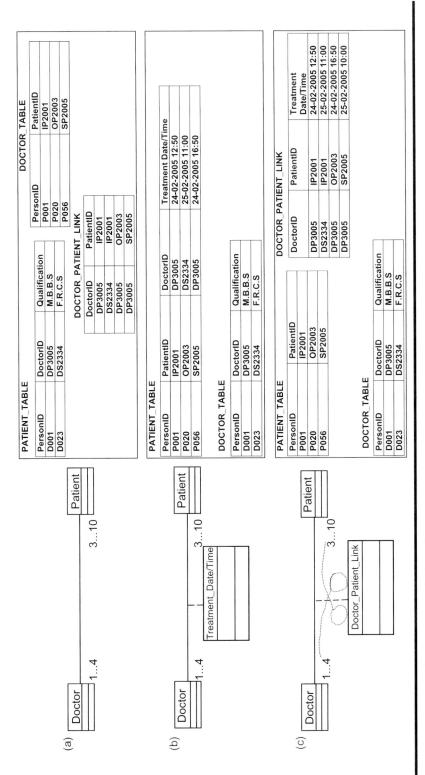

Figure 13.9 Multiplicities & association class.

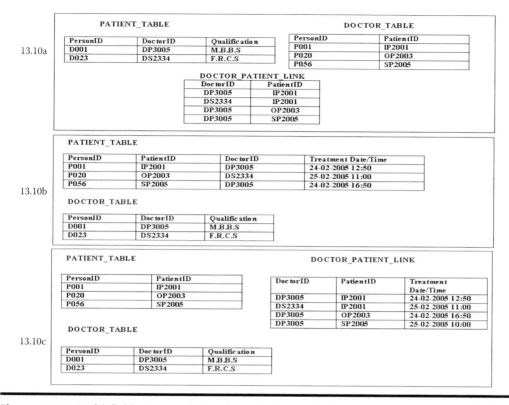

Figure 13.10 Multiplicities & association class: (a) Doctor-Patient have "many to many" relationship, (b) An attribute "Treatment_Day/Time" is used to connect the two tables and (c) the idea situation of creating a "Doctor_Patient_Link" association (or link) table between Doctor-Patient. With design (c) the multiplicities between Doctor-Patient will shift to the association table.

A similar case is the mapping of an association class. An association class, in an object-oriented design, represents a class that stores the information and behavior of an association, instead of the associated classes. Figure 13.10 shows such a class.

A doctor treats a patient and may treat 3 patients or a maximum of 10 patients. In this case an association class, such as treatment, stores the information about this treatment such as date/time. It should be noted that this information is only stored when a Doctor object is associated with a Patient object and not before this, and thus requires an association class.

Mapping an association class differs in various cases and depends on multiplicities. In Figure 13.10b, mapping will result in two tables, one for each class, with the key for Doctor appended to the table storing patients. However, the association class is not mapped to a table. Instead, the attributes date/time are appended to the Patient table. This further exhibits a limitation in relational databases storing associated objects.

This mapping will change if the multiplicities change. Consider Figure 13.10c, which shows the same association class but different multiplicities in the association. In such a scenario, the mapping will result in three tables instead of two, as many-to-many multiplicities are not directly implemented in a relational database. In this mapping, the association class is directly mapped to a table, which has keys of both Doctor and Patient along with its own attribute, TreatmentDate/Time. This is shown in the result of mapping in Figure 13.10c.

Mapping Aggregation: Composition and Shared Aggregation

An aggregation relationship (discussed in Chapter 9) includes composition (classes are composed of other classes) and shared aggregation (wherein a class is shared by many other classes).

In the case of mapping a composition relationship in object-oriented design to relational storage, there is a need to understand the object's lifetime and corresponding storage in the rows of corresponding relational tables.

To demonstrate this concern, consider Figure 13.8 again. The class diagram includes a composition between the `Prescription` class and `PrescriptionLine` class. To map this, first both classes will be mapped to individual tables. Then, as per the rule explained previously, the key of the associating class will be appended to the table corresponding to the associated class. Thus, `PrescriptionLine` will contain `PresID`, the key of `Prescription`. The only variation would be that whenever a Prescription object is destroyed, care has to be taken to destroy all the related `PrescriptionLine` objects. This is achieved through the inclusion of `PresID` in the key of `PrescriptionLine`, i.e., the primary key of `PrescriptionLine` will be a composite key of `PresLineID` and `PresID` together.

Shared Aggregation and Reference Table

The aggregated classes should be mapped to one group of tables, rather than multiple table groups spread across various physical data models. This approach to design helps in the maintainability of the system because the changes to the tables are localized to a particular group of tables.

Aggregation in design implies that the object's lifetime is dependent on the aggregating object. Therefore, whenever the aggregated object is destroyed during system execution, the corresponding rows spread across multiple tables are also deleted in order to maintain the consistency of the data model. In the case of shared aggregation, there is more than one object sharing or requiring the aggregated object. Therefore, the aggregated object that is being shared needs to exist independently.

This design concept is better illustrated in Figure 13.11. There, the Doctor class is aggregating the `SpecialityCode` class. `SpecialityCode` stores the speciality codes for Doctor and its corresponding description such as affiliation.

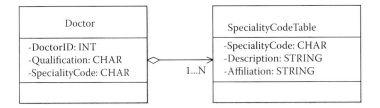

`SpecialityCodeTable` stores the speciality codes for the `Doctor` and their corresponding and detailed description, affiliation etc.
Although the speciality code "belongs" to the Doctor (and therefore, we have shown an aggregation), still the *same* speciality code can and will be used by many other doctors. Hence this is known as a "shared" aggregation. Shared aggregation appears in database design whenever there is a need to model a "reference table."

Figure 13.11 Shared aggregation (reference table).

Although the speciality code "belongs" to the doctor (and therefore, there is an aggregation), the *same* speciality code is used by many other doctors. This is known as a "shared" aggregation. Mapping this design to relational storage results in two tables, one for each class.

The access key for the Doctor table will be appended to the `SpecialityCode` table. However, the key of the `SpecialityCode` will only be `SpecCodeID`. This key will not include the key of Doctor (see composition explained in the previous section). Shared aggregation is a database design concept that helps model (among other things) a "reference table" that contains data referenced by multiple other tables.

Persistence in Practice for HMS

Persistence Design for Patient-Related Classes

Figure 13.12 shows an example of how <<table>> classes are put together to create the relational database design that stores persistent objects of a system. In the case of HMS, although many more tables will be required, a simple class diagram that enables storage of the patient's details is shown.

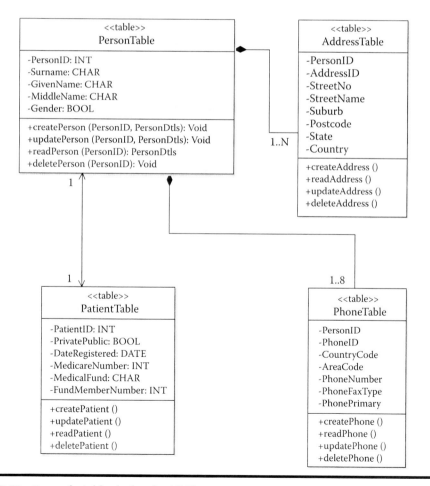

Figure 13.12   Example table design for HMS.

The PersonTable stores all objects belonging to the <<entity>> Person class. Note that this is true even if Person is an abstract class (which is the most likely case). Person will contain only the common attributes of all types of persons in the system. This is shown by the various attributes listed in the Person class. Attributes like Surname, GivenName, MiddleName, and Gender are common to all persons whether they belong to the Patient class or the Staff class. This is the application of generalization (within Inheritance). These <<table>> classes utilize the CRUD operations discussed earlier in the chapter. PersonTable is shown in an aggregation relationship with AddressTable and PhoneTable.

The one-to-many relationship between Person and these two other tables is also shown by the multiplicities in this figure. The PhoneTable is also used in storing fax numbers. Finally, the relationship between PersonTable and PatientTable is an association in this database design, versus the inheritance relationship in entity design. This is because when it comes to data storage, the inheritance relationship is meaningless and not implementable in a relational structure.

The placement of keys in the diagram is also important, as shown in Figure 13.12. In the case of one-to-many relationships, the associating class is converted into a table and the attributes of the associated class is appended. To reduce the data redundancy, the class with the "many" multiplicity is taken as the associating class. In the Figure 13.12 the AddressTable and the PhoneTable are the associating classes because they have their own "many" relationship, and the PersonTable becomes the associated table. The attribute PersonID, which is the key of the PersonTable, is appended to the AddressTable and the PhoneTable.

Additional Example of Persistence Design in HMS

Figure 13.13 provides another example of HMS implementation. The four tables presented here are PatientTable, StaffTable, BookingTable, and VacationTable. Both association and aggregation relationships appear in this diagram. The BookingTable is associated with both the PatientTable and the StaffTable. This often happens in the real world, where one entity is related to multiple entities. In such cases the BookingTable becomes the associating table and the PatientTable and the StaffTable both become the associated tables, with the keys of both the table (PatientID and StaffId) being appended to the BookingTable. The VacationTable is shown to have an aggregation relationship with the StaffTable as the existence of records in the VacationTable is very closely associated with the StaffTable. There has to be a staff record, so that the vacation can have a related record. Similarly, whenever the staff records are updated or deleted, the VacationTable also needs to be updated or deleted.

Incorporating Database Interface Pattern in HMS Persistence Design

Although the previous two database designs using the <<table>> classes are able to store and retrieve data, they can still be further improved by application of the principles of robustness discussed in Chapter 15.

Figure 13.14 shows such a database interface pattern using a sequence diagram that separates the <<boundary>> from <<entity>> and <<table>> classes using a <<control>> class. Using this <<control>> class uncouples the Patient form from the Patient table and Patient entity, ensuring that changes made to the table in the relational database do not require the modification of the Patient form.

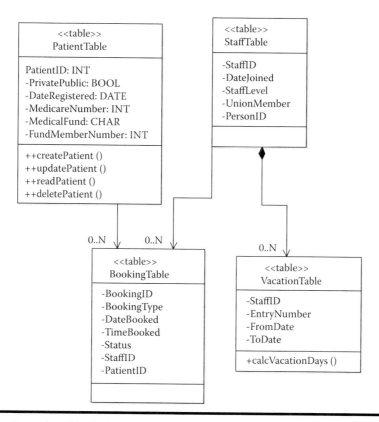

Figure 13.13   Example table design for HMS.

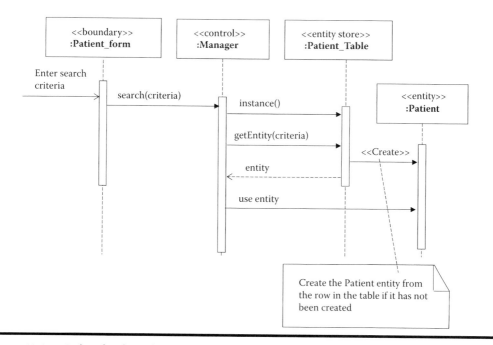

Figure 13.14   Using database interface pattern in designing persistence in HMS.

Common Errors in Interpreting Database Modeling and How to Rectify Them

Common Errors	Rectifying the Errors	Examples
Treating all objects as persistent	Only <<entity>> objects are candidates for persistence, and <<table>> objects enable that persistence to happen.	Patient needs to be stored, but PatientForm need not be stored.
Ignoring persistence till late in design	Start with the persistent design as soon as entity classes are identified.	With the identification of the Patient class in the problem space, discussions on its storage should begin immediately.
Not understanding association tables	These tables do not have any business logic in them; they are a means to relate two other tables that have a many-to-many relationship.	Many doctors can see many patients. The doctor-patient relationship is many to many. This will require an association table between the two that only stores the identifiers of doctor and patient. Such an association (or link) table will have no business logic in it.
Placing CRUD in entity classes	Use CRUD only in <<table>> classes.	Create, read, update, and delete are standard database functionalities; they are not business functions and therefore they should not appear in, say, Patient class.
Storing <<entity>> classes directly in tables.	Entity classes should contain business logic; they should then pass the data to table classes that store and manage the data.	Patient class contains business logic; PatientTable contains the data corresponding to the patient but no business logic.

Discussion Questions

1. What is persistence? How does it differ from transience in software design?
2. What are the advantages and limitations of different storage mechanisms for objects?
3. How can an object be mapped to a relational storage? Discuss with an example.
4. What is an association table? Discuss its use with examples.
5. Discuss CRUD method types with examples.
6. How is robustness applied in relational databases?

Undertake the following practical exercise:

7. Create a simple class diagram containing three classes: Vehicle, Car, and Truck. Provide TWO attributes for each of these three classes.
8. Create a rough sketch of a relational table that will store the objects belonging to the aforementioned three classes.
9. Ensure you have tried all three options—single table, two tables, and three tables—in your database design.
10. Enter TWO objects PER table, corresponding to the classes.
11. Try and read the two-table design to recreate a Car object.
12. Repeat the preceding step to recreate a Truck object.
13. Create a simple association relationship in a separate class diagram showing Driver and Car.
14. Apply a multiplicity of 1 on the driver side and N on the Car side.
15. Add/modify your table designs to handle storing of TWO objects belonging to Car and TWO belonging to Driver.
16. Now, modify the multiplicity on the Driver side to N. This makes it a many-to-many multiplicity.
17. Modify your table designs to handle this multiplicity and show where and how the KEYS or IDs will have to be placed.
18. Create a class diagram corresponding to the tables you have designed. Stereotype all classes on that class diagram as <<table>>.

Team Project Case Study

1. Identify classes in HMS that need to be stored in a relational database (DB). You will find that for some <<entity>> classes there is a need to create the corresponding DB/Table classes, and stereotype them appropriately.
2. You are expected to create AT LEAST FOUR <<table>> classes per package, although more may be possible and required by your design. Your tables (database classes) should be sufficient to store all your entity classes. (*Hint: the entity to table classes are not one-to-one. For example, two entity classes may be stored in one table.*)
3. Show association relationship between the tables and the entity classes that will be stored by the tables.
4. Stereotype all table classes as <<table>>.
5. Give careful thought to multiplicities when KEYS to your tables are specified.
6. For many-to-many multiplicities, create association (link) tables.

Endnote

1. David A. Taylor.

Chapter 14

Dynamic Modeling with State Machine Diagrams

Learning Objectives

- Understand dynamic modeling with state machine diagrams (SMDs)
- Use SMDs in analysis (model of problem space) and design (model of solution space)
- Build a SMD using a set of steps
- Study examples of SMDs for boundary, entity, and control objects in design

Introduction to Dynamic Modeling with State Machine Diagrams

This chapter discusses state machine diagrams (SMDs). These diagrams (occasionally also called state charts and state transition diagrams) are used for modeling the dynamic aspect of a system in both the problem and solution space.

In the problem space, SMDs model the states, conditions, and transitions of business entities, whereas in the solution space, SMDs model the states, conditions, and transitions of technical objects including interface and control objects.

In the model of the problem space (MOPS), SMDs are also a good mechanism to identify the business rules associated with an entity. These rules are captured as conditions on the SMDs. Changes or transitions in states of an object occur based on these conditions.

In the model of the solution space (MOSS), SMDs provide advanced modeling techniques for the dynamic (real-time) aspects of a system. The conditions and transitions on SMDs provide detailed design-level information to programmers on how an object changes its state.

SMDs can also be used to model the states of other models within a system such as a use case or even the system. In most practical situations, though, SMDs are used to model the states of an object belonging to a class.

As discussed in the introduction to object-oriented fundamentals, objects display the characteristics defined by classes. Each object can display the same characteristic in various ways. While the class defines the object, it does not exist at runtime like an object. Therefore, classes do not have states that can change over time. Classes, however, do contain the methods (operations) that bring about changes to the objects that are created from these classes.

State Machine Diagrams for Dynamic Modeling

An SMD shows the various states in which an object can exist. States typically describe the values of attributes of an object. Objects (not classes) can actually store the data and use the methods described in classes. Since multiple objects can be instantiated from a class, each of these objects can have different state depending on their attribute values throughout their own runtime.

Consider, for example, two dog objects (aDog and bDog) created from a Dog class. The class Dog does not have a state, but the dog objects do. This Dog class has a few attributes such as Name, Breed, Age, Microchip, Action, and Feedtime. At a point in time, aDog an be sitting (Action="Sitting"); at the same point in time, bDog can be jumping (Action="Jumping"). Sitting and Jumping are the values of the attribute Action. The state of an object is based on the values of one or more of its attributes. States for each object can be different, depending on various conditions experienced during the life of an object.

States represent dynamic situations or conditions of an object. These situations can include the object performing some action or, alternatively, waiting for an event. These states are all shown in an SMD. The events or messages that cause the transition of an object from one state to another and the actions that result from a state change are also shown in an SMD.

Since a class can spawn a potentially unlimited number of objects, an SMD is not created for every object in a system. Instead, a sample subset of objects with significant dynamic behavior of their own are used to model a SMD.

Being runtime dynamic diagrams, they model objects and not classes (although modeling tools will usually show the name of the class in an SMD). This dynamic nature of the SMD is ideal for major real-time modeling exercises.[1]

Notations of State Machine Diagrams

Figure 14.1 shows the modeling notations used to create a typical SMD. They are states, transitions, guard conditions, and actions that result from the triggering of transitions, start and stop states, nested states, and notes.

- States are represented by rounded rectangles. States represent the condition of an object at a particular point in time.
- Actions that precede all transitions are placed as an entry action within the state. Likewise, actions that accompany the exiting of a state are placed as exit actions within the state.
- Behavior that occurs within a state is called an activity. An activity starts when the state is entered. Activity is completed or is interrupted by an outgoing state transition.
- A guard condition determines if an object changes from one state to another. If the condition is satisfied, then the value of the attribute that determines the state is changed. This results in a change in the state of the object. Therefore, a guard condition checks attribute values that, when true, results in a transition.

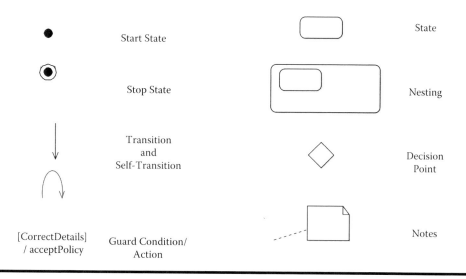

Figure 14.1   Notations in a state machine diagram.

■ Sometimes, a condition is fulfilled for a transition—but the transition results in the same state as before. This is called self-transition and is shown by the semicircled arrow in Figure 14.1 (e.g., an account object has a positive balance of $500; then a message triggers a withdrawal of $100; despite the lower balance, the state of the account remains positive in terms of its balance).

■ Start and stop (initial—represented by a large dot, and final—represented by a bullseye) states are two special states of an SMD shown in Figure 14.1. The start and stop are pseudo-states. They model the starting point and the stop point of an SMD. Each diagram must have one and only one start state (for exceptions, see the later discussion on nesting) because the object needs to be in a consistent state when it is created. The second special state is a stop state. Unlike a start state, an object can have multiple stop states or may not require any stop states (in which case the object is never deleted—a common situation with the Internet of Things devices).

■ States within states are represented by nesting. A higher-level state (e.g., account is in open state) can contain lower-level states (e.g., open-current or open-overdrawn). Each can be modeled by SMDs.

There are a few ways to transition out of a state. The first is automatic and occurs when the activity of a state completes and a transition occurs. The second type of transition is based on external action—typically a message sent to one object from another object after a condition has been satisfied. An arrow that points from the originating state to the successor state represents a state transition. Yet another way for objects to transition to a state is through a decision point, shown by a diamond in Figure 14.1. This decision point shows two potentially different states to which an object can transition depending of the condition on the decision point.

State Machine Diagrams for Patient Object in Problem Space

State machine diagrams in problem space help in modeling the business rules around a business entity. For example, these states can be documented in the requirements model using a state table (e.g., as shown in Table 14.1). This table lists the identification of each state and corresponding

Table 14.1   States Table for Patient Object

State Identification	State Name That Succinctly Describes the State of an Object	Comments Describing the State of a Patient Object
0	Registered	The patient is registered in the HMS system.
1	Admitted	The patient is admitted to the hospital.
2	Operated	The patient is operated upon for a particular problem.
3	Recovered	The patient is in the recovery state after the treatment.
7	Consulting	This state is for an outpatient (nonsurgical).
9	Released	The patient has been released from the hospital.

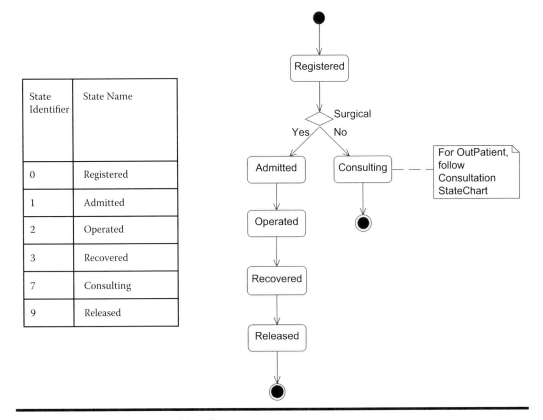

Figure 14.2   Patient state machine diagram.

state names. Note, this table does not show the transition between states. The SMD corresponding to this table is shown in Figure 14.2 as follows.

The identifier of a state shown in Figure 14.2 need not be in a particular sequence; also, in case of nesting, this identifier can take on two parts or digits (e.g., 00, 10, 70, and so on) to represent the higher- and lower-level states, respectively.

"Patient" State Machine Diagram

Figure 14.2 shows a simple SMD for various states of a Patient object. The pseudo start state is followed by the Registered state for a Patient. This state is followed by a decision point, where the system queries whether the patient is Surgical (requires surgery) or general Consulting (i.e., does not require surgery). If the patient is Consulting, the state "changes" to that and finishes. Alternatively, a surgical patient changes the state to Surgical and is Admitted to the hospital. The patient then progresses through the Operated, Recovered, and Released states. Guard conditions are not shown in this simple diagram, but they do appear when relevant, especially in a detailed SMD.

"Consultation" State Machine Diagram

The SMD shown in Figure 14.3 demonstrates the use of "nesting" for the Consultation object in the HMS. The Consultation object starts with an Open state, which progresses to the Closed state. These are the two superstates for Consultation. Within each of these super states are substates.

For example, within an Open superstate, the Consultation object can be either Available or Booked. When in the Booked state, the Consultation object may be Cancelled and reverts back to Available. However, when the consultation is being provided, the Consultation object moves from the Booked state to the Provided state. As a result, the superstate for the Consultation is Closed. From Provided the Consultation moves to the state of Billed. At the end of billing the state diagram finishes. Notes help provide additional explanations and clarifications on this SMD.

"Bill Payment" State Machine Diagram

Figure 14.4 shows an example of an SMD for a Bill Payment object. The states shown in this diagram are Generated, Issued, Paid, Overdue, and Defaulted. The transitions from Generated to Issued to Paid are straightforward. However, when an Issued bill remains unpaid past its due date, it transitions to an Overdue state. The guard condition for this transition is time-based.

Note how a partial payment of this Overdue bill self-transits the object and keeps it in Overdue state because the bill remains partly unpaid. Later, if the bill is fully paid, the state changes to Paid, whereas if it is not paid, the state changes to Defaulted.

Advanced State Machine Diagram for Patient Object in HMS in Solution Space

The following examples of SMDs are in the solution space. There is additional depth in these diagrams, and classes (objects) with different stereotypes other than <<entity>> are also modeled with SMDs in the solution space.

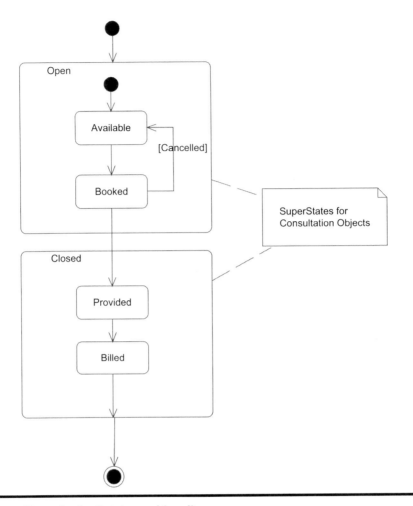

Figure 14.3 **"Consultation" state machine diagram.**

State Machine Diagram for "Patient" in HMS

Figure 14.5 gives an advanced SMD for the Patient object. The major states for the Patient object, as shown in this diagram, are InHospitalQueue, Registering, Registered, BookingAppointment, Admitted, InTreatment, Recovering, and Discharged. Some of these states are also nested, resulting in substates.

This SMD starts with a start state followed by a condition MedicalProblemOccurs, which is not curable locally (wherever the person may be). When the patient object encounters such a condition (which, in this case, may not be a part of the software system), the state of the object changes to InHospitalQueue.

The transition from InHospitalQueue to Registering is automatic (although it can be based on an event such as availability of administration staff).

Registering is shown as a major state that has nested substates within it. Each nested state has the start state that specifies where to start reading the nested states and corresponding substates. As a part of the Registering state, the Patient starts providing his details (like name and address) and therefore is in the ProvidingDetails state. Once all the details required

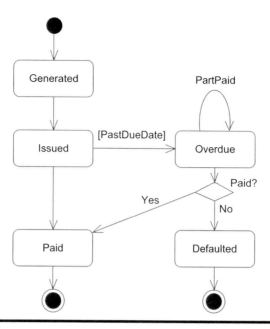

Figure 14.4   Bill payment state machine diagram.

for the registration have been provided by the patient, and the message "register details" hits the `Patient` object, the state of the object changes to `RegistrationInProgress`.

In case of invalid inputs detected during the `Registration` process (when the Patient object is in the `RegistrationInProgress` state), the state of the patient is reverted back to `ProvidingDetails` and the patient is asked to provide (or reenter, depending on how this model is implemented) his details. Note that while these substate changes are going on, the superstate continues to remain "Registering."

Following a successful registration process, the patient enters the state of `Registered`. This state is now showing any activities or actions at this stage. However, in some cases where enhancement to the model is expected, modelers may create such states in anticipation of filling them in later on.

After the `Registered` state, the Patient object is queried for details of the `NatureOfSickness`. This query helps make a decision as to whether the `Patient` needs to book a consultation or needs to be admitted to the hospital for treatment. (Note that various other scenarios in this transition are possible, and here only one common scenario is shown.) This decision point is resolved by evaluating the answer from the Patient object: If the answer is `NormalSickness`, then the `Patient` transitions to the `BookingAppointment` state; however, if the sickness is of a serious nature, or if the patient is being admitted in an emergency, the Patient object immediately transitions to the `Admitted` state.

In the state of `BookingAppointment`, the `patient` transitions through various substates—providing his medical details, providing convenient times for an appointment, and books the appointment. Finally, the BookingConsultation state is reached, after which the `Patient` transitions to the state of `Consultation`.

The transitions of states from `Admitted` to `InTreatment`, from which the patient progresses to the state of `Recovering` and then to the state of `Discharged`, are all straightforward. However, in practice, each of these states has potential for numerous substates. This patient SMD finally ends in two stop states, which are the pseudo-states shown at the end.

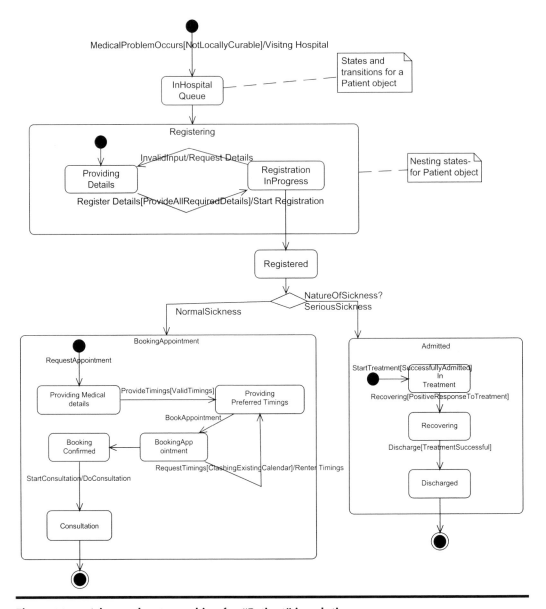

Figure 14.5 Advanced state machine for "Patient" in solution space.

State Machine Diagram for "Patient_Form" Boundary Object in HMS

SMDs provide an opportunity to model the states of a <<boundary>> object, which is instantiated from a graphical user interface (GUI) class. While these states for boundary objects are important, they are not as complicated (and do not contain the many business rules) as the states for an entity object in design.

Figure 14.6 shows an example of an SMD for the Patient _ Form object. This SMD can be read from the start state and enters the Created state when the form is instantiated. Once the form has been created, it enters the state of Displaying. A user can input data on the form, indicating the form is in Entering mode. Once the user finishes entering the data in the form,

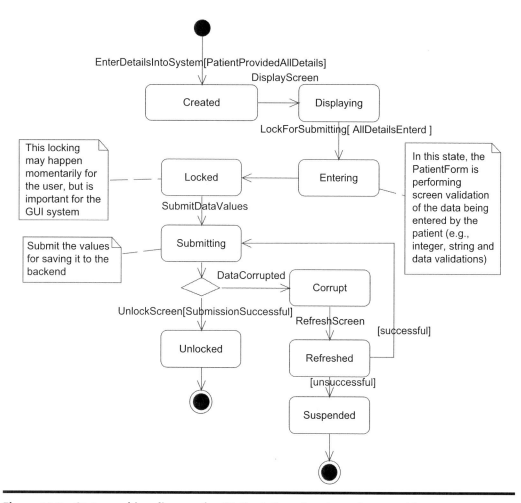

Figure 14.6　State machine diagram for "Patient_Form" <<**boundary**>> **object.**

it transitions to a `Locked` state, wherein the form object is locked for submission. The guard condition ensures that all the details have been entered in the form. The object then enters the state of `Submitting`, where the data are transferred to the control class for further processing. If the submission of the form is successful, the object moves to an `Unlocked` state wherein the SMD ends.

In case the data are corrupted (or the screen is unable to display the information), the form object moves to the state of `Corrupt`. Upon receipt of the `Refresh Screen` message, the object changes the state to `Refreshed`. If `Refreshed` is successfully performed, the state reverts back to `Submitting`. However, if the `Refresh` is unsuccessful, the object is suspended, and a drastic step, outside of this SMD, will be required to get the object back on track.

State Machine Diagram for "ConsultationManager," a Control Object in HMS

The SMD for the controller class (i.e., an object instantiated from a <<control class>> `ConsultationManager`, is shown in Figure 14.7. The `start` state is followed by the

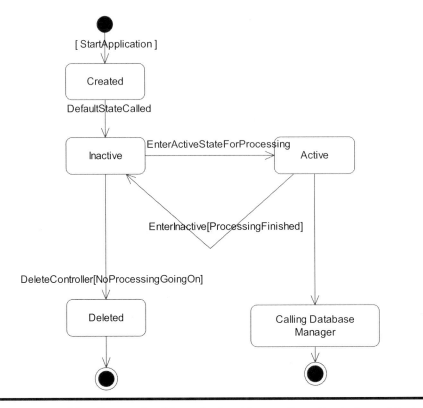

Figure 14.7 State machine diagram for "Consultation Manager" <<Control>> object.

`Created` state, where the object is created. The `ConsultationManager` object then enters the default state of `Inactive`. When an event, such as `EnterActiveStateForProcessing`, is received, the object enters the `Active` state. Upon completion of the processing, the `ConsultationManager` again enters the default state of `Inactive`. When the event `DeleteConroller` is received by the object, the object is deleted and enters the state of `Deleted`. The guard condition ensures that no processing is going on when the delete event is called. The state machine then follows to the `stop` state. The Active state may also lead to the control object calling the corresponding database manager, resulting in the state of `CallingDatabaseManager`. This is where the `stop` state is reached.

Steps in Building a State Machine Diagram

The following steps are followed in building an SMD.

- Select an object in the system that is important or complex.
- Carefully understand the stereotype of that object—whether it is an entity, interface, controller, or table.
- Examine the attributes of the object (from the class documentation) to see if they reveal possible states for the object. For example, a Patient object may have an attribute that describes at what point the patient is in her visit to the hospital, such as being admitted, being operated on, or in recovery.

- Determine the sequences and events are involved in changing the state of this object. An object changes state because some event has occurred or because of the passage of a certain amount of time (e.g., a bill will become unpaid after 30 days). These events are organized into a logical progression the object moves through.
- Apply transitions to the states of an object to show the progression of the object from one state to another.
- Add guard conditions associated with the event, where applicable.
- Determine whether there are any nested states that can be incorporated into this diagram. If a number of related states can be logically grouped together under a common state, then consider moving them to a substate that is nested within that common state in the main diagram.
- Add explanatory notes to clarify the diagram.
- Explore other elements within the system that may need state modeling (e.g., a special use case). Modeling of the states of such an element can follow steps similar to the preceding ones.

Common Errors in Modeling State Machine Diagrams and How to Rectify Them

Common Errors	Rectifying the Errors	Examples
Drawing an SMD like a flow chart (activity diagram)	List clearly all the states for ONE object. Ensure these states are not activities.	Revisit activity diagrams and compare them with state diagrams. For example, in Figure 14.2, there are no activities, only states.
Having more than one start state	This is the single starting point to read the SMD. Remove all others (except within a nested substate).	See Figure 14.2, which clearly shows a single start state.
Differentiating between self-transition and no transition	When a nested message hits an object but the object does not change state, it is a self-transition.	Consider for a `Bill` object an "overdue" state. If only half the bill is paid, it's a message, but the bill remains in the same state.
Not understanding an unconditional transition	Understand that it occurs by default when an activity is completed.	See Figure 14.2. The transition from admitted to operated is unconditional transition; it occurs when the admitted state is completed. No explicit condition is shown in the transition in this diagram.

Common Errors	Rectifying the Errors	Examples
Confusing a decision point (diamond) and a guard condition	Use decision point when transition can occur to potentially more than one state.	See Figure 14.2 where the decision point (surgical?) appears as a diamond. Based on the answer to this query, the state of an object can go toward surgical or consulting.
Showing states for a class rather than an object	Although the class appears in discussions and in the modeling tool, the states are always for an object.	Figure 14.2 shows the states of a patient. Although the class name seems to appear in this diagram, actually all the states belong to an object Patient. See also the aDog and bDog example in the chapter.
Not showing a start state within a nested state	It is important to treat a nested substate diagram similar to a state diagram; therefore, it will have a start state.	Figure 14.3 has an open state with nested substates within it. There is a need to show the start state within that substate of open; since the state is then transitioning directly to another substate (provided), there is no need to show a start state in the second nested state (closed).

Discussion Questions

1. Why is an SMD considered a dynamic model?
2. An object is shown in an SMD. True or false? Discuss with example.
3. Compare a SMD with an activity diagram and discuss the differences between the two diagrams.
4. Compare an SMD with a sequence diagram and discuss the differences between the two diagrams.
5. Discuss the pseudo-states in an SMD. What is their purpose and conditions for use?
6. What is a transition? Discuss why a transition occurs without a guard condition in the SMD?
7. Is there a decision point in SMD?
8. Discuss the difference between a decision point in an SMD and an activity diagram.
9. What is the importance of nesting in SMDs?
10. Why is a start state important within a nested substate?
11. Discuss the effect of self-transition on a state—with examples.

Team Project Case Study

1. Revisit ALL your classes in your class diagrams drawn within separate packages.
2. Select the two most important/complex classes from each package.

3. Draw an SMD corresponding to each of these two classes. *(Hint: You are drawing SMDs for an anonymous object corresponding to the class.)*
4. Add appropriate guard conditions, nesting, self-transition, and notes. This information is derived by revisiting the use case documentation and by revisiting the sequence diagrams.
5. Add suitable substates to any one of your SMD within each package *(this may not always be necessary in practice, but here it is required as part of your case study).*
6. Observe the difference in which states are created for <<entity>> and the rest of the stereotypes in your diagrams.

Endnote

1. Douglass, Bruce Powel. (1999), *Doing Hard Time Developing Real-Time Systems with UML, Objects, Frameworks, and Patterns.* Addison-Wesley, Object Technology Series, 1999.

Advanced Software Engineering Design Concepts: Reuse, Granularity, Patterns, and Robustness

Learning Objectives

- Understand the various levels, types, and approaches in reusability of software
- Know the impact of granularity of class designs on the reusability and maintainability of systems
- Apply design patterns to enhance the quality of class diagrams
- Apply the concept of robustness in object-oriented design in order to improve the maintainability of systems
- Understand basic system architecture (software specific) and correlate it to package diagrams

Introduction

This chapter discusses some advanced concepts in software engineering that are of particular value in solution and architectural modeling spaces (MOSS, MOAS). These advanced concepts are based on the earlier discussions of class and sequence diagrams.

The focus of this discussion is creating a software design that is robust, reusable, and of high quality. Such good-quality design has value for the organization beyond the current project. The discussion in this chapter includes reusability, understanding "with" and "for" reuse, granularity in object-oriented designs, and applying design patterns. Relevant aspects of a development process that support quality design are also mentioned.

Reusability in Software Engineering

Reusability is considered a major contribution of object orientation (OO) to the field of software engineering. This is because OO offered the first opportunity for software developers to use an existing class again, without modification, in a new class. Reuse provides value in terms of improved productivity and enhanced output quality.

Levels of Reuse

Understanding the various levels of reuse within software development provides a good starting point to appreciate reusability. Figure 15.1 shows three different level of reuse prevalent in software engineering:

- Code-level reuse—occurs when a new class is based on an existing, fully coded class.
- Design level reuse—can occur when an bases all its new design is based on existing designs and available design patterns.
- Analysis-level reuse—can occur at an organizational level across multiple projects. Requirements identified in one project can be reused (with suitable modifications) in another project. Such analysis-level reuse requires an organization-wide reuse culture.

Code-Level Reuse

Code-level reuse occurs when a class reuses another class. This implies the use of any function (or attribute) of the base class by the inherited class. Code-level reuse also includes reuse of classes in the language of implementation and the development environment.

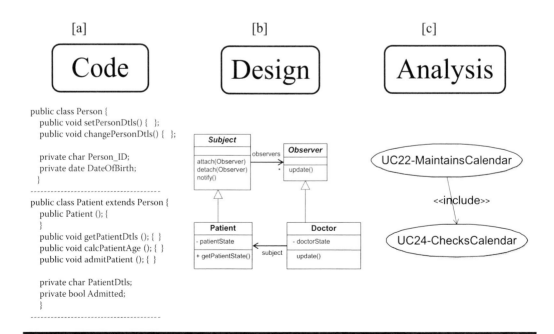

Figure 15.1   Level of reuse in OO.

Figure 15.1a shows this basic reuse on the left-hand side. The code example shows how a new `Patient` class is created inheriting the `Person` class. All the properties and relationships of `Person` are available to `Patient` without an explicit declaration again in `Person` class. The code-level reuse depends on the programmer's knowledge of the development environment and the availability of existing classes.

Design-Level Reuse

Reuse at the design level is based on class designs, components, frameworks, packages, and services. Reuse at this level is important as it occurs at a higher level than the code-level reuse and, therefore, has a bigger impact on a project. For example, reusing an entire executable library or calling a complex analytical service has a much greater impact on development as compared with reusing a class. This is the reuse at the design or "pattern level" that provides major benefits to the software project. This is the reuse in a project that also provides value across multiple projects.

Figure 15.1b shows this second form of reuse wherein classes and their relationships can be modeled based on an existing design or pattern. Figure 15.1 shows a design based on Gamma's (Gamma et al. 1995) `Observer` pattern (discussed later in this chapter). The inheritance between `Subject` and `Patient` is not based on the semantic meanings behind the classes but, rather, on their implementation characteristics. The inheritance of `Patient` and `Doctor` classes from the corresponding `Subject` and `Observer` classes facilitates implementation of the `Observer` pattern with minimal effort on the part of the system designer. Figure 15.1b shows how an entire suite of classes can be reused based on their design characteristics in implementation.

Analysis-Level Reuse

The third form of reuse is at the analysis level, shown on the right in Figure 15.1c. At this level, requirements are documented and reused from the use cases provided by the UML. Use-case-to-use-case relationships facilitate this reuse. The $<<$include$>>$ relationship between two use cases enables requirements reuse at the analysis level. For example, one of the use cases `MaintainsCalendar` has a need to check the `Calendar` details. At the same time, other modules like "booking appointment" and "reschedule consultation" also need to check the calendar. In such a scenario, a new use case `ChecksCalendar` is developed. Later, other use cases that need to use this use case could include it for their implementation. This reuse is shown in the Figure 15.1 where the `MaintainsCalendar` use case includes the `ChecksCalendar` use case.

Reuse Strategies in Software Projects

Reuse strategies provide greater value in software projects than code-level reuse. These reuse strategies need to be carefully thought out, agreed upon by all stakeholders, and incorporated into the software development processes. Strategic reuse results in productivity and quality gains for the project and the organization.

Reuse increases productivity as the reused classes and components are not designed from scratch. The reused classes and components also need not be tested again (except for the new interfaces with the inherited classes). Thus, basing a class on an existing classes reduces coding as well as testing effort—thereby enhancing quality and improving productivity. Such reuse, however, requires a strategic approach that goes beyond one project and into all projects within the organization.

Encapsulation Facilitates Reuse

In addition to inheritance, encapsulation also contributes to reusability in OO—resulting in productivity and quality gains. As discussed in OO fundamentals in Chapter 1, encapsulation "wraps" class attributes by its functions or methods. Since data and functions are "encapsulated" together in a class, potential errors in logic and execution can be easily pinpointed to a specific class. This narrowing down of errors in OO does not occur easily in procedural designs because there the errors can occur and flow through any part of the system without being localized.

With object-oriented designs, if an error is "thrown" by an object while it is retrieving the values of certain attributes, that error is relatively easily traced to that specific object and the code for its corresponding class. Furthermore, due to encapsulation, the error remains entrapped within the class and will not percolate through the rest of the system.

The preceding discussion suggests that once a class is designed, developed, tested, and placed in a module (or a component or service), then that module can be distributed and reused widely. Such reuse of that module requires minimal effort limited to testing the new interface for the newly designed class.

A reused class has higher quality characteristics than a newly written class, particularly if it has already been reused before. This is because as classes get reused, they also get tested through that reuse in real-life situations. Thus, the more a class gets reused, the higher is its quality.

For encapsulation to succeed, it must be a part of the design standard in a project and therefore part of project culture (as discussed next). Care should be taken to ensure that encapsulation does not degenerate into an exercise of data hiding. Simply hiding data or attributes behind a function does not provide the same quality benefits as those resulting from encapsulation.

As a simple example, consider the Patient class in the HMS and the attribute `MedicareNumber` in that class. If `MedicareNumber` is accessed using a `+getMedNo()` method, then what is achieved is data hiding—hiding the data by a function. If, instead of `+getMedNo()`, a function is provided that has a business logic to it, such as `+getCoverDetails()`, which contains a Medicare number as well as other fields, then an entire business functionality is encapsulated in the class.

Reuse as a Culture

Reuse culture in a project needs a strategic approach by the project management. One helpful concept in understanding reuse at an organizational level is shown in Figure 15.2. This figure shows two "types"* of reuse:

1. Refining the class or component for *future* reuse, resulting in the project's being the "producer" of reusable elements;
2. Incorporating reusable classes and components in the next project, or "consuming" them.

The former needs a generalization of classes and may be called "for" reuse, whereas the latter is called "with" reuse. The strategic aspect of these two types of reuse across more than one project is shown in Figure 15.2. Project 1 is shown as producing the reusable components, and Project 2 is consuming or "reusing" them.

---

* Or categories, to separate this grouping of reuse from the earlier discussion on levels of reuse around Figure 15.1.

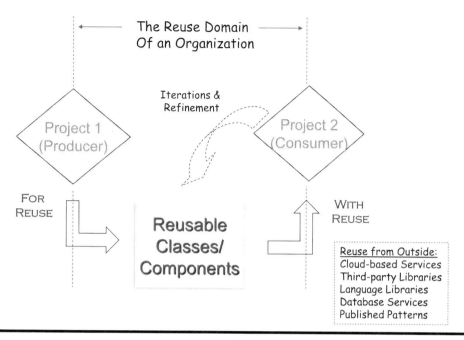

Figure 15.2 "With" and "for" reuse—part of reuse strategy.

Generalization versus Specialization in Reuse

The modelers and developers who work on Project 1 are making an additional contribution (to their normal work) to produce reusable components. This is working "for" future reuse. Such reuse work benefits the modelers and developers who work on Project 2. The Project 2 people are undertaking their modeling work "with" reuse, so they rely on the work done by the Project 1 staff.

An example of "for" reuse is generalization of an Animal class to Living class. Such a design has sufficient functionality that caters not only to the needs of the current project but also those of future projects. *Extra* effort is needed in the first "producer" project, particularly in the area of quality assurance, as well as quality control or testing. This is because the class has to be specified, documented, and tested not only for its application now, but also for unknown future usage.

This extra effort is offset by the relatively *less* effort needed in the quality area when "with" reuse occurs, as components are expected to be quality assured for all their basic features and need to be retested for the variation occurring due to their usage. For example, a new class Cat, modeled on Animal, is an example of specialization ("with" reuse). Here, Cat enjoys the advantages of all the design and testing effort by the developers of the Animal and Living classes.

Granularity in Object-Oriented Design

The "for" and "with" reuse considerations impact requirements of future or concurrent projects *explicitly* as development proceeds to satisfy the current project's requirements. The size of an average class has a bearing on the ability of the project team to successfully create such a "feed forward" mechanism. The size of a class is the basis for discussions on granularity in this section.

Granularity means, for a given functionality, designs can be created with a few large classes (coarse granular design) or a large number of smaller-sized classes (fine granular design).

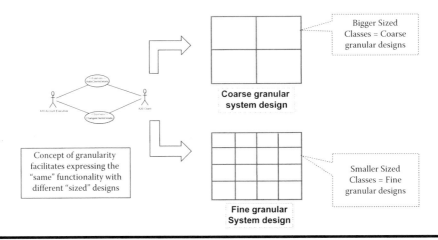

Figure 15.3 The concept of granularity in object-oriented designs.

The concept of granularity further states that the average size of an object/class in an object-oriented system is an important consideration in the successful reuse in design.

This concept of granularity is demonstrated in Figure 15.3, wherein the same functionality (roughly denoted by a use case diagram) is shown capable of being implemented by either 4 coarse granular classes or 16 fine granular classes.

Fine granular classes take more effort to produce, but they are more reusable. This is because a large number of smaller-sized classes lend themselves to "better fit" in newer scenarios/requirements than larger-sized (coarse) classes. The flip side of this situation is that finer granularity designs require extra attention to quality, as there are a larger number of classes used for a given functionality. Furthermore, it is not only the classes themselves but also their relationships that need to be tested. Regardless of the case (fine or coarse), it is essential for system architects and system designers to keep in mind this vital concept in creating their object-oriented designs.

Design Patterns in Software Design Engineering

What Are Patterns?

Patterns are recurring "thought processes" that are captured in abstractions. These "higher-level" abstractions can then be reused in newer designs without the designers having to undergo the same rigors as starting from scratch.

Design patterns have provided one of the most popular approaches to reusing software and designs, especially in the context of object orientation. Due to the popularity of design patterns, other patterns of value have also appeared on the software engineering scene. These are:

■ Analysis patterns, which describe and model recurring phenomena during analysis in the problem space[1]
■ Design patterns, as discussed earlier, are recurring phenomena in solution space (Gamma et al., 1995)
■ Architectural patterns, which are recurring phenomena that occur as organizational constraints on the system being developed
■ Game patterns, which are recurring sociopsychological phenomena in software projects (Unhelkar, 2003, 2005)[2,3]

Origins of Patterns

The idea of patterns capturing design expertise originated with the architect Christopher Alexander. *The Timeless Way of Building* (1977)[4] remains essential reading for the idea of patterns, which has been developed into design patterns as elements of reusable object-oriented software by Gamma et al. (1995). According to Alexander, "Each pattern describes a problem which occurs over and over again in our environment, and then describes the core of the solution to that problem, in such a way that the solution can be used a million times over, without ever doing it the same way twice." Even though Alexander was talking about patterns in buildings and towns, the concept holds equally true in object-oriented design patterns.

Coplien (1991)[5] further defines a pattern as both a description of the thing being built and a process for building it, *a solution to a problem in a context* and that which resolves the forces at play for a given design decision. This definition is helpful in discovering patterns and applying them to software engineering projects. The models created and the *process of* creating those models find guidance through the aforementioned definition.

Structure of a Pattern

Formally, a pattern can be described by the following four essential elements of a pattern (Gamma et al., 1995):

- The *pattern name* describes the design problem, its solutions, and consequences, in a word or two.
- The *problem* describes when to apply the pattern.
- The *solution* describes the elements that make up the design, their relationships, responsibilities, and collaborations.
- The *consequences* are the results and trade-offs of applying the pattern.

Using Patterns in the Solution and Architectural Modeling Spaces

Patterns formalize reusability at the conceptual level (Figure 15.1b). Experienced designers can identify recurring class hierarchies, associating classes or access sequences, and put them together in such a way that they can be applied to various practical design problems.

As Gamma et al. (1995) say: "These patterns solve specific design problems and make object-oriented designs more flexible, elegant, and ultimately reusable." Since they capture not only system parts but also the rich relationships between them (Coplien, 1991)[5], patterns describe a system architecture that is broader than any object or class hierarchy.

Once described and documented in a catalog, design patterns serve as a source of proficiency that only experience can provide—facilitating reuse through efficient and flexible designs. Patterns also address the issue of object size and number—helping in deciding what should be an object. For example, Gamma et al. describe the `Facade` pattern, which represents complete subsystems as objects, and the `Flyweight` pattern, which describes how to support huge numbers of objects at the finest granularities.

Thus, it is seen that by capturing and documenting the recurrent behavior that is apparent to the experts, patterns provide reusability and quality to object-oriented software engineering. Design patterns, in particular, provide the aforementioned value mostly in the solution space

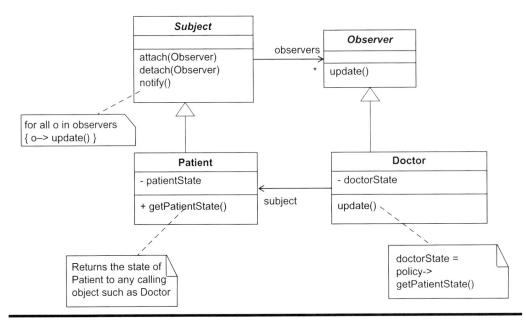

Figure 15.4 Using a design pattern in HMS (Based on the `Observer` pattern work by Gamma et al.).

(MOSS). However, together with analysis and architectural patterns, the value of reuse and quality is maximized in the architectural space (MOAS). This is because of the organizational-level decisions made in the architectural space based on constraints and parameters.

Figure 15.4 demonstrates the use of patterns in software architecture and design. The `Observer` pattern has been described in detail by Gamma et al. in their popular work on design patterns. In that pattern, they capture the essence of a situation where one class (`Observer`) depends on another class (`Subject`). Any change in the subject's state influences the `Observer`. The abstract classes representing `Observer` and `Subject` are specialized into `concreteObserver` and `concreteSubject`.

Consider, from a design viewpoint, the need for Excel data to be represented in some graphical way (like a graph or pie chart). In this scenario, the actual data in the Excel sheet are the `Subject` and the graphs are the `Observer`. In terms of classes, this can be explained as follows. Consider that state of `object B` depends on the state of `object A`. Whenever the state of `object A` changes, `object B` has to recompute its state in order to remain consistent.

In the HMS domain, this pattern can be interpreted as shown in Figure 15.4. In that figure, the `concreteObserver` is replaced by the `Doctor` and the `concreteSubject` by the `Patient` classes. This design indicates whenever there is a change in any details of `Patient`, the `Doctor` is affected. Changes in the state of `Patient` (say, `InTreatment patient`) affect the way the `Patient` is treated by the Hospital.

This design, shown in Figure 15.4, will have the advantage over a design developed from scratch because in basing the design on the `Observer` pattern, the knowledge and experience of Gamma et al. is being reused. Needless to say, this design is further modified and extended to satisfy the complete implementation needs of the hospital domain, but it is certainly a better start than thinking of the `Patient-Doctor` association from scratch—resulting in better quality.

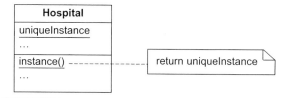

Figure 15.5 Singleton pattern (another example in HMS, based on Gamma et al.'s work).

Often, in a system there is only one instance of an object that needs to be created, and it is then accessed by the entire system. In such cases, there is a need to control the instantiation and access of such a single object. Examples of such objects include communication, database access, window manager, and print spoolers. These objects are required globally in the system. Having multiple instances of such classes would lead to inconsistency in the system.

The Singleton pattern facilitates design creation wherein classes based on this pattern can be instantiated only once. Thus, Singleton patterns result in global objects that are encapsulated and can be checked for the existence of only one object.

Figure 15.5 shows an example of how a Singleton pattern is used in the HMS. This example shows a class from the HMS, which needs to have only one single instance. The Hospital object is unique, in HMS, as only one instance of it is required when the system is executed. This is achieved by basing it on the Singleton pattern. Without such a pattern, the part of the system where Hospital is instantiated has to be "hand coded" by the designer and developer to ensure single instantiation.

Robustness in Design

Dependencies of Classes

Robustness in design is a concept that explores dependencies between classes. This extent of dependency, or coupling, between classes is one of the traditional challenges of software engineering. If a class depends heavily on another class, then naturally a change in one class affects all other classes that depend on that class. As a result, changes in one class can influence other classes to the extent where it becomes almost impossible to change one part of the system without affecting many other parts.

Simply stated, the higher the dependency of classes on one another in a system, the less robust the system is. Conversely, if the classes are less dependent on one another, then changes in one class will have less influence on other classes in the system. As a result, the system is said to be robust. Thus, robustness is an approach to design that ensures the ability of one part of a solution to change without affecting the rest of the system.

Identifying Lack of Robustness

Consider Figure 15.6. Note that the two <<entity>> classes, Patient and Schedule, are tightly coupled. Even though these classes are associated with the <<boundary>> class Patient _ Form, the entire design is tightly coupled. Changes in one class (and corresponding object at runtime) impacts the other classes directly.

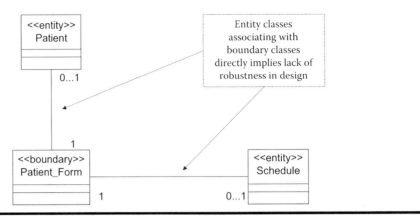

Figure 15.6 Identifying lack of robustness.

Rules of Robustness

Robustness is a specific design construct in which the controller (or manager) class is inserted between entity, boundary, and database classes. For example, the Patient class may not directly associate with the Doctor class, or, more specifically, the Patient class may not invoke or create a Doctor class, and vice versa. Instead, an object manager (or a class with any other name that is a <<manager>> or a <<controller>> stereotype) is introduced between the two aforementioned classes. This object manager assumes the responsibility of creating and managing a list of active objects.

The concept of robustness discussed here derives from an earlier, well-known SmallTalk pattern called MVC*, or model view controller pattern. In MVC, the model (or <<entity>> stereotypes in UML-based designs) and the view (or <<boundary>> stereotypes) are separated by the controller (or <<controller>> stereotype). When applying robustness, the following rules are incorporated (shown in Figure 15.7) in the designs:

- Boundary (interface) classes cannot talk to (associate with) each other
- Entity classes cannot talk to (associate with) each other
- Boundary and entity classes can talk to control classes
- Control classes can talk to (associate with) each other

Note that in practice, these rules of robustness can also be extended to the <<table>> and <<entity>> relationship; this means that the <<entity>> classes, when required to store details in corresponding <<table>>, cannot do so directly. Instead, <<entity>> classes go through another <<control>>, typically the DatabaseManager class, to store details in <<table>>.

Incorporating Robustness in Design

Figure 15.8 shows how a <<control>> class is inserted in the design shown earlier in Figure 15.6. The class diagram in this figure shows the separation of the Patient_Form from the Patient class by the ConsultationManager control class. The Patient class is also separated from the other entity class Schedule.

---

* MVC pattern.

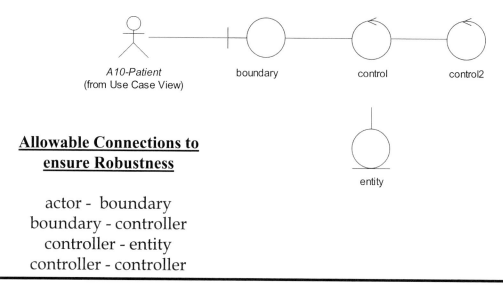

**Allowable Connections to
ensure Robustness**

actor - boundary
boundary - controller
controller - entity
controller - controller

Figure 15.7   Rules of robustness.

The class diagram shown on the left-hand side of Figure 15.8, with the stereotypes labeled on the classes, is repeated on the right-hand side of the figure with icons. This use of icons makes the diagram more readable—making it easier to spot robustness (or lack thereof). In practice, robustness is limited to creating entity and boundary objects; once the objects are created, they may end up sending and receiving messages to each other—despite incorporating a control class.

Figure 15.9 shows an additional example, now through a sequence diagram, of how robustness is implemented in practice. Once the PatientRegistrationForm receives a message

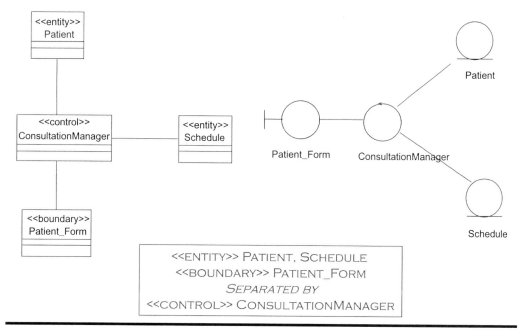

Figure 15.8   Incorporating robustness in design.

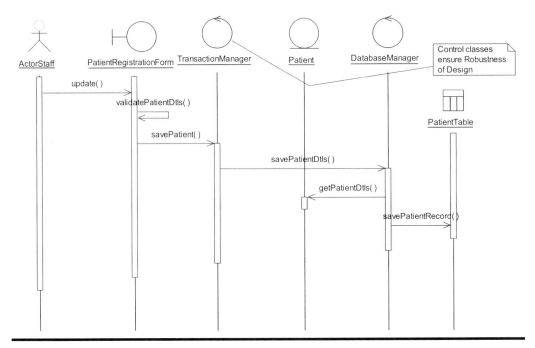

Figure 15.9   Effect of robustness on the process of saving patient's registration details.

to update() the details of Patient, it does an internal validatePatientDtls(). It then sends a message savePatient() to TransactionManager, which is the <<control>> class (object in this case because it is an instance-level sequence diagram). This control object then passes the message to another control object called DatabaseManager, which in turn calls the Patient object to get the details of the Patient that need to be saved in the database. On receiving the Patient details, the DatabaseManager sends them to the PatientTable for saving.

In practice, this robustness, implemented through two control objects in this sequence diagram, has a potential negative impact on the performance of the system. This is because of the need for messages to travel through additional controller objects. The balancing act here is to sacrifice a small part of performance to gain design flexibility and robustness.

System Architecture and Design Process

The advanced design concepts discussed thus far provide significant value in the building of a model of architectural space (MOAS). Following is a discussion on building such a system architecture model.

Project roles like a system designer, system architect, and project manager need to come together and work strategically to achieve reuse granularity and robustness. Techniques like creating a prototype (executable) and refining the requirements support the earlier discussion on reuse and quality. Operational considerations (requirements of the system when it is in operation) also come into play in developing MOAS. Here are the activities and tasks that are relevant in developing good system architecture.

Survey existing architecture and design of the system (and other systems within the organization):

■ Understand current system architecture and design needs of the system
■ Relate the current system architecture to the existing enterprise architecture (EA) of the organization
■ Understand current operational requirement as specified in creating a model of problem space (MOPS)

Incorporate Patterns

■ Recognize a "patternable" situation in current design
■ Identify suitable design patterns that can be used in the current design
■ Experiment with available patterns to see which ones are most appropriate to use
■ Incorporate suitable patterns in your designs
■ Undertake a walkthrough of designs "with" selected patterns

System Architecture Creation

■ Create information architecture for the system
■ Create database architecture to enable persistence functions for the system
■ Execute architectural prototype (this and the next task relate to prototyping process component) to enable understanding of architectural needs
■ Check current system architecture against architectural prototype

Operational Requirements Confirmation

■ Ensure performance requirements are handled by the system architecture
■ Ensure volume requirements are handled by the system architecture
■ Ensure that the architecture is scalable, which will enable the system to grow as the needs of users of the system grow
■ Ensure that the security requirements of the system are incorporated into the architecture. In a Web application in particular, there has to be a balance between the performance and security requirements

Figure 15.10 shows a basic system architecture for the HMS. Based on an understanding of the infrastructure of the system, the architecture is split into three parts: user interface, business rules, and database. These three layers are interspersed with four functional layers: `Patient`, `Staff`, `Consulting`, and `Account`.

In practice, many more functional divisions are possible. The crisscross between the functional and infrastructure layers of the system is the basis for creating packages. Therefore, such an architectural diagram is also drawn very early in a project (refer again to the discussion on creating packages in Chapter 3).

Each cross section of this architecture can be a package, as shown in Figure 15.10. Alternatively, the GUI and the database can each be put together in a package, and the functional sections can be placed in packages of their own. The underlying idea of such divisions is to create manageable subsystems represented by packages.

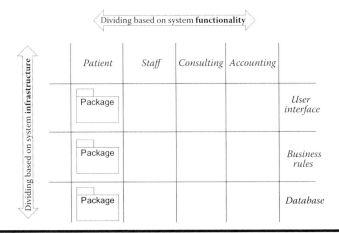

Figure 15.10 **Basic system architecture considerations.**

Common Errors in Reuse, Granularity, Patterns, and Robustness and How to Rectify Them

Common Errors	Rectifying the Errors	Examples
Only thinking of "with" reuse and not "for" reuse	Create a strategy to develop reusable class for future use; ensure people understand that "for" reuse requires an additional contribution and management is prepared to acknowledge that contribution for future benefits.	See Figure 15.1, where both aspects of reuse are presented.
Creating classes with random size	Review granularity needs of project and ensure a balanced size for the classes within the solution space.	Revisit Figure 15.3 and the discussion around it to understand granularity in practice.
Not separating design reuse from runtime reuse	Design reuse focuses on structure of classes using inheritance; runtime reuse is based on "calls" to services already instantiated.	See Figure 15.1 for examples of different types of reuse; then consider the difference between design and runtime reuse.
Thinking of design patterns as implementation patterns	Design patterns are precisely that—thought processes abstracted. They need to be converted to implementation for specific real-life situations.	See Figures 15.4 and 15.5 as practical examples of implementing design patterns.

Common Errors	Rectifying the Errors	Examples
Going "extreme" in terms of robustness	Not every practical design adheres to robustness—mainly because such robustness can add significant overheads in runtime.	Revisit Figure 15.9 to understand how robustness is applied in practice.
Ignoring the process and steps in creating system architecture and design	Following the process for system architecture and design helps in reuse and quality.	For example, design classes "with reuse" by utilizing classes "for reuse" developed in the previous iteration/project.
Not separating the functional and technical aspects of the architecture	The functional and technical layers of the system architecture crisscross each other. Functional layers represent the behavior of the system, whereas the technical layer represents the database, rules, and interfaces.	Revisit Figure 15.10 to further understand the difference between the functional and technical layers of the system. Use that information to create a basic system architecture.

Discussion Questions

1. Discuss the concept of reuse within software engineering. What are the different types of reuse and how does each benefit a project?
2. How is a code-level reuse different from a design-level reuse? Which one requires a more strategic approach? Why?
3. How is reuse with inheritance different from reuse with encapsulation? Discuss with examples.
4. Productivity and quality are considered two advantages of reusability. Explain with examples.
5. List and explain an advantage of "with" and "for" reuse.
6. List and explain a challenge of "with" and "for" reuse.
7. What is granularity of design? Discuss with an example.
8. Discuss why a fine granular design has greater overheads as compared with coarse granular designs.
9. What are the different types of patterns? Discuss design patterns in particular with examples.
10. List two practical advantages of using design patterns—with an example.
11. Describe the `Observer` pattern in terms of its use with Patient and Doctor classes (Figure 15.4).
12. Discuss the Singleton pattern and how it can be used in practice.
13. What is robustness? What are its advantages?
14. What is the overhead associated with robustness? Answer with an example.
15. Explain why a good system architecture can form the basis for good test designs.
16. What are the basic system architecture considerations? Which of the two considerations have priority if the project is technology driven?
17. How does a system architecture help in the creation of packages?

Team Project Case Study

1. Consider reusability issues, discussed in this chapter, in the context of your team project. In particular, document the three levels of reuse outlined in Figure 15.1, as applicable to your team project.
2. Discuss the challenges of "with" and "for" reuse in your project. Are you likely to apply "with" reuse in this new project? Why? Document your thoughts.
3. Consider the generalization and specialization of classes in order to enhance reuse in your overall system design.
4. Apply the principle of granularity in your design to see if classes can be made "FINER" or smaller-sized to facilitate their reuse in subsequent projects and iterations.
5. Consider a design pattern like `Observer`, `Singleton`, or `Façade`. Apply that design pattern in any of your class diagrams. (This will require all members of the project team to sit together and discuss which class diagram is suitable for application of the design pattern.)
6. Introduce robustness in your design. Create controller (manager) classes that separate entity and interface classes and entity and table classes. (*Note 1:* interface and table classes are discussed with stereotypes in Chapter 10, and table designs, in particular, are discussed in Chapter 13. The robustness discussion here will update those designs. *Note 2:* Robustness may not be achieved in all cases; therefore, it is important to only demonstrate your understanding of robustness in one particular part of your design, and not in all of your design.)
7. In addition to class diagrams, robustness should also be applied in sequence diagrams in any ONE of your packages.
8. Create a system architecture diagram for your project (similar to Figure 15.10), and, as a result, see if the package diagram drawn earlier (Chapter 3) needs to be modified. Note your observations in your report.

Endnotes

1. Fowler, M. (1997), *Analysis Patterns: Reusable Object Models*, Reading Mass.: Addison-Wesley.
2. Unhelkar, B. (2005), "Stop Playing Games!: Transactional Analysis and IT Leadership," *Cutter IT Journal*, Vol. 18 (No. 4), April, 2005, pp. 13–18.
3. Unhelkar, B. (2003), "Games IT People Play", *Information Age*, publication of the Australian Computer Society, June/July, 2003, pp. 25–29.
4. Alexander, Christopher (1979). *The Timeless Way of Building*. Oxford University Press. ISBN 978-0-19-502402-9.
5. Coplien, J., (1991), Advanced C++ Programming Styles and Idioms, Addison-Wesley Professional, Reading: MA.

Chapter 16

Interface Specifications: Prototyping

Learning Objectives

- Understand system interfaces and their different types
- Specify interfaces and relate them to use case descriptions
- Create graphical user interface (GUI) specifications based on actor–use case relationship
- Create mockups (user interfaces), navigation maps (flow diagrams), and storyboards for mobile applications
- Use different types of prototypes (functional/interface, technical, and architectural) in software engineering

Introduction to Interfaces

This chapter discusses the fundamentals of interfaces and their specifications. These interfaces are the mechanism used by external entities to interact with a system. Actors, as part of use case models, represent those external entities. Therefore, actors form the basis for identifying interfaces to systems. Actors may be more appropriately considered "roles" that *require* interfaces in order to interact with the system. The different types of interfaces for software systems are:

- User interfaces (UIs)—most common within these interfaces are the graphical user interfaces (GUIs) typically made up of screens or forms; there can also be specialized Web UIs and mobile or handheld user interfaces.
- Device interfaces—these interfaces provide mechanisms for a system to interact with physical devices. Examples of devices include key card readers, machine sensors, and Internet of Things. The interface mechanism for these devices is different from the standard GUI as it includes audio, video, photographic, and biometric formats.

- Printer interfaces—these are interfaces of a system with a physical printing device. Therefore, these are a special type of device interface. Although most online system functionalities do not require a printer, there is still a need to have printer interfaces from both legal and usage viewpoints.
- External system interfaces—enable exchange of information with external systems. Examples of external systems include a partner organization's systems, government provided databases, external electronic services, mobile services, and existing legacy systems.

Each of the aforementioned interfaces needs to be specified, designed, developed, and tested. Thus, these interfaces have their own life cycle that is a subset of the software development life cycle. During analysis, interfaces are identified and *specified*—but not designed. Design of the interfaces includes knowledge of the environment where the solution operates, the data and analytics of the system to be displayed, and knowledge of the implementation language that makes it possible to present the interfaces and contents to the user.

Interface specifications and designs contribute to the quality of the software solution. Interfaces provide users with the ability to interact with the system by enabling data inputs and receive outputs (analyzed or processed data) in an effective, efficient, and pleasing way. Since it is the UIs that the end users see and use, UIs play a major role in the user's satisfaction with the system.

The principles of usability and usage-centered designs that apply to software solutions are discussed at length by Constantine[1] and Hudson.[2] User experience analysis (UXA)[3,4] as a subdiscipline of business analysis is prominent in developing good Web-based and mobile software solutions. As the focus of UIs shifts from simply designing great graphics to satisfying the overall goal of the user, additional factors such as screen depths, navigation hierarchies, and storyboards come to prominence.[5]

Specifying Interface Requirements

Interface specifications include details of what is required for the actor to interact with the system. The UI specification document begins with its name, title, and some descriptive information on how the interface is used by the actor. Thus, an interface specification document includes:

- The goals of the actor in interacting with the system (also documented in use cases),
- List of interfaces (based on the variety and number of interactions an actor will have with the system), and
- Navigation and dependencies (based on the process flows documented in use cases but now revised based on the interfaces).

The UML standard plays a minimal role in modeling a UI. There is no UML diagram to model an interface. Use case documentation, however, provides the basis for starting the interface specifications as it contains the actors and their goals in interacting with the system. UIs can be specified using templates, and their corresponding prototypes elicit additional user requirements and refine them.

An example template that can be used in specifying interfaces is provided here. This specification template has an interface identifier, a unique number and a name to the interface, the list of actors who use the interface, and the list of use cases where this interface is used. In specifying device interfaces, this documentation may additionally contain a brief description of the data and a format for data interchange. Another example where this interface specification template can be used is a printer interface, wherein the data to be sent to the printer and the format for printing are specified.

> **Interface Identifier:**
> <This is the number and name of the interface being specified>
> **Actors:**
> <A list of the actors who interact with the system through this interface>
> **Use Cases:**
> <List of use cases or one-line description of the use case in which this interface appears>
> **Short Description:**
> <Description of the interface in a few lines>

Interface Specifications for HMS

This section has examples of specifications for GUIs, printer interfaces, and external system interfaces for the hospital management system (HMS). These examples are the best way to appreciate and understand UIs and creating their specifications.

User Interface Specifications for HMS

What follows are examples of interface specifications for the HMS. These brief specifications are developed iteratively in a project as the development progresses. The actors mentioned in these specifications belong to the use cases specified and documented (recap the detailed discussions on use cases in Chapter 5).

> **User Interface Identifier:** UI10-PatientRegistrationForm
> **Actors:** A10-Patient, A80-Administrator
> **Use Cases:** UC10-RegistersPatient; UC12-MaintainsPatientDetails
> **Short Description:** This UI enables the creation of registration details for a first-time patient at the hospital. This same UI also enables maintenance of a patient's registration details. Specific registration details of the patient for this interface are available in the respective use cases.

> **User Interface Identifier:** UI12-PatientMedicalProfileForm
> **Actors:** A60-Doctor, A10-Patient
> **Use Cases:** UC14-CreatesPatientMedicalProfile; UC16-UpdatesPatientMedicalProfile
> **Short Description:** This UI enables the creation of a medical record for a first-time patient registering at the hospital. Partial details may be entered by the patient. This interface also enables maintenance of a patient's medical profile details. Specific medical profile data for the patient are described in the respective use cases.

User Interface Identifier: UI20-CalendarMaintenanceForm
Actors: A50-Staff
Use Cases: UC20-CreatesCalendar; UC22-MaintainsCalendar
Short Description: This UI deals with the creation and maintenance of personal calendars specifically for the staff at the hospital. The interface allows the hospital staff to query their roster times, enter details on their preferences, and request vacations. Specific calendar data are described in the respective use cases.

User Interface Identifier: UI30-ConsultationMaintenanceForm
Actors: A10-Patient
Use Cases: UC30-BooksConsultation;
Short Description: This UI enables the patient to interact with the system to book a consultation with a physician. The interface needs to access and display data from the physician's schedule to enable booking and maintenance of "consultations" by the patient online.

User Interface Identifier: UI50-BillPayInternetForm
Actors: A10-Patient
Use Cases: UC56-PaysBillOnInternet; UC50-PaysBill
Short Description: This UI enables the patient to undertake payment of their bill online. It enables online payments by popular methods such as credit cards, electronic transfers, PayPal, and so on.

User Interface Identifier: UI00-LogInForm
Actors: A00-User
Use Cases: UC00-LogsIn
Short Description: This UI provides a facility for registered users to log in to the hospital system. Login data are found in the `LogsIn` use case. This interface also allows for the recovery of forgotten passwords.

Printer Interface Specifications for HMS

Interface Identifier: DI00- PrintRegistrationForm
Actors: A10-Patient, A80-Administrator
Use Cases: UC10-RegistersPatient; UC12-MaintainsPatientDetails
Short Description: This printer interface provides a facility to select a printer and change its settings to print a selected form—in particular the registration form data collected through UI10-PatientRegistrationForm. This interface utilizes the features of most standard printer drivers to enable functionalities such as printing on both sides of a paper, printing in high/ low resolutions, and printing in color.

External System Interfaces for HMS

External System Interface Identifier: I90-GovernmentHealthRegulatorySystem
Actors: A90-GovernmentHealthRegulatorySystem
Use Cases: UC10-RegistersPatient
Short Description: This system interface allows for verification of the Medicare details of a patient. These relevant Medicare details are made available by the external system provided by the government—with published interfaces that can be used to "plug in" the services associated with Medicare data.

Examples of User Interface Designs for HMS (Initial Iteration)

Once the interfaces are specified, they are designed in detail. Following are some examples of UIs for HMS in the initial iteration of design. Each UI has its data described as attributes within classes/programs that manipulate and display those data. These interfaces are iteratively designed and developed. Prototyping, discussed later in this chapter, also plays an important part in enabling interface design. The interface examples outlined next can be considered as the initial prototypes that evolve into the final interfaces for the system.

Figure 16.1 shows a sketch of the GUI that will be used in `UC10-RegistersPatient` and `UC12-MaintainsPatientDetails` use cases to capture or update the details of a patient. Example details include the name of the patient, address, date of birth, details of next of kin, and Medicare data. Since this form is an initial sketch in the first iteration in the problem space, it does not provide specific design-level details such as color, size of text boxes, and so forth. The specific quality design features of this interface are marked in Figure 16.1.

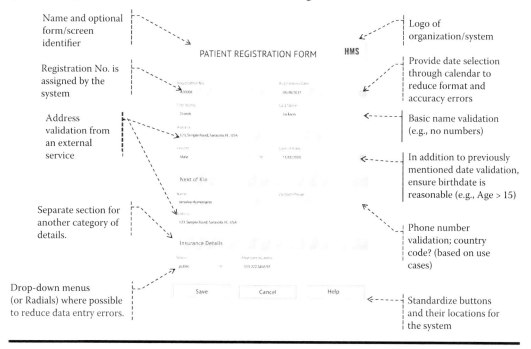

Figure 16.1   User interface of PatientRegistrationForm.

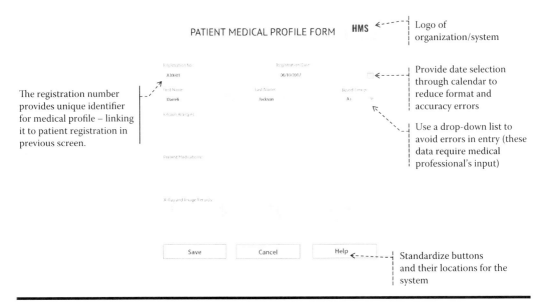

Figure 16.2 User interface of PatientMedicalProfileForm.

Figure 16.2 shows a sketch of the GUI used in recording the medical profile of a patient by the doctor. The same form may show the history of treatments, if there are any. This form is used in use cases UC14-CreatesPatientMedicalProfile and UC16-UpdatesPatient MedicalProfile. The captured medical profile details include the blood group, known allergies, present medications, and details of any medical report. It also shows the same information about the patient such as name, admission date, and patient number to avoid any mistaken updates by the user. This form is at an early stage of MOPS and therefore does not show additional details related to the patient medical profile such as blood pressure or other test records, for example. The quality design features of this interface (in addition to those in Figure 16.1) are marked in Figure 16.2.

Figure 16.3 shows a sketch of the GUI used in maintaining calendar information by staff. This form is used in use cases UC20-CreatesCalendar and UC22-MaintainsCalendar. The calendar information includes booking dates with time and vacation dates. Furthermore, the interface also shows staff ID, name, staff level, and the staff ID of the person to whom the user is reporting. The UI also confirms with the user that he is updating his own calendar. The additional quality design features of this interface are marked in Figure 16.3.

Figure 16.4 shows a sketch of the GUI used in paying bills by the patient. This form is used in UC55-PaysbillByCard. The captured bill information includes the biller code, bill number, and billing date, for example. As with the previous interfaces, this is the sketch of the interface in its initial iteration and, therefore, does not contain the final or polished details of the solution-level interface (such as colors and size of text boxes). The additional quality design features of this interface are marked in Figure 16.4.

Specifying the Flow of User Interfaces (HMS Example)

UI flow diagrams, occasionally also called storyboards, screen navigation diagrams, or navigation maps, model the relationships and dependencies between UIs. Site maps complement these flow

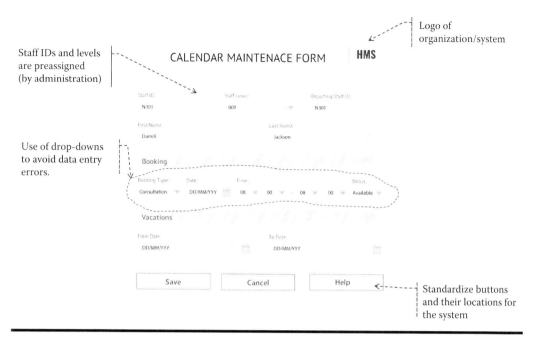

Figure 16.3   User interface of CalendarMaintenance form.

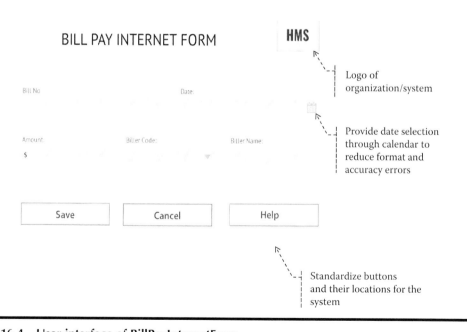

Figure 16.4   User interface of BillPayInternetForm.

diagrams by representing the relationships between various pages of a website or screens (in a mobile app). While site maps show the static aspect of interfaces, when it comes to execution of the system, interfaces appear in different sequences. For example, the same Web page appears multiple times for the same (or different) user and in different sequences. There is a need to model this flow and interdependencies between screens. The most practical way to do so is by creating a flowchart that shows the screens in the flow. Since the UML provides an activity diagram as a flowchart, in practice it is helpful to use the activity diagram itself to create this navigation map. The screens are represented by objects in this activity diagram. Such use is not based on the UML standard but, instead, a practical way to show the navigation of screens.

The flow diagrams themselves provide an excellent opportunity to undertake a holistic inspection of the entire solution from a usability viewpoint. The holistic inspection is important because it goes beyond the accuracy and usability of a single screen and, instead, focuses on a group of screens and their sequence.

Organizing use case descriptions in a series of numbered steps is a good starting point to understand and develop UI flow diagrams that show the navigation of different screens/forms (Constantine and Lockwood, 2001).[6] The preconditions in use case documentation can be used to ascertain correct ordering of use cases. For example, "Staff member should be valid, and should have a valid login" preconditions for use case UC22-MaintainsCalendar appropriately fixes the order of usage for functionality "Maintains Calendar." It is only available for staff members once they log in to the HMS.

Alternative courses of events also provide indications for structuring the UI flow. For example, if a staff member has not filled the minimum number of hours required in a weekly roster while maintaining the calendar, the system should not proceed to RosterConfirmationForm. The explicit relationships among use cases based on Include and Extend dependencies is yet another input in organizing UI flow. For example, the extension UC55-PaysbillByCard in use case UC50-PaysBill indicates that the system control should proceed to BillPayCard form if the patient selects the option to arrange a BPay payment (bill payment via an online bank account).

Figure 16.5 shows a basic example of UI flow or a navigation map for the UIs for actor A50-Staff. The staff actor has to log in to the HMS using UI UI00-LoginForm. This login is followed by UI20-CalendarMaintenanceForm, which provides the ability to update the calendar. This flow is based on the precondition of use case UC22-MaintainsCalendar.

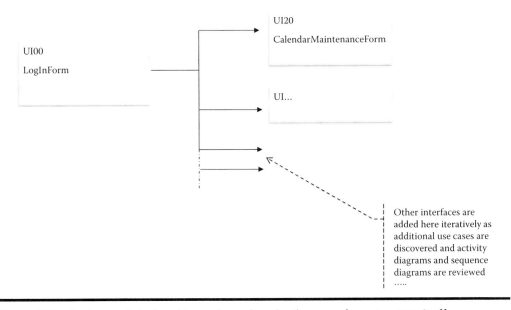

Figure 16.5   Basic user interface hierarchy and navigation map for actor A50-Staff.

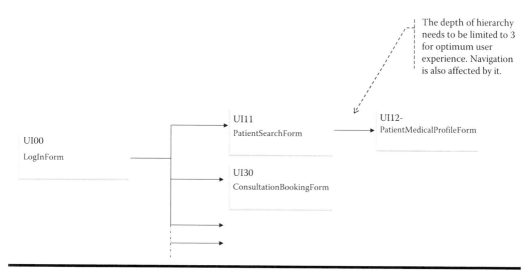

The depth of hierarchy needs to be limited to 3 for optimum user experience. Navigation is also affected by it.

Figure 16.6   Basic user interface hierarchy and navigation map for actor A60-Doctor.

Similarly, iterating through the use cases for actor A50-Staff will help complete the UI flow diagram.

Figure 16.6 shows the UI flow or navigation map for the user interfaces for actor A50-Doctor. The doctor actor has to log in to the HMS using user interface UI00-LoginForm. Then, if there is a need to update the medical profile of the patient, that profile is searched using UI11-PatientSearchForm. Once the patient is successfully located, the corresponding medical profile of that patient can be updated using UI12-PatientMedicalProfileForm. Note that since A60-Doctor is inherited from A50-Staff, the doctor can also navigate to UI20-CalendarMaintenanceForm. The flow for A50-Staff is previously identified and hence is not shown here separately for A60-Doctor.

Mobile Applications Interfaces

Figure 16.7 shows examples of mobile application interfaces. These interfaces are also call mockups. The UI design challenge in mobile apps is to capture and provide detailed and comprehensive information within limited space and time in a user-friendly manner. The specific quality design features of this interface are marked in Figure 16.7.

Storyboards help in understanding the navigation between screens. They also help understand the value that a user is seeking from a mobile application. Figure 16.8 shows a storyboard for a mobile application.

Printer Interfaces

Printed reports are an important part of system interfaces. These outputs (also known as reports, printouts, or hard copies) are a one-way output of the system. Despite the increasing use of electronic media for display and receipt of information, printed output continues to play an important part in business applications. This could be for a number of reasons including, for example, legal and taxation requirements that require hard copies of the output to be printed and preserved. Medical

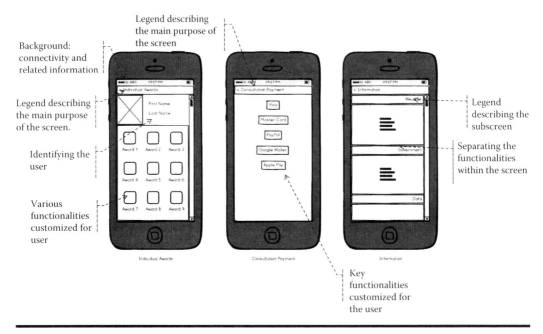

Figure 16.7 Designing mobile application interfaces with Mockups.

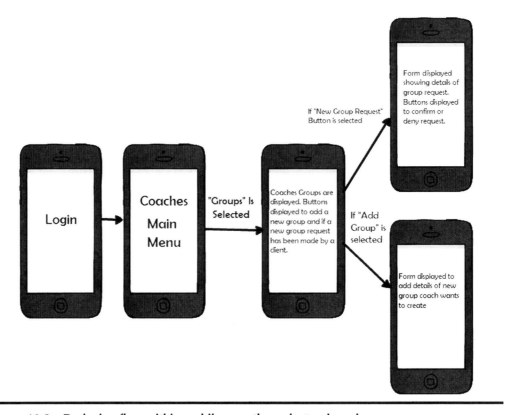

Figure 16.8 Designing flow within mobile apps through storyboards.

records, diagnostic results, prescriptions, and even pay slips and tax reports are common examples of printouts coming out of an HMS. These examples illustrate the need to create and maintain documentary evidence of system outputs. This requires that system designers pay careful attention to designing and developing printer interfaces.

Figure 16.9 shows a basic "printing" architecture. This figure incorporates a printer database between the output of the system and the printer. In other words, the system does not directly print. Instead, the system sends output data to an intermediate "Print Database" from where the actual reports are printed. This approach to printing separates the responsibility of printing from that of the business logic. Thus, in this approach, none of the <<entity>> classes in the system do the printing; instead, these classes send the data to the "Print Database," which then formats and prints the data.

There are two major aspects to designing a printer interface:

Static—this aspect deals with the actual layout of the printed output. Examples of issues that deal with the static design of printer outputs are:

■ What information needs to be printed?
■ Who is the user of this information?
■ What is the actual documentation need of this user (the reason for the printout)?
■ What is the documentation need on the printout (e.g., date and time of printing, page numbers to be carried forward)?
■ What are the header and footer requirements on this report?
■ What are the front and back page requirements of this report?
■ Validation of data including, for example, data range, decimal points, and currency overflows.
■ Need for control totals that will verify the printed totals and give a summarized view of the reports.
■ Incorporating "preprinted" part of the report (this is the preprinted form that minimizes actual storage and printing of repetitive or standard information by the system).

Dynamic—this aspect of printing deals with the behavior of classes when a printout is created. Examples of dynamic issues dealing with printing are:

■ What is the sequence for the printouts—for example, should a patient's details always be printed before the diagnostic results?
■ What is frequency of printing—daily, weekly, monthly, yearly?
■ What are the security requirements when the reports are printed?
■ What approach should be adopted to minimize data transmission between the system and the final printout?

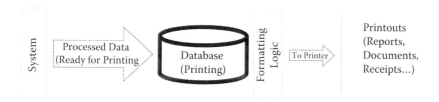

Figure 16.9   Basic architecture of sending system processed data to a printer.

Both static and dynamic aspects of printing must be considered in designing printer outputs. Relevant UML diagrams, such as class and activity diagrams, can and should be used in designing printer outputs. The classes that deal with the printing can be stereotyped as <<printer>> classes. This is because even though they are interfaces, they are a specific kind of interface.

User Interface Design Considerations

The business analyst is initially responsible for the UI specifications. These specifications are analyzed during UI design to create detailed and implementable interface classes. The details of the GUI design include positioning of fields on the screen, dependencies and cross-checks between fields, and dependencies between screens. Consider the UI specifications for interfaces: UI10-PatientRegistrationForm, UI12-PatientMedicalProfileForm, and UI20-CalendarMaintenanceForm.

These specifications simply describe the name, the primary actors, the use cases, and some more information of the UIs. During this design phase these specifications are reviewed to improve the sketches created during analysis. Usually, this reviewing happens by a walkthrough of each step within the use case specification that provides details of the GUI. The resultant GUIs can then be organized according to the actors (users) who will be using them. Simultaneously, minute details of the design, commonly known as colors, fonts, and graphics, are added.

Organizing Interface Classes

In almost all interface designs, the GUIs are derived from existing graphic support provided by the development environment (typically the language of implementation). For example, windows, scroll bars, and radio buttons are not designed from scratch but, rather, incorporated in the interface design from the available technologies.

Most of these small yet important and numerous functionalities required in a GUI are usually available through a Form object and inherited by the GUI under design. For example, a Patient_Detail_Form interface inherits from a Form object provided by the development environment that makes the basic, desired GUI functionality available to the interface designs rather than developing those functionalities from scratch.

While common interfaces are provided by the development environment, they can also be created and reused by the designers themselves. Creation of such common interfaces has been discussed by Kruchten et al. (2001),[7] wherein they are called "central boundary classes" and "primitive boundary classes." A common interface class is created that represents the primary window for the actor interaction. Then the rest of the interfaces required for that actor can inherit the common functionality provided by the common interface class. This applies the principles of reuse, which result in improved quality and productivity because all generic interface requirements for a specific actor are moved to the common interface class. Application of this principle of creating inheritance hierarchies for interface classes is illustrated in Figure 16.10 in the context of HMS.

Figure 16.10 shows a hierarchy of interface (or boundary) classes, all derived from a main HMSmainForm class. This class itself is based on classes provided by the development environment. The actor-specific classes that provide the common interfaces for the actor are the StaffCommonForm and the PatientCommonForm. The rest of the interface classes are based on these common classes, resulting in the advantages of quality and productivity.

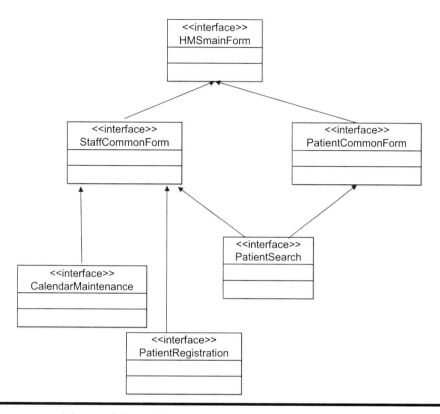

Figure 16.10 Deriving modeling of interfaces based on a central boundary class.

For example, if `CalendarMaintenance` is derived from the `StaffCommonForm`, then by default it will have `StaffID` and other relevant data, positioned at the right place, all available to it. Similarly, `PatientSearch` can be based on `PatientCommonForm`, providing all necessary fields and their positions to the `PatientSearch` interface. However, since `PatientSearch` can also be performed by staff, when it is used by a staff member, it is based on the `StaffCommonForm`. This multiple inheritance scenario is a practical scenario in UI designs, although it may not exactly conform to the discussion on multiple inheritance in Chapter 11.

Usability in GUI Design

Usability describes the ease with which a user can interact with the system. Usability also describes the value that the system adds to the user's goal in using the system. Thus, discussions on usability need to consider not only creating good UIs, but also improving the way the interfaces get used, resulting in the completion of user functions. Well-designed UIs increase productivity, decrease time and costs associated with user training and support, reduce user errors, and improve maintainability of the UI from the designer's viewpoint.

Usability facilitates easy learning and adoption of the interface by users who are familiar with the system. For example, for users familiar with using Web-based applications, the existence and positions of the common OK, Cancel, and Help buttons is well known. Since most users are likely to be familiar with these three buttons, they should appear in familiar positions and order in a well-designed interface.

Naming all the fields and buttons in an interface is also an important aspect of usability. Each field and button should be clearly named to represent the function it performs. Cryptic or extremely long names for buttons and field descriptions in an interface can cause unnecessary confusion. For example, having "PID" or "Number" to represent `PatientNumber` or Patient identification is not a good design. Another common example is the use of the "Save" button. Although "`Save`" can be used in UIs, it may be preferable to use "`Update`" or "`Register`" on the button to further clarify the meaning behind the button.

An overall principle to remember in designing interfaces is the focus on prevention, rather than correction, of errors. For example, if the user is entering "Date of Registration" for a patient, the system should first present the user with "Today's Date" and then allow the user to change it. This approach is helpful in preventing errors compared with the approach where by the user is asked to enter the date (or any other data) from scratch.

Continuous cross-checking and validation of the user's actions prevent erroneous data from entering the system. For example, if a user mistakenly presses the cancel button after filling out the information in the interface UI10-`PatientRegistrationForm`, the system should verify from the user for the action before executing it.

With good UI designs, a large number of fields on screens are validated immediately, rather than being validated by the entity classes *after* the data have been transmitted from the interface classes. For example, entry of a valid date is almost always a function of the interface class and not the entity class. However, once the date has been entered, whether or not it is semantically a correct date (e.g., date of birth should not be greater than today's date) is the responsibility of the entity classes, not interface classes.

Finally, the interfaces should be designed with aesthetics in mind. For example, information in an interface commonly runs from left to right and not the other way around—the patient's first name appears to the left of the patient's last name. Overcrowding on screens should be avoided, and colors should be used to convey meaning and be pleasing to the eye.

User Categories in GUI Design

The tests and inspections for UIs vary in results, depending on the type of users selected. The expertise of the users can play an important part in determining the usability of the system. During interface inspections, it is advisable to select an "average" user, who is not an expert or a novice. Therefore, it is important to understand the general categories or grouping of users, in terms of user expertise.

Users can be very roughly categorized as novice, intermediate, and expert. Good UI design begins by considering the intermediate or average user of the system; however, it will then have to specifically consider the characteristics of the other two user types as well. Furthermore, good UI design incorporates the ability of the interfaces to *change* depending on the evolving expertise of the user.

Following are the user categories and their corresponding design aspects.

■ Novice—this user needs a lot of help and support in using the system. Tool tips and comprehensive help are invaluable to this user. Everything that the user needs initially should be available and visible to the user. Examples of how to use the system, and corresponding brief demos of the same, are very helpful to this user. The novice user is likely to follow the "80–20" principle—that is, he will use for 80% of the time only 20% of the features of the system.

■ Intermediate—this user is the "average" user mentioned earlier, the one who is not a novice but is also not an expert user of the system. This user is generally familiar with the most common features of the system but is eager to explore further and use some additional functionalities to achieve his goals. Good UI design should help such a user by providing basic help and examples and also prompting the user for additional functionalities that he is likely to use if he knows about them.

■ Expert—increasing expertise of use means that users are increasingly able to remember screens and their sequences. This can be achieved by designing interfaces that conform to the project, organization, and industry standards. An expert user needs minimal help and support from the system. Therefore, the UI should also be designed in a way that enables users to achieve their goals with minimal support from the system. This category of user does not need all the help and examples that a novice user needs. Therefore, excessive help should be avoided, as it would be a hindrance to the user. An expert is a user who may use the "clever" and, occasionally, even archaic features of the system. This should, of course, be anticipated and provided for, in terms of relevant helps and examples.

Prototyping

Prototyping is an important part of modeling and is extremely valuable in improving the quality of software being developed. Specifying UIs benefits immensely from prototyping. UI prototypes improve the usability of interfaces, eventually improving the quality of interface specifications.

As noted earlier, there are no specific UML notations or support for UI prototyping. However, classes together with judicious use of stereotypes specifically help prototyping. Prototyping is conducted in all three modeling spaces as follows:

■ Functional prototype (including interface prototype) in the MOPS,
■ Technical prototype in the MOSS, and
■ Architectural prototype in the MOAS.

These prototypes and their importance in enhancing quality are discussed next.

Functional Prototype

A functional prototype deals with the functional aspect of a system. Therefore, this prototype verifies the flow within and between use cases. The UI prototype can be used as part of a functional prototype, although in some cases the functionality of the system can be prototyped without a physical screen—such as by using a set of cards representing interfaces. A functional prototype is particularly relevant to end users involved in the specification process. Functional prototypes help in finding missing requirements, in managing expectations, and in improving the usability of the system through UI prototyping.

A functional prototype is created during requirements modeling in the problem space. Prototypes in the problem space need not be executables. The purpose of this prototype is to extract as much of the functional requirements as possible from the user. Therefore, this prototype can be a collection of mockup screens as shown in the earlier section of UIs for the HMS.

While requirements modeling itself may not be focused on GUI design, the prototypes created in the MOPS can be extended for UI modeling. The prototyping activities create forms and screens in order to get a "look and feel" of these GUI elements as early as possible in the life cycle. Prototyping also helps in experimenting with navigation and flow of screens. Functional prototypes can also be used to set the expectations of (a) the users and (b) management. By showing what a system can and can't do early in the MOPS, it is possible to review and refine the objectives and the scope of the system with users.

Technical Prototype

A technical prototype illustrates the technical feasibility of a system. It tests how a solution fits together in the solution space. Therefore, this prototype provides a lot of information to the system designer as to whether a particular technology is ideal for the solution, whether that technology (such as a compiler for a programming language or a third-party component library) satisfies the needs of designers and programmers and whether the designs have the technical capability to resolve some business problem. This prototype is very helpful to system engineers as it enables them to understand what is technically feasible. Therefore, by observing the technical prototype from a distance, the user and analyst can together work out whether their specifications are technically feasible. The creation and discussion of technical prototypes is beyond the scope of the current discussion.

Architectural Prototype

Although the creation of a detailed architectural prototype is beyond the scope of the current discussion, the constraints placed by the architecture of the enterprise is of immense interest to the business analyst as well as the system engineer. An architectural prototype deals with the architectural feasibility of the system. The possible areas of a software solution where architectural prototyping plays an important part are middleware, architecture, database, and security. Like technical prototypes, architectural prototypes usually involve an executable.

The architectural prototype explores the possibilities of the system in the architectural (background) modeling space. Therefore, industry, business, and technical knowledge in the context of the organization is most helpful in creating architectural prototypes in the MOAS. Such knowledge comes with experience in the industry and the organization rather than from only education or research.

Prototyping and Quality

Prototyping in all three spaces (MOPS, MOSS, and MOAS) enhances the quality of the system being developed. Functional prototypes engineer "quality" requirements in the problem space, whereas technical prototypes model operational and other language-specific requirements.

There is also a need to provide a continuous feedback loop between prototyping and the original requirements. Such feedback ensures prototyping is used to its best advantage—to elicit requirements, as well as to test technical feasibility.

While some object-oriented practitioners advocate evolving prototypes into full solutions, it is usually not advisable to convert a prototype into a solution. Most ideal prototypes help extract requirements from users, help identify potential pitfalls of a solution, and ascertain the likely performance and volume issues that the system will face when it goes into production. Prototyping is also a fine act of balancing—too little prototyping and there is not enough to extract the level of requirements desired or test the technology sufficiently; too much prototyping and the project itself tends to become a prototyping project, which is not the aim of prototyping.

Prototypes, by their very nature, are incomplete. They serve a specific purpose—eliciting requirements, validating technical feasibility, and applying architectural constraints. Beyond that, attempting to complete prototypes is not advisable. Exceptions to this advice is where prototypes themselves evolve into the final UI.

Common Errors in Interface Specifications and Prototyping and How to Rectify Them

Common Errors	Rectifying the Errors	Examples
Assuming GUIs are the only interfaces	Explore other interfaces such as printer interfaces right from the beginning of requirements modeling.	See different types of interfaces introduced earlier in this chapter.
Expecting users to not make mistakes in interacting with the system	Start interface designs with potential mistakes in mind and provide mechanisms to reduce entry errors.	See the remarks in Figures 16.1 to 16.4.
Creating fixed UI designs	Provide opportunities for users to customize their interfaces.	Design a patient registration interface that will *change* as the patient gets more used to the interface (making it easier for the Patient user to customize the interface).
Creating mockups without storyboards	Mockups and storyboards are iteratively created.	See Figures 16.7 and 16.8 together.
Not delineating between functional and technical prototype	Functional prototypes can be created to capture and validate behavioral requirements; technical prototypes can be created to validate operational/ nonfunctional requirements.	See the discussions on functional and technical prototypes later in this chapter.

Discussion Questions

1. What are the different types of interfaces to a software system? Discuss with examples.
2. What is the difference between specifications and designs of an interface?
3. Why is it important to design interfaces as if they were a system in their own right? And why is it important to follow a process for specifying and designing interfaces? (*Hint: they are the key to user experience.*)

4. List four or five key features that you will use to create a high-quality GUI? *(Hint: drop-down lists and radial buttons to prevent wrong user data entry, for example.)*
5. Why is it important to have a similar look and feel for most screens in a software or mobile application?
6. Why is a printer interface important even when most of the business functions are moving online?
7. What are the situations where a system needs external system interfaces? Answer with examples.
8. Why is navigation and depth of hierarchy as important as designing a good GUI?
9. What is the importance of actors in a UI flow diagram?
10. What are the ways other than a visual graphic for users to interact with a system?
11. What is prototyping? What are the different ways to prototype a system? Answer with examples from each of the ways to prototype.
12. What is the difference between a functional and a technical prototype? Answer with examples.
13. How is prototyping helpful in creating good UIs?
14. Why should prototypes not evolve into final solutions? What are the exceptions to this advice?

Team Project Case Study

1. Revisit the use cases documented in earlier requirements modeling work (Chapters 5 and 6). Identify and specify (using the template provided in this chapter) at least FOUR UIs per package.
2. Identify and specify at least ONE printer interface for your case study.
3. Create ONE UI flow diagram per package corresponding to an actor using the interfaces identified in (1) above.
4. Identify and specify TWO devices for your case study (device interfaces may include, for example, printer, card readers for security ID cards, and barcode readers for inventory).
5. Discuss and document briefly the specifications of an external interface to a service for your case study system; identify and document four or five potential mockups for a mobile interface to your system.
6. Develop a navigation map for your mockups identified.
7. Consider the creation of a functional prototype (not necessarily an executable) for the interface specifications identified here.

Endnotes

1. *Constantine on Peopleware*, Yourdon Press Computing Series, New Jersey: Prentice Hall, 1995.
2. Hudson, W. (2001) *A User-Centered UML Method*. In Object Modeling and User Interface Design: Designing Interactive Systems, Harmelen, M.V., (ed.). Addison-Wesley.
3. Unhelkar, B., *User Experience Analysis Framework: From Usability to Social Media Networks*—Cutter Executive Report, April 2013, Data Insights and Social BI, Vol. 13, No. 3, Boston, USA.
4. Unhelkar, B., *Beyond the Who of User Experience Analysis* – Cutter Executive Update—Vol 15, No. 17, Business Technology Strategies practice, Cutter Boston, USA.
5. For example, Kruchten et al. (2001) recommend a screen hierarchy depth to three in order to optimize user navigation experience Kruchten, P, Ahlqvist, S., and Bylund, S., 2001, User Interface Design in the Rational Unified Process, Harmelen, M.V., (ed.), *Object Modeling and User Interface Design*, Addison-Wesley.

6. Constantine, L. and Lockwood, L. (1997), *Software for Use: A Practical Guide to the Models and Methods of Usage-centered Design,* Reading Mass.: Addison-Wesley, 1997. (see also www.foruse.com.) Constantine, L.L., and Lockwood, L.A.D. 2001, "Structure and Styles in Use Cases for User Interface Design," in *Object Modeling and User Interface Design,* Harmelen, M.V., (ed.), Addison-Wesley.
7. Kruchten, P., Ahlqvist, S., and Bylund, S., 2001, "User Interface Design in the Rational Unified Process," in *Object Modeling and User Interface Design*, Harmelen, M.V., (ed.), Addison-Wesley.

Implementation Modeling with Component, Deployment, and Composite Structure Diagrams

Learning Objectives

- Understand components and their representation in the UML
- Creat component diagrams in the architecture modeling space
- Understand the dependency relationship in component diagrams
- Review the composite structure diagram of the UML
- Understand deployment diagrams and creating them in the architecture modeling space
- Learn the processes around the implementation (component and deployment) diagrams

Introduction

This chapter discusses the last set of UML diagrams. These diagrams tend to be "architectural" in nature, forming the model of architecture space (MOAS). Architectural space incorporates the needs and limitations of the organization placed on the system.

The diagrams discussed here are called implementation diagrams because they are very close to the written code (implementation) of the system. For example, if an organization has a certain available bandwidth, a specific database, or a need to create distributed components across dispersed application servers, then these constraints are reflected in implementation diagrams.

This chapter also discusses the runtime composite structure of classes (objects and components) shown by the composite structure diagram. A composite structure diagram is also helpful in understanding system implementation.

Component Diagrams

Understanding a Component

What follows are some of the significant characteristics of components in software:

- A component is a large and cohesive collection of classes in implementation. A component in a physical module of code comprises many classes that are orchestrated to carry out functions.
- Objects and classes form the building blocks of components. Thus, in object orientation (OO) terms, classes are *realized* by components. Components are not object-oriented in a strict sense and many OO fundamentals do not apply to them. For example, components don't inherit the way classes do.
- Components, being a collection of cohesive classes, are static-structural in nature. Since the components are encapsulated by interfaces, all messages to and from the component are through those interfaces. So long as the interfaces remain the same, components are replaceable.
- Components realize a set of classes in implementation. Furthermore, through a set of interfaces, components provide a simple and higher-level reuse of a suite of classes simultaneously.

Relevance of Component-Based Software Development

Components play an important role in software development projects. This is because components are large, coarse granular entities, which makes it easier to use and reuse them in software solutions.

Developing components "for reuse" requires significantly more effort than their use. This is because the creation of components requires understanding the underlying class structure, its realization, and its potential deployment. The discussion in this chapter focuses more on the production (creation) of components "for reuse" rather than "with reuse."

Components facilitate "plug and play" architecture, enabling software developers to use and reuse large pieces of code. The concept of "plug and play" components is similar to computer hardware components. Hardware engineers are not concerned with the individual "chips" that store the data but, rather, with a collection of chips that are treated as a cohesive component. If a chip is found to be faulty, it is cheaper to replace the entire component than locate and fix an individual chip inside the component.

This replaceable and reusable architecture requires standardization of components and their interfaces. Standardized components with well-defined interfaces improve quality, facilitate reuse and thereby increase productivity in software development projects.

Component standardization plays a vital role in service-oriented architecture (SOA). Services as components provide wrappers to legacy "entities;" these services are called upon by new software applications. Componentized services are typically provided on the Cloud as utilities, analytical solutions, data storage, and security.

The concept of granularity, discussed in Chapter 15, also applies to components. Components can be bigger or smaller in size, with their corresponding advantages and limitations. For example, the maintainability of a software solution is influenced by the component size—the coarser the size, the easier it is to replace but more difficult to modify, and vice versa.

Component-based systems are half-way between ready-to-go software packages (e.g., ERP packages like SAP™ and Peoplesoft™) and in-house "handcrafted" software systems. Creating systems based on components provides greater flexibility than packaged solutions but not as much as with in-house systems. Component-based systems have productivity and quality gains due to the reuse of prefabricated components and services.

Types of Components

Technically a component represents a physical piece of the implementation of a system, including software code (source, binary, or executable) or the equivalent, such as a script or command file. There are a few types of components in software solutions. Examples of some of these components are as follows:

- Design time—these components are made up of a collection of classes that are already put together in a design that can be readily used. Examples are design patterns.
- Link time—these components are ready to use libraries that can be directly inserted in the current system design by linking to them.
- Runtime—these components are executables that can be used to provide some service to the system. An example is agents on the net.
- Distributed (DCOM/CORBA) components—facilitate interaction across dispersed software systems.
- Service-oriented components—are offered as a service (AaaS).[1]

Representing Components with UML

Figure 17.1 shows the UML notation for a generic component. A component is rendered as a box with two tabs. The tabs represent the fact that components can be used through interfaces. However, actual interfaces are shown using a circle at the end of a line, as shown in Figure 17.1. A line from interface to component means the component implements the interface. Additional and more sophisticated representations are also available but rarely used.

Components may also be stereotyped, like most other elements of the UML. The major relationship between two components is that of dependency, as shown in Figure 17.1, with an example of one component (Schedule) dependent on another (Doctor). Finally, notes can be added to component diagrams for further explanations.

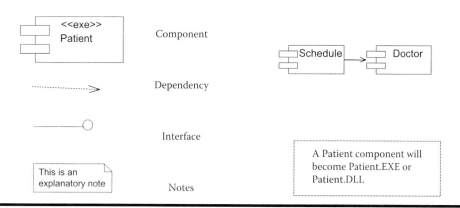

Figure 17.1   Notations in a component diagram.

Component Characteristics and Types

Components, like classes, are created at design, link, and runtime. Following is a brief description of major categories of components that can all be design, link, and run time. Components may also be stereotyped using these categories. These types or categories are as follows:

- Application components deal with a collection of classes containing business logic in them.
- Database components deal with the storage and retrieval of data.
- Security components enable provision of security-related interfaces that can be directly incorporated into a design.
- GUI components provide interface standards and partial implementation.
- Printer components enable faster implementation of printer classes by making printing routines available.
- Utility components support component-based development by providing utility support, such as dates, math, and rate calculations.
- Analytical components provide data analytics such as from Big Data.
- Internet of Things components encapsulate analytics within devices.

As mentioned earlier, components do not inherit from other components the way classes inherit from classes. Encapsulation in components is also different from class encapsulation. The OO fundamentals, including encapsulation, apply *within* components. Outside of the component there is only an interface (or a suite of interfaces) that facilitates interaction of the rest of the system with this component. Therefore, encapsulation of a component merely implies "hiding" of all classes internal to the component and exposing the public interfaces of the public classes through the component interface.

Figure 17.2 shows how the components relate to each other in practice through interfaces. The component-to-component relationship presented in this figure is through an <<interface>> stereotyped class. However, there can be multiple interface classes for a component and multiple relationships with the interfaces.

The interface contains a named set of operations that characterize the behavior of an element. In a component design, the use of interfaces avoids dependency on a specific implementation and allows "plug and play" or swapping of components.

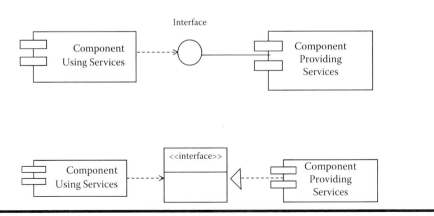

Figure 17.2 Component relating through interfaces.

Component Diagrams for HMS

Figure 17.3 is an example of a component diagram for the HMS. This diagram shows the staff component and how it relates to classes. On the left-hand side of Figure 17.3 is a class diagram that shows the relationship between various staff-related classes. The way in which these classes that are put together (compiled, linked, and built) and realized is shown by the staff component on the right. Therefore, it is highly likely that the <<component>> stereotype shown here as an example will be replaced by the <<dll>>, <<exe>>, or <<service>> stereotype.

Figure 17.4 shows another example of a component diagram in the HMS and illustrates the dependency between the application components and those provided by the language of implementation (Java in this case). Staff, Patient, and Schedule are all components that depend on the Java components for their own implementation. Thus, these application components end up having a .JAVA extension of their own. If the implementation is in C++, then one component would represent the .CPP and another one the .HPP files.

Practical Component Diagram Showing Interdependencies and Packages for HMS

Figure 17.5 shows how it is possible to model components and the particular packages where they reside. `Patient`, `Staff`, and `Scheduling` subsystems are represented by the three packages in this figure. The components of `Patient`, `Staff`, `Schedule`, and `Calendar` are shown in the corresponding packages. A `Database` package is also shown in this diagram. A component diagram drawn in this manner provides an excellent high-level architectural view of the system.

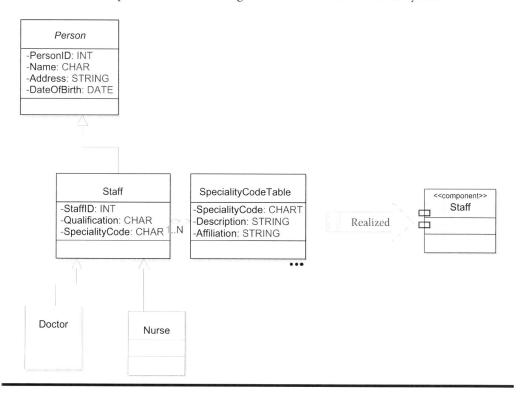

Figure 17.3   Staff component realizes classes for HMS.

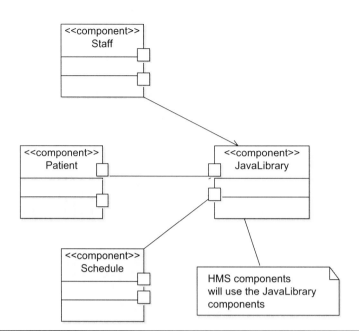

Figure 17.4   Practical component diagram for HMS showing Java library dependency.

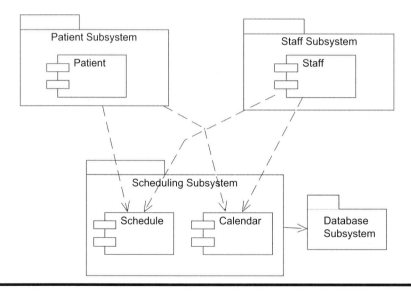

Figure 17.5   Practical component diagram showing interdependencies and packages for HMS.

Strengths and Weaknesses of Component Diagram

What follows are some of the strengths of component diagrams:

- Components show how classes are realized in implementation.
- Component diagrams provide the means to create an executable (implementation) model of a system.

■ Component diagrams represent how the software is physically structured and how its components (or sub-systems) relate to each other.

■ Interfaces used in a component diagram help in facilitating well-organized reuse of multiple classes simultaneously.

■ Component diagrams help in creating a good, efficient architecture as the components within these diagrams can also be applied to nodes in deployment diagrams (discussed next).

■ Component diagrams facilitate reuse by breaking software into reusable parts, which in turn increases overall quality.

What follows are some of the weaknesses of component diagrams:

■ Component diagrams can be too coarse grained and do not show finer details of implementation.

■ Component are not object-oriented in nature and require special care to ensure they are encapsulated and reusable.

■ Component diagrams often have circular dependencies between components.

■ Mapping component diagrams to deployment diagrams is not always easy and may not be supported by modeling tools.

■ Component diagrams are implemented in many different ways by modeling tool vendors; therefore, they are subject to varied interpretations.

Composite Structure Diagram

A composite structure diagram shows the runtime position of objects and components. This diagram was introduced in UML 2.0. Its current use is limited to showing the structure of runtime elements on a system.

Figure 17.6 shows a composite structure diagram for a small part of the HMS. This diagram shows two runtime instances: the staff object and the calendar object based on the calendar component. The calendar component provides two interfaces: `DateCalculate` and

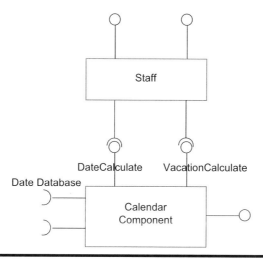

Figure 17.6   Composite structure diagram for HMS component.

VacationCalculate; any other runtime entity (object or component) can access these interfaces and get the Calendar component to perform the work. The interface provided is shown as a full circle at the end of the line, and the required interface is a semicircle at the end of the line.

The staff object needs the two interfaces—called "required." There is also a required interface shown for the Calendar component, which needs the data to be fetched from the database. (Note that the terms object and component have been used interchangeably here. While objects are understood as runtime entities, a similar concept is implied in terms of components here. All components mentioned here are runtime entities and, hence, equivalent to an instance of a large collection of objects.)

Deployment Diagrams

A deployment diagram shows the configuration of runtime processing nodes and the component instances and objects that are executed on those nodes (processors). Such a diagram is part of the the physical deployment of a system. As a result, a deployment diagram is the only diagram in UML that incorporates hardware. Since the deployment diagram shows all of the nodes in a physical network, their interconnections, and the corresponding processes they execute, it becomes an important part of the system architecture. This diagram influences, and is influenced by, the operational requirements of the system.

UML Notations on a Deployment Diagram

Figure 17.7 shows the notations on a deployment diagram. The notations include the processor, the connection (using links), nodes, and notes. Runtime objects and runtime component instances are executed on processors.

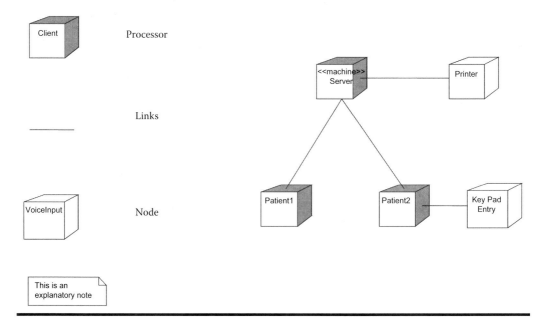

Figure 17.7   UML notations on a deployment diagram and a sample deployment diagram.

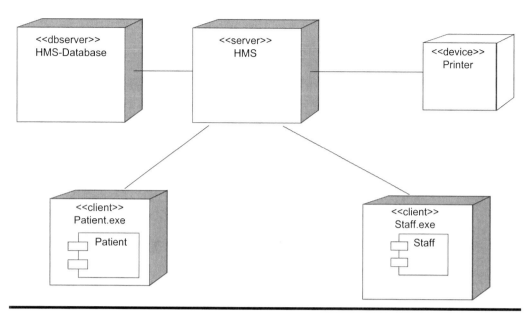

Figure 17.8 Deployment diagram with HMS components and their distribution.

A node is a physical object having memory and processing capabilities. Printers and keypad readers are common examples of nodes in a deployment diagram. A node is shown as a cube, and the connection is a line drawn between nodes. An instance of a node has a name and, optionally, a stereotype. On the right-hand side of Figure 17.7 is an example deployment diagram.

Figure 17.8 shows another example of a deployment diagram specifically for the HMS. The primary node for the HMS is the server, to which a database is linked on one side and a printer device on the other. Two client nodes (machines) run separate components of the HMS—the Patient subsystem and the Staff subsystem. Each are linked back to the server node. The creation of such a diagram is extremely helpful in understanding where the hardware pieces of the system are and how they fit in with the software components.

Note that a deployment diagram is an instance-level diagram. Hence, the processors shown are real instances (like objects) of the system. It is not practically possible to show all the hardware elements of a system in this one diagram. For example, if a hundred users are going to log in to the HMS at a given point in time, it is not possible to show a hundred terminals in the diagram, nor is it required.

Notes are used to clarify the number of elements expected in a system. Stereotypes and constraints can also be used to specify the number of hardware elements in this diagram. These hardware numbers are likely to be influenced—even dictated—by the operational requirements. Hence, deployment diagrams represent some aspects of the operational requirements that also influence those requirements.

Figure 17.9 shows yet another example of a typical hardware diagram showing the deployment architecture of the HMS. In this diagram, the elements are represented by their actual icons rather than the standard cube with the stereotype labeled on it. This makes the deployment diagram easily readable. However, use of these icons stretches the diagram from the standards, requiring additional explanations to clarify the intended meanings behind the diagram.

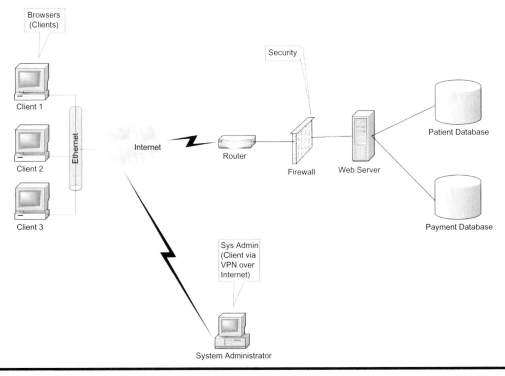

Figure 17.9   Deployment diagram—Another example.

The hardware elements shown in the deployment diagram in Figure 17.9 are as follows:

- The `client machine` representing the computers used by the users such as patients and staff members (these users are all users of the client machine)
- The `Internet Cloud`, which shows how these client machines are connected to the server
- The Ethernet, which provides the local connectivity for the client machines
- The system administrators machine, which connects to the Internet and performs the administration functions on the HMS; this system administrator displays virtual private networking (VPN) connectivity over the Internet
- The HMS `server`, which is shown as a Web server
- The router, which facilitates the Web server's connection to the Internet
- The firewall, which protects the server from external intrusions
- The two database machines hosting the database servers—one for Patient and another for Payment database tables

In addition to what is expressed in Figure 17.9, this deployment diagram can also contain additional considerations in terms of the size and placement of machines (e.g., server speed and size), bandwidth requirements, and security points in the architecture (especially important when the privacy of medical transcripts and security of financial transactions, such as settlement of bills, is involved) and connectivity [shown through VPN in this diagram, but it may be more complex than this]. The server side of the architecture needs special considerations in a Web application—particularly content management. There is also a need to consider issues related to the integration of legacy applications.

Process Around Implementation Diagrams

Implementation diagrams (as do all other diagrams) benefit when the modelers follow a process. Such a process includes activities and corresponding tasks that help create the implementation diagrams. The sequence and selection of activities and tasks shown in what follows depend on the needs of the project. Therefore, the following is only an indicative list of those activities and tasks during implementation:

■ Environment creation deals with the creation of the development environment where the designs are implemented. This requires, among other things, installation of the environment (e.g., a programming language editor) and getting ready for coding.

■ A requirements model is required for further explanation of use cases and activity diagrams as well as preparing for subsystem reviews when the packages are developed.

■ System design appraisal includes the part of the process that finalizes important issues such as the development language, the specific support required in terms of design patterns, and reusable components (class libraries) that support the coding effort. Furthermore, with such a system design appraisal, there may be an optional need to modify the designs created earlier. Such modifications should be factored in the process of system design and implementation.

■ System architecture appraisal requires a critical quality-specific view from the background space. All operational specifications must be considered in such an appraisal, and architectural inputs such as Web services must be considered.

■ Coding—this is the most significant activity in implementation, and it includes writing of code based on the system designs and possible code generation through the UML modeling tool and writing of test harnesses for the coded classes (discussed in Chapter 19).

■ Updating reusable component libraries with classes and class hierarchies that are "for reuse."

■ Creating a technical prototype to facilitate as well as verify the system design and architectural appraisals.

■ Building is the final activity to enable the creation of executable code. However, this activity is carried out iteratively with other activities in implementation. Building the system includes linking all the components in the system, then building the executable, and finally executing it. Furthermore, building also includes incorporation of reusable link-time component libraries.

■ Testing, at a unit level, is an important part of implementation. However, it will iterate with the comprehensive testing activities outlined in the quality control process component in Chapter 9. During implementation, though, testing beyond just unit testing needs to be considered. Designing and coding for testing of components, system, and integration are a part of the activities conducted along with implementation.

Common Errors in Implementation Modeling with Component, Deployment, and Composite Structure Diagrams and How to Rectify Them

Common Errors	Rectifying the Errors	Examples
Treating component diagrams as object oriented	Components are large blocks of code that may contain object-oriented fundamentals within them—but not across each other.	See Figure 17.3, where on the right side is the staff component. This component has hardly any object-oriented fundamental associated with it.
Trying to access components directly and not through their interfaces	Such designs can crash during execution as interfaces localize and control component access.	See Figure 17.2 for a good example of how to access components through their interfaces.
Confusion between structural and runtime components	Structural components appear in designs; runtime components are similar to services hosted on the Cloud.	Figure 17.3 shows a structural component staff; when executed, staff can use other runtime components (services).
Not realizing that deployment diagrams are the only hardware diagrams in UML	Deployment diagrams are hardware diagrams in the architectural space.	See Figures 17.7 and 17.8; these architecture type diagrams only contain hardware nodes and links.
Not mapping components to nodes on deployment diagrams	All components need a "home" or a physical node on which they reside and from where they are executed.	See Figure 17.8, which is a deployment diagram containing two components, patient and staff.

Discussion Questions

1. What are the two implementation diagrams in the UML? Explain also why they are called implementation diagrams.
2. Why is a component diagram static-structural in nature? Explain with an example.
3. What are the possible stereotypes for a component?
4. What is a circular dependency on a component diagram?
5. What is the difference between a staff component and a staff class?
6. What do you understand by "realizing" a component? Discuss with an example.
7. Why are components not considered object-oriented in nature?
8. What are the advantages of a coarse granular component from a software maintenance viewpoint? What are its disadvantages?
9. What is a composite structure diagram? What purpose does it serve?

10. What is the only hardware diagram in the UML? Answer with an example sketch.
11. What is a node? How is it different from a link in a deployment diagram?

Team Project Case Study

1. Identify and draw a detailed component diagram for your case study. At this stage, you are required to produce only ONE diagram that shows the major components of your solution together; hence the team will have to work together in creating this diagram.
2. For this exercise, focus only on the components, not on their relationships.
3. Map a cohesive set of classes to each of the components. This mapping of classes to components (also called "realization") will be achieved in two to three attempts (i.e., it won't be achieved in the first instance). Note that in practice, the language of implementation will provide some ready-made components, which will become part of your solution design.
4. Create ONE composite structure diagram in your design.
5. Create ONE deployment diagram for your solution; this diagram must contain the details of the hardware architecture of your system—namely, the application servers, database servers, client machines, printers, other devices, and so on.
6. Annotate the diagrams with stereotypes, notes, and other explanatory material.

Endnote

1. Unhelkar, B. (2017), *Big Data Strategies for Agile Business,* CRC Press.

Quality of UML Models with Syntax, Semantic, and Aesthetic Checks

Learning Objectives

- Appreciate the meaning of quality of UML models
- Separate the various quality functions in a software project: management, assurance, and control (testing)
- Understand the strategic and tactical aspects of software testing
- Apply verification and validation techniques to enhance the quality of UML models
- Apply syntax, semantics, and aesthetic quality checks to enhance the quality of UML models

Introduction

This chapter focuses on quality *of* UML models—which is different from the quality *by* UML models. Most studies on quality agree on the fact that modeling with UML improves the quality of the software solution. This is now obvious because efforts at modeling requirements, design, and the architecture improves communication, resulting in a much better understanding of the requirements and the solution. The quality of the software solution is enhanced by modeling. But what about the quality of the models themselves?

Software engineering with UML is not complete without a dedicated discussion on the quality of UML models. This chapter draws attention to the work required in assuring the quality of the UML models. Since the models are not executables, an approach different from regular testing of software is required to assure the models' quality. To achieve the objective of model quality, this chapter outlines syntactic, semantic, and aesthetic checks for the verification and validation (V&V) of UML models.

In addition to the quality of models, the overall quality function within a software project and an organization is also of interest in this chapter. Separating quality management from quality assurance (the process of assuring quality) and then from quality control (or testing) is the starting point for organizing the overall quality function.

Quality Management, Assurance, and Control (Testing)

Figure 18.1 shows the three aspects of quality in a software project: Quality Management, Quality Assurance and Quality Control; and the Strategic versus Tactical emphasis of these aspects of Quality management (QM) is the strategic and organizational aspect of quality. QM deals with planning and organizing the quality function for a project and an organization. For example, QM deals with organization-wide policies and procedures for quality, budgeting for and creating a good-quality development and test environment, creating and managing teams (staffing), selecting and using processes and standards, and handling the overall quality culture (sociology).

Quality assurance (QA) deals with the selection, configuration, and deployment of the software development and maintenance processes. A software process reduces errors and increases success in acceptance testing. Using templates to create deliverables and ensure compliance with project standards is important for assuring the quality of UML models. QA includes techniques to verify and validate models. These techniques are grouped into syntactic, semantic, and aesthetic checks in the three modeling spaces (Unhelkar, 2005).[1] QA results in an overall improvement in the quality of models and is an important part of the discussion in this chapter.

Quality control (QC) or testing deals with executing the developed product to ensure it does not contain errors. Testing requires tactical skills on the part of testers. Since testing involves the "detection" of errors, it is also occasionally referred to as "policing" work. Testing essentially includes passing a suite of varied test data through the actual software components that have been developed. This testing work aims to find the maximum number of errors and ensure they are fixed before the system is released for production (discussed in greater detail in Chapter 19).

Quality Assurance and Model Quality

As mentioned in the introduction, while models enhance quality, the quality of the models themselves does not receive enough attention. QA in this discussion focuses on the quality of the UML

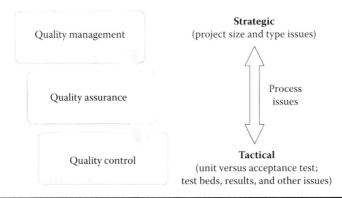

Figure 18.1 Three aspects of quality in a software project—quality management, quality assurance, and quality control—and the strategic versus tactical emphasis of these aspects.

models themselves. Model quality depends on detailed verification and validation of the UML diagrams.

UML-based modeling effort in the three modeling spaces (MOPS, MOSS, and MOAS) produces a large number of "noncode" artifacts. These models are substantial assets of the project that transcend both data and code. A careful approach is needed for the software models themselves to undergo QA.

Verification and Validation

Verification and validation are two important terms in the QA of models. Verification is the syntactic correctness of software and models, whereas validation deals with semantic meanings and value to the users of the system. V&V prevent and detect errors, inconsistencies, and incompleteness. V&V comprise a set of activities and checks to enhance model quality.

Based on definitions by Perry (1991),[2] verification confirms software functions correctly, whereas validation ensures the software meets the needs of the user. Thus, verification comprises a separate set of activities that ensure the model is correct. Validation, however, works to ensure that the model correlates to the requirements of the users (that is, the solution being modeled is meaningful to the users of the system). Therefore, validation of models deals with tracing the software functions to the requirements specified by users.

The subjective nature of quality implies it cannot be easily quantified. A practical way to handle this subjectivity is to start with a "checklist" for QA. This quality is iterated more than once to incrementally improve model quality. The correctness of models is *verified* by a suite of checklists that deal with the syntax of the models, whereas the meaning and consistency behind the models is *validated* by creating a suite of checklists dealing with the semantics of the models.

Thus, verification requires more "concrete" skills like knowledge of the programming language syntax; validation, however, requires more abstract skills. Some of this V&V deals with the visual aspects of the model, while other facets deal with the specification, construction, and documentation aspects of the model. Once augmented with aesthetic checks, this complete suite of checklists provides a "quantifiable" aspect of measuring quality and can be used as a "benchmark" for developing further qualitative understanding.

Syntax, Semantics, and Aesthetics Verify and Validate Artifacts, Diagrams, and Models

Since UML is a language for visualization, quality checks are primarily applied to UML-based diagrams and models. Therefore, the V&V effort also focuses on the visual aspects of models. Preventing errors from appearing in UML models and ensuring they are syntactically, semantically, and aesthetically correct are the goals of V&V of UML models (Figure 18.2).

Thus, to assure the quality of a UML artifact, there are three types of V&V checks: syntax, semantics, and aesthetic. These checks are based on the following premises:

■ All quality models should be syntactically correct, meaning they adhere to the rules of the modeling language (UML 2.5) they are meant to follow.

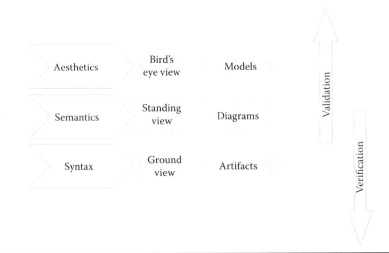

Figure 18.2 Syntax, semantics and aesthetics verify and validate artifacts, diagrams, and models.

- All quality models should represent their intended semantic meanings and be consistent in representing that meaning.
- All quality models should have aesthetics. This means that software models are symmetric, complete, and *pleasing* in what they represent. Aesthetics exhibit the creativity and far-sightedness of their modelers.

While the syntax and semantic checks outlined here have close parallels with the work by Lindland et al.,[3] the last of the three, the aesthetic part of model quality, also finds some discussions in Ambler (2003),[4] under the umbrella of "styles."

Application of Syntax, Semantics, and Aesthetics to UML Notations

The words syntax, semantics, and aesthetics reflect the techniques or means of accomplishing the V&V of models. These techniques directly relate to UML models. The quality of UML models is greatly enhanced by applying syntactic, semantic, and aesthetic checks.

Quality Models—Syntax

All languages have their own syntax. However, two major characteristics of the UML differentiate it from programming "languages" (e.g., Java, XML):

- UML is a visual language, which means it has a substantial content comprising notations, diagrams, and specifications.
- UML is a modeling language, which means the primary intention is not to be compiled and used in the production of code (as programming languages are).

Although a diagram itself cannot be compiled, incorrect syntax affects the quality of visualization and specification. Syntactic errors at the diagram level percolate down to the construction level and eventually into the software code.

Modeling tools help enormously to ensure minimum syntactic errors. Consider, for example, a UML class diagram created in a modeling tool. Most modeling tools provide a selection for visibilities (and create default visibilities like private for attributes). Modeling tools also ensure syntactic correctness, such as not allowing modelers to set multiplicities on inheritance hierarchy.

Syntactic checks ensure that each UML-based model conforms to the Object Management Group (OMG) standards and guidelines. In addition, the notations, diagram extensions, annotations, and the corresponding explanations in the diagrams all follow the syntactic standard of the UML.

Figure 18.3 shows a Dog class modeled by a rectangle. The major focus of the syntax check in this diagram is that the rectangle is the right notation—that of a class. The syntactic check ensures the correctness of the rectangle by making sure it is not an ellipse or an arrowhead (both of which would be syntactically incorrect when using UML's notation).

In terms of UML models, a syntactic check is a checklist of everything that needs to be verified to comply with the official UML standard. Permissible variations to these diagrams are allowed provided those variations comply with the OMG metamodel. These permissible variations to the diagram then becomes a project-specific part of the syntactic checks. Conformance with syntactic correctness is a great aid in communications, especially when these diagrams are read by different groups of people in different organizations across countries (a typical software outsourcing scenario).[5]

Quality Models—Semantics

A software program can compile and execute correctly and yet may not be of any value to users. Similarly, a UML model may be syntactically accurate and yet may not convey the intended meaning of the user. Such a model, although syntactically correct, misses out on the important semantic correctness.

Consider, for example, Figure 18.3. The real dog is abstracted and represented by a rectangle with the word "Dog" written in it. Writing the word "Dog" within the rectangle is syntactically correct. But what if the user was actually talking about a "Cat"? If a class dog is specified for an

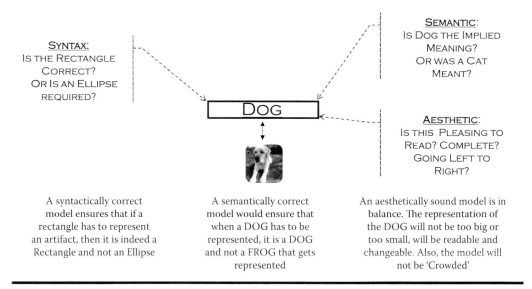

Figure 18.3 Application of syntax, semantics and aesthetics to UML notations.

object Cat, the meaning behind the model is corrupted, even though the model is syntactically correct.

The semantic aspect of model quality ensures not only that the diagrams produced are correct but also that they faithfully represent the underlying reality as expressed by users. For example, business objectives stated by users need to be correctly reflected in use case diagrams, and corresponding business rules, constraints, and pre- and postconditions need to be recorded in corresponding use case documentation.

Once again, models in general are not executable, and therefore it is not possible to verify and validate the purpose of a model by "execution." Consequently, model quality needs alternative evaluation techniques. Walkthroughs and inspections (Unhelkar, 2003)[6] are frequently used techniques for semantic checks.

Another example of such techniques in use case modeling is to *personify* each actor and use case and *play act* through the diagram as if the people were objects themselves. For example, testers walk through use cases and verify the purpose of each actor and use case and determine whether they depict what the business really wants. This is the semantic aspect of verifying the quality of a UML model, supplemented by actual (non-UML) use case descriptions (e.g., Cockburn, 2000).[7]

Quality Models—Aesthetics

Syntactic and semantic correctness is necessary but not sufficient for quality. QA of UML models needs to ensure their aesthetic quality as well. Aesthetics imply style. For example, a code (or any deliverable) may be accurate (syntactically) and meaningful (semantically) but lack in style. Style impacts the presentation, readability, and understandability of UML models.

Granularity (discussed in detail in Chapter 15) is a factor that affects styles on a UML diagram. The level of granularity affects not only the reusability but also the understandability of the models. For example, how many rectangles (classes) are there in a diagram (as against the previous two checks: "is that a class notation?" and "what is the meaning behind this class?" respectively)? A MOSS containing 4 class diagrams, each with 25 classes and numerous relationships, may accurately represent a business domain model but may not be aesthetically pleasing. Instead, the classes need to be appropriately balanced and appear in an aesthetically pleasing format. In the preceding example, the aesthetic check will suggest creating more class diagrams and spreading the classes across those additional diagrams. A MOSS with 10 class diagrams each with 10 classes is aesthetically better than one with 4 class diagrams with 25 classes each. Theoretically, a mega class can compose an entire system. Thus, one class diagram with four classes can easily model an entire solution (not wrong from a UML viewpoint, but visually disorganized).

Aesthetics are improved through experience. Aesthetics also improve through the use of benchmarks and a good suite of metrics (e.g., 7 ± 2 elements such as a class or a use case in each diagram). Such aesthetically pleasing models offer a high level of satisfaction primarily to the members of the design team, but also to all other stakeholders of the project.

Quality Techniques and V&V Checks

The three aspects of quality checks—syntax, semantics, and aesthetics—are not independent of each other. A change in the syntax may change the meaning or semantics behind a sentence or a diagram. While syntax gets checked minutely and for each artifact, an error in syntax may not be limited to the error in the language of expression.

This happens frequently in UML models, wherein the syntax and semantics may depend on each other. For example, the direction of an arrow showing the relationship between two classes affects the way in which that class diagram is interpreted by the end user. Similarly, the aesthetics or symmetry of diagrams facilitates their easier understanding making the semantics clearer and the diagrams themselves more comprehensible to readers.

Quality techniques of walkthroughs, inspections, reviews, and audits are most helpful in assuring the quality of UML models. The V&V of models through their syntactic, semantic, and aesthetic checks is accomplished by applying the aforementioned techniques as follows:

- *Walkthroughs* are carried out mainly by individuals or a close-knit small team. This is a check of the UML model that helps identify and remove syntactic errors. Modeling tools reduce the work needed in walkthroughs.
- *Inspections* are more rigorous than walkthroughs, and they are usually carried out by a person or team other than the one that created the artifact. Inspections are undertaken with the goal of finding both syntactic and semantic errors.
- *Reviews* increase in formality and focus on working in a group to identify errors. The syntactic checks are less important during reviews because they are at a minute level within each diagram, and if the QA process is followed correctly, the syntactic errors should all be identified and removed by this point. In formal reviews, therefore, the semantic and aesthetic quality of a model starts to become important.
- *Audits* are formal V&V that are carried out by parties external to the project and, perhaps, even to the organization. As a result, audits involve only spot checks for syntactic correctness but focus substantially on semantic and aesthetic checks of the entire model.

Levels of Syntax, Semantics, and Aesthetics as Applied to UML-Based Diagrams

The Syntactic, Semantic, and Aesthetic checks apply to a diagram or a model made up of many diagrams. Alternatively, they can also be applied to a single artifact within a diagram. Thus, it is not necessary to have all types of checks applying to all artifacts, diagrams, and models produced.

The three levels of checks of diagramming elements apply as follows:

- Artifacts (or "things") and the specifications of these artifacts are checked primarily for syntactic correctness; semantic and aesthetic checks follow. Syntax checking is equivalent to the ground-level view of artifacts and their notations.
- UML diagrams are checked thoroughly for their semantic meaning; the syntactic checks are minimal as they are already completed at the artifact level; aesthetic checks follow. This is the equivalent of a standing view of a model. Finally comes V&V of the models (MOPS, MOSS, MOAS) together with relevant UML diagrams and their specifications. Provided syntax and semantic checks are done carefully, this model-level checking focuses primarily on the aesthetics of the models. This is the bird's-eye view of checks, with the aesthetics checking the symmetry and consistency of the models resulting in improved readability, comprehensibility, and communicability of the models.

This understanding of the levels of checks helps in focusing on the intensity of the checks and is very helpful to ensure the efforts at quality improvement are well balanced. This is further explained in the following subsections.

Syntactic Checks and UML Elements (Focus on Correctness)

Syntactic checks are applied to individual artifacts (elements, notations) in UML diagrams. For example, in applying syntactic checks to a use case diagram, first they are applied to the artifacts that comprise the use case diagram (e.g., actors and use cases). In another example, of a class diagram, these basic syntactic checks apply to *a* class first and whatever is represented within the class. Since these artifacts are the basic building blocks from which the diagrams and models are created in UML, checking their correctness is the primary activity in assuring quality.

This syntactic check for an artifact is followed by checking the validity of the diagram in which the artifact exists. The focus of quality check thus moves from one element to the entire diagram.

Syntactic checks for the elements and the diagrams that comprise the elements assure correctness of the UML diagrams. As a result, the intensity of syntactic checks need not be very high when, eventually, the entire model is checked.

Semantic Checks and UML Diagrams (Focus on Completeness and Consistency)

Semantic checks deal with the meaning behind an element or a diagram. Therefore, the focus of these checks is the completeness of the meaning behind the notation (as against the correctness of representation in the syntactic checks). Consider, for example, a class `Car`. The semantic checks for model of `Car` would be: "Does the Class `Car` as named in this model actually represent a car? Or is it actually representing a truck?" Note that a truck named `Car` is syntactically correct as long as it has clearly defined name, attribute, and operation. Only semantic checks would reveal the error that the name `Car` does not represent trucks.

The meaning of an element of the UML depends on many other elements and the context in which it is used. Semantic checks are therefore performed at a higher level than the syntactic checks. This means shifting the attention away from checking the detailed correctness of representation and focusing on the purpose of representation. Therefore, the focus on quality checks is not just one element in the diagram but the entire diagram. Semantic checks thus become more intense at the diagram level, rather than just at the element level.

Taking the `Car` example further, semantic checks also deal with consistency between diagrams that would include, for example, dependencies between `doors` and `engine` and between `wheel` and `steering`. In UML terms, while a class door may have been correctly represented (syntactically correct) and may "mean" a `door` (semantically correct), still the dependencies between `door` and `car` or between `door` and `driver` (or even `door` and `burglar`) need detailed diagram-level semantic checks.

Semantic checks also include cross-diagram dependency checks. These checks are applied to more than one diagram. Semantic checks also focus on whether a class has a unique and coherent set of attributes and responsibilities. In the car example, check whether Driver-related operations also appear in Car? This would be semantically incorrect. Thus, semantic checks apply to each of the UML diagrams specifically as well as to the entire model in general.

Aesthetic Checks and UML Models (Focus on Symmetry and Consistency)

Aesthetic checks of UML diagrams and models add a different dimension to the QA activities because they don't deal with correctness or completeness. Instead, aesthetic checks focus on the overall consistency and symmetry of UML diagrams and models. These aesthetic checks are at the bird's-eye view of the model.

By conducting these aesthetic checks at a very high level, a lot more is visible—not just one diagram, but many diagrams, their interrelationships, and their look and feel. This requires that aesthetic checks be conducted at certain "checkpoints," where a certain amount of modeling is complete. Therefore, aesthetic checks also require knowledge and understanding of the process followed in the creation of the models and the software. The process ensures that the aesthetic checks are applied to the entire model, as compared with one element or a diagram.

In UML terms, having created a `Car` class, the aesthetic checks involve verifying the dependency of `Car` on other classes and their relationships with persistent and GUI classes' cross-functional dependencies. This requires crosschecking between various diagrams of the UML that contain the `Car` class as well as their consistency. Furthermore, aesthetic checks, being at a bird's-eye level, are focused on checking whether this `Car` class has too many or too few attributes and too many or too few responsibilities. For example, if the `Car` class has too many operations including that of "driving itself," the entire model would become "ugly." Thus, a good understanding of aesthetic checks results in diagrams and models that are visually pleasing and easy to read.

Finally, aesthetic checks look at the entire model (MOPS, MOSS, MOAS) to determine whether those models are in balance. For example, if a class diagram in a model has too many classes, aesthetic checks ensure a redistribution of classes.

Thus, together the syntactic, semantic, and aesthetic checks make sure that the artifacts produced in UML, the diagrams representing what should be happening in the system, and the models containing diagrams and their detailed corresponding documentation are all correct, complete, and consistent.

Common Errors in Quality Assurance and Testing of UML Models and How to Rectify Them

Common Errors	Rectifying the Errors	Examples
Quality assurance is the same as testing	Quality assurance is prevention of errors; quality control is testing or detection of errors.	See the discussions in the introduction to this chapter where the three terms associated with quality are described: management, assurance, and control.
Assuming that UML models don't require quality checks	Create syntactic, semantic, aesthetic checklists for each UML model and undertake the checks at various levels described in this chapter.	See discussions in this chapter; also, revisit the discussions on notations of each UML diagram in previous chapters.

Common Errors	Rectifying the Errors	Examples
There is only one level of checking for quality of UML models	There are three distinct yet related levels of checks: syntax, semantics, and aesthetics.	See the discussions around Figure 18.2.
Assuming a UML model is correct if its syntax is correct	A syntactically correct UML model can still be semantically wrong. Be sure to check the semantic meaning behind the model.	See Figure 18.3.
Aesthetics of a UML model are a robust standard	Aesthetics depend on perception rather than being dictated. Aesthetic quality is highly subjective and hence will change for different organizations.	Revisit the discussion on aesthetic quality in this chapter.
Verification and validation are not that different	Verification and validation are two different and important parts of quality function.	See the discussion in this chapter on each of these terms and what they mean. For example, Verification = Is this use case right/correct? Validation: is it the right use case to represent this business process?

Discussion Questions

1. What are the three main quality functions in an organization?
2. What is quality assurance? How does it differ from quality control?
3. What is a quality management function in an organization? Answer with examples of activities performed in quality management.
4. What is the purpose of testing in software projects? Discuss why having a good quality assurance process reduces the effort in testing?
5. What is the difference between quality of models and quality by models?
6. What are verification and validation? How do the two differ? Explain with examples.
7. Discuss the three different types of checks to improve the quality of UML models.
8. Why do you think syntactic checks require concrete knowledge of solutions development, whereas aesthetic checks require abstract skills?
9. What is the impact of granularity of design on the quality of UML models? Also discuss which particular aspect of the quality of UML models is most impacted by granularity decisions.

Team Project Case Study

1. Undertake a review of all the packages you have developed thus far with UML models (these will be four to five packages depending on the number of students working on a project team).
2. For each package, discuss the approach to take to assure the quality of the models within those packages.
3. Create three separate outlines of syntactic, semantic, and aesthetic checks you will perform within MOPS, MOSS, and MOAS (these models are not separately delineated files but a group of UML diagrams that specify requirements, design, and architecture).
4. Document the list of checks based on the preceding step.
5. Apply each of the three checks created earlier to the UML diagrams.
6. As with the development process, iterate here for the quality process: first apply the syntactic checks, then the semantic and aesthetic checks to one diagram (say, a use case diagram within Package-1). Based on how your V&V efforts proceed (in a workshop), update the list of checks.
7. Now apply the refreshed checklist to a few more diagrams—and ensure that the checks are updated with discoveries of new items in your checklist.
8. Each type of UML diagram requires its own syntactic, semantic, and aesthetic checks. This checklist is created based on the elements on each UML diagram, its purpose, and its appearance to the reader.
9. Remember to create and apply cross-diagram checks: these are checks on the quality of dependencies of one diagram on another (e.g., a class diagram getting updated by a sequence diagram).

Endnotes

1. Unhelkar, B., (2005), *Verification and Validation for Quality of UML Models, John Wiley and Sons*, (Wiley Interscience), July, 2005; Clothbound, Pages 290+. ISBN: 0471727830 (Foreword by Prof. Brian Henderson-Sellers, UTS, Sydney, Australia).
2. Perry, William (1991), *Quality Assurance for Information Systems*, MA: QED Information Sciences.
3. Lindland, O.I., Sindre, G. and Sølvberg, A., (1994), *Understanding Quality in Conceptual Modeling*, IEEE Software, March 1994, 42–49.
4. Ambler, 2003, The Elements of UML 2.0 Style by Scott W. Ambler, Cambridge University Press. 9-May-2005 United Kingdom.
5. Unhelkar *Sourcing Methods: Philosophy and Approach* (16,000 words), Cutter Executive Report, July, 2008, Vol 9, No. 3, Sourcing and Vendor Relationship Practice.
6. Unhelkar, B., (2003), *Process Quality Assurance for UML-based Projects* Pearson Education (*Addison-Wesley*), Boston, 2003; (394 Pages + CD. Foreword by Vicki P. Rainey, Raytheon Corporation, USA). ISBN 9 780201-758214.
7. Cockburn, A. (2000), *Writing Effective Use Cases*, Addison-Wesley.

Software Testing: Plan, Design, and Execute

Learning Objectives

- Plan and organize testing in software projects
- Appreciate different approaches to testing
- Create test designs corresponding to packages
- Create test harnesses for class testing
- Create functional test cases for use case testing
- Create sample test data using equivalence partitioning and boundary values
- Document steps in executing test cases and collating results
- Planning operational testing (e.g., testing for performance, volume)

Introduction

Quality control (QC), popularly known as testing, plays a significant role in any software development and maintenance project. The purpose of testing is to detect errors. These errors can occur in requirements, design, models, and programs. Errors can also exist in test cases written to detect errors. The main purpose of testing is to verify the correctness of a software program.

This chapter discusses the planning and organizing of testing in a software project. This discussion includes creating test plans and designs, understanding types of tests, creation of test data, and execution of tests.

Testing Needs in a Project

Testing requires an understanding of "what" is being tested, a process discipline (that is "how" to test including how to categorize data for testing), creating test cases, identifying testing tools, and sourcing testing skills.

Effective testing artifacts include a strategy for testing (i.e., having a carefully thought-out and well-documented approach to testing a specific software product), a properly documented test plan, test cases (with positive and negative scenarios), a good test architecture, test data, and traceability of testing.

The detailed and unit-level test includes designing and creating "test classes" that will test the actual solution classes by checking their algorithm and by passing a carefully constructed set of data through the classes that have been developed. The challenges in designing test classes and incorporating them in test designs are an important part of this discussion.

In most practical projects, testing can use about a third of the allocated project time. However, in practice, testing is the first activity that gets cut if the project is running short on time. This is because the visible impact of testing is not felt immediately but usually after the system has gone into production. Therefore, it is important that testing be made an integral part of the overall development process.

Various Types of Testing

Figure 19.1 shows the various types of tests to consider during test planning. These are:

- Unit test—tests the functionality of small units in the model and in the system, such as use cases and classes. Unit tests are usually technical tests of the code, and they require writing test harnesses and creating test data.
- Component test—where the functionality of an entire component or subsystem comprising a number of classes is tested.
- System test—where the functionality of an entire system, together with interdependencies between system components, is tested. When the project reaches this system test level, it is also ready for full performance and load tests.
- Integration test—tests an entire system as well as its interfaces with all other systems and databases already in production. Integration tests benefit from an existing enterprise

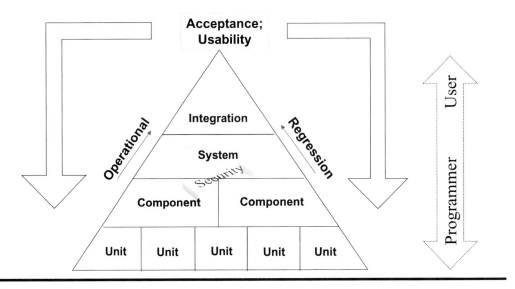

Figure 19.1 Test types.

architecture that provides information on all existing systems and their alignment to each other.

■ Acceptance test—conducted by system users independently of the developers before accepting the system. Developers are available to answer queries, set up the test environment, and support the users; but they do not justify their work—instead, acceptance test results are studied together by the project team to identify potentials for improvement.

■ Operational test—tests the system for its features when it will be in operation. Operational requirements (also known as nonfunctional requirements or NFRs and discussed in Chapter 20) include performance, volume, security, and scalability, to name a few. A test database and environment that can replicate the actual load of the system as much as possible is required for operational testing.

■ Regression tests—performed over an entire system after errors are fixed in any package of the system. Regression testing can occur during development, as well as during the operation of the system. Regression testing ensures that not only is the newly fixed part of the system working, but also the existing functionality of the system is not affected by newer fixes. Automated testing tools play a significant role in ensuring that regression testing is carried out effectively and efficiently.

■ Security tests—while considered part of operational testing, security testing is shown orthogonal to the other tests in Figure 19.1. This is because security testing needs to occur at any and all stages of testing of the software solution. Starting with the unit test, the security of the solution needs to be tested at all other stages of development—and beyond. Penetration tests, defensive and offensive hacking tests, and functional security checks are part of this security testing—which becomes very technical in nature.

Formal reporting of test results to stakeholders leads to an understanding of the status of the project, the reliability of the system in production, and whether any strategic decisions, especially those related to system release (e.g., delaying the release), need to be made.

Test Strategy Influencing Factors

The strategic aspect of testing includes discussion within a project on the scope of testing, the time and cost of required resources, where to source them from, and other high-level complexities.

The risks associated with not testing some parts of a solution and the cost of defect prioritization are also considered in test planning. Although testing itself is tactical in nature, it requires a strategic approach at the start of the project to provide quality benefits to the software solution.

The type of UML-based project influences the creation of the test plan. For example, the test plan for an integration project focuses on the interfaces between the newly developed system and the corresponding legacy application. A test plan for a package implementation project focuses on the accuracy and relevance of the use cases for testing.

The size of the project also influences the approach to testing. For larger projects, a much bigger system testing life cycle has to factor in the costs and time for rework resulting from testing. In large projects, testing starts as soon as the first package is developed and, as such, is a part of the iterative and incremental development life cycle. Small projects, on the other hand, may focus on one-off testing of the entire product; small projects may have relatively few walkthroughs and inspections as compared with large projects.

Criticality of the project is also important in quality control. After the basic testing of the system has been accomplished, the scope of testing may be narrowed to focus only on the critical aspects of the system. For a project with extensive regulatory compliance, requiring audit and external approval, a defect-based prioritization approach can be used.

Organizing the Testing of Software

Organizing the testing function starts in the very early stages of the software project. The test strategy defines the types of testing, the expected outcomes, how the testing is to be completed, when testing occurs, tools used, roles and responsibilities, reporting, and acceptance criteria. The key roles and responsibilities for final approval of test results are also a part of the test strategy.

Figure 19.2 shows the test plan as a key document in organizing testing based on the test strategy. Test plans contain *test designs* that are at the package or subsystem level. Test designs benefit by considering use-case-based versus class-based testing (discussed later). Finally, the *test cases* are at the detailed unit level. These three aspects of test organization are discussed next.

Test Planning

The test plan is an important document that is based on the strategy for testing. The test plan details the resources required for the tests, the timeline for scheduling test designs and test cases, the procurement and use of tools for testing, and the approach to documenting and retesting errors and creating and maintaining the test environment.

A good test plan also specifies the anticipated effort in modules to be tested and the resources available to do so. A good test plan aims to start the testing activity as soon as the first package is implemented. This requires the test plan to be developed during the initial iteration of the software process. It is also important to focus on the customer-oriented external product attributes of functionality, reliability, and usability of software (Younessi, 2002)[1] when creating the overall test plan.

The schedule of the test plan (perhaps within the quality or project plan) should also include specific dates for the completion of individual tests and the responsible team member(s). Cloud-based

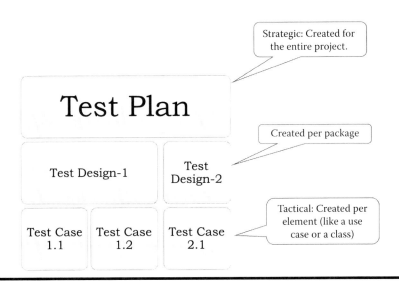

Figure 19.2 Test organization.

testing tools provide a database to record and report software incidents and enable analysis of the test results and making educated guesses on the risks associated with testing.

The following details are expected in a test plan:

- The objective or purpose of undertaking testing; while this is usually straightforward (improving quality and reducing the errors), testing can take various forms and have various objectives (e.g., ensuring a software package is compliant with a regulatory need or testing the performance to ascertain quality of service from a third-party vendor).
- People and processes involved in testing—these are the resources used for testing, the place from where they will be sourced (e.g., in-house, outside), and their skill levels; updating the people skills to ensure it is at par with the needs of testing is a part of this section of the project plan.
- The overall acceptance criteria—similar to the objective of the entire testing exercise, the acceptance criteria are also a strategic section within the test plan document. This is the statement that describes under what conditions the system will be "accepted" by the users.
- List of test designs—derived from the process used to create the entire testing environment, these test designs usually map to the packages within the software models. Test designs contain specific information that deals with testing the packages and subsystems of the software solution.
- Methods and processes to use for testing in detail—these are the descriptions of the activities and tasks used in testing a software solution. Standards (such as ISTQB and ISO9001) can provide inputs into the approaches and methods to be used in testing.
- Approaches to testing—based on a combination of vertical-horizontal, black-white boxes and so on (explained in detail later in this chapter).
- Approach to tracing the tests to their original requirements—through a traceability matrix.
- The responsibilities and schedule for testing based on the resources available, how development is progressing (e.g., interative, incremental, parallel will produce modules that are ready for testing before the entire system is developed).
- Approach to reporting errors and retesting—this is a description of how retesting and regression testing (that is, full testing of the solution after a bug/error is fixed in one part of it) will be carried out. Making provision for retesting is a challenging project management exercise because it is very difficult to predict what will be discovered during the testing phases of the software development exercise.

Traceability Matrix

A traceability matrix is considered as part of test planning. This matrix, however, is important enough to be an independent document of its own. The treacability matrix is owned by the quality manager together with the users. For smaller projects, though, this matrix can be a part of the test plan mentioned earlier.

The traceability matrix, as its name suggests, traces test cases to the source of corresponding requirements being tested—essentially the use cases. The traceability matrix reveals whether a requirement can be traced to a test case. If not, either the test cases are inadequate or some requirement has not been met. Modeling tools often provide traceability tools that can be used in reporting on this activity. Traceability is an ongoing activity that starts with the first iteration test case creation.

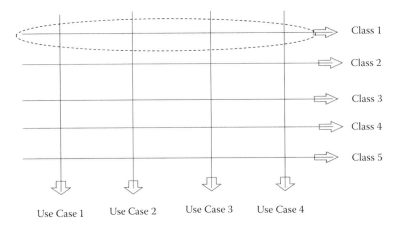

A technical test case tests a class for all its operations; as
such, it results in a testing of some functionalities of
numerous use cases. This technical testing is different from
acceptance testing, where the unit of test is a use case
and not a class.

Figure 19.3   Use-case-based versus Class-based test designs.

Use-Case-Based versus Class–Based Test Design

Use cases and classes have primarily different foci in software modeling—use cases focus on requirements in the problem space and classes on design in the solution space. Furthermore, the relationship between use cases and classes is many to many as shown in Figure 19.3. Test designs for these two crucial software modeling elements need to consider these aforementioned factors and the potential overlap between use case and class testing in test designs.

Classes, especially in the solution space, are owned by solution designers. Use cases in the problem space are closer to users and business analysts. As a result of this demarcation, acceptance test cases that belong to users and business analysts focus on testing the quality of use cases, whereas technical test cases include writing test harnesses. Test harnesses are a set of classes that are written only to test the main classes by automatically passing test data and executing the functionality. Test harnesses test all classes in the system by testing their data-handling and processing capabilities.

Test designs also focus on individually executable parts of a system—e.g., subsystems such as packages. This focus results in a testing approach and a suite of test cases that are specific to the particular package. For example, test designs for a patient package verify and validate all aspects of creating and managing patient details, whereas the test design for a database package contains test cases that verify and validate the performance and security aspect of the hospital management system (HMS) database.

Test designs corresponding to each package also consider the number of classes to be tested and their corresponding complexity. For each class, there are many test cases testing different functionalities.

Test designs further incorporate extra test cases that deal with testing an entire component or a package—as against individual classes. For example, a set of test cases within a test design tests the Date class, and another set of test cases may test the Account class. However, a good test design ensures there will be additional test cases that test the working of the two classes together and the results they provide together to the calling classes.

Test Approaches

Test approaches are a part of test strategy. Test approaches help determine the type of tests to design, the kind of data to create for the tests, and the skills of the people required to undertake testing.

The type and size of project as well as the criticality of the classes being tested play an important part in enabling testers to develop a sound test approach. The test approaches discussed here are not exclusive to each other. Most test designs incorporate some aspects of each of the test approaches discussed here. Keeping the test approaches in mind while creating test designs makes them more exhaustive and accurate.

The different approaches to testing are highlighted in Figure 19.4. These approaches deal with:

- Visibility of testing—black box versus white box testing
- Automation of testing—conducting manual tests versus use of automated testing tools
- Slicing of tests—vertical (functional) or horizontal (technical)
- Partitioning of data—equivalence partition and boundary values

These approaches are discussed in further detail next.

Visibility of Testing—Black Box versus White Box Testing

Black box–white box testing deals with the openness or closedness of the element being tested. Black box tests are only concerned with the inputs and outputs of the system, whereas white box testing goes into detailed checking of logic in the functions and procedures of software. A white box approach is ideal for verifying the internal details of a class design; black box testing is used in acceptance testing of use cases.

Automation of Testing—Manual versus Automated

Manual or *automated* testing is based on the people and tools used in testing. In manual testing the tester executes the test cases physically and checks the results manually. In contrast, in

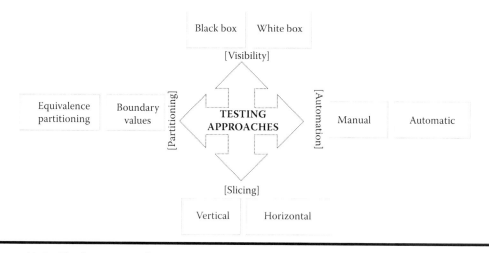

Figure 19.4   Testing approaches.

automated testing an automated testing tool is used to verify the software. Automated testing can help in regression testing—wherein all parts of the system are tested (even though they have not changed) to ensure that a change in one part of the system does not create errors in other parts.

Slicing of Tests—Vertical (Functional) or Horizontal (Technical)

Vertical or *horizontal* testing indicates behavioral versus technical slicing of the system for testing. Vertical division of the system means dividing it into subsystems from the application viewpoint and incorporating those divisions into test designs. For example, a hospital application divided into packages of patient, consultation, and staff is tested for these packages only.

Horizontal slicing of tests is based around its infrastructure rather than its functionality. For example, horizontal slicing for testing the HMS implies testing the entire system first for data only, followed by testing the business objects and the GUI—cutting across all packages and programs.

Partitioning of Data—Equivalence Partition and Boundary Values

Equivalence partitioning and boundary values indicate how test data are sampled for testing (Meyers, 1979).[2] Equivalence partitioning is applicable to any variable that makes up the data entity. All available data are divided into equal partitions, and then samples from each partition are selected to create a sample suite of data for testing. The edges of the equivalence partitions are the boundary values. Thus, test data based on boundary values are made up of data from the edges of the partitions.

Test Architecture

Figure 19.5 shows a technical architecture of the testing classes used in testing of the HMS. This figure shows a small section of a comprehensive testing architecture and highlights the carefully designed test architecture (almost like designing a part of the system itself). All classes in Figure 19.5 are stereotyped as <<tester>> to classify them as classes responsible for testing.

Figure 19.5 shows the HMSbaseTester class, which is an abstract class. This class will contain the common functions required of testing. They are createTestObject(), runTest(), and updateTestResults(). These operations are overloaded by the operations in lower-level classes.

The second-level classes, which also apply to each stereotype of class in the system, are BoundaryTester, EntityTester, and TableTester. These classes are entrusted with the common functions for testing these specific types of classes. For example, BoundaryTester has functions that deal with displaying forms, filling them up with data, and validating the fields on the forms. EntityTester class has the most common functions required of entity classes, such as get() and set() functions, whereas classes derived from the EntityTester have their own specific functions to test out the business logic of the actual entity classes; TableTester deals with the common functions required to test database classes in an actual system and therefore may contain functions related to loading of the database, then checking the CRUD functionality (create-read-update-delete functionality, discussed in Chapter 13) as well as checking for data integrity. These three classes, however, are in the middle tier of the testing architecture.

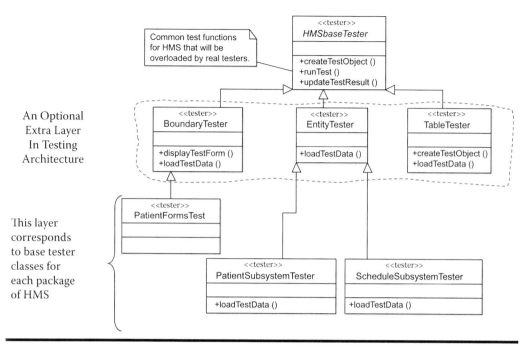

Figure 19.5   A possible test architecture for HMS.

Figure 19.5 also shows `PatientSubsystemTester` and `ScheduleSubsystemTester` classes. These are superclasses, which represent the base functionality that needs to be tested for the corresponding `Patient` and `Schedule` packages. Such superclasses are created for each package and entrusted with the common test functionalities for that package.

Test Designs

Test Designs in Solution Space

Test designs are created based on the understanding of the system at a subsystem or component level. Packages provide a starting point for the test designs. Test designs give a broad coverage of the required functionality rather than the lower-level test cases for each unit of the system. The test designs resulting from package diagrams as well as from the use case documentation in MOPS ensures modularity in approaching testing. The user can also contribute to these test designs, which can then be used to conduct acceptance tests.

Test Design Format

A typical format of a test design contains the following:

- Name—this identifies the test design under consideration, which may be stored as a document. The name should ideally reflect the nature of the test design. It may be the name of a package prefixed by "Test" as in TestPatient.

- Module—indicates details of the subsystem, package, or any other module within the target system that is specified by the test design. It contains a brief description of the type of package being tested, the preparation required for the package (creating test data or procuring a domain expert's services, for example), and the various categories of test cases needed.
- Dependency—to indicate the other test designs on which this test design depends. This is helpful when creating test cycles, or the test design itself may be created based on the test cycles. For example, the dependency of the TestPatient test design is TestConsultation—one should ideally be testing the creation and maintenance of clients after the user codes and passwords for the overall system have been tested.
- List of test cases—this is a list of test cases that make up the test design. All test cases belonging to this test design are listed together with a brief one-line description. Test cases may be numbered and grouped according to the needs of the test design (for example, all interface test cases may be grouped together in a test design document, separately from all database access test cases).

Test designs focus on packages in the solution space. Once implemented, packages (or subsystems) are considered individually executable parts of the system. This requires test designs to consider the approach to testing the package, the type of data required, the dependency of the package with other packages, and the operational requirements on the package. This results in listing and understanding the number of classes of each stereotype in the package. Test designs may also lead to creating a separate test package within each package or a separate test package altogether in the system.

Test Designs for Components

Since components are executable units of code within a package, test designs are also used for individual components. Furthermore, test designs contain test cases for individual classes within the components. Thus, the dependency of components and classes within the components on each other has to be tested and needs to be incorporated into the test design. Furthermore, at times, operations between two or more classes may also depend on each other (usually specified through a sequence diagram), requiring carefully creating test cases that handle this dependency.

Extra test cases are required to test the entire component—as against individual classes. For example, a set of test cases within a test design may test the Date class, and another set of test cases may test the Schedule class. A good test design ensures there is a third group of test cases that test the working of the schedule based on the valid and invalid data entered in the Date class.

Thus, the earlier test cases are considered unit tests for the classes, whereas the one described later are a test case based on some functionality in the system that goes beyond the individual operation of a class, i.e., the scheduler accepting valid dates and between a certain range. This concept of interdependencies is extended in test designs to include numerous types of classes, components, and packages that depend on each other.

Reusability in Test Designs

Reusability in test architecture and design implies that the base classes enhance the ability of the test designers to come up with a good suite of test classes that ensure not only thorough and effective testing but also efficiency in creating test designs and execution of test cases. Reusability in test designs helps the test designers learn from past projects and incrementally increase their repertoire of test cases. Test harnesses and test cases used in the initial iterations of software projects can be reused for testing later iterations.

Attention to reuse helps in creating test data from existing test beds. Finally, test classes used in the collation of test results also lend themselves to reuse and should be accordingly incorporated into test architecture and designs.

While considering reuse in testing, though, it is important to note that classes that are going to be reused ("for reuse" as discussed in Chapter 15) need to be thoroughly tested not only for their current functionalities but also for the potential reuse through inheritance and association in the subsequent projects that are going to use them ("with reuse").

In addition to testing reusable classes in great detail, it is also essential to provide an opportunity for the users (consumers) of these classes to extend the test classes to create their own test classes. Therefore, for a reusable class library, a suite of test classes that lend themselves to reuse should also be provided.

Test Cases in Solution Space

Test cases form the basis of the testing effort particularly in the solution space. Writing good test cases is as important as writing good use cases. Therefore, it is important to revisit Chapter 5, where writing good use cases was discussed. There it was mentioned that good use cases are the starting point for good test cases. This is because acceptance test cases require the tester to step through use cases.

Test cases are written for technical testing of classes and components. These test cases are the basic unit of technical testing based on a small piece of testing code. Test cases also test the basic unit of the software under development. Thus, a test case would document the steps undertaken in conducting the tests for a class.

Test Case Format

The format to document test cases varies depending on what is being tested. For example, a test format for a test case that is testing a GUI is different from one testing a database. Following is a general test case format that can be extended and used for design:

- Identification—a name and number to identify a test case
- Purpose—the reason for the test (e.g., verifying business logic or checking the validity of fields on a screen). This purpose may dictate the type of tester class.
- Prerequisites—elements that are necessary before the test can be carried out. These prerequisites relate to a particular test case. The prerequisite for the entire test design for the module is documented separately.
- Input—the data to enter in the system, made up of valid and invalid sets of test data.
- Actions—the activities or steps required on the part of the tester to carry out the test. Actions may not be required in detail for technical test cases because these actions are part of the test harnesses.
- Expected output—determines whether the test was a success or failure.
- Actual output—or a placeholder for recording the result as the test case gets executed.
- Administrative details—of the tester carrying out the tests, for example.

Table 19.1   Test Data

INPUT for "Patient Medicare Insurance Number" – a 6-Digit INTEGER Field	Comment
312521	Typical valid standard input. Accept; Pass.
999999	Another valid input on the boundary. Accept; Pass.
123A45	An invalid input. System should reject it for the test to be a success (Pass).
1 3 5	Another invalid input: spaces between numbers are not allowed; system should reject for test to Pass.

Test Data

Creating a good sample of test data is important in successful testing. Each test case and test design should be able to draw from a broad range of data to create the sample test data. Each test design should also be able to match actual output with the expected output, especially in automated testing.

The test data are an input file containing a large number of data records made up of both valid and invalid inputs. Table 19.1 provides an example of these two important categories of data. These are the input data for `Patient` class, testing its "`Patient Medicare Insurance Number`" – a six-digit INTEGER field. The valid inputs ensure that the class is able to accept and process the input that it is meant to accept. The invalid inputs test the ability of the class to reject the input that it is not meant to accept.

These two sets of data are entered in the input file, and a corresponding set of expected results is entered in another file. The actual output can then be matched against this file of expected results to ensure verification of test results. Testing tools use this approach to not only conduct regular testing but also regression testing, which requires a large amount of routine testing that does not need human interaction.

Masking and Blending of Test Data

For certain tests, issues like data leakage and privacy are of concern. Who can test and what they can test are important. Therefore, details like account numbers, names, and other identification sources need to be masked before testing can be performed. For example, a credit card number 1234 1234 1234 1234 will be masked as xxxx xxxx xxxx xx34. Similarly, only the last digits of a passport number are supplied. Related to masking is the blending of data. This merges data and substitution, e.g., real names with fake names. The code for masking and blending is itself tested to ensure the results are correct and not causing false test results.

Acceptance Test Cases for Hospital Management System

The following section contains acceptance test cases for the HMS. These test cases are owned by users and business analysts. They are based on corresponding use cases (discussed in Chapter 5).

Test Case for "RegistersPatient"

Identification: Test case for use case UC10-RegistersPatient (Chapter 5)
Purpose: Input valid details of patients.
Prerequisites: Has to be a first-time patient
Admin: Carried out by Harry Potter

Input	Actions	Expected Output	Actual Output
Name: (surname, first name middle initial) Smith, David L Address: (house no., street no., street, town, state, posta code) Unit 45, 34, Gaffao St., Wahroonga, NSW, 2047, AUS Date of birth: (YYYY MM DD) 1965 12 24 Telephone no.:(99 9999 9999) 03 9002 4002 Medicare no.: (M999999) M123456 Status: (private/public) public	The name, address, date of birth, telephone number, Medicare no., and status (whether public or private patient) are to be entered in the given format.	New patient should be created with a patient number generated by the system.	New registered patient in the name of Smith, David L with patient ID : P 3001, who is a public patient with a Medicare no. of M123456.
Name: Hassel, 123 L Address: 45, Hassler St., Mt. Anan NSW 2333. Date of birth: 1965 12 24 Telephone no.: 03 9003 5002 Medicare no.: M788456 Status: Private	The name, address, date of birth, telephone number, Medicare no., and status (whether public or private patient) are to be entered in the given format.	New patient should NOT be created due to WRONG name data format entry. An error message should be generated.	Display message: Invalid name: given name contains numerical characters.
Name: Yallop, Graham N Address: 44, Nomess St., Erinsborogh SA 2333. Date of birth: 21 10 1966 Telephone no.: 03 8003 4544 Medicare no.: M243534 Status: Private	The name, address, date of birth, telephone number, Medicare no., and status (whether public or private patient) are to be entered in the given format.	New patient should NOT be created due to wrong D.O.B. data format entry. An error message should be generated.	Display message: Invalid date of birth. The format is YYYY MM DD. Please reenter.

Test Case for "MaintainsCalendar"

Identification: Test case for use case UC22-MaintainsCalendar (Chapter 5)
Purpose: This use case deals with the maintenance of personal calendars by hospital staff
Prerequisites: A valid staff member with a valid login
Admin: Carried out by Ron Wesley

Input	Actions	Expected Output	Actual Output
Login: wes123 Roster Preference: 21 Week start date 22-11-2004 Hours: 38	The staff member logs in. Clicks for his calendar. Enters the preferred roster number and weekly hours.	Calendar should be created/updated for the login staff member indicating his new work hours.	Roster for week starting 22-11-2004 Monday 1.00–8.30 pm Tuesday 1.00–8.30pm Wednesday 1.00–8.30pm Thursday 1.00–8.30pm Friday 1.00–9.00pm
Login: adn123 Roster Preference: 22 Week start date 22-11-2004 Hours: 50	The staff member logs in. Clicks for his calendar. Enters the preferred roster number and weekly hours.	Calendar should NOT be created/updated for the login staff member indicating his new desired work hours exceed the maximum allowed per week.	Display message: Invalid entry due to work hours >38 per week.
Login: 122223 Roster Preference: 21 Week start date 22-11-2004 Hours: 35	The staff member fails login due to wrong login.	The staff member should NOT be able to log in due to wrong login data format.	Display message: Invalid login. Please reenter.

Test Case for "BooksConsultation"

Identification: Test case for use case UC30-BooksConsultation (Chapter 5)
Purpose: This use case describes the process by which a patient is able to book a consultation session with a doctor.
Prerequisites: Patient should be registered in the system.
Admin: Carried out by Janalee and Tyler

Input	Actions	Expected Output	Actual Output
Patient ID: P 3001 Details: Throat problem Preferred Doctors: Dr. Bartlett Dr. Casper Dr. Chatfield Appointment: Dr. Bartlett 22/11/2004 at 9.00am Special Comments (optional): "Fasting for blood test"	The patient clicks to Book a Consultation session via the hospital's website and input his patient no. and details of his illness. Then the system would provide a list of doctors and the patient will give three choices for doctors.	An a Appointment time and date are to be displayed with a doctor, out of three choices provided by the patient.	Display message: Your Appointment Room No. 222 Dr. Bartlett On 22/11/2004 at 9.00 am. Please be present at the lab (room 232) half an hour early to take blood sample if required.
Patient ID: 20030	The patient clicks to Book Consultation via the hospital's website and input his patient no. The system rejects the patient as his patient number is not correct.	Patient is not allowed to log in due to wrong login. A message should be generated accordingly.	Display message: Invalid patient no. Please reenter.
Patient Id: P 5002 Details : Throat problem Preferred Doctors: Appointment: 22/11/2004 at 9.00am Special Comment: (Optional)	The patient clicks to Book a Consultation via the hospital's website and input his patient no. and details of his illness. He also inputs a consultation time. He didn't input his preference of doctors.	An a Appointment time and date are not to be displayed with a doctor due to not entering his choice of doctors. A message should be generated accordingly.	Display message: Please give choice of doctors to book a consultation.

Test Case for "PaysBill"

Identification: Test case for use case UC50-PaysBill (Chapter 5)
Purpose: This use case describes the process by which a patient pays his medical bill.
Prerequisites: Patient should be registered in the system.
Admin: Carried out by Ravi and Andy

Input	Actions	Expected Output	Actual Output
Patient login: P2003 Payment type: Cash/Check/Card/ BPay	Patient logs in and the bill is displayed. After checking the details the patient will opt for a payment type. (BPay)	A printed bill for customer as an invoice to be settled.	Invoice No. 200303 Amount to be settled: $125 Date of Payment: 02/10/04
Patient login: 12343X	Patient tries to login but fails as the login is incorrect.	Prompt saying "Invalid Login/ Password. Please Try again.	Display message: "Invalid login. Please try again."

Test Case for "PaysBillOnInternet"

Identification: Test case for use case UC56-PaysBillOnInternet (Figure 5.6 in Chapter 5)

Purpose: This use case describes the process by which a patient pays his medical bill over the Internet by credit card.

Prerequisites: Patient should be registered in the system.

Admin: Carried out by Andy and Allison

Input	Actions	Expected Output	Actual Output
Patient login: P2003 Payment type: Credit card Credit card no. 1111 2222 2222 3333 Valid until: 06/05 Type: VISA	Patient logs in and the bill is displayed. After checking the details the patient will opt to pay the bill online. Once the bill is checked, the card details are to be entered. Card will have to be authenticated.	A receipt indicating the receipt number for the payment made.	Payment Authenticated. Receipt No. 200303 Amount: $ 3333.00
Patient login: P3432 Payment type: Credit card Credit card no. 1111 2222 3433 3333 Valid until: 06/03 Type: VISA	Patient will opt to pay the bill online. Once the bill is checked, the card details are to be entered. Card will have to be authenticated.	A receipt indicating the receipt number for the payment made.	Display message: Invalid credit card. Please enter credit card number again.

Test Case for "CashChequePayment"

Input	Actions	Expected Output	Actual Output
Patient login: P2003 Payment type: Cash/cheque	Patient logs in and the bill is displayed. After checking the details the patient will opt for a payment type of cash/check. (PayPal for example)	A printed bill for customer as an invoice to be settled.	Invoice No. 200303 Amount paid: $3333.00 Date: 22/11/2004 Payment method: Cash
Patient login: 123432	Patient tries to log in but fails as the login is incorrect.	Prompt saying login error.	Display message: Invalid login. Please try again.

Identification: Test case for use case CashChequePayment – (UC57)

Purpose: This use case describes the process by which a patient pays his medical bill by cash or check.

Prerequisites: Patient should be registered in the system.

Admin: Carried out by Alexis and Alexa

Class-Based Approach to Test Cases in the Solution Space

This section discusses test cases in the solution space. The focus here is technical testing of design-level classes. Therefore, all technical test cases and their corresponding test harnesses focus on testing a class as a unit of testing (as against a use case in the acceptance testing discussed in the previous section). However, because of the many-to-many relationship between use cases and classes, each test case for a class also tests some functionalities of numerous use cases. This impact of class-based testing on use cases was shown earlier in Figure 19.3.

Test Harnesses

In an object-oriented design, a class is called upon by other classes for the functionality it offers. This call is made to the operations or methods of the class by other classes. Classes do not execute on their own but are called by other classes. Thus, to start a system, a starting class is required. This starting class depends on the operating environment (for example, in Java, this starting point is the class loader in Java Virtual Machine, or JVM, provided by the language).

It may neither be practical nor necessary to use the JVM and test the entire system every time. On the other hand, it may be necessary to test a class at its smallest level, as it is written by the programmer. This regular and incremental testing at the smallest unit of the system requires that there be some test methods coded in the class itself.

This requirement is achieved by writing a test class to specifically invoke the class being tested and all its operations. Such a test class is called a test harness. For example, in a Java environment, in order to test the `Patient` class, first create a `main()` function inside `Patient`. Normally, a Java application needs only one class with a main method that is the starting point for the application. However, having a main method within classes other than the "starting class" allows for the code for testing to reside within the class, and thus the class can be "unit" tested independently of other classes.

EXAMPLE CODE 19.1

```
class Patient {
// private:
  int PatientID;
  String name;
  ADDRESS address;
  DATE Date-of-birth;

//operations
// public:
+ <<business>> getPatientName (): BOOL;
+ getSerialNumber(): BOOL;
+ changeAddress(): BOOL;
  <<maths>> calculateAge(): AGE;
-   <<database>> saveDetails(Sno, Details): Void;
-
//test operations
static void main(String args[])
aPatient = New Patient;
aPatient.getPatientName();
aPatient.getSerialNumber();
aPatient.changeAddress();
aPatient.calculateAge();
aPatient.saveDetails();

}
```

The preceding class shows how all the functions of Patient class will get tested. Creating the test harness, sending of test messages, and, optionally, recording the results automatically are shown in a sequence diagram in Figure 19.6. As seen in that figure, test harnesses ensure that every operation of the class gets tested. However, test harnesses should concentrate on thoroughly testing functions whose implementation is likely to change over time to allow for extensibility of the function and, thus, the system. This is because the changeability of functions is likely to create bugs in the system rather than the standard functions.

Verifying Test Cases

Once the test cases are designed and created in the specified format, it is essential to verify that the test cases are correct. They can be cross-checked against the results from an existing system, provided the calculations and other outputs have not changed, or the outputs can be verified against sample manual outputs and other calculations performed by expert users of the system. Walkthroughs of the test cases in a workshop are also extremely helpful in verifying that the test cases and test harnesses are correct.

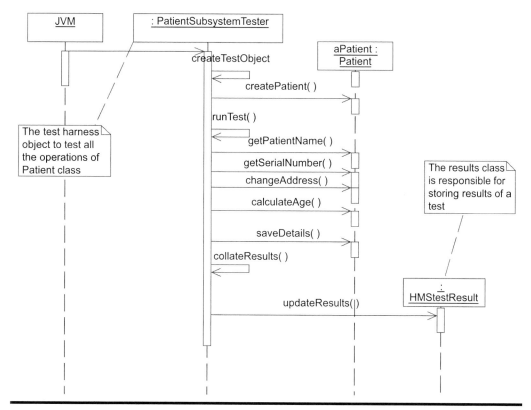

Figure 19.6   Sequence diagram depicting behavior of a test harness.

Operational (NFR) Testing

Operational testing is a separate, dedicated activity within technical testing. Operational tests are designed, written, and executed much like test cases for classes, as discussed earlier.

Operational testing requires a separate approach and design. Therefore, the entire operational test is placed in the testing package separately. Operational (nonfunctional) specifications, discussed in Chapter 20, provide the criteria for the success or failure of these tests.

Some Operational Tests

Some of the operational tests include the following:

- Performance testing—testing the system for its performance under various conditions. Testing tools are a valuable aid in testing the response time of a component or a system. However, response times should be calculated under varying load conditions. Testing a response with minimal load on the system may give a false impression of the success of the test.
- Volume testing—the ability of the system to handle a specific volume of transactions under operational conditions. Examples of volume tests include the ability of the system to insert/ update a large volume of data in its database and its ability to hold data in its entity objects during operation of the system.

■ Security testing—the ability of the system to allow or block data through proper authentication and other security mechanisms. While logging in and passwords are a routine part of the functionality of the system, security testing deals with testing specific security classes and third-party security components that may have been used in the system.

■ Scalability testing—the ability of the system to handle increasingly more load when possibly using additional functionality of the system. For example, if the system can handle 500 instances of the Patient object today, can it hold 50,000 instances of the Patient object in a year's time? Another example of scalability testing is testing the ability of the system to store an increasing amount of data and an increasing number of users of the system.

Common Errors in Testing in Solution Space and How to Rectify Them

Common Errors	Rectifying the Errors	Examples
Testing a technical class without a test "harness"	Write a test harness to correspond to the technical classes.	See Example Code 19.1 and the discussion on test harnesses.
Forgetting to test the component	Ensure that the test designs include testing of components in addition to classes.	See the earlier discussion on test designs.
Not planning for operational testing	Include operational (NFR) tests at the beginning of test planning. Start conducting operational tests as soon as the first module (package) is developed.	See discussion on operational (NFR) testing in the chapter.
Not basing acceptance tests on use cases	Acceptance tests are performed by users before they accept the system. Since the requirements are specified in use cases, acceptance tests must be based on use cases.	See the examples of acceptance tests cases for HMS in this chapter.
Creating insufficient test data	Ensure a broad range of test data covering major requirements are available.	See the discussion in the chapter on test data creation by sampling from equivalence partitions and boundary values.
Assuming all testing is either manual or automated	Actual testing is a balance of manual and automated tests.	See Figure 19.4 on testing approaches.

Common Errors	Rectifying the Errors	Examples
Not understanding the difference between positive and negative testing	Positive testing is where "good" data are accepted by the class; and negative testing is where "bad" data are rejected by the class	Revisit discussion on valid and invalid data for testing.

Discussion Questions

1. Discuss the important issues of creating a comprehensive test plan for a software development project.
2. Discuss the difference between a test plan and a test design.
3. Discuss how you will position test cases within test designs.
4. What is a traceability matrix? Explain with an example.
5. Describe various test approaches that can help create a good test design.
6. What is a boundary value and equivalence partitioning in creating test data? Answer with an example of test data.
7. Provide an example of test data that is suitable for positive testing versus negative testing.
8. What is the importance of automated testing? *(hint: regression testing)*
9. What is regression testing? Discuss in the context of manual versus automated testing.
10. Why is testing of security orthogonal to all other tests for a software system? *(Revisit Figure 19.1.)*
11. Explain a test architecture by creating its sketch.
12. Write a generic acceptance test case for an example use case (like those documented in Chapter 5 for the HMS).
13. Write a generic test case for a business class appearing earlier in Chapter 8 for the HMS.
14. Write a generic test case that will test some of the operational requirements (this may be completed after you have finished reading Chapter 20).

Team Project Case Study

1. Create a detailed test plan explaining objectives, planning of resources, timings, and the justification of such detailed testing for your system.
2. Create test designs—one per package—for your system indicating various tests to be carried out by whom and in what order. Also mention how the test data will be created for the ensuing test cases.
3. Write TWO detailed test cases for EACH use case in your system.
4. Provide inputs/actions/expected results in your test cases.
5. Ensure you have added a set of valid and invalid inputs to test the use cases.
6. Develop a traceability matrix that matches requirements to test cases.
7. Create a suite of Test classes that will test out ALL classes in your design. This requires you to create a separate class diagram that only shows all your test classes. Thus, you will have ONE separate class diagram per package that will model all the test classes used to test that package. Create a separate stereotype called <<tester>> in your design, and apply that stereotype to all these test classes.

8. Although the number of test classes need not be exactly the same as the number of actual classes you are testing, still it is imperative to ensure that the test classes are sufficient to test all other classes in your system. In case of this project work, the number of test classes should be half the number of classes you have entered in your design.

9. THREE categories of classes will be tested: the <<boundary>>, <<entity>>, and <<table>> classes. The test classes for <<boundary>> classes will be testing the display and accept functions; the test classes for <<entity>> will test the business logic—and therefore, they will be derived from the test cases you wrote during analysis; and the test classes for <<table>> classes will be responsible for testing the CRUD functionality. Create a common test class for each category of tester classes, then derive your test classes from that common test class.

10. In addition to the aforementioned test classes, you will also create another suite of test classes that are COMMON to the entire design. These test classes will test the entire functionality of the system together, as against the individual classes and components. Therefore, these test classes may correspond to the test cases written for use cases. These test classes will also be responsible for OPERATIONAL testing. That will require that these test classes create a substantial "test bed" for testing using the logic of "equivalence partition" and "boundary values." These test classes are placed in another separate class diagram and then stored, possibly in a separate package.

11. Ensure that the test database contains a sufficient set of valid and invalid data for testing of all packages. Therefore, the test database should contain a set of test tables that have data for each package.

12. Create a class that can be used for automatic recording and collation of test results—although a detailed design of the result and collation aspect of testing is not required at this stage (as, in practice, this will be provided by an automated test tool).

13. Create a separate section in your report that deals with test reporting, collation of results, and action to be taken based on the results of testing. Note that in this design exercise, you are not actually carrying out the testing but are ensuring that you have designed for the testing in sufficient detail to cater to all actions resulting from testing.

14. Create operational tests for NFRs (you will need to revisit this after studying the NFRs in the next chapter).

15. Update the test plan with the approach to testing, as well as the details of the test designs.
    a. Ensure there is a provision for regression testing in your project plan.
    b. Develop a test defect report for a project showing test results and the tracking of test case numbers to requirements.

16. Create separate test cases for operational requirements (operational requirements are discussed in Chapter 20 next).

Endnotes

1. Houman Younessi. Object-Oriented Defect Management of Software, ©2002 |Prentice Hall.
2. Meyers, G., Badgett, T., and Sandler, C., 1979, The Art of Software Testing, 3rd Edition, John Wiley & Sons, Inc., Hoboken, New Jersey. ISBN-13: 978-1118031964. http://www.softwaretestinghelp.com/what-is-boundary-value-analysis-and-equivalence-partitioning/ accessed October 19, 2017.

Chapter 20

Nonfunctional (Operational) Requirements Specification and Application

---

Learning Objectives

- Understand and specify nonfunctional requirements (NFRs)
- Learn the various types of NFRs
- Recognize two major categories of NFRs: constraints and quality
- Apply NFRs at various levels within a project and an organization
- Study specific NFRs, such as performance, volume, accessibility, operating platform, usability, and security
- Study common nonfunctional parameters that apply to aforementioned NFRs: security, user experience, Big Data (velocity, variety), and the Cloud
- Identify critical issues in capturing and analyzing operational requirements

Nonfunctional (Operational) Requirements

This chapter focuses on the important topic of nonfunctional (operational) requirements (NFRs). It is important to capture and implement these requirements in designing and developing a software solution. These are the requirements of a system when it is deployed (that is, when the system is in operation). Therefore, they are also called operational requirements. The functionality or behavior is outside the scope of NFRs. For example, an activity diagram is not suitable to model an NFR because its flow or behavior model is not a part of the operational requirements of the system.

NFRs address issues such as the performance of an entire system under normal business transactions, scalability of a system for varying customer counts, and security of a system deployed over a web-based architecture. Additionally, security, volume, quality of service (QoS), and maintainability are also part of NFRs. The parameters of a system that are not part of its functionality (workflow) but are crucial for a good user experience are the focus of this discussion on NFRs.

NFRs and UML

The aforementioned operational (nonfunctional) requirements cannot be modeled with, say, a use case or an activity diagram. The UML does not have specific modeling constructs (notations or diagrams) for NFRs because its major focus is modeling the functional (behavioral) requirements. NFRs, however, can appear in various ways in UML diagrams. For example, notes, constraints, and tags are used as mechanisms to annotate UML diagrams with NFRs. Component and deployment diagrams in the architectural (background) modeling space are most appropriate for depicting NFRs in them.

The notes feature of the UML in particular is a great help in specifying NFRs. Notes are used in use case, activity, and class diagrams to highlight the operational needs of a system. For example, a note in a use case diagram highlights the maximum number of users for that use case in a day or a year.

Source of NFRs

Architectural and operational constraints of an organization are the major sources of NFRs. For example, a limitation (constraint) of having a Windows 8 operating system impacts the way in which a software solution can be deployed in an organization. As a result, the software solution must be able to operate on Windows 8 across the entire organization. A smart phone's operating system (e.g., iOS or Android, plus the corresponding version number) is another example where the organization's policies stipulate the operational requirements of this system (mobile application in this case).

The enterprise architecture (EA) of an organization limits the type and size of contents, analytics, knowledge creation, and customer interactions. These EA factors are an important source of NFRs. The technology boundaries and limitations of the organization impact the NFRs.

In addition to the operational requirements of the software developed, some additional constraints impact the NFRs. These are the project- and organizational-level constraints that are different from those that directly belong to the software solution. What follows are examples of some of these factors that influence NFRs in a software project:

- The existing technical environment of the organization, its capabilities, and its limitations
- The existing tools and technologies that are used in software projects
- The current project context, budgets, resources, and their limitations
- The type, size, and criticality of the project
- The processes in operationalizing the software solution
- Legal and compliance experts (i.e., lawyers), who influence the way in which a system is developed and deployed, providing yet another source of operational requirements that bind the solution

These NFRs eventually influence the perception of the end user. The front end of a software solution (such as on a website or a mobile application) is limited by the performance parameters at its back end. For example, if a web page of an application freezes due to low bandwidth, the user is not interested or able to perceive that underlying nonfunctional parameter. The overall perception of the user, called "user experience," suffers due to poor operational performance. NFRs are crucial in enhancing the user experience, and they deserve separate and dedicated attention in software modeling and development.

Types of Nonfunctional Parameters

Figure 20.1 shows examples of the most common nonfunctional parameters of a system. These nonfunctional parameters are stated as requirements in the early stages of software development. NFRs of the system are not isolated, independent requirements, even though they are presented here as such. Instead, these NFRs depend on each other and are applied together to the software solution based on the constraints of the EA.

What follows is a summary of NFRs (as highlighted in Figure 20.1). A detailed discussion of each of these NFRs follows later in this chapter:

- Performance (bandwidth)—usually specified in terms of the speed of response expected from a system. The performance requirement for an Internet-based deployment depends on the available bandwidth. Factors such as available processing power and amount of data to be processed, for example, also impact performance.
- Scalability (time)—the expected growth and use of the system over time. Scalability includes system parameters such as data storage and performance related to the system as the number of users grows. Scalability requirements are dependent on the time factor (growth and demand over next day, month, or year).
- Volume (databases)—the size of the database expected when the system is in operation, for example. Data space for current usage as well as backup and mirroring of operational databases is part of this requirement.
- Availability (QoS)—examples of these requirements include permissible downtime for maintenance, number of times a system is allowed to be offline, and expected QoS for different types of system failures.
- Operability (platforms)—almost all systems in operation today require a back-end operating system and a front-end browser technology. This requirement specifies the type of operating platform and the browsers used for the system. Owing to dynamically changing devices and locations (in the case of mobile interfaces), the specifications of browsers become very important. The entire range of browsers and operating systems and their versions is vital in specifying this NFRs.

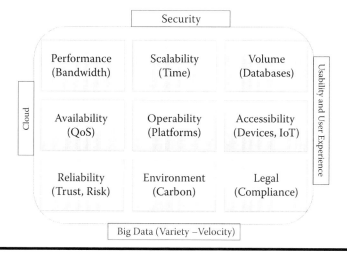

Figure 20.1 Types of nonfunctional parameters in an organization/system/project [architectural (background) modeling space].

■ Accessibility (devices, IoT)—these NFRs deal with the ease of access for user devices. This ease of access needs to consider users that may have special needs (e.g., if users are asked to enter captcha characters to authenticate they are not robots, then those characters should also be available in an audio format to ensure some users are not disadvantaged). Accessibility is not limited to the needs of users; it is also a mandated, regulator requirement (discussed later in this chapter).

■ Reliability (trust, risk)—this NFR is based on the criticality of the system. For example, an aircraft navigation system can have a reliability specification that is closer to Twelve Sigma (versus Six Sigma)—implying a one in a billion, rather than a one in a million, defect.

■ Environment (carbon)—the increasing importance of environmental consciousness in business implies a requirement to specify the carbon content of a system. While some business systems may not directly contribute to carbon emissions, their effect on back-end data servers increasingly come into calculations for overall carbon emissions of the organization (Unhelkar, 2011).[1] Alternatively, carbon emission management systems have more detailed specifications for their carbon capacity that is specified as nonfunctional as well as functional requirements.

■ Legal (compliance)—financial systems invariably have requirements for tracking and auditing. While some of these requirements are functional in nature (e.g., logging the details of the auditor), others that deal with creating an audit trail and backups may not directly be functional. Instead, the legal requirements are specified as nonfunctional and require careful walkthroughs and inspections for their verification in the system.

Each of the preceding NFRs is impacted by four other nonfunctional (operational) parameters. These four parameters are shown in Figure 20.1 (and discussed in greater detail later in this chapter). These nonfunctional parameters are as follows:

■ Security (levels)—this requirement varies widely, going from a specific function or use case in a system through to the organizational policies in terms of access to its Web portals. Examples of security requirements include encryption (e.g., 128 bit), passwords policies, and browser requirements.

■ Usability and user experience—this requirement applies to all other requirements shown in the center of Figure 20.1. While usability itself deals with the ease of use of a typical user interface of the system, user experience deals with the overall "take away" of the user when interacting with the organization through the system. Thus, all nonfunctional parameters in the middle of Figure 20.1 influence and are influenced by user experience.

■ Big Data (velocity and variety)—this is shown as a higher-level requirement in Figure 20.1 that influences and is influenced by all other requirements in the center of that figure. While Big Data–related requirements are newer (as compared with the early procedural and also object-oriented approaches to software engineering), it is important to factor these requirements within the overall NFRs of any new system. This is particularly true with the velocity of data coming into the system—such as when an IoT device (a fitness wrist watch, a blood-pressure-monitoring device, or a carbon-emission-recording device) collects and sends data to the system. Furthermore, Big Data also adds to the challenge of nonfunctional parameters due to the variety of data—audio, video, and graphics, for example.

■ Cloud—Cloud computing has brought a vital parameter in the discussion on NFRs, because most new software systems (including and especially mobile applications) store their data in the Cloud. Even corporate systems that have in-house databases are moving those databases to a private Cloud. For example, the capacity, availability, scalability, and reliability parameters are influenced by the Cloud computing architecture. With the back-end data on the Cloud and the processing (analytics) also shifting to the Cloud, the availability of the system and its reliability depends on that of the Cloud—and the intermediate network that carries the connectivity to the Cloud.

Composite Agile Method and Strategy and Prototyping for NFRs

The Composite Agile Method and Strategy (CAMS), discussed in Chapter 4, encourages detailed discussion, modeling, and prototyping of the solution to enable handling of these NFRs. Chapter 16 discussed the important role of prototyping in modeling software.

Prototyping enables simulation of the technical environment in which the NFRs are applied. Thus, creating a prototype for the NFRs becomes vital at the start of a project. Business analysts collaborate with both technical and business specialists to create prototypes and ensure through testing that the NFRs are eventually met when the system is fully developed and integrated. There is no point, for example, in discovering that 128-bit encryption will not work for a specific application once the application has been fully developed. NFRs are tested as early as possible in a project by creating technical prototypes.

To help improve estimations and assumptions, CAMS recommends formally involving business analysts and users early in a project. The architects and solution designers, together with business analysts, explore NFRs and undertake their proof-of-concept prototypes. Business analysts working closely with business stakeholders, architects, and solution designers—especially when it comes to NFRs—is an important part of CAMS in practice.

NFR Categories: Qualities and Constraints

NFRs are broadly categorized into two parts: the various "qualities" or attributes of a system in operation and the corresponding "constraints" on the system. Figure 20.2 shows these two major categories of NFRs:

The constraints are usually derived from the EA, whereas the qualities tend to be specified at the system architecture level.

Constraints:

■ These are the limitations on the system architecture and design. Adhering to the constraints during system architecture and design ensures the proper functioning of the deployed system within those organizational parameters. Examples of constraints at various levels include:
  – organizational (e.g., 100 mbps bandwidth)
  – project (e.g., $350 k budget)
  – timeframe (e.g., must be live by some date)

Qualities:

■ organizational (e.g., 3-second response time)
■ project (e.g., every requirement subject to walkthrough)
■ acceptability (e.g., 1 defect per million; or 23 hours 58 minutes uptime per day)

Business analysts, together with key business users AND architects, are in an excellent position to investigate and specify these NFRs. Furthermore, business analysts can also outline the acceptance criteria (tests) for these NFRs.

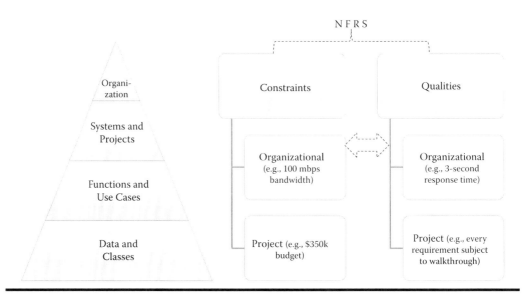

Figure 20.2 Two major categories of NFRs compete—constraints (architects stating what the system can't do) and quality (business stakeholders stating what they want from the system in a function).

The *qualities* (occasionally also grouped under the various "-ilities" required) of the system are specified by the business analysts in collaboration with the users and domain experts. The *constraints* on the system are usually dictated by the enterprise architects who are aware of the organizational parameters applicable to the system.

NFR Challenges

NFRs have a tendency to be ignored in the early part of the development life cycle. This happens occasionally, as these NFRs are not the behavior of the system and, therefore, not easy to document and model.

Another difficulty with NFRs is that they start becoming relevant when at least some part of the system has been developed. For example, specifying and testing the performance of a system is not something to be modeled with a UML diagram; instead, it can only be verified when the system is available in a production-equivalent environment.

Interaction between the key business stakeholders and domain experts is thus necessary to capture NFRs. However, even those interactions are not sufficient for successful capture of NFRs at the start of the project. This is because when it comes to NFRs the experts make educated estimates (guesstimates) to determine NFRs. For example, the number of accounts expected to be opened in the first year of a banking application (10,000? Or 100,000?) can be "anybody's guess." Estimates are made at the beginning of the project and then refined as the iterative and incremental development of the system progresses. An iterative and incremental approach to NFRs ensures the architecture of the system will be capable of handling the NFRs.

Owing to the guess work involved in NFRs, it is also a good idea to pair these requirements with corresponding *assumptions*. With the example of 100,000 accounts expected to be opened in the first year, assumptions can be fairly accurate when correlated with online marketing and the bank's social media. As can be seen, these requirements are crucial in satisfying the needs and "experience" of the users of the system when in operation and also its eventual acceptance.

Capturing NFRs in CAMS

Business stakeholders and domain experts participate in workshops, usually organized by business analysts, to discover these otherwise unfamiliar and unclear requirements. Lack of standardized modeling constructs (especially in a pure Agile approach) for NFRs also means they are not visually modeled. Furthermore, the business stakeholders may not fully know NFRs up front.

The uptime required of a system or the resources required to achieve that uptime may remain uncertain and unmodeled at the start of a project. Opening up the discussions on NFRs in the requirements modeling workshops is an ideal way to start capturing these NFRs. For example, if the business is demanding a 3-second response time for any query on its new solution (a performance-related *quality* expected of the system), then the enterprise architect can say, "No, that will not be possible as we only have a certain bandwidth available—100mbps." Once this is discussed (although not necessarily sorted out or resolved) up front, it opens up doors for the business stakeholders to either increase their budgets to achieve the quality they are expecting of the solution or, alternatively, lower their expectations. If these NFRs are left untouched or not discussed until later stages of the solution, then the expectations and the offerings of the solutions will not match.

CAMS AND NFR TESTING

There is no one-to-one relationship between functional and nonfunctional requirements. However, a careful inspection of the functional requirements can always throw light on the NFRs. Many NFRs apply at the project and organizational levels but not at an individual functional level. This could be another reason why NFRs usually lag behind functional requirements. Testing NFRs can also lag behind—"since there is no system, there is not much that can be checked for performance."

Creating an early prototype of the system where the NFRs can be tested is encouraged in CAMS. Instead of only focusing on the implementation of functional requirements, the enterprise architect and the solutions designer can work together to load the databases and run the prototypes against these test databases. This is the way NFR specifications (including performance, scalability, and security), and their incorporation in the solution is carried out in CAMS.

Because NFRs apply across the organization, business stakeholders may not fully understand the level at which these requirements are applied to a software system. The business analyst highlights an NFR and its relationship to cost and time. The qualities the business stakeholders expect of a system need to have associated costs and time, both of which go up as the expectations of the business increase. Note these are not new expected functionalities, nor are they associated with the higher quality of those functionalities (requiring higher rigor in testing). These qualities in NFRs are the characteristics of the system when it will be in operation. Higher demand of NFRs from the system have corresponding costs and time that need to be factored into the project.

For example, stakeholders agree to the highest possible security, 24×7 uptime, and mirroring of data to improve global performance. Unless business analysts show a direct relationship between each of these NFRs and the corresponding costs and times required to achieve the requirement, these NFRs will continue to appear (and increase) as the project progresses.

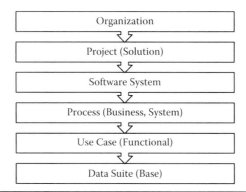

Figure 20.3   NFRs associated with a software solution are specified and applied at various levels within the organization and in the project.

NFR Levels

NFRs are not limited to a system. Instead, NFRs are sourced from and applied at various levels within an organization. Understanding the level of applicability of NFRs is most helpful in deciding where and how they influence the system under development. NFRs can be part of the overall EA, apply at a specific system level, or apply to a single unit of functionality. It is important to identify the levels of NFRs and use them for enterprise and system architecture and the corresponding verification and validation of these architectures. Figure 20.3 shows the various levels of NFRs:

- Organization-level NFRs are applicable across the entire organization. Therefore, organizational-level NFRs apply to all projects and systems that are developed (or procured) for the organization. Examples of these NFRs include policies relating to electronic access, available bandwidth, data warehouse resources, and HR requirements relating to users.
- Project (solution)-level NFRs relate to the solution produced by the project. This is the overall solution, which is more than just the software system. For example, operational procedures and rules associated with the solution can be specified as NFRs at this level. These are the rules applicable to the solution when it is operational. (Note: These are different from the business rules embedded within the software solution.) When specified at the software system level these NFRs apply to the development, deployment, and operation of the software solution in practice. For example, the requirement of a particular operating system or the version numbers of a browser are requirements that can relate to the operation of a software system but not necessarily to the entire organization.
- Process (business, system)-level NFRs are part of managing the processes associated with the solution. Thus, these requirements include detailed business rules that are not part of any visual model. The system-level technical rules that describe dependencies of the solution on other (typically external) elements of the system are part of this level of NFRs. The reason for associating rules with process-level NFRs is that these rules are applied across the entire process, cannot be visually modeled, and are embedded within the solution with no direct visibility to users (and, therefore, no interfaces). Despite the hidden nature of rules for processes, they need to be specified as part of NFRs.
- Use case (functional)-level NFRs are the requirements that apply at an individual use case level (versus the aforementioned rules and requirements that apply at a process level). Since a business process can comprise many use cases, the NFRs at this functional level help

differentiate the requirements that are specifically applicable to only one use case. For example, an entire inventory process may have a stringent audit requirement overall; but NFRs related to an audit for a particular use case that deals with internal staff moving inventory from warehouse to shop front may not have the same stringent audit requirements. Thus, use-case-level NFRs modify or specialize those that apply to the entire process.

■ Data suite (base)—NFRs here relate to a piece of data or a table that contains the data. NFRs for a data suite also apply to the entire database. For example, an NFR related to an amount field within account (typical banking application) can specify a legal (compliance) need for four decimal points. Another NFR at the database level can specify a need to create a mirror image of the entire database to ensure improved performance and availability for a crucial business function.

The remaining sections in this chapter go into further details on some of the important NFRs discussed thus far.

Performance

Performance requirements specify the speed or the response time required of a software solution. This performance criterion plays an important role in determining the efficiency and effectiveness of the system. Thus, this performance criterion contributes to the overall user experience. In case of large and complex systems, subsystems have their own performance requirements. For example, the performance requirement for an external facing patient-related process in the HMS is stringent (3 seconds per page), but for an internal staff-related process it can be more relaxed (5 seconds per page).

Due care should be taken in defining the performance criteria of a system at a very early stage in the creation of a MOPS. During this early stage of development, systems (especially large and complex systems) are divided into subsystems and packages (Chapter 3). Performance criteria are specified for each of these subsystems, and then the criteria are applied to the overall system.

Leaving the specification of performance criteria for later is a project risk because once a solution is developed, it becomes difficult to rearchitect and redesign it to fulfill the performance criteria. The iterative and incremental basis for a software process is most valuable in handling the risks associated with NFRs and, in particular, performance of the solution.

UML models have a direct, standardized mechanism to show performance requirements. CAMS, however, encourages documentation of NFRs on story cards—whose normal format is meant to list functional requirements of the system. Approaches such as PRIMA-UML[2] are worth exploring by project teams trying to get the performance requirement right in the early modeling stages.

Response Times and Performance

Performance of a system, for most practical purposes, is equated to response time—that is, the time taken by the system to handle a user request. End users are looking for increasingly faster response times, regardless of the type of processing being performed. Demand from users is based on increasing expertise in using a system, the increasing number of functions that they are required to perform, and the psychosocial factors influencing human needs from systems and devices. The increasing demand from users is thus a part of scalability requirements of the system that need to be incorporated into discussions on expected performance from the system.

Without due considerations to the many factors influencing performance criteria, the system design will not be able to meet the performance objectives demanded by users. The lack of good system performance can damage customer relationships with the organization (e.g., when a system has poor response, customers will invariably turn away from the system). Internal organizational processes also suffer due to poor system performance resulting in productivity losses and revenue losses. If the system needs a redesign to improve its performance, there will be additional costs to the project and the associated risk of opportunity costs (due to missed market windows). In extreme cases, the entire solution is scrapped as performance tuning efforts may not be sufficient and projects may need to be cancelled.

Performance challenges arise mainly due to a lack of attention to NFRs in the early stages of the software development life cycle (SDLC). The lack of attention can be a result of difficulty in eliciting realistic performance requirements from users. Since performance testing requires a simulated technical environment (a sufficiently populated database and an executing system), this testing also gets postponed in the SDLC. Furthermore, with the use of external, reusable service-oriented components in building software systems, performance issues can also depend on those external services. Finally, the communication mechanisms (including network protocols, security needs, volume, and velocity of data) also influence the performance of the system.

System designers need to continuously keep the "expectation time" by the user in mind when designing systems. It is important to communicate to users the balance between demanding higher performance time and the costs associated with fulfilling those demands. A random expectation time for system response is not helpful in setting the goals and the designs for the system. Additionally, the response time should not be so fast as to escape the user's attention span. Performance requirements and their satisfaction is a balancing act between technology, design and development, and user expectations.

RESPONSE TIME AND PERFORMANCE ANALYSIS

The basic response times for various functions have been discussed in detail by Miller (1968)[3] in his research work on response times in human–computer interactions. The expected response time that users feel is necessary is almost instantaneous at about 0.1 second. This happens in situations where no special feedback is necessary and all that is required is to display a result. One second is regarded as the maximum delay the system can allow before interrupting the user's flow of thought. Even though such a delay would be felt, it will not disrupt the user's attention on his/her task. Ten seconds is the maximum timeframe and the user should have his/her attention focused on a dialog box (progress indicator). This provides expected finish time of the process so users do not lose patience and start working on other tasks.

Outsourced Projects and Performance

An important factor influencing performance is outsourcing of software development. Usually, outsourcing of work is equated to advantages including significant cost savings, assured availability of trained IT staff, flexible resource utilization, and minimal setup costs. Routine low-level tasks can consume a large portion of a company's resources, and this could be a reason to utilize outsourcing, which may significantly reduce the amount of resources needed to perform these day-to-day low-level tasks and indirectly lower company expenses.

Despite the fact that outsourcing offers several advantages, there are multiple challenges associated with it. For example, if the outsourcing vendor is not able to understand the requirements and, in particular in Agile projects, not able to participate in the development collaboratively, the performance of the overall system suffers.

Service-level agreements (SLAs) directly apply to performance analysis. The SLAs should clearly state the scope and nature of all services required. The level of performance should also be clearly stated. Factors like throughput time, turnaround time, and system availability are some of the key issues that directly affect system performance. A well-established, well-equipped, and efficient vendor who can participate from the early requirements phase of the system understands the performance needs much better than a vendor only contracted to "code."

Bandwidth

Bandwidth availability at an organizational level is closely associated with system performance. Bandwidth may be a constraint placed on the system from the IT infrastructure of the organization itself. Existing organizational communications networks and those that will be carrying the software solution are integral to performance. Also, data communication processes (such as sending and receiving Big Data to/from the Cloud) need to be studied, modeled, and incorporated into the system design. Bandwidth can have a key effect on the timely delivery of information.

Network bandwidth is the capacity to deliver a certain amount of data in a given time. Applications demanding high bandwidth load networks internal and external to the organization.

Bandwidth specifications for a software solution should include the minimum acceptable data transfer rate. This transfer rate, however, needs to vary depending on different loads—which can vary depending on the time of day, location of access, and other factors. In the example HMS, the modules that only exchange static and information can perform even with a bandwidth of 64 kbps. The HMS modules that undertake intense analytics and that involve the transfer of multimedia information like patient video clippings and medical images need a much higher bandwidth like 4 Mbps.

Scalability

Scalability is an NFR of a system that deals with incrementally increasing the workload. This scaling up of the system demand places constraints on its resources as the expected response time from the users is still the same. Scalability-related issues become a concern especially when the system is successful in its operation because the more successful a system is in providing value, the greater the demand on its services from users. Scalability requirements cover a range: scaling up to the increasing number of users, the distribution of analytics, user interfaces and multimedia capabilities, data transmission and storage, and end-user equipment access and its usage.

Scalability can thus be both a technical requirement and also a business requirement based on the functionality utilized. Thus, scalability is a requirement that can be entered within a use case documentation as an estimate of how many users are likely to use that particular use case in the month, quarter, or year after the launch of the system.

Technically, the scalability requirement can specify the techniques and tools to distribute and balance the data workload over the network. This data distribution also helps in transmission over multiple channels and parallel sessions. Because Internet and e-commerce sites grow at an exponential rate, scalability forms one of the core issues to be analyzed in project sustainability.

Balanced scaling of technical resources (especially Cloud-based resources) results in improved access protocols, value for the money spent on storage, and overall satisfaction for the owner stakeholder of the project.

Scalability and Hardware

Scalability issues may also have hardware constraints. To cope with higher loads, there may be a need to add more processors or more servers, depending on the type of problems that exist. Each additional processor can boost the overall server performance. In addition, good multithreading architecture techniques can help load distribution and increase system performance, which results in good scalability. E-commerce websites involve a high level of inquiries at the back end, which is a resource-consuming task. A common procedure is to use a separate database server that removes, for example, some of the load off the central server.

The architecture of the system should be flexible enough to allow the additional hardware to be added, as this helps in the scalability of the project. The deployment diagrams used in the model of architectural space should help in developing a stable system without scalability problems.

HMS Example of Scalability Requirement

Examples of scalability requirements of the HMS include a situation where, say, the system initially handles 1000 transactions per day, 3 months after release, the system needs to be scaled up to handle 5000 transactions per day. The initial release capacity of the back-end database space on the Cloud is 1 TB; with exponentially growing multimedia and related contents for medical data, the back-end capacity requirements are set to grow to 5 TB in the first year. Thereafter, close monitoring of data needs is required to ensure the system can scale up to handle the demands of both data storage and processing.

Volume

The volume requirement specifies the total data size required for the system. This volume includes the local databases, Cloud-based servers, data stored locally on computers and smartphones, and the like. With advances in Big Data and corresponding Cloud technologies, volume (size) of data becomes even more important for the success of the system.

The HMS is expected to be used heavily by staff and patients. The rough estimate of website transactions is 500 per day. The HMS needs to handle data—their ingestion, quality, transfer, and secure storage—efficiently. A Cloud-based server is geared up to handle the load of the HMS—which starts with a 1 TB space on the server. Estimations of volume needs are based on the number of new patients per day (100) and returning patients (150) that are handled specifically by the HMS in the first year of its operation. Apart from the patient's personal details, there is a large amount of multimedia data like videos of surgical procedures, antenatal videos, recovery methods, other health-related videos, audio, pictures, and graphics that need to be stored in various formats.

Operating System

The operating system (OS) and corresponding operating environment of the system are decided at the start of the project. These OS requirements are not as difficult to ascertain as some of the other NFRs. However, deciding on the OS and its version is crucial for the development effort—and the users and system architects need to discuss this requirement together, with the users specifying why they need the solution to operate on a particular operating platform and the architects fulfilling that requirement within the organization's given parameters.

In addition to the existing OS and environment, the compatibility and future growth issues also need to be incorporated to handle this requirement. As a simple example, a system developed for the Windows platform cannot work in the UNIX environment and raises issues such as compatibility and portability. With the use of compatible interfaces, data can still be transmitted as services across these otherwise heterogeneous platforms; but the execution of the system across multiple platforms is a key NFR that requires both business and technical inputs.

In case of the HMS, users, business analysts, and software developers get together to decide that the Windows operating platform is most ideal for the current user base (typically the staff). These stakeholders also set the minimum working conditions for the successful functioning of the system—such as Windows 7 or higher. The browser requirements can be Internet Explorer v.9 and above and Google Chrome—with its ability to carry out all system functions including browsing, data entry, editing, and saving contents on a page.

Mobile OS

Typically mobile applications operate on Apple iOS and Android OSs. These OSs provide the basis for application functions. Their additional features include security and performance tuning. The requirements for an OS are based on the need to manage resources, handle the needs of the business process, address analytical demands on the device (as compared with the back-end Cloud-based analytics), and provide security.

Accessibility

Accessibility is an important NFR that enhances user experience. Designing easy-to-access software solutions requires an understanding of the physical characteristics (and limitations) of users and their usability needs. Accessibility requirements are also part of legal and compliance needs of most government bodies dealing with software solutions. Similar to physical accessibility needs, government regulations also stipulate software accessibility needs[4] that must be met by software solutions before the solutions are released.

An important part of accessibility requirements is to ensure they are satisfied not only during design, development, and testing, but also when the system is fully deployed. Therefore, work associated with satisfying accessibility requirements continues well beyond the release of the software.

Examples of accessibility requirements for the HMS include the ability of users (especially patients) to handle color (highlighting important information with color; color blind users can still get the information), selective enlargement of contents on the screen, context-based tool tips, layout arrangement to correspond to the logical workflow of an actor, and alternative access to keyboard and mouse (e.g., audio/sound inputs and output). With increasing use of IoT devices to monitor patient parameters, the requirements of the HMS are focused on minimal intervention and input from the user (patient). Thus, automation is the key criteria for the use of IoT devices that provide data to HMS.

Reliability and Maintenance

The reliability and maintenance requirements of a software system translate to the availability of the system when the users need it most and the ability of the system to come back online after changes (maintenance).

Software maintenance comprises the postdelivery activities, which are performed for system stability and functioning. Maintenance is generally regarded as one of the major resource-consuming activities. An iterative and incremental approach also helps in the maintenance cycle (as opposed to a new development cycle) as it enables planning for piece by piece maintenance of fully encapsulated packages.

Apart from general system maintenance, database maintenance also forms a crucial part of this NFR. The maintenance policies should clearly describe objectives, functions, processing details, and verification procedures. The database maintenance policies describe the process of data backup, data cleaning, and scheduling. The policy also has a priority schedule to complete high-priority tasks before general tasks. The maintenance process includes defining, measuring, and improving risk analysis and quality assurance.

Validation also forms a major part of the maintenance policy and ensures the system performs in the desired way. For example, in the HMS project, keeping the system up-to-date with regular patches to various components and classes is a vital part of the solution—and requires incorporating these activities in the iterative and incremental maintenance life cycle of the system. For example, each package of the HMS can be updated every month—provided there is no impact of one change on other packages.

Maintenance also deals with regular backups and mirroring of HMS data. Furthermore, archiving data (patients and doctors who are no longer with the hospital) also requires a planned approach—and needs to be specified as a maintenance NFR at the start of a project. This type of maintenance removes the load from the central server and increases the overall efficiency of the solution.

Environment

As mentioned earlier, increasingly, there is a need to incorporate environmental requirements within the solution design. These are the requirements that deal with sustainability and the environment as related to business. Since these requirements are not behavioral, they fall under the NFR category.

For example, the total computer hardware involved in the development of a solution produces certain carbon contents; similarly, operationalizing a solution results in carbon generation and a corresponding impact on the environment. Complex server technologies and Cloud-based deployments are equally responsible for carbon emissions by the organization. The corresponding cooling effort for computing hardware needs to be incorporated in carbon calculations. Therefore, the deployment of a system needs to consider these environmental parameters of the system.

HMS requirements can specify, for example, that the total carbon generated during the development effort will be 100 KT (kilo tons). An estimate of the carbon production can also be made (e.g., 1 KT per user per month). Furthermore, these environmental requirements stipulate certain internal hardware requirements (e.g., low-carbon-emitting screens) and recycling of machines when they are no longer in use (e.g., 3 years from the date of release of HMS).

Legal and Compliance

Most software solutions have to deal with legal and compliance requirements. These requirements emanate from the business situation and the geographic region where the solution is developed and deployed. These legal requirements in the NFR category are different from the legal requirements that are part of the system logic. For example, if a legal requirement specifies the addition of 10% tax on every scale (e.g., a VAT or a GST tax), then that becomes part of the functional requirements of the system. Examples of legal requirements in operationalizing a system include hosting the system, mandatory reporting of activities, and privacy issues of data storage.

Security

Security is by far the most crucial NFR of a software system. Earlier, in Figure 20.1, security was shown on top of the box—influencing all other NFRs. This influence is important to note because, from a system architecture viewpoint, each NFR needs to be balanced with the security needs of the system. Hypothetically, the most secured system in the world is the one that simply cannot be accessed; but without access such a system is meaningless. The philosophy and implementation of security deals with the balancing act of allowing relevant access to the right (authorized) people at the right time and place. Thus, security is a continuously changing, dynamic NFR of a system.

Security also has a large functional component. For example, the functionality associated with the now ubiquitous user code/password access is easily modeled with a use case and a corresponding activity diagram. However, the number of users accessing the system at any given point in time and ensuring that access is secure is part of the NFR related to security. The number of security levels, their types, their encryption needs, physical security of servers, computers, and handheld devices, and the implementation of firewalls are important nonfunctional parameters influencing the development of a software application. All issues related to security that do not fall under the functional or behavioral aspect of a system are considered, documented, prototyped, and verified through NFRs.

There are four security factors that influence all levels of security in a software system. These four influencing factors, shown in Figure 20.4a are confidentiality, integrity, accountability, and availability. Confidentiality requirements of the system describe the issues related to nondisclosure of information to unauthorized users. Integrity requirements ensure that information in the system is manipulated only by authorized users who have proper access rights (control) to do so. Accountability requirements specify which users are authorized and for what specific time. Availability requirements ensure that authorized users are not denied service when they need it.

Each of these four requirements are applied to the levels of security (shown in Figure 20.4b) provided for a system. These security levels are described next:

- Physical security
  - Physical access to servers—when maintained in-house (as compared to Cloud) needs to be limited to authorized users.
  - Physical location of servers, networks, and devices should be such as to ensure their security; these machines should be accessible to those responsible for their maintenance but otherwise should not be physically visible to other users.
  - Mobile device access and potential loss of a device need to be factored into the security of a system; for example, ensuring data are stored on the back-end server rather than a physical device so the loss of the device does not translate to a loss of data.

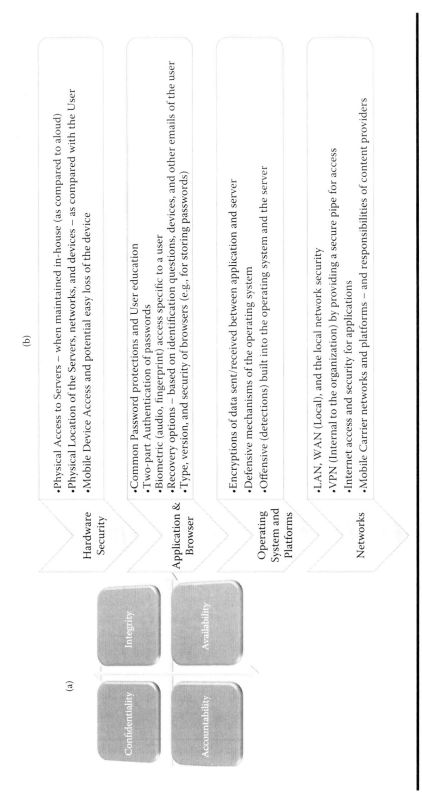

Figure 20.4 Software and mobile application security: (a) influencing factors and (b) levels.

- Application and browser
  - Common password protection mechanisms (such as length and composition of passwords) and corresponding user education in terms of using browsers (e.g., not saving passwords in the browser)
  - Two-part authentication of passwords as a process (this will be a functional model although it is discussed here as part of NFRs).
  - Biometric (audio, fingerprint) access specific to a user—reduces the opportunity for unauthorized access and increases accountability
  - Recovery options based on identification questions, devices, and other emails of the user ensure the integrity of access for a particular application and device.
  - Type, version, and security of browsers (e.g., if used for storing passwords—although that is not recommended) to ensure confidentiality and accountability of users
- Operating system and platforms
  - Encryptions of data sent/received between application and server maintain the integrity of data.
  - Defensive mechanisms of the operating system ensure confidentiality and integrity of the solution.
  - Offensive detections built into the operating system and the server also ensure confidentiality and integrity of the solution.
- Networks
  - LAN, WAN (local), and local network security to ensure authorized access for users.
  - VPN (internal to organization) by providing a secure pipe for access that simulates in-house access.
  - Internet access and security for applications to ensure confidentiality and integrity of the solutions.
  - Mobile carriers networks and platforms—and responsibilities of content providers also to ensure confidentiality and integrity of the solutions.

Usability and User Experience

Applying Usability Requirements to Software Solutions

Chapter 16 discussed application of the principles of usability and usage-centered design to software systems. The flow of control between screens is part of the functional aspects of requirements that was also discussed in Chapter 16. Usability requirements discussed here are considered nonfunctional only to the extent that they deal with static, structural aspects of interfaces. For example, the colors and button positions on the screen of a mobile application are part of the nonfunctional aspects of the system. Usability applies in conjunction with almost all other NFRs.

Usability also describes the value the system adds to the user's goals. Discussions on usability need to consider not only creating good user interfaces, but also improving their ultimate value to users. Well-designed user interfaces enable users to complete their tasks, increase productivity, decrease time and costs associated with training, reduce user errors, provide user support, and improve maintainability of the interfaces.

Usability facilitates easy learning and adoption of the interface by the users who are familiar with the system. For example, for users familiar with using web-based applications, the existence and positions of the common OK, Cancel, and Help buttons are well known. Since most users are likely to be familiar with these three buttons, they should appear in their familiar positions and order in a well-designed interface.

The naming convention of all fields and buttons in the interface is an important aspect of usability. Each field and button should be clearly named to represent the function it performs. Cryptic or extremely long names for buttons and field descriptions in an interface can cause unnecessary confusion. For example, having "PID" or "Number" to represent `PatientNumber` or patient identification is not a good design. Another common example is the use of the "`Save`" button. Although "`Save`" can be used in user interfaces, it may be preferable to use "`Update`" or "`Register`" on the button to further clarify the meaning behind the button.

Designing to Prevent Errors

An overall principle to remember in designing interfaces is the focus on the prevention, rather than correction of errors. For example, if the user is entering "Date of Registration" for a patient, the system should first present the user with "Today's Date" and then allow the user to change it. This approach prevents an error that might be typical where the user is asked to enter the date (or any other data) from scratch. There should also be continuous cross-checking and validation of the user's actions to prevent erroneous data from entering the system. For example, if a user mistakenly presses the cancel button after filling out the information in the interface UI10-`PatientRegistrationForm`, the system should ask the user to verify the action before executing it.

With good user interface designs, a large number of fields on screen can be validated immediately, rather than being validated by the entity classes "after" the data have been transmitted from the interface classes. For example, entry of a valid date is almost always a function of the interface class and not the entity class. However, once the date has been entered, whether or not it is semantically a correct date (e.g., date of birth should not be later than today's date) is the responsibility of entity classes, not interface classes.

Finally, the interfaces should be designed with aesthetics in mind. For example, information on an interface commonly runs from left to right and not the other way around—patient's first name appears on the left of patient's last name. Overcrowding on screens should be avoided, and colors should be used to convey meaning and be visually pleasing.

Big Data (Velocity, Variety)

Big Data is a wide-ranging term that describes—as its name suggests—large quantities of data; additionally, these data are coming into the system at a very high speed (most likely because it is generated by machines, in additions to humans) and contain variety. The variety of data is characterized beyond text—made up of audio, video, graphic, unstructured descriptions (blogs, emails), and machine generated. Each of the aforementioned characteristics of Big Data needs to be kept in mind in designing and developing new software applications. This is because most new applications deal with some element of Big Data—either in sourcing data, analyzing them, or, as discussed in the next section, storing it on the Cloud.

Cloud

As discussed earlier in this chapter, Cloud computing is integral to most new systems and plays a vital role in ensuring that the nonfunctional or operational requirements of the solution are satisfied.

Cloud computing describes a system where users can connect to a vast network of computing resources, data, and servers that reside somewhere else, usually on the Internet, rather than on a local machine, LAN or in a data center.[5]

While the Cloud is the default mechanism to store data, its importance in software solution goes beyond data storage. The processing associated with a software, its sourcing and sharing of data, and the ability of the software to enable collaboration at a time and place of the user's choosing are something enabled by the Cloud.

Thus, the actual execution of the applications and analytics also occurs on the Cloud. The Cloud obviates the need to install software and analytical applications locally on a user's devices. As a result, computing becomes a utility where analytical applications are available on demand.[6] The NFRs discussed earlier—including performance, volume, scalability, security, and operational platforms—are all affected by the Cloud. This is because the Cloud renders the entire back end of an organization virtual.

The Cloud thus forms a key part of the system architecture for a software solution. The impact of the Cloud on the nonfunctional parameters of a software solution needs to be explored in early requirements gathering stages and, later, through regular testing before and during deployment of the solution.

Common Errors in Handling NFRs and How to Rectify Them

Common Errors	Rectifying the Errors	Examples
Not giving enough attention to NFRs because they cannot be visually modeled	NFRs should be considered as important as functional requirements; the way to extract NFRs is by the creation of prototypes (e.g., technical, interface, business).	See the early discussion in this chapter and the one on prototyping in Chapter 16.
Not realizing that the user experience from a software solution depends to a large extend on its NFRs	Undertake a series of formal workshops to document NFRs.	Revisit Figures 20.1 through 20.3 to understand the depth and breadth of NFRs and write a practical requirement corresponding to each heading.
Presuming security to be an entirely separate entity that can be somehow added later on to the software solution being developed	Start discussing security with every use case and with every activity diagram.	See the discussions in this chapter and then revisit the documentation of use cases to add security to it.

Common Errors	Rectifying the Errors	Examples
Volume and performance will be tested only at the end of the system development life cycle	These two NFRs in particular cannot wait for the system to be fully executable. Instead, start testing these requirements with initial modules of the software release.	See the discussions in this chapter.
NFRs are all at the same level	NFRs are at different levels and, therefore, need to be documented at the relevant levelsorganization, project, process, use case, and data.	See Figure 20.3 for the various levels of NFRs.
Usability is the same as user experience	Usability deals with the precision of design; user experience is the overall takeaway by the user from the system.	See the discussion in this chapter on usability and user experience; also revisit discussions in Chapter 16.
Cloud is meant to handle on data storage	Cloud computing is integral to most new software applications. The Cloud can handle not only data but also analytics and processing. Cloud also facilitates collaborations amongst systems, databases, and businesses.	See the discussion in this chapter on Cloud.

Discussion Questions

1. List two key NFRs from the ones discussed in this chapter. Explain your answer with reasons and examples.
2. List two NFRs that you think are not relevant in a given situation. Explain your answer with reasons and examples.
3. Argue why NFRs are difficult to capture early on in a project. Also argue your approach to capturing these NFRs as best you can during analysis work. *(Hint: lack of an operational solution early on in a project.)*
4. Why is prototyping considered important in capturing NFRs? Which NFR in particular will you capture first using a prototype?
5. Which NFRs are commonly applicable to all other NFRs in most modern-day projects? Why? *(Hint: revisit Figure 20.1.)*
6. Explain the two major categories of NFRs: qualities and constraints. Your answer must contain examples of both categories.
7. There are many levels at which NFRs apply. List the levels of applicability of NFRs with examples.
8. Which level of NFR is most relevant to an ERP software package being implemented? Why? *(Hint: a ready-made ERP package needs to meet the quality of service it promises.)*

9. Compare the NFR for scalability with volume. Explain why simply handling the volume NFR is not sufficient for a software project to be successful.
10. What do you understand by the term quality of service? Why is this QoS important for successful operation of a system?
11. Why is security considered an NFR? Discuss the importance of security across all other NFRs discussed here.
12. What is usability? Why is usability included within the overall user experience of a software solution?
13. Changes in operating systems (platforms) can create major problems for an otherwise functionally perfect system. Discuss this statement in the context of NFR capture and implementation.
14. Which other NFR is close to the legal and compliance requirement of a system? Why?
15. With the advent of IoT devices, accessibility and usability requirements are becoming extremely important. Discuss this in the context of unique characteristics of actors (users) of a system. *(Hint: such as elderly or infants, who may have these devices but may not have easy access to them due to limited movement.)*
16. Cloud computing is more than storage of data. Discuss this statement in the context of the NFRs of a system.
17. Consider how you would build a prototype (technical) to implement NFRs.

Team Project Case Study

1. Revisit your project work thus far and examine the key business objectives and the high-level requirements for each package.
2. Create a subsection in your project document called the nonfunctional requirements subsection. Review Figure 20.1 and create an entry for each heading in that figure; now write the "assumed" NFR for your system for each of these headings. *(Hint: in practice, this exercise will be iteratively carried out by building a business and a technical prototype for the system.)*
3. Each of the aforementioned NFRs can contain two categories—a requirement that is a quality or need of a user and a requirement that is a limitation or constraint coming from the technology and organizational resource viewpoint.
4. Explore at least one use case, one class, and a component diagram from the point of view of NFR. Add an NFR to each of these diagrams as a note.
5. Ensure that EACH NFR that you write for the preceding item is TESTABLE.
6. Explore a Cloud-based system architecture. Make note of how the Cloud architecture impacts your system deployment.
7. Write an independent subsection on the performance requirements of your entire system. This is a requirement that applies to the entire system (versus the performance of a particular package or use case).

Endnotes

1. Unhelkar, B., (2011), *Green ICT Strategies & Applications: Using Environmental Intelligence*, Boca Raton, FL, USA: CRC Press (Taylor and Francis /Group/An Auerbach Book), April, 2011. Authored ISBN: 9781439837801. Unhelkar, B., *Environmentally Responsible Business Strategies for a Green Enterprise Transformation*, Vol. 13, No. 2, February 2010, Business-IT strategies resource centre, Cutter Executive Report, Boston, USA.

2. PRIMA-UML: a performance validation incremental methodology on early UML diagrams" by Vittorio Cortellessa, Raffaela Mirandola; Published in Science of Computer Programming, Vol 44, Issue 1, July 2002, pp. 101–129 by Elsevier http://www.sciencedirect.com/science/article/pii/S0167642302000333.
3. Miller, 1968.
4. http://ocfo.ed.gov/coninfo/clibrary/software.htm.
5. Kay, Russell. "QuickStudy: Cloud Computing." *Computerworld*, 4 August 2008 (www.computerworld.com/action/article.do?command=viewArticleBasic&articleId=321699).
6. Big Data Strategies for Agile Business, B. Unhelkar, 2017. CRC Press.

Emerging Information Technologies and Modeling

Learning Objectives

- Explore the possibilities of using UML beyond contemporary software development (Big Data, NoSQL, IoT, Cloud, mobile, social media)
- Consider UML usage for social-mobile-analytics-Cloud (SMAC) stack modeling
- Model web services with UML (XML, SOAP, WSDL, UDDI)
- Review model-driven architecture and executable UML

Emerging Information Technologies and Modeling

The UML is used in many ways to model various domains, technologies, and processes. Chapter 1 argued for the various ways in which the UML can be used (Figure 1.14). All those purposes of UML are also applicable in modeling systems and processes around emerging information technologies. This last chapter explores the possibilities of using UML in modeling new and emerging information technologies.

Since the advent of the Cloud, services have gained further prominence in software solutions. Therefore, this chapter also delves into the modeling of services (typically on the Cloud) using the UML. Model-driven architecture (MDA) and executable UML are also discussed here to enable an understanding of how they can influence future software development efforts.

Emerging information technologies include (but are not limited to) the following:

- Cloud-based services that utilize the ubiquitous Internet connectivity to provide utilities and analytics as services
- Big Data technologies and analytics that enable new insights for business decision-making
- NoSQL databases that enable storage of unstructured data (including audio and video) and their management

- Internet of Things (IoT) at both the industry and personal levels utilizing highly connected devices to capture data and provide results based on set parameters
- Social-mobile-Cloud working together to provide a homogeneous suite of technologies for collaboration and personalization
- Artificial and business intelligence to capitalize on technical ability to process and correlate insights
- Machine learning to enable an ongoing ability of computers to continue to identify patterns and personalize responses
- Virtual and augmented reality to provide location-independent support for complex procedures, defense applications, and games

SMAC Significance

The underlying quartet for these emerging technologies is the social-mobile-analytics-Cloud (SMAC) stack[1] shown in Figure 21.1. Each element of the SMAC stack is influenced by the fundamentals of software engineering discussed in the opening chapter. As a result, software development initiatives based on these new and emerging technologies stand to benefit from modeling.

The SMAC technologies are used more effectively as a quartet rather than singularly.[2] This is so because a business solution is not realistic or practical if it uses only one of these SMAC technologies. For example, staff with mobile devices and laptop computers but with no access to the Cloud may not be able to execute their business processes satisfactorily. Similarly, a mobile device

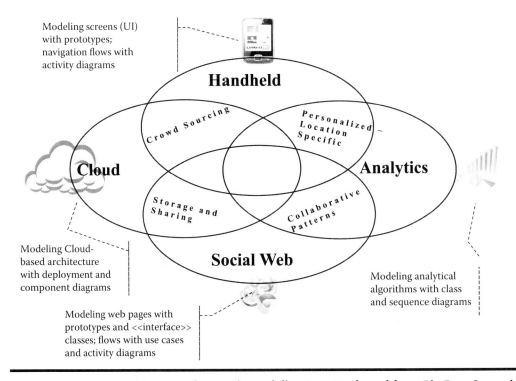

Figure 21.1   Opportunities to apply UML in modeling SMAC (adapted from *Big Data Strategies for Agile Business*, B. Unhelkar, CRC Press, 2017).

is useful to an end user when it provides relevant analytical results in an easy-to-understand pre-sentation. The SMAC stack supports innovative business models, impacts product directions, and enables the creation of new actionable knowledge.

Figure 21.1 summarizes the SMAC stack and the ways in which each of the four technologies (social media, mobile, analytics, and Cloud) can use the UML. This figure only provides a starting suggestion for UML use and is by no means comprehensive.

Service Orientation (Analytics, Utilities)

The popularity of Big Data and analytics and their availability on the Cloud imply the possibilities of offering analytics as a service.

Figure 21.1 also shows that the UML can be used to carry out the modeling of various aspects of emerging technologies. The UML diagrams of interest in modeling services, for example, are class diagrams and sequence diagrams; occasionally component diagrams of the UML also play a role in modeling Cloud-based services.

Analytics comprises statistical algorithms and their corresponding implementations using pro-gramming constructs. Analytics enables utilization of data by processing them to generate action-able knowledge or insights. Popular analytics includes descriptive, predictive, and prescriptive analytics—each playing a specific role in business decision-making. Analytics can occur in the background on a server, in the Cloud, or locally on a social website or in a mobile app. Analytics is influenced by context and granularity.

Analytics can be offered as a service on the Cloud. Analytics as a Service (AaaS) is an area of software solutions that gains immensely through modeling. The service interfaces, modeled with <<boundary>> stereotypes, can contain the parameters, pointers, and return values of the entire service. The business processes that use AaaS can be modeled with use case and activ-ity diagrams.

Big Data services ingest wide-ranging data sources and varying data types (including unstruc-tured data) with delivery across organizational boundaries. Additional impacts to services include audit, compliance, regulatory, and security issues. These factors can be incorporated into the func-tional models and nonfunctional prototypes of new software solutions.

An enterprise-architecture-based approach to incorporating Cloud analytics in business pro-cesses reduces risks of technical surprises later in the transformation of organizational processes.[3] The various shared, operational, and customer services need a robust, underlying architectural model to enable use of the service-intelligence platform that allows customers to create their own self-serve analytics.[4]

Internet of Things

The Internet of Things (IoT) is a rapidly emerging technical domain comprising devices with smart analytics. IoT benefits from modeling as follows:[5]

- Modeling the data distribution service (DDS) protocol for the IoT (by creating class and sequence models to represent network interoperability for connected devices)
- Modeling automotive (self-driving) processes using activity and state machine diagrams

- Standard for threat information sharing (or "threat modeling")
- Modeling self-learning algorithms to enable IoT devices to provide personalized and localized insights depending on the priorities of the user
- Create a commonly acceptable standard for modeling across myriad IoT devices and their networks
- Enable a simple component model that is agnostic to middleware, thereby enabling communications, and service guarantees

Mobile and Social Media Applications

The SMAC quartet (Figure 21.1) influences and is influenced by the economic, social, and process dimensions[6] of an organization. In adopting Big Data, each of these four elements of SMAC stack need to be considered from an organization's existing technology setup (through its EA), financial situation, people (including their skills and attitudes), and business processes (with business process models). With increasing sophistication, social media and mobile are so closely intertwined that it is not possible to make a clear difference. "SoMo" is the best way to refer to this group of social and mobile technologies and applications.

- Social media—Comprises wikis, blogs, forums, communities, feeds, tagging, bookmarking, avatars, forums, and statuses—each representing a technology and its application that enables socialization. Social media are thus a conduit for the generation of social information, connecting people, and the formation of communities and groups. For example, Facebook, LinkedIn, and Twitter connect people and generate data while riding on the communication capabilities of the underlying infrastructure. Social media also comprise tools for sharing knowledge and experience.
- Mobile—Comprises technologies and applications that primarily take the social media aspect mentioned earlier and make it location independent. Mobile devices, mobile Internet, WiFi, and near field communications are examples from this mobile domain. The IoT takes the location and time independence of mobility to the next level of being ubiquitous. IoT (especially as sensor devices) generates large volumes of data at high velocity without user intervention. These devices are further personalized to the data and information needs of the user. Also, when web services (WSs) are made available on handheld devices, they make use of wireless XML (WML), which is a subset of XML. UML can be used to model this WML like XML (XML is discussed later in this chapter).

Cloud Integration

Cloud computing represents a suite of interconnected storage devices (servers) made available through the connectivity of the Internet based on a common interface. Since the Cloud is not within the physical boundaries of an organization, there is no locally owned data center to hold the organizational data. The Cloud is elastic, offering more or less space and features depending on the needs and budget of the user (as is evident through popular Cloud offerings by Google and Amazon). The Cloud represents key features of scalability and shareability that are of immense importance in the Big Data world.

Virtual and Augmented Reality

Augmented reality (AR) and virtual reality (VR) technologies are deployed in games, high-risk training (e.g., pilots), and simulations. Devices and technologies around VR and AR can utilize UML modeling in almost all aspects of their development. For example, the requirements for solutions based on these technologies can be modeled with the UML diagrams in MOPS. The components, services, and deployment of these solutions can benefit by the MOAS and MOSS.

Robotics and Machine Learning

Robotics and machine learning contain areas of software development that need to be modeled formally. Therefore, UML has the potential to add value to these developments. Machine learning has a range of applications that make use of devices (e.g., IoT), back-end Cloud computing (for storage), and Big Data analytics (for processing high-velocity data). Coupled with robotics, machine learning impacts business applications by automating them, making them more personalized and reliable. Machine learning, together with IoT, plays an increasingly important role in carbon sensing and monitoring —thereby contributing to environmental consciousness and sustainability initiatives by businesses.

Modeling the Not Only SQL Databases

The ability of NoSQL databases to accommodate the lack of data structure creates opportunities for business processes to use data as is. Since the external reality does not have a schema, the natural representation of that reality within NoSQL databases makes it possible to generate new and unique insights. Ample storage space, distributed architecture, and high processing power make this possible.

NoSQL databases are schema less to the extent that they allow adding data with varying structures. Beyond that, NoSQL databases need the same management and maintenance as SQL databases. In order for the data to remain useful (i.e., performing metrics, analytics, etc.), a schema becomes necessary. In the absence of a schema, it becomes difficult to handle unstructured data. Thus, while a NoSQL database has no enforced schema, the analysis data end up requiring a schema.

UML thus has a role to play in modeling schemas (even though temporary) and enabling applications to utilize them. Most practical analytical applications need to integrate the structured SQL format with the incoming unstructured Big Data in order to provide a meaningful, holistic, 360° view desired by users.

Figure 21.2 shows these different types of data stores that comprise relational (SQL), object-oriented (OO), key-value pairs (NoSQL), and associated large unstructured storages (also NoSQL). As mentioned, the relational and OO databases still remain important in the Big Data world. This is because of the large amount of enterprise data that has been stored over many years, which is an organizational asset.

Figure 21.2 highlights the need to analyze large amounts of ad hoc, high-velocity data in order to produce actionable insights. These data are often very difficult to model because they have very few underlying rules in terms of source and structure. The processing of these data is also not straightforward. Instead, processing occurs in stages. The data from NoSQL databases first need to be cleansed and brought together in a staging area where they can be processed. NoSQL designs

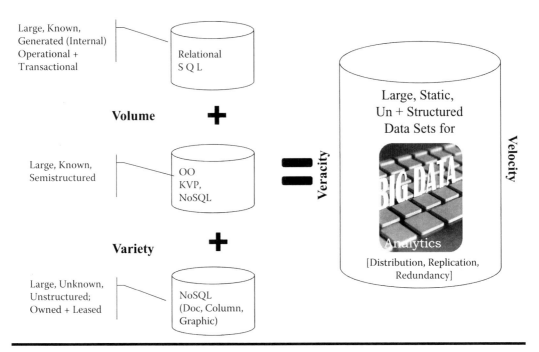

Figure 21.2 Modeling challenges in the Big Data space—with multiple types of data (e.g., structured, transactional, and unstructured) stored in SQL and NoSQL databases (typically in the Cloud).

need to ascertain the purpose or usage of data, its access pattern, and the currency (period for which the analytics will remain current or valid) and then determine the storage solution. UML plays a role in creating models for these NoSQL designs in the solution space. The distributed database architecture of NoSQL databases is also modeled in the architectural space (MOAS) with component and deployment diagrams of the UML.

Service Orientation Based on the Cloud

Service orientation under WSs are a combination of component technologies, distributed computing, and the Internet (Lan and Unhelkar, 2005)[7]. Cloud-based WSs are advances on model-specific interactions.

Distributed component object model (DCOM), common object request broker architecture (CORBA), and remote method invocation (RMI) are middleware technologies that have evolved into service orientation. Middleware technologies are specifically designed and constructed to suit specific applications, hardware, and other related components within an organization or with business partner organizations.

With the advances in software systems it is increasingly important for them to communicate through the Internet. This requires information to be exchanged across varied hardware, software, and operating platforms. WSs are an XML-based suite of technologies that help in interaction between varied software applications.

Document-based XML enables easy exchanges between software applications on a wide variety of platforms. The possibility of clustering departments within one organization or organizations together to offer a wide variety of services is endless.

Designing with Services

Figure 21.3 shows a practical scenario with WSs. The figure is divided into two parts by the client and the service provider interfaces. Central to the client view is the "virtual HMS." This virtual HMS provides a unified view of the hospital management system to clients, which comprise the interactive physical user, the programmatic client, and the interactive wireless client.

The integrated services interface (virtual HMS) itself comprises many disparate services. Applications from different service providers—that would otherwise not be related to each other—come together in this scenario. For example, for the HMS, the pharmacies, laboratories, insurance companies, accounting, and the registration and discharging services have all come together under the umbrella of a local registry to enable an integrated services interface.

Services on the Cloud have a public interface. Services are located and used by the virtual HMS. Most modern-day software applications have components made available through the Internet for other applications to use. This offering and consumption of application components across the Internet is described by an umbrella term "Web Services (WSs)."

The ability for WSs to exchange procedure calls and data through the use of XML-based HTTP protocols (discussed next) allows applications from the service providers to interface and communicate through the boundaries of the corporate firewalls. This enables usage of these applications through globally "advertised" and consumed interfaces. These WS-based facilities can also be used to tap into the otherwise "trapped" data within legacy systems, encapsulating and making them available for use on the Internet.

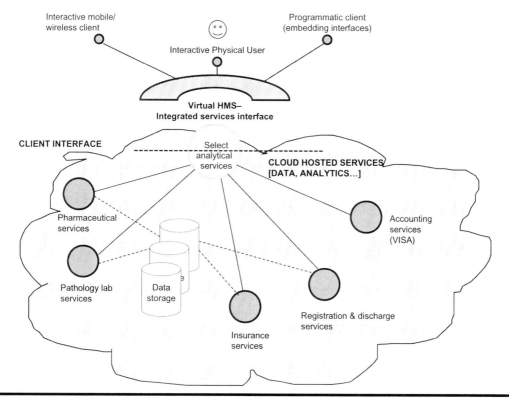

Figure 21.3 Designing an integrated services interface with Cloud-background for use by clients (physical users and technical programs).

Core Elements of Web Services

WSs provide the next level in enabling applications to "glue together" by providing an ability to *publish, locate,* and *consume* applications. The World Wide Web Consortium (W3C) has the following definition of a WS:

"A Web service is a software system identified by a Universal Resource Identifier (URI) whose public interfaces and bindings are defined and described using eXtensible Markup Language (XML). Its definition can be discovered by other software systems. These systems may then interact with the Web service in a manner prescribed by its definition, using XML-based messages conveyed by Internet protocols."

WSs are applications designed and built around components of software that can be invoked using standard Internet protocols. Web services can also be viewed as a framework upon which applications can be built. The current standards for WSs can be considered in the context of three relatively distinct layers as follows:

- The XML/SOAP protocol and packaging layer provides the basic means of transferring document-based information and data across the Internet
- The WSDL definition layer helps in defining the meaning behind services
- The UDDI discovery layer helps in publishing and locating services

XML/SOAP

XML (eXtensible markup language), together with simple object access protocol (SOAP), provides the basic technology for communication between applications. XML/SOAP is at the center of WS-based applications. XML basically enables the interchange of structured documents over the Internet independently of the platform, language, and tool in which the interchanging applications are developed and deployed.

XML-based communication directly sends and receives information, leaving the internals of the "other application" hidden. As a result, XML has been extensively used in electronic data interchange (EDI), multimedia publishing, and workflow management applications. However, because of its document-centric nature, XML tends to be bulky and performs in a non-real-time manner for business-to-business (B2B) applications.

The basic protocol used by applications using XML is hyper text transfer protocol (HTTP), typically used by web browsers—e.g., Netscape, Internet Explorer—to access websites. Other protocols include FTP, telnet, SMTP, and MIME.

When it comes to business applications, XML is wrapped by SOAP, which provides a framework to invoke services across the Internet. SOAP is text-based encoded XML running over HTTP that describes the rules to process messages. Thus, SOAP can be considered an envelope that provides the framework for packaging message information, resulting in an interface to a WS.

Web Services Description Language

Web services description language (WSDL) provides the definition of interfaces to WSs. This definition is required because, although XML facilitates communication between two applications, it is essential to understand the "meaning" behind these applications. This is done for two purposes in the use of WSs—the definition as well as consumption of WSs. The applications that want to provide services define them through WSDLs, and these WSDLs are consumed by the user of the service.

Universal Description, Discovery, and Integration

Universal Description, Discovery, and Integration (UDDI: www.uddi.org) makes the application and its services "known" to the external business world and facilitates the ability of users of those services to locate and consume those services. Thus, UDDI is a "meta service" for locating and consuming WSs. UDDI is useful in both internal (to the organization) and external (public) deployments of WSs—working effectively like an electronic "yellow pages."

Web Services and Modeling

Modeling and Usage of Web Services

Figure 21.4 also shows where UML can be used in modeling WSs. In fact, all layers of WSs can benefit by the application of the UML. However, as mentioned at the start of this chapter, the two UML diagrams relevant here are class diagrams and sequence diagrams. Class diagrams can be used to represent XML/SOAP documents as well as a WSDL definition. The interactions between various applications in sending and receiving XML-based messages can be modeled with sequence diagrams. Specifically, the UML can be used to model WS components as follows:

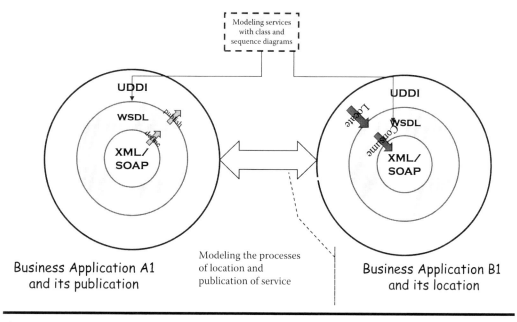

Figure 21.4 Modeling various layers of services to facilitate location, publication, and consumption of those services.

Web Service Metamodels and Dynamics

In considering the modeling of WSs with UML, it is helpful to consider a metamodel for WSs. This is shown in Figure 21.5 using UML notations. In this figure, the WS is shown with a <<service>> stereotype. This "service layer" defines the programmatic interface for other applications to interact with the WS, usually in the form of an XML file. Such businesses register their services with a directory service provider, such as UDDI.

This can be considered a "discovery layer," typically implemented with UDDI and stereotyped as <<directory>> in Figure 21.5. A UDDI provides a standardized way in which WSs can be centrally registered, located, published, and controlled.

The ptient–client application—shown with the stereotype of <<client>>—will go to the <<directory>> to locate a particular service. Having located the service, the client goes to the registration <<service>> and consumes the service that it requires. The possible implementation of the service provider can be in <<java>> and the registration service may need to interact with the legacy application possibly containing legacy data related to the patient registration service.

This diagram also highlights the way in which UML stereotypes can be used to represent various WS elements. For example, <<xs>> can be used to stereotype all classes that represent XML schemas, whereas <<wsdl>> can be used to stereotype UML classes that represent a WSDL.

The lower part of the diagram depicts what is considered Web engineering, whereas the upper part, including the UDDI directory service, is a WS-based design. Finally, in a WS-based design, as depicted here, the entire interaction is automated through service interfaces.

The difference between a normal web application and a WS-based application is further clarified with a sequence diagram. In Figure 21.6, a Patient object sends a message searchServiceProviders() to the directory (UDDI). When finding a service provider for the type of service required, the Patient object locates that specific service from the service provide; in this case, it is the registration service. The Patient object then goes to the Registration object to locate and consume the service it requires through getRegistrationService().

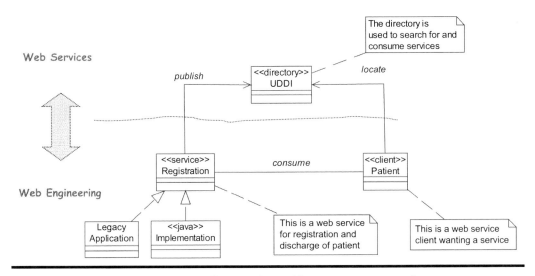

Figure 21.5   A meta-model for modeling services with UML (HMS example).

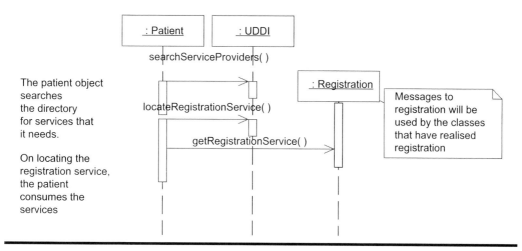

Figure 21.6 Sequence diagram explaining the dynamics of Web services.

The UDDI object in this sequence diagram makes this a WS-based application. In the absence of the UDDI object, the `Patient` object goes directly to the `Registration` object to seek the services it requires. This implies that the Patient object *knows* where to go and what to look for the job being performed, in the WS scenario by UDDI.

Model-Driven Architecture and Web Services

The OMG's model-driven architecture (MDA™) offers advances in modeling by providing a high-level model that is independent of implementation. The MDA capitalizes on the existing OMG standards of the UML, meta-object facility (MOF), and the common warehousing metamodel (CWM). The MDA takes the concept of modeling with UML a step further by creating a business view (which is completely independent of technology and simply deals with the business processes), the platform independent model (PIM) creates a business model based on UML, and then the platform-specific model (PSM). The PSM can be used in software architecture that uses, integrates, and implements technologies such as Java, XML, or web application servers.

Executable UML

In Chapter 1, the discussion around the purpose of the UML included "Construction." UML has poor visibility for use as a compilable language ("construction"). However, "executable UML" is based on the possibility of creating code directly from a model.

The initial model for this purpose is the PIM. A model compiler can take the PIM, which is based on the UML, as an input and directly produce code from it.

The opportunities for executable UML (or any approach similar to the UML) used in practice are phenomenal, but so are the challenges. For example, although the ability to rapidly produce code is crucial in software projects, the challenges appear in terms of maintainability and efficiency of the code produced, both of which are likely to suffer with the conversion of UML model to code. This is because the code produced directly from models is not as efficient as individually designed class codes. Maintenance for this code requires more effort than "handcrafted" code. However, these limitations are offset by the speed at which systems can be designed, developed, and deployed.

Discussion Questions

1. According to you, what are the two key emerging technologies that benefit from modeling?
2. Why is the SMAC stack important in modeling emerging technologies?
3. What are the important aspects of modeling Cloud technologies? Answer with respect to the emerging aspects of the Cloud that impact analytical solutions.
4. What is Big Data? Why is it important to model business processes that use Big Data technologies and analytics?
5. Why is modeling of services most crucial in modern software systems?
6. What is XML? Why do you need XML in most modern-day applications?
7. How would you model XML, WSDL, and UDDI using the UML?
8. Discuss how WSDL and UDDI can form the basis of service-oriented models of software systems.
9. What is model-driven architecture? How can it help in software development?
10. What is executable UML? Discuss the advantage and challenges in its usage.
11. Consider modeling a mobile application using the technologies discussed here.

Team Project Case Study

1. Reconsider your entire system architecture MOAS in light of emerging technologies. Consider a couple of emerging technologies for your software solution. How will you incorporate these emerging information technologies in your solution? (You are simply exploring and pointing out the opportunities—and not going into the details of it.)
2. Explore the web services that can be used by your team project case study. This will require you to think in terms of the various services that your system can offer, that can be registered in a directory, and that can be made available to potential consumers of these services. You may consider additional packages to represent external services.
3. Demonstrate your understanding of your WSs using notes in your class diagrams and sequence diagrams, which point out where you can consider it worthwhile using WS.
4. Incorporate the Cloud within your system architecture. Discuss the importance of the Cloud in the context of your team project.
5. Create a brief description of this understanding in your project report for each package. Note: In practice, WS architecture will appear much earlier in the software development life cycle than appearing here. However, you can still modify your designs slightly to reflect the incorporation of WSs (e.g., by changing stereotypes of some of your classes or adding new WSDL classes to your existing designs or incorporating UDDI classes).

Endnotes

1. SMAC stack.
2. See this Cutter IT Journal issue for varied discussions around these four technologies and especially their interdependencies, Vol 26, No 2, pp 26.
3. Hazra, T., and Unhelkar, B. (2016), Leveraging EA to Incorporate Emerging Technology Trends for Digital Transformation, *Cutter IT Journal*, (theme—Disruption and Emergence: What Do They Mean for Enterprise Architecture?), Vol 29, No 2, pp 10–16.
4. Sherringham, K., and Unhelkar, B., "Service Management in Big Data," Proceedings of the System Design and Process Science (SDPS2016) conference, December 4–6 2016, Orlando, FL, USA.

5. Extending OMG's discussion on IIoT.
6. Unhelkar, B., *SMAC with Agile*—Cutter Executive Update, 2014, 4 of 5, Vol.15 , No.9, Agile Product & Project Management Practice, Boston, USA; and Unhelkar, B., "SMAC with Agile and Big Data," Computer Associates Webinar series on Big Data 2014; and
7. Lan, Y., and Unhelkar, B. (2005), *Global Enterprise Transitions, IDEAS Group Publishing*, 2005, Total Pages 240. ISBN: 1591406250.

Appendix A: Case Study Problem Statements for Team Projects

Common Note for All Case Study Problem Statements:

GoodMead Hospital's hospital management system (HMS)—part of the running thread for examples in this book for modeling with the UML

    OzAir Airline, Agro Farm, and Desi Travels—experiential learning for medium- to large-sized team projects for modeling with the UML

    Lucky Insurance—experiential learning for large and collaborative team projects for modeling with the UML

The case study problem statements appearing here are as close to real-life software engineering projects as is possible in an educational setting. Based on the underlying philosophy of experiential learning, these problem statements are put together for students learning UML-based modeling in all three modeling spaces (Model of Problem Space [MOPS], Model of Solution Space [MOSS], and Model of Architecture Space [MOAS]).

    An important part of these case studies is that they are geared toward students working on a team of software engineers. The emphasis in these projects is on the word "team." This is because students need to learn early and quickly that a large amount of real-life modeling and software development work is undertaken in teams.

    Typically, software projects start with a business problem or an opportunity that is discussed and debated to arrive at a common understanding of the overall scenario. This scenario provides the business context for the software engineering project. Initially, this scenario is a couple of descriptive pages, usually not fully developed (in fact, incomplete), sometimes confusing, and always changing.

    The problem statements given below describe such scenarios. These case study problem statements set the business context for the UML-based software modeling exercises undertaken by students in teams. These problem statements are slightly better organized than what you will discover at the end of the first brainstorming meeting. However, they are purposefully not very tightly defined.

*The main idea here is to give you, the students, a basic sketch of the business and what it wants from the software project. You are then free to develop the scenario further depending on how you understand the context in which the project is to be executed. The focus of these case studies is **not** the accuracy of the problem domain itself but rather how the students understand, model, and express themselves through UML.*

The requirements for these case study problems start by a description of the business situation. This business situation provides the basis to identify the key business objectives for the project. The software engineering project starts from there onward—following the software development life cycle (including Agile), creating the MOPS, MOSS, and MOAS, and utilizing the tools and techniques discussed in this book.

*The software system in the following case studies is to be developed by a group of consultants (**You**). The scope of this book is limited to software modeling. That's why actual implementation of the solution (i.e., development, testing, and deployment) is not expected in these case studies. Eventually, however, the solutions you model are implemented in a technical environment (e.g., Java-based environment, together with an appropriate back-end database such as Oracle or SQLserver, with Cloud service from providers such as Amazon AWS or Microsoft Azure). Support for mobile processes is also an integral part of these projects, although that implementation is also beyond the scope of this exercise.*

Your project team is made up to four to six team members. Assume you have some experience in the software industry. You are involved in creating and successfully deploying software solutions for various types and sizes of projects across a range of organizations. You are capable of understanding the business objectives of the project keeping the business context in mind; you are able to extract and document user requirements for the project; then, based on the business context, you are able to decide the type and size of the software engineering project. Within that project, you have the skills and tools to model, architect, design, and deploy the solutions. You also verify and validate the quality of your models and plan and organize the testing of the eventual solution.

Students are encouraged to delve deeper into the requirements given below; they can brainstorm in a workshop setting to ascertain what the user really wants out of the system and how the user is going to use the system to achieve his/her business goals. The students should be able to appreciate how these requirements can be further correctly, completely, and consistently modeled using the software engineering fundamentals together with the UML.

GoodMead—Hospital Management System

[Special Note: This particular case study on a hospital management system (HMS) is the basis for the running example in the book. Reading this case study problem statement gives you, the readers, a good background for the examples. Advanced students can further read and modify this case study problem statement and use it to develop more detailed and additional examples.]

GoodMead is a **hypothetical** large hospital in a metro city within a fully developed country (say, Sydney, Australia). This hospital provides diverse types of health-related services in pediatrics, gynecology and obstetrics, orthopedics, radiology, dentistry, sports medicine, and so on.

A detailed review of the current systems and methods of the hospital was carried out. The review is a part of a comprehensive e-business strategy aimed at modernizing the hospital's information technologies and systems. This included a review of the following processes: patient admission, staff scheduling, maintaining patient records, managing laboratory test results, identifying and utilizing historical medical records, managing drugs, managing inventory, allocating funds, and utilizing facilities.

As a result of the review and ensuing discussions by the board of GoodMead, a new "program of work" has been commissioned. This program of work comprises key IT projects dealing with new development, integration, transformation, and extension activities. The aim is to provide a fully integrated software solution that is on the Cloud. Cost effectiveness and efficiency in providing patient services, effective use of hospital resources, and compliance with current and upcoming regulations are some of the key goals of this strategy.

The new software development project is approved by the board in conjunction with a reputed consulting company—MethodScience. The project is called HMS (hospital management system). HMS has a dedicated business objective, separate budget, a project director, three project managers, and a team of analysts, designers, developers, and testers.

The brief given to this HMS project is to develop an Internet-enabled, Cloud-based software solution that will handle all current and future hospital management processes. Successful implementation of HMS should result in ease of access to patients and staff, quicker registration and tracking of patients' details, and in general a smoother day-to-day operation. HMS is aimed at providing value to patients, staff, administrators, and regulators. HMS is also meant to enhance collaboration of GoodMead with other business entities (such as pharmacies, laboratories, and police and ambulance services).

The project director for the HMS is working closely with the principal consultant of MethodScience to seek advice on software development processes, architectural frameworks, software engineering approach (object-oriented), design standards (they have agreed on the UML 2.5), CASE tools for modeling (they have agreed on StarUML, although some users are comfortable using Visio), and testing approaches. The decision as to which implementation technology should be used is yet to be made by the technical architects of the system (e.g., whether the system will be implemented in .NET or J2EE and which corresponding Cloud platform will be used). Expertise from the medical administration domain is sought to capture and enhance the hospital's business processes and ensure legal compliance.

A recent senior level workshop carried out over two days included the program director, all three project managers, principal consultant, senior business architects, consulting enterprise architects, and special advisors from the field of medical technology. The following summarizes the resolutions in point form:

1. The hospital has a large outpatient department (OPD) that provides medical consultations and prescriptions, usually during the day. There are at least two shifts, as the OPD is open from 8 a.m. to 10 p.m.; the OPD is staffed with doctors, physicians, nurses, receptionists, and various other related roles. The OPD is the first area of the hospital that needs to be upgraded for its business processes and support systems.

2. The hospital has 10 sophisticated operating theaters. There is a large number of pre- and postsurgical activities (including pre- and postnatal activities). Many processes around the aforementioned activities are not documented. Instead, the staff carries them out based on their knowledge and experience. The processes that require mandatory documentation are not very well supported by the software system. There is an urgent need to upgrade these processes, which include not only dealing with the patients' medical procedures and corresponding legal documentation (such as signing of authority to perform certain medical procedures and nomination of next of kin) but also optimization of facilities management.

3. Diagnostic tests, including blood tests, x-rays, and so on, are carried out on the hospital's premises. However, the ownership and operation of these laboratories are independent of

GoodMead hospital. Therefore, there is a need for coordination and collaboration between the software systems used by the laboratories and HMS.

4. The hospital is continuously in touch with various pharmaceutical organizations that manufacture drugs; this enables the hospital to get the latest information on existing and new drugs and new medical experiments and allows it to provide input on those experiments and trials. Thus, the senior team sees great opportunity for knowledge sharing and collaboration in the areas of provisioning drugs, availability of latest instruments and medical technologies, and exchange of innovative ideas in medical research.

5. Staff-related processes (e.g., checking availability of physicians and surgeons and scheduling nursing and support staff) are not currently optimized. Many processes are manual, and occasionally administrative staff uses physical notepads, diaries, and whiteboards to check the availability of and book doctors. HMS should be able to handle the scheduling of consultations of patients with the respective medical staff and scheduling work rosters for nurses and administrative staff.

6. Internal administrative systems (such as booking of surgeries in operating rooms or leaving schedules of nurses) either use tools such as a local Access database created by people with no software engineering background or, much worse, on whiteboards. These administrative functions are to be moved to the Internet-enabled, Cloud-based system that will be managed remotely.

7. Security in terms of storage and access of data and patient privacy have come out on top as key concerns and risks from a legal and compliance viewpoint. The government regulatory specialist on board in this project has advised that patient data are part of a government initiative on electronic medical records (EMRs). The EMR initiative enables sharing of data on the Cloud to enable emergency services to access it based on preauthorized IoT devices. Privacy of those data remains on the highest compliance needs of government regulatory bodies and cannot be compromised under any circumstances.

8. User interfaces of the software solutions are specified and designed with usability in mind. HMS is to be used by a wide age range of user groups—young and old, and users with disabilities. HMS needs to comply with the government requirements on the accessibility of the system.

9. Performance and security of HMS are separately specified as nonfunctional requirements and they are part of the agreement between the program director and the board.

10. A range of relative cross-functionalities (such as sports information) needs to be included to attract and keep nonpatients at the site as well. The purpose of it is to keep the community aware. This is part of GoodMead's social responsibility

11. Creating efficiencies in operational processes of the hospital is vital to handling the reduction in charities and partial government funding to the hospital. HMS is meant to provide those operational efficiencies and corresponding metrics and measurements to prove its success.

12. There is no software architecture at all in the hospital. Development of HMS will be based on a robust enterprise architecture that will cover any system that exists within the hospital and then the corresponding system architecture for HMS.

13. A part of this project is the creation of a comprehensive Not only SQL (NoSQL) database that can handle multimedia files. These files contain selected past consultations in audio and video forms, email messages in unstructured format, and summaries of medical journals and newspaper reports. These data and their associated analytics are available to various authorized users such as doctors, consulting doctors, patients, and service providers (such as biowaste cleaners).

14. The use of NoSQL/multimedia databases is a strategic decision that aims to provide optional extensions to the project. This extension is to incorporate the use of remote consultations by doctors and registered nurses through audio and video media using high-speed connectivity.
15. The development process for HMS is to follow composite Agile (CAMS). Thus, the entire HMS development team is trained in the use of Agile and all its associated techniques and practices.
16. Testing of the HMS solution will be carried out both internally and externally (alpha and beta) in an iterative and incremental manner.

Bibliography

Ambler, S. (2004), "The Object Primer," in *Agile Model Driven Development with UML 2.0* 3rd ed., New York: Cambridge University Press. ISBN#: 0-521-54018-6.

Armour, F. and Miller, G. (2001), *Advanced Use Case Modeling*, Reading, MA: Addison-Wesley.

Bandwagon. *Sloan Management Review*, 35(1), 73–86.

Basili, V., Briand, L., Condon, S., Kim, Y.-M., Melo, W. L., and Valett, J. D. (1996), Understanding and predicting the process of software maintenance releases. *Proc 18 Intl Conf on Software Engineering*, Berlin, Germany.

Beck, K. (2000), *EXtremeProgramming Explained: Embrace Change*, Reading, MA: Addison-Wesley.

Beizer, B. (1984), *System Testing and Quality Assurance*, New York, NY: Van Nostrand Reinhold.

Bennett, K.H. and Rajlich, V.T. (2000), Software Maintenance and Evolution: A Roadmap. Published in the ACM Press, "The Future of Software Engineering," ACM Press 2000, ISBN-1-58113-253-0.

Binder, R.V. (1999), *Testing Object-Oriented Systems*, Reading, MA: Addison-Wesley.

Boehm, B.W. (1986), "A Spiral Model of Software Development and Enhancement," *ACS Software Engineering Notes*, 11(4), 14–24.

Booch, G. (1994), *Object-oriented Analysis and Design*, 3rd Edition. Upper Saddle River, NJ: The Addison-Wesley Object Technology Series.

Booch, G., Rumbaugh, J., and Jacobson, I. (1999), *The Unified Modelling Language User Guide*, Reading, MA: Addison-Wesley.

Canosa, J., *Introduction to Web Services, Embedded Systems Programming*. Retrieved from https://www.embedded.com/design/connectivity/4023907/Introduction-to-Web-Services; accessed October 19, 2017.

Cantor, M. (1998), *Object Oriented Project Management with UML*, Wiley, USA. Also see the companion site for this book: http://www.wiley.com/legacy/compbooks/cantor/; accessed October 15, 2017.

Card D. and Comer E. (1994), "Why Do So Many Reuse Programs Fail?," *IEEE Software*, 11(5), 114–115.

Caudwell, P. (2001), *Professional XML Web Services*, Birmingham: Wrox Press

Cho, J. (2008), *Issues and Challenges of Agile Software Development with Scrum*, Colorado State University-Pueblo, Issues in Information Systems, vol. IX, no. 2.

Cockburn, A. (1997), "Goals and Use Cases," *Journal of Object-Oriented Programming*, 10(5), 35–40.

Cockburn, A. (2000), *Writing Effective Use cases*, Reading, MA: Addison-Wesley.

Coffin, R. and Lane, D. (2007), A Practical Guide to Seven Agile Methodologies, Part 1, Jupitermedia Corporation. Retrieved from http://www.devx.com/architect/Article/32761/1954

Constantine, L. (1995), *Constantine on Peopleware*, Yourdon Press Computing Series, Upper Saddle River, NJ: Prentice Hall.

Constantine, L. (2001), *The Peopleware Papers: Notes on the Human Side of Programming* (Yourdon Press computing series). Upper Saddle River, NJ: Prentice Hall. ISBN-13: 978-0130601230.

Constantine, L. and Lockwood, L. (1997), *Software for Use: A Practical Guide to the Models and Methods of Usage-centered Design*, Reading, MA: Addison-Wesley. (see also www.foruse.com).

Constantine, L.L. (1997), "The Case for Essential Use Cases," *Object Magazine*, 7(3), 72–80.

Constantine, L.L. and Lockwood, L.A.D. (2001), "Structure and Styles in Use Cases for User Interface Design," in *Object Modelling and User Interface Design*, M. V. Harmelen (ed.), Reading, MA: Addison-Wesley.

DeMarco, T. and Lister, T. (1987), *Peopleware: Productive Projects and Teams*, USA: Dorset House Publishing Company.

Douglass, B. P. (1999), Doing Hard Time Developing Real-Time Systems With UML, Objects, Frameworks, and Patterns, Object Technology Series. Reading, MA: Addison-Wesley.

Fowler, M. (1996), "A Survey of Object-oriented Analysis and Design Methods," OOPSLA'96 Tutorial No. 45, 6–10.

Fowler, M. (1997), *Analysis Patterns: Reusable Object Models*, Reading, MA: Addison-Wesley.

Fowler, M. (2003), *UML Distilled*, 3rd ed., Reading, MA: Addison-Wesley.

Frakes, W.B. and Isoda, S. (1994), "Success Factors of Systematic Reuse," *IEEE Software*, 11(5), 14–19.

Gabriel, R. (1993), "The Quality Without a Name," *Jrnl of Obj Or Prog*, 6(5), 86–89.

Gamma, E., Helm, R., Johnson, R., and Vlissides, J. (1995), *Design Patterns: Elements of Reusable Object-Oriented Software*, Reading, MA: Addison-Wesley.

Glass, R. (1997), *Software Runaways: Monumental Software Disasters*, Upper Saddle River, NJ: Prentice Hall.

Glenford, M. G., Badgett, T., and Sandler, C. (1979), *The Art of Software Testing*, Hoboken, NJ: John Wiley & Sons, Inc.

Goldberg, A. and Robson, D. (1983), *The Interactive Programming Environment*, Reading, MA: Addison-Wesley. ISBN: (978-)0201113716.

Goldberg, A. and Rubin, K. (1995), *Succeeding with Object: Decision Frameworks for Project Management*, Reading, MA: Addison-Wesley.

Graham, I. (1994), *Migrating to Object Technology*, Reading, MA: Addison-Wesley.

Graham, S. (2001), *Building Web Services with Java: Making Sense of XML, SOAP, WSDL, and UDDI*, Indiana: SAMS Press.

Greatrex, C., (KPMG Director) (1996) "Achieving Excellence through Effective Management of your IT project," *Proceedings of IT Project Management by AIC Conferences*.

Hammer, M. and Champy, J. (1994), *Reengineering the Corporation*, St Leonards, NSW: Allen and Unwin.

Hans-Erik, E. and Penkar, M. (2000), *Business Modelling with UML; Business Patterns at Work*, OMG Press.

Henderson-Sellers, B. (1997), *Book of Object-oriented Knowledge*, 2nd ed., Upper Saddle River, NJ: Prentice Hall.

Henderson-Sellers, B. and Bulthuis, A. (1997), *Object-oriented Metamethods*, New York: Springer.

Henderson-Sellers, B. and Edwards, J. M. (1994), *Book Two of Object-oriented Knowledge: The Working Object*, Upper Saddle River, NJ: Prentice-Hall.

Henderson-Sellers, B. and Serour, M. (2001), "Creating a Process for Transitioning to Object Technology," *IEEE 2000*, 436–440, 00896731; Also presented at *TOOLS USA 2001*.

Henderson-Sellers, B. and Unhelkar, B. (2000), *OPEN Modelling with the UML*, Reading, MA: Addison-Wesley.

Henninger S. (1994), "Using Iterative Refinement to Find Reusable Software," *IEEE Software*, 11(5), 48–59.

Hudson, William (2001), "A User-centered UML Method," in *Object Modeling and User Interface Design: Designing Interactive Systems*, Mark Van Harmelen (ed.), Reading, MA: Addison-Wesley.

Humphrey, Watts (1995), *A Discipline for Software Engineering*, Reading, MA: Addison-Wesley.

Hutt, A. (1994), *Object Analysis and Design, Description of Methods*, OMG/Wiley.

Jaaksi, A. (1997), "Our Cases with Use Cases," *Jrnl. Of Obj Or Prog*, 10(9), 58–65.

Jacobson, I. (1993), "Time for a Cease-Fire in the Methods War," *Jrnl of Obj Or Prog*, 6(3), 20–25.

Jacobson, I., Booch, G., and Rumbaugh, J. (1999), *The Unified Software Development Process*, Reading, MA: Addison-Wesley.

Jacobson, I., Christerson, M., Jonsson, P., and Overgaard, G. (1992), *Object-Oriented Software Engineering: A Use Case Driven Approach*, Reading, MA: Addison-Wesley.

Jacobson, I., Griss, M., Jonsson, P. (1997), *Software Reuse*, Reading, MA: Addison-Wesley.

Jalote, P. (2000), *CMM in Practice: Process for Executing Software Projects at Infosys*, Reading, MA: Addison-Wesley.

Kriendler, J. (1993), "Cultural Change and Object-oriented technology," *Jrnl of Obj Or Prog*, 5(9), 6–8.

Kruchten, P., Ahlqvist, S., and Bylund, S. (2001), "User Interface Design in the Rational Unified Process," in *Object Modelling and User Interface Design*, M. V. Harmelen (ed.), Reading, MA: Addison-Wesley.

Lacity, M. and Hirschheim, R. (1993), The Information systems Outsourcing

Lan, Y. and Unhelkar, B. (2005), *Global Enterprise Transitions*, Hershey, PA, USA: IDEAS Group Inc.

Lanier, J. (1997), "The Frontier between Us," Special Anniversary issue on 50 years of computing, Communications of the ACM, 40(2), 55–56.

Lauder, A. and Kent, S. (1999), "Two-Level Modelling," in *Technology of OO Languages and Systems, (TOOLS 31)*, Jian Chen, Jian Lu, Bertrand Meyer (eds.), Nanjing, China: IEEE Computer Society, 108–117.

Lewis, J. and Neher, K. (2007), "Over the Waterfall in a Barrel – MSIT Adventures in Scrum," IEEE Computer Society, Washington, DC.

Lim, W. C., "Effects of Reuse on Quality, Productivity, and Economics," *IEEE Software*, 11(5), 23–30.

Lorenz, M. and Kidd, J. (1994), *Object-oriented Software Metrics*, Upper Saddle River, NJ: Prentice-Hall.

McGregor, J. and Sykes, D. (2001), *A Practical Guide to Testing Object-Oriented Software*, Reading, MA: Addison-Wesley.

Meyer, B. (1991), "Object-Oriented Software Construction," In *The Importance of Being Humble*, 2nd ed., Upper Saddle River, NJ: Prentice Hall, PTR, Section 19.4.

Meyer, B. (1995), *Object Success*, Upper Saddle River, NJ: Prentice Hall.

Meyers, G. (1979), *The Art of Software Testing*, USA: John-Wiley and Sons.

Miller, R. B. (1968). "Response Time in Man-Computer Conversational Transactions." *Proc. AFIPS Fall Joint Computer Conference*, 33, 267–277.

Nygaard, K. (1999), *Keynote Address, Technology of OO Languages and Systems, (TOOLS 31)*, J. Chen, J. Lu, B. Meyer (eds.), Nanjing, China: IEEE Computer Society, 108–117.

OMG White Paper on Security (1994) OMG Security Working Group, Issue 1.0 April 1994.

Perry, W. (1991), *Quality Assurance for Information Systems*, MA: QED Information Sciences.

Rosenberg, D. and Scott, K. (1999), *Use Case Driven Object Modelling with the UML*. Reading, MA: Addision-Wesley.

Rosenberg, D. and Scott, K. (2001), *Applying Use Case Driven Object Modelling with the UML*. Reading, MA: Addision-Wesley.

Rumbaugh, J. "Modeling & Design: Designing bugs and dueling methodologies," JOOP Jan'92, pp. 50–56.

Rumbaugh, J., Jacobson, I., and Booch, G. (1999), *The Unified Modelling Language Reference Manual*, Reading, MA: Addison-Wesley.

Schneider, G. and Winters, J. P. (2001), *Applying Use Cases, Second Edition a Practical Guide*, Object Technology Series, Reading, MA: Addision-Wesley.

Schwaber, K. and Beedle, M. (2001), *Agile Software Development with Scrum*, Upper Saddle River, NJ: Prentice Hall.

Scott, K. (2004), Fast Track UML 2.0, Apress.

Shaw, M. and Garlan, D. (1996), *Software Architecture: Perspectives on an Emerging Discipline*, Upper Saddle River, NJ: Prentice Hall.

Sommerville, I. (1989), *Software Engineering*, Reading, MA: Addison-Wesley. p. 352.

Thomas, D. and Jacobson, I. (1989), Managing Object-oriented Software Engineering Tutorial, TOOLS '89, Paris, 13–15 November 1989. This has been further developed by Henderson-Sellers, B. (1993), "The Economics of Reusing Library Classes," *Jrnl of OO Prog*, 6(4), 43–50.

Torres, R. J. (2002), *Practitioner's Handbook for User Interface Design & Development*, Upper Saddle River, NJ: Prentice-Hall.

Unhelkar, B. (1995), "The MOSES Experience," *Object Magazine*, p. 51.

Unhelkar, B. (1997), "Developing a Financial Market Analysis Product: A MOSES Case Study," in *Developing Business Objects*, A. Carmichael (ed.), SIGS, pp. 113–140.

Unhelkar, B. (1997–98), *Effect of Granularity of Object-oriented Design on Modelling an Enterprise and its Application to Financial Risk Management*, Ph.D. Thesis, University of Technology, Sydney: 1997–1998.

Unhelkar, B. (1998), "*Effect of Granularity of Object-oriented Design on Modelling an Enterprise and its Application to Financial Markets*," Doctoral thesis, Univ. of Technology, Sydney.

Unhelkar, B. (1999), *After the Y2K Fireworks: Business and Technology Strategies*, Boca Raton, FL: CRC Press.

Unhelkar, B. (2001), "DeMystifying the UML" *Information Age*, publication of the Australian Computer Society, pp. 56–61.

Unhelkar, B. (2003), *Process Quality Assurance for UML-based Projects*, Reading, MA: Addison-Wesley.

Unhelkar, B. (2005), "Practical Object Oriented Analysis," *Cengage (first published by Thomson Publishing)*, Australia, March, 2005. Pages 221; ISBN 0-17-012298-0.

Unhelkar, B. (2005), "Practical Object Oriented Design," *Cengage (first published by Thomson Publishing)*, Australia, July, 2005. Pages 220+. ISBN 0-17-012299-9.

Unhelkar, B. (2010), *Agile in Practice: A Composite Approach*, (16,000 words), Cutter Executive Report, Jan 2010, USA. Vol 11, No 1, *Agile Product and Project Management Practice*.

Unhelkar, B. (2013), *The Art of Agile Practice: A Composite Approach for Projects and Organizations*, Boca Raton, FL: Taylor and Francis, ISBN 9781439851180.

Unhelkar, B. and Henderson-Sellers, B. (1993a), "Evaluating the Role of Reuse in Object-Oriented Systems," *Proceedings of the First Australian Conference on Software Metrics, ACOSM'93*, J. Verner (ed.).

Unhelkar, B. and Henderson-Sellers, B. (1993b), "The Role of Granularity in the Reuse of Object-oriented Systems," *Proceedings of ACOSM'93 First Australian Conference on Software Metrics*, Sydney, Australia, June Verner (ed.), Australian Software Metrics Association, November 18–19 1993, pp. 51–66.

Unhelkar, B. and Mamdapur, G. (1995), "Practical Aspects of Using a Methodology: A Road Map Approach," *Report on Object Analysis and Design (ROAD)*, 2(2), 34–36, 54.

Van Harmelen, M. (ed.). (2001), *Object Modelling and User Interface Design: Designing Interactive Systems*, Reading, MA: Addison-Wesley.

Winblad A., Edwards S., and King D. (1990), *Object-Oriented Software*, Reading, MA: Addison-Wesley, pp. vi.

Wohlin, C. and Ahlgren, M. (1995), "Soft Factors and Their Impact on Time to Market," *Software Quality Journal*, 4(3), 189–205.

Younessi, H. (2002), *Object-Oriented Defect Management of Software*, USA: Prentice Hall PTR.

Younessi, H. and Henderson-Sellers, B. (1997), "Cooking Up Quality Software: Object-oriented Software Development Process," *Object Magazine*, 7(8), 38–42.

http://www.uml-diagrams.org/

http://www.agilemanifesto.org/

http://www.omg.org/spec/UML/2.5/

https://www.ibm.com/software/rational (earlier Rational.com – www.rational.com Rational company's website containing details of Rational's Object Software Engineering (ROSE) CASE tool for UML. Rational is now owned by IBM and known as IBM Rational.

https://www.researchgate.net/publication/229001868_The_future_of_UML [accessed Jul 6, 2017].

ISO/IEC 19505-1:2012 (UML 2.4.1 Infrastructure) http://www.iso.org/iso/iso_catalogue/catalogue_tc/catalogue_detail.htm?csnumber=32624

ISO/IEC 19505-2:2012 (UML 2.4.1 Superstructure) http://www.iso.org/iso/iso_catalogue/catalogue_tc/catalogue_detail.htm?csnumber=52854

www.MethodScience.com. Practical experiences in using and training with UML.

www.omg.org: Contains details of standard UML are available. Site also contains details on CORBA, and the Unified Process Model, which is the upcoming effort by OMG to standardize processes.

www.sei.cmu.edu: The Carnegie-Mellon University's Software Engineering Institute's site. This is the Institute responsible for the five levels of CMM – Capability Maturity Models.

www.BPMN.org

Index